Turbo Pascal®

By EXAMPLE

que

Greg Perry

Turbo Pascal® By Example

Publisher
Lloyd J. Short

Associate Publisher
Rick Ranucci

Publishing Manager
Joseph B. Wikert

Development Editor
Ella Davis

Production Editor
Jodi Jensen

Editors
Bryan Gambrel
Kezia Endsley
Rebecca Whitney

Technical Editors
Rich Jones
Michael G. Staton

Production Director
Jeff Valler

Production Manager
Corinne Walls

Imprint Manager
Matthew Morrill

**Proofreading/Indexing
Coordinator**
Joelynn Gifford

Production Analyst
Mary Beth Wakefield

Book Designer
Michele Laseau

Cover Designer
Jean Bisesi

Graphic Image Specialists
Dennis Sheehan
Jerry Ellis
Susan VandeWalle

Indexer
Johnna VanHoose

Production
Claudia Bell, Paula Carroll,
Michelle Cleary, Brook Farling,
Kate Godfrey, Bob LaRoche,
Laurie Lee, Cindy L. Phipps,
Caroline Roop, Linda Seifert,
Lisa Wilson, Phil Worthington,
Christine Young

Composed in Palatino and MCPdigital typefaces by Prentice Hall Computer Publishing.
Screen reproductions in this book were created by means of the program Collage Plus
from Inner Media, Inc., Hollis, NH.

About the Author

Greg Perry has been a programmer and trainer for the past 14 years. He received his first degree in computer science, then he received a Masters degree in corporate finance. He currently is a professor of computer science at Tulsa Junior College, as well as a computer consultant and a lecturer. Greg Perry is the author of 10 other computer books, including *QBASIC By Example*, *C By Example*, and with Marcus Johnson, *Turbo C++ By Example* (all published by Que Corporation). In addition, he has published articles in several publications, including *PC World*, *Data Training*, and *Inside First Publisher*. He has attended computer conferences and trade shows in several countries, and is fluent in nine computer languages.

Acknowledgments

Special thanks to Chris Land, who wrote the code examples for this book. I appreciate his diligence and attention to detail.

I also appreciate my editors—Ella Davis, Jodi Jensen, Bryan Gambrel, Rebecca Whitney, Rich Jones, and Michael Staton—who kept me on track so that readers can have an accurate and readable text.

Gary Farrar was one of the primary reasons for this book's accuracy and clean readability. Gary is an excellent example of the pupil who surpassed the teacher. I am grateful for your help, Gary.

The Tulsa Junior College administration continues to support my writing. More importantly, Diane Moore, head of the Business Services Division, puts up with my antics and motivates me to look forward to each day.

When Dr. Richard C. Burgess and his wonderful wife Ellen recently stepped back into my life, they filled a void. Rick, you are the reason I am who I am today. Ellen, you have always been *simpatica, molta!*

As always, my beautiful bride Jayne, my parents Glen and Bettye Perry, and of course, Luke, the bischon, are my closest daily companions. It is for them that I work.

Trademark Acknowledgments

Que Corporation has made every attempt to supply trademark information about company names, products, and services mentioned in the book. Trademarks indicated below were derived from various sources. Que Corporation cannot attest to the accuracy of this information.

IBM is a registered trademark of International Business Machines Corporation.

MS-DOS is a registered trademark of Microsoft Corporation.

Turbo Pascal is a registered trademark of Borland International, Inc.

Overview

Contents

Part III Input and Output

Part IV Control Statements

Part VII Disk File Processing

Introduction

Turbo Pascal By Example is one of several books in Que Corporation's new line of *By Example* titles. The philosophy of these books is a simple one: Computer programming concepts are best taught with multiple examples. Command descriptions, format syntax, and language references are not enough for a newcomer to truly learn a programming language. Only by looking at numerous examples, in which new commands are used immediately, and by running sample programs, can programming students get more than just a feel for the language.

Who Should Use This Book

This book offers instruction at three levels: beginning, intermediate, and advanced. Text and numerous examples are aimed at each level. If you are new to Turbo Pascal, and even if you are new to computers, this book attempts to put you at ease as you gradually build your Turbo Pascal programming skills. If you are an expert with one of the forms of the BASIC language and want to learn a more structured language, this book is also for you.

The Book's Philosophy

This book focuses entirely on programming *correctly* in Turbo Pascal, by teaching structured programming techniques and proper program design. Emphasis always is placed on a program's readability rather than "tricks of the trade" code examples. In this changing world, programs should be clear, properly structured, and well-documented. This book does not waver from the importance of this philosophy.

This book teaches you Turbo Pascal with a holistic approach. Not only do you learn the mechanics of the language, but you learn tips and warnings, how to use Turbo Pascal for different types of applications, and a little of the history and interesting asides of the computing industry.

Whereas many other books build single applications, adding to them a little at a time with each chapter, the chapters in this book are stand-alone chapters that show you complete programs which fully illustrate commands introduced in the chapter. There are programs for every level of reader, from beginning to advanced.

This book contains more than 200 sample program listings. These programs show ways that Turbo Pascal can be used for personal finance, school and business recordkeeping, math and science, and general-purpose applications that almost everyone with a computer can use. This variety of programs shows you that Turbo Pascal is a powerful language that is easy to learn and use. Experienced programmers can learn what they need by skipping to those programs that demonstrate specific commands.

Appendix E provides a complete application that is much longer than any of the other programs in the book. This application tries to bring together your entire working knowledge of Turbo Pascal. The application is a computerized book collector's inventory system. As you work through the chapters of the book, you learn how each part of the program works. You might want to modify the program to better suit your own needs. You can change it to keep track of other information, such as a compact disc and record collection.

EXAMPLE

An Overview of This Book

This book is divided into eight parts. Part I introduces you to the Turbo Pascal environment. Starting with Part II, the book presents the Turbo Pascal programming language in six logical parts. After mastering the language, you can use the book as a handy reference. When you need help with a specific Turbo Pascal programming problem, turn to the appropriate area for numerous code examples that describe that part of the language.

To give you an idea of the book's layout, here is a description of each part of the book:

Part I: Introduction to Turbo Pascal

This part explains what Turbo Pascal is by describing a brief history of the Pascal programming language and then presenting an overview of Turbo Pascal's advantages over its predecessors. This part describes your computer's hardware, how you start and end Turbo Pascal, and the fundamentals of using the Turbo Pascal editor to enter and run programs.

Part II: Primary Turbo Pascal Language Elements

This part teaches the rudimentary Turbo Pascal language elements, including variables, comments, math and string operators, and introductory output commands. Starting in the earliest chapter, you write your first Turbo Pascal programs while you learn the foundation of the Turbo Pascal language.

Part III: Input and Output

Without the capability to receive input from the user and display results, Turbo Pascal would be limiting. Fortunately, Turbo Pascal supplies a rich assortment of commands that enable you to enter and display information in whatever format best serves your application. You learn how to store and compare data, as well as format your output to the screen and printer.

Part IV: Control Statements

Turbo Pascal data processing is most powerful because of the looping, comparison, and selection constructs it offers. This part shows you how to write programs that correctly flow and control computations to produce accurate and readable code.

Part V: Data Structures

Turbo Pascal offers single- and multidimensional arrays that hold multiple occurrences of repeating data but do not require a great deal of effort on your part to process. By learning the fundamentals of sorting and searching parallel arrays, you begin to build powerful routines you can use later in your own programs.

Part VI: Subroutines

The reusability of a language determines whether programmers continue to use it or discard it for another. The authors of Turbo Pascal produced a block-structured, fully separate subroutine and function procedural language that enables you to define the scope and visibility of variables and how you want to pass them between procedures and functions. Along with the built-in numeric and string functions, this part of the book describes the many options available when you start to create your own library of procedures and functions.

Part VII: Disk File Processing

Your computer would be too limiting if you could not store data to the disk and retrieve that data into your programs. Disk files are required by most real-world applications. This part describes how Turbo Pascal processes sequential and random-access files and teaches the fundamental principles needed to effectively save data to a disk.

Part VIII: Appendixes

The appendixes supply support information for the rest of the book. You will find a comprehensive ASCII table, answers to all the chapter review questions, and a keyword reference. Appendix E includes the complete program listing for the book collector's inventory system.

Conventions Used in This Book

The following typographic conventions are used in this book:

♦ Code lines, functions, variable names, and any text you see on-screen appear in a special `monospace` typeface.

♦ Placeholders within code are in *`italic monospace`*.

♦ User input following a prompt is in **`bold monospace`**.

♦ Filenames are in regular text font, usually all uppercase.

♦ New terms, which can be found in the Glossary, are in *italic*.

Icons Used in This Book

Three icons are used to indicate examples at a certain level of difficulty.

Level 1 　　　　Level 2 　　　　Level 3

Three additional icons are used to identify material shown in a box.

Tip   Caution   Note

Pseudocode is a special way of explaining a section of code with an understandable, English language description. You often see pseudocode before a code example.

Pseudocode

Diagrams Used in This Book

To further increase your understanding of Turbo Pascal, this book includes numerous *margin graphics*. These margin graphics are similar to *flowcharts* you might have seen before. Both employ standard symbols to represent program logic. You might have heard the adage, "A picture is worth a thousand words." Rather than wade through a lot of code, you sometimes can more easily look at this book's margin graphics to get a feel for the overall logic before dissecting programs line-by-line.

Throughout this book, these margin graphics are used in two places. Some graphics appear when a new command is introduced, to show you how the command works. Others are placed where new commands are shown in example programs for the first time.

No attempt is made to give you complete, detailed graphics of every statement in each program. The margin graphics are kept simple to give you an overview of the statements you are reading about at the time.

The following symbols are used in margin graphics. Their meanings are described next to each one.

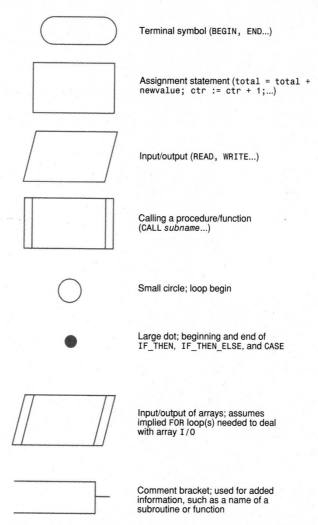

Terminal symbol (`BEGIN`, `END`...)

Assignment statement (`total = total + newvalue; ctr := ctr + 1;`...)

Input/output (`READ`, `WRITE`...)

Calling a procedure/function (`CALL` *subname*...)

Small circle; loop begin

Large dot; beginning and end of `IF_THEN`, `IF_THEN_ELSE`, and `CASE`

Input/output of arrays; assumes implied `FOR` loop(s) needed to deal with array `I/O`

Comment bracket; used for added information, such as a name of a subroutine or function

Figure I.1. Symbols used in margin graphics, and their meanings.

The graphics presented here are easy to interpret. Their goal is to be self-explanatory, even if you have not fully learned the commands they represent. The margin graphics, program listings, program comments, and program descriptions presented in this book should give you many vehicles for learning the Turbo Pascal programming language.

Part I

Introduction to Turbo Pascal

Welcome to Turbo Pascal

Turbo Pascal 6.0 is the latest version of the Pascal programming language from Borland International. Whether you are a novice, intermediate, or expert programmer, Turbo Pascal contains the programming tools you need to help your computer perform the way you want. This chapter introduces you to Turbo Pascal, briefly describes the history of the Pascal programming language, shows the advantages of using Turbo Pascal, and introduces hardware and software concepts.

What Turbo Pascal Can Do for You

Have you ever wished that your computer could perform exactly what you want? Maybe you have searched for a program that keeps track of your household budget exactly as you prefer. Perhaps you want to keep the records of a small business (or a large one) with your computer, but no program is available that prints reports to your liking. Maybe you have thought about a new use for a computer and would like to implement that idea. Turbo Pascal provides you with the power to develop new uses for your computer.

Turbo Pascal supplies outstanding programming tools to help you concentrate on the important job: the program you are writing. Turbo Pascal removes the tedium from programming by supplying a full-screen editor, online help, mouse support, an integrated debugger, and extensions that add structure, power, and flexibility to the Pascal language.

If you have never programmed a computer before, you will discover that programming in Turbo Pascal is rewarding. Becoming an expert programmer in Turbo Pascal, or any other computer language, takes some time and dedication on your part. Nevertheless, you can start writing simple programs with very little effort. When you learn the fundamentals of Turbo Pascal programming, you can build on what you've learned and hone your programming skills. As you write more powerful programs, you will start to discover new uses for your computer, and you will use your programming skills to develop programs that other people can use as well.

The Background of Pascal

Before jumping into Turbo Pascal, you should know a little about the origins and evolution of the Pascal programming language. Programming the early computers was a complex job at best. Several programming languages were available, such as COBOL, FORTRAN, and Assembler, but each was confusing to beginning programmers and hard to learn. In addition, programs were becoming larger and more difficult to maintain. One reason for all this difficulty was that these early languages did not have sufficient built-in structure.

In the early 1970s, Niklaus Wirth created a language to teach structured programming. He named his language *Pascal* after the 17th century mathematician Blaise Pascal. Although Pascal was originally designed as a tool for teaching, Pascal has been hugely successful for general programming purposes.

Turbo Pascal and Microcomputers

In the 1970s, NASA created the *microchip*, a small wafer of silicon that occupies less space than a postage stamp. Because computer components could be placed on small microchips, the computers did not take up as much space as their predecessors did. NASA produced these small computers because the agency wanted to send rocket ships to the moon with onboard computers. Earth-bound computers could not deliver split-second accuracy to the rockets because radio waves require a few seconds to travel between the Earth and the moon. Through development, these microchips became small enough that a computer could travel with a rocket and accurately compute the rocket's trajectory.

The space program was not the only beneficiary of the miniaturization of computers. The microchip was used also as the heart of the *microcomputer*. For the first time, computers could fit on desktops. These microcomputers were much less expensive than their larger counterparts. Many people started buying them, which helped create the home and small-business computer markets. Today, a microcomputer is typically called a *PC*, or *personal computer*.

PC usage has continued to grow into the multimillion-dollar industry it is today. No one expected the tremendous growth and power increases that followed the early computers.

The Evolution of Turbo Pascal

Although Pascal compilers were available for the early PCs, they were expensive and awkward to use. When Borland International introduced Turbo Pascal 1.0 in the fall of 1983, it was reasonably priced, easy to use, and well-written. However, the major innovation was probably its built-in editor. If the compiler found an error, it loaded the problem file into the editor and positioned the cursor at the appropriate line. It was not long before Turbo Pascal became the *de facto* standard for Pascal.

As Turbo Pascal improved, PCs also became more powerful. Today, the large amount of memory and computing power that accompanies computers is complemented by newer versions of Turbo Pascal. These new versions are written to take advantage of that added computing power. Turbo Pascal now contains an Integrated Development Environment (IDE) and includes many helpful features that aid programmers.

Before diving into Turbo Pascal, take a few minutes to familiarize yourself with some of the hardware and software components of your PC. The next section, "An Overview of Your Computer," introduces you to parts of the computer that Turbo Pascal interacts with, such as the operating system, memory, disks, and input/output (I/O) devices connected to your PC. If you are already familiar with your computer's hardware and software, you might want to skip to Chapter 2, "The Turbo Pascal Environment," and begin using Turbo Pascal.

An Overview of Your Computer

Your computer system consists of two parts, the hardware and the software. *Hardware* is all the physical parts of the machine. Hardware has been defined as "anything you can kick." Although this is a rough definition, it helps illustrate that your computer's hardware consists of the things you can see. *Software* is the data and programs that interact with your hardware. The Turbo Pascal language is an example of software. You will use Turbo Pascal to create even more software programs and data.

The Computer's Hardware

Figure 1.1 shows a typical PC system. Before using Turbo Pascal, you should have a general understanding of what hardware is and how your hardware components work together.

The System Unit and Memory

The *system unit* is the large box component of the computer. The system unit houses the PC's main microchip. You might hear this main microchip called the *CPU*, because its more formal name is the *central processing unit*. The CPU acts in a manner similar to a traffic cop: it controls every operation of the computer system. The CPU is analogous to the human brain. When you use the computer, you actually are interacting with the CPU. The rest of the hardware enables the CPU to send results to you (through the monitor and printer). You also give instructions to the CPU through the hardware (the keyboard).

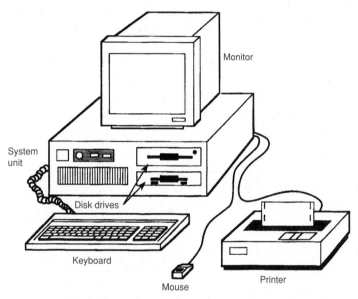

Figure 1.1. **A typical PC system.**

The system unit houses the computer's internal *memory* as well. The memory has several names. You commonly hear it referred to as *RAM* (for *random-access memory*). The CPU searches for software and data in the RAM. When you run a Turbo Pascal program, you are instructing your computer's CPU to search RAM for the program and carry out its instructions. Turbo Pascal uses some of your RAM when you start it.

RAM is one of the most important components of your computer's hardware. Without it, your computer would have no place for its instructions and data. The more RAM your computer has, generally, the more work the computer can do.

Byte: The amount of memory taken up by one character.

The amount of RAM is measured by the number of characters it can hold. PCs usually hold a maximum of about 1 million characters in RAM. In computer terminology, a character is called a *byte*, which can be a letter, a number, or a special character such as an exclamation point. Turbo Pascal can only work in "conventional" RAM, which is 640,000 bytes. If your computer has 640,000 bytes of RAM, it holds a total of 640,000 characters.

All those zeros following RAM measurements quickly become cumbersome. You often see the shortcut notation, *K* (which comes from the metric system's *kilo*, meaning 1,000), in place of the last three zeros. Therefore, 640K means 640,000 bytes of RAM.

The Power of 2

Although K means approximately 1,000 bytes of memory, in reality, K equates to 1,024 bytes. Computers are based on *off* and *on* states of electricity, which are called *binary states*. At its lowest level, a computer does nothing more than turn electricity on and off with millions of switches, called *transistors*. Because these switches have two possibilities, the total number of states of electricity in the computer is a power of 2.

The closest power of 2 to 1,000 is 1,024 (which is 2 to the 10th power). The inventors of computers designed memory so that it is always added in kilobytes or multiples of 1,024 bytes at a time. Therefore, if you add 128K of RAM to a computer, you actually are adding a total of 131,072 bytes of RAM (128 multiplied by 1,024 equals 131,072).

Because K is actually more than 1,000, you always get a little more memory. Although your computer might be rated at 640K, it really holds more than 640,000 bytes—655,360 to be exact.

Tape is to music as RAM is to characters.

The limit of RAM is similar to a cassette tape's storage limit. If a cassette tape is manufactured to hold 60 minutes of music, it does not hold 75 minutes of music. For programs in this book, the total characters that make up your program, any program data, and the computer's system programs cannot exceed your RAM's limit.

Generally, 640K is ample room for anything you would want to do in Turbo Pascal. Computer RAM is relatively inexpensive today.

If your computer has less than 640K of memory, you should consider purchasing additional memory to bring its total RAM up to 640K. You can put more than 640K in most PCs. This additional RAM is called *extended* or *expanded memory*. Expanded memory is memory you add to an original PC or XT. Extended memory is memory you add to an AT (286 and above). Typically, you need to use special techniques to access this extra RAM. Many Turbo Pascal programmers do not need to worry about RAM past 640K.

The computer stores Turbo Pascal programs to RAM as you write them. If you have used a word processor before, you have used RAM. As you typed words in your word-processed documents, the words appeared on the video screen. The words also went to RAM for storage.

Despite RAM's importance, it is only one type of memory in your computer. RAM is *volatile*. In other words, when you turn the computer off, all the RAM is erased. Therefore, you must store the contents of RAM to a nonvolatile, more permanent memory device (such as a disk) before turning off your computer. Otherwise, you lose your work.

Disk Storage

A *disk* is another type of computer memory, sometimes called *external memory*. Disk storage is nonvolatile. When you turn off your computer, the disk's contents are not erased. This is important to remember because after typing a long Turbo Pascal program into RAM, you do not want to retype that program every time you turn on your computer. Therefore, after creating a Turbo Pascal program, save the program to the disk. It remains there until you retrieve it.

Disk storage differs from RAM in ways other than volatility. Disk storage cannot be processed by the CPU. If you have a program or some data on disk that you want to use, you must transfer it from the disk to RAM. That is the only way the CPU can work with the program or data.

If all this sounds complicated, you only need to understand that data must be brought into RAM before your computer can process it. Most of the time, a Turbo Pascal program runs in RAM and brings in data from the disk as it needs it. Later in the book, you will find that working with disk files is not difficult.

There are two types of disks, *hard disks* and *floppy disks*. Hard disks (sometimes called *fixed disks*) hold much more data and are many times faster than floppy disks. Most of your Turbo Pascal programs and data are stored on your hard disk. Floppy disks are good for making backup copies of information on hard disks and for transferring data and programs from one computer to another. The removable floppy disks sometimes are called *diskettes*. Figure 1.2 shows two common diskette sizes, the 5¼-inch diskette and the 3½-inch diskette. Before using a new box of diskettes, you must format them for use on your computer. *Formatting* writes a pattern of paths called *tracks* where your data and programs will go. Before you use new diskettes, check the *MS-DOS Reference Manual* that came with your computer.

TIP: Some disks are already formatted when you buy them, which saves you the time and trouble of formatting them yourself.

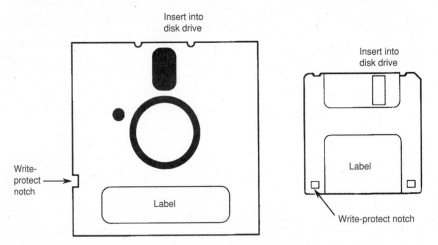

Figure 1.2. A 5¼-inch diskette and a 3½-inch diskette.

Disk drives hold the disks for use in your computer. Usually, the disk drives are part of your system unit. The hard disk stays sealed inside the hard disk drive, and you never remove it. You must insert and remove floppy diskettes to and from exterior disk drives.

Disk drives have names. The computer's first floppy disk drive is called A:. The second floppy disk drive, if you have one, is called B:. The first hard disk (many computers have only one) is called C:. If you have more than one hard disk, the rest are named D:, E:, and so on.

The size of the disk is measured in bytes, just as RAM is. Disk drives hold more data than RAM; in fact, they hold millions of bytes of data. A 40-million-byte hard disk is common. In computer terminology, a million bytes is a *megabyte*. Therefore, if your hard disk is a 20-megabyte hard disk, it holds about 20 million characters of data before it runs out of space.

The Monitor

The television-like screen is called the *monitor*. It is sometimes called the *CRT* (which stands for the primary component of the monitor, the *cathode ray tube*). The monitor is one place where the computer's output can be sent. If you want to look at a list of names and addresses, you can write a Turbo Pascal program to list the information on the monitor.

The advantage of reading output on-screen over printing on paper is that screen output is faster and does not waste paper. Screen output, however, is not permanent. When text is *scrolled* off the screen (displaced by additional text being sent), it is gone and you might not be able to see it again.

All monitors have a *cursor*, which is usually a blinking underline. The cursor moves when you type letters, which appear on-screen, and marks the location of the next character you will type.

Monitors that can display pictures are called *graphics monitors*. Although most PC monitors can display graphics and text, some can display only text. With Turbo Pascal, you can draw your own pictures on a graphics monitor. If your monitor cannot display colors, it is called a *monochrome* monitor.

Your monitor plugs into a *display adapter* located in the system unit. The display adapter determines the amount of resolution and the possible number of on-screen colors. The *resolution* refers to the number of row and column intersections. The higher the resolution, the sharper the graphics and text appear. Some common display adapters are the Hercules, MDA, CGA, EGA, and VGA display adapters.

The Printer

The *printer* provides a more permanent way of recording your computer's results. It is the "typewriter" of the computer. The printer prints Turbo Pascal program output to paper. You usually can print anything that appears on-screen. You can even print checks and envelopes with your printer.

The two most common PC printers are the *dot-matrix printer* and the *laser printer*. A dot-matrix printer is inexpensive and fast; it uses a series of small dots to represent printed text and graphics. When printing text, most laser printers are even faster than dot-matrix printers, and their output is much sharper. Laser printers are more expensive than dot-matrix printers, so their speed and quality come with a price. For many people, a dot-matrix printer provides all the quality and speed needed for most applications. Turbo Pascal can send output to either type of printer.

The Keyboard

Figure 1.3 shows three typical PC keyboards. Most of the keys are the same as on a standard typewriter. The letters and numbers in the large center of the keyboard produce the characters that you type on-screen. When you want to type an uppercase letter, press one of the *Shift* keys before typing the letter. Pressing the *Caps Lock* key displays every letter you type as an uppercase letter. When you want to type one of the special characters above a number, press the Shift key (even when you have Caps Lock on). For instance, to type the percent sign (%), press Shift-5.

You can use the *Alt* and *Ctrl* keys in conjunction with other keys, just as you did with the Shift key. Some Turbo Pascal commands and programs require you to hold down the Alt or Ctrl key while pressing another key. For instance, when Turbo Pascal prompts you to press Alt-F, you should press the Alt key, then press the F key while still holding Alt.

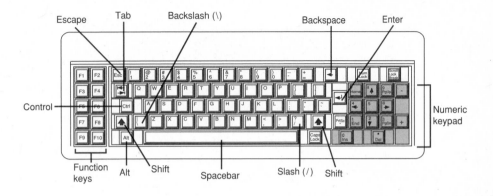

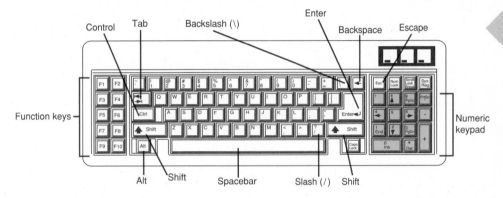

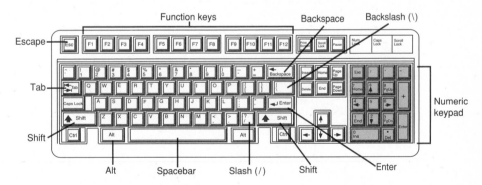

Figure 1.3. Three PC keyboards.

The key marked *Esc* is called the *Escape* key. In Turbo Pascal, you press this key to escape from something you have started. For instance, if you prompt Turbo Pascal for help and then you no longer need the help message, pressing Esc removes the help message from the screen.

The group of numbers and arrows on the far right side of the keyboard is called the *numeric keypad*. People familiar with a 10-key machine might prefer entering numbers from the keypad rather than from the top of the alphabetic key section. The numbers on the keypad work only when you press the *Num Lock* key. Pressing the Num Lock key a second time executes the arrow keys but not the numbers. Many keyboards have separate arrow keys that enable directional movement of the cursor while the keypad is being used solely for numbers.

The arrows enable you to move around the screen. Use the arrows to move the cursor from one area of the screen to another. To move the cursor toward the top of the screen, press the up-arrow key. To move the cursor to the right, press the right-arrow key, and so on. Do not confuse the Backspace key with the left-arrow key. *Backspace* moves the cursor back one character and erases as it moves. The left-arrow key simply moves the cursor backward without erasing.

The keys marked *Insert* and *Delete* are the editing keys on the keyboard. Later, you will see how to change program text within Turbo Pascal using these keys. If you have used a word processor before, Insert and Delete work in Turbo Pascal programs in the same manner that they work in the word processor's text. If you do not have separate keys labeled Insert and Delete, you may have to press the Num Lock key and use the keypad keys 0 (or Ins) and period (or Del) to perform text insertion and deletion.

Page Up and *Page Down* are the keys you press when you want to scroll the screen (move text on-screen) up and down. (On some keyboards, additional keys read PgUp and PgDn.) Your screen acts like a camera that scans your Turbo Pascal programs up and down. You can move the screen down the text (like panning a camera) by pressing the Page Down key, and up the text with the Page Up key. Like Insert and Delete, you might have to use the keypad if these actions are not on keys by themselves.

The keys labeled *F1 through F12* (some keyboards go only to F10) are called *function keys*. The function keys are located either across the top of your alphabetic section or to the left of it. These keys perform advanced functions. When you press one of them, you usually want to issue a complex command to Turbo Pascal, such as zooming a window. The Turbo Pascal function keys do not produce the same results as they might in another program, such as your word processor. They are *application-specific*.

Later, you will see examples that use the keyboard for different commands and functions in Turbo Pascal.

> **CAUTION:** Because computer keyboards have a key for number *1*, do not substitute the lowercase *l* to represent a *1* as you do on many typewriters. To Turbo Pascal, a *1* is different from the letter *l*. You also must be careful to use *0* when you mean zero, and *O* when you want the uppercase letter *O*.

The Mouse

The mouse is a relatively new input device. The *mouse* moves the mouse cursor to any location on-screen. If you have never used a mouse before, you should take time to become skillful in moving the mouse cursor with it. Chapter 2, "The Turbo Pascal Environment," explains the mouse's use in Turbo Pascal. You also can issue Turbo Pascal commands and select items on-screen by pointing to them with the mouse and pressing a button on the mouse.

Some mouse devices have two buttons, whereas others have three. Most of the time, pressing the third button produces the same result as simultaneously pressing both keys on a two-button mouse.

The Modem

The *modem* enables your PC to communicate with other computers over telephone lines. Some modems sit in a box outside your computer. Such modems are called *external modems. Internal modems* reside inside the system unit. It doesn't matter which one you have because they operate identically.

A modem is frequently used to speed things up by overcoming the distance between two computers.

Many people have modems so that they can share data between their computer and a friend's or coworker's computer. You can write programs in Turbo Pascal that communicate with your modem.

A Modem by Any Other Name...

You probably have heard the term *digital computer*. This term originates from the fact that your computer operates on binary (on and off) digital impulses of electricity. These digital states of electricity are perfect for your computer's equipment, but they cannot be sent over normal telephone lines. Telephone signals are called *analogsignals*, which are much different from the binary digital signals used by your PC.

Telephone lines are fine for analog signals, but they behave poorly when they send digital signals. Therefore, before your computer can transmit data over a telephone line, the information to be sent must be *modulated* (converted) into analog signals. The receiving computer then must *demodulate* (convert back) those signals to the digital information.

The modem provides the means by which your computer signals are *mod*ulated and *dem*odulated from digital to analog and back. Thus, the name of the device that modulates and demodulates these signals is *modem*.

The Computer's Software

No matter how fast, how large, or how powerful your computer's hardware is, the software determines what work actually gets done and how the computer does it. Software is to a computer what music is to a stereo system. You store software on the computer's disks and load it into your computer's memory when you are ready to process it, much like you store music on cassettes and compact discs so that you can play it later.

Programs and Data

No doubt you have heard of *data processing*. This is what computers really do: they take data and transform it into meaningful output. The meaningful output is called *information*. Figure 1.4 shows the *input-process-output* model. This input-process-output model is the foundation of everything that happens in your computer.

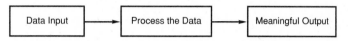

Figure 1.4. Data processing at its most elementary level.

In Chapter 2, "The Turbo Pascal Environment," you will learn the mechanics of programs. For now, you should know that programs you write in Turbo Pascal process the data you input into those programs. Both data and programs compose the software. The hardware acts as a vehicle that gathers the input and produces the output. Without software, computers would be worthless, just as an expensive stereo would be useless without some way of processing music so that you could hear it.

The input originates from input devices, such as keyboards, modems, and disk drives. The CPU processes the input and sends the results to the output devices, such as the printer and the monitor. A Turbo Pascal payroll program might obtain its input (the hours an employee worked) from the keyboard. It would then instruct the CPU to calculate the payroll amounts for each employee in the disk files. After processing the payroll, the program would print checks on the printer.

MS-DOS—The Operating System

MS-DOS must be loaded into your computer's RAM before you can do anything with the computer. MS-DOS stands for *Microsoft Disk Operating System*. MS-DOS, commonly called *DOS* for short, is a system program that permits your Turbo Pascal programs to interact with hardware. DOS is always loaded into RAM when you start your computer. DOS really controls more than just the disks; DOS is there so that your programs can communicate with all the hardware on the computer, including the monitor, keyboard, and printer.

Figure 1.5 illustrates the concept of DOS. It is the "go-between" for your computer's hardware and software. Because DOS understands how to control every device hooked to your computer, it stays in RAM and waits for a hardware request. For instance, printing the words *Turbo Pascal is fun!* on your printer requires many computer instructions. You do not need to worry about all those instructions, however. When your Turbo Pascal program wants to print something, it actually tells DOS what to print. Because DOS always knows how to send information to your printer, it acquires your Turbo Pascal program requests and does the dirty work of routing that data to the printer.

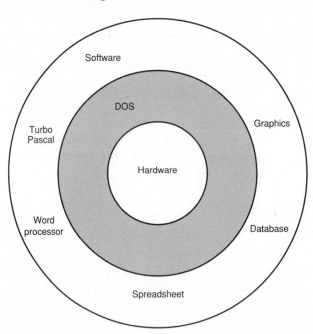

Figure 1.5. MS-DOS is the intermediary between the software and the hardware.

Many people have programmed computers for years without really learning why DOS is there. You do not need to be a DOS expert or even know more than a few simple DOS commands to be proficient with your PC. Nevertheless, DOS performs some operations more conveniently than Turbo Pascal, such as formatting diskettes. As you learn more about the computer, you might see the need to better understand DOS. For a good introduction to using DOS, check *Using MS-DOS 5*, Second Edition, published by Que Corporation.

NOTE: As mentioned earlier, DOS always resides in RAM and is loaded when you start the computer. This is done automatically so that you can use your computer and program in Turbo Pascal without worrying about how to get DOS into RAM. It is important to remember that DOS always uses some of your total RAM.

Figure 1.6 illustrates the placement of DOS and its relationship to Turbo Pascal and your Turbo Pascal program area in RAM. The 640K of RAM usually is pictured as in Figure 1.6: a bunch of boxes stacked on top of each other. Each memory location (each byte) has a unique *address*, just as everybody's house has a unique address. The first address in memory is 0, the second RAM location's address is 1, and so on until the last RAM location (which comes thousands of bytes later).

DOS reserves part of the first few thousand bytes of memory. The amount of RAM that DOS reserves varies with each computer's configuration. When working in Turbo Pascal, the Turbo Pascal system sits on top of DOS, leaving the remainder of RAM for your program and data. This explains why you can have a total of 512K of RAM and still not have enough memory to run some programs; DOS is reserving some of the memory for itself.

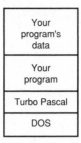

Figure 1.6. After memory is reserved for MS-DOS, Turbo Pascal, and a Turbo Pascal program, the remaining space is all you have for data.

Summary

Whether you are new to Turbo Pascal or are an experienced programmer, Turbo Pascal is a language that suits almost all your programming needs. Turbo Pascal is all you require to produce computer programs that make the computer work the way you want it to.

This chapter presented the background of Turbo Pascal by walking you through the history of the Pascal programming language. Turbo Pascal did not forget its roots, so it is an easy language that beginning programmers can learn. Turbo Pascal, however, offers some of the most advanced programming language commands that exist today. The rest of this book is devoted to teaching you Turbo Pascal. Chapter 2, "The Turbo Pascal Environment," explains the Turbo Pascal screen and environment so that you can start writing Turbo Pascal programs.

Review Questions

Answers to the Review Questions appear in Appendix B.

1. What is RAM?

2. How is RAM measured?

3. What is the main difference between RAM and a hard disk?

4. Which usually holds more data: RAM or the hard disk?

5. What is the name of the device your PC uses to communicate over telephone lines?

6. What type of device is the mouse?

   A. Storage device

   B. Input device

   C. Output device

   D. Processing device

7. What key do you press to turn on the numbers on the numeric keypad?

8. What is the main advantage of Pascal over other languages?

9. What was the main innovation of Turbo Pascal?

10. What program controls your computer?

11. Why do we say that RAM is volatile?

12. True or False: The greater the resolution, the better graphics look on-screen.

13. How many bytes is 512K?

14. What does *modem* stand for?

The Turbo Pascal Environment

Turbo Pascal offers an array of helpful tools, such as a full-screen editor, pull-down menus, helpful advice, mouse support, and an integrated debugger. These tools make up the Integrated Development Environment (IDE).

This chapter introduces the following topics:

♦ Starting Turbo Pascal

♦ Understanding Turbo Pascal's screen

♦ Using Turbo Pascal's menus

♦ Getting help in Turbo Pascal

♦ Leaving Turbo Pascal

This chapter shows you how to use the IDE.

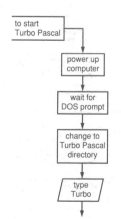

Starting Turbo Pascal

To begin using Turbo Pascal, start your computer. On most systems, a DOS prompt appears, similar to the following:

```
C:\
```

If your PC displays a menu on start-up and Turbo Pascal is not a menu option, you can't start Turbo Pascal until you choose the menu option that exits the menu and takes you to DOS. If you use Turbo Pascal often, you might want to add the Turbo Pascal start-up command to your menu. If you don't know how to do this, contact the person who installed the menu program on your computer.

When you have installed Turbo Pascal and have accepted the installation's suggested directory, Turbo Pascal is located in the \TP directory on your hard disk. To load Turbo Pascal on most computers, you only need to type CD\TP, press Enter, and then type TURBO in either uppercase or lowercase letters. After you type TURBO and press Enter, the Turbo Pascal opening screen appears (see Figure 2.1).

Figure 2.1. The Turbo Pascal opening screen.

If an error message occurs, the directory with Turbo Pascal may be named something other than \TP. In such a case, you might have to contact the person who set up your computer to find where Turbo Pascal is installed.

With one simple technique, you can start Turbo Pascal from any directory. You should add \TP (the directory where Turbo Pascal is stored) to your PATH command in AUTOEXEC.BAT. After adding this path, you can start Turbo Pascal. See Que's *Using MS-DOS 5* for more information on the PATH command.

Proper Start-Up

There is a proper sequence to follow when turning on your computer. The sequence is easy to remember with the following rule:

The boss always comes to work last and is the first to go home.

Have you had bosses like that? Your computer's start-up sequence should follow that rule: the system unit (the "boss" that holds the CPU) should come to work last. In other words, turn on everything else first, including the printer, monitor, and modem. Only then should you turn on the system unit. This keeps system unit power surges to a minimum and protects circuits inside the unit.

When you are ready to shutdown the computer, turn off the system unit first (the boss goes home first). Then, turn off the rest of the equipment in whatever order is most convenient.

TIP: If your computer equipment is plugged into a switched surge protector, it is acceptable to use the single switch for all your equipment, including your system unit. The surge protector ensures that power reaches the system unit as evenly as possible.

Starting Turbo Pascal from Windows

If you use Microsoft Windows, one of the easiest ways to start Turbo Pascal is to select the File Manager, open the \TP subdirectory, and click twice on TURBO.EXE. Figure 2.2 shows Turbo Pascal being started from the File Manager screen.

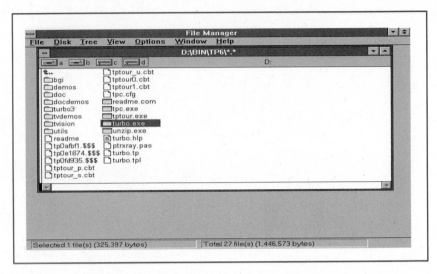

Figure 2.2. Starting Turbo Pascal from the Windows File Manager.

Turbo Pascal works in all Windows modes. A Turbo Pascal .PIF file is not supplied with Turbo Pascal, however, and no Window icon for Turbo Pascal exists. (You must run Turbo Pascal as a DOS application.) You can, however, switch from Turbo Pascal to another Windows application by pressing Ctrl–Esc, just as you do with any Windows-based application.

After mastering Turbo Pascal, you may want to consider using Turbo Pascal for Windows (TPW). TPW is a separate product designed to develop Turbo Pascal programs as Windows applications.

Starting Turbo Pascal with Command-Line Options

You can add several options to the Turbo Pascal start-up command. These options, listed in Table 2.1, modify the Turbo Pascal environment to alter the way it starts. With some options, you can place a + or - after the option to turn it on or off. Other options require a number. Some options will make more sense when you learn more about Turbo Pascal. Typically, you use command-line options when you want to start Turbo Pascal in a slightly different way. All the following options may be set directly in the IDE.

Table 2.1. Turbo Pascal start-up command-line options.

Option	Meaning
/C	Use this option with the filename of a particular configuration file. The filename must follow the /C with no spaces.
/D	Use this option if you have either two video cards or two monitors.
/Enn	Use this option to change the size of the editor heap from a default size of 28K to a maximum of 128K. Used mostly with a slow disk.
filename	Use this option to load the ASCII Turbo Pascal program called filename into the editor when Turbo Pascal starts. This is faster than starting Turbo Pascal and then selecting menu options to load the program. The filename must be a valid Turbo Pascal program with a .PAS extension.
/G	Use this option to direct the IDE to save another 8K buffer for debugging graphics programs in EGA, VGA, or MCGA mode. This is often used when you do not have two monitors.
/L	Use this option if you have an LCD screen.
/N	Use this option for older CGAs (Color Graphics Adapters) that flicker during screen updates.
/Onn	Use this option to change the IDE's overlay heap size. The default is 112K, the minimum is 64K, and the maximum is 256K.
/P	Use this option if you need to restore the EGA palette registers when a screen is swapped.

continues

Table 2.1. Continued.

Option	Meaning
/S	Use this option to specify where the swap file should be located. For example, if you have drive E: set up as a RAM drive, use /SE:\. The swap file is a temporary file (of form TP*hhhhhh*.$$$ where *h* is a hex digit) used by the editor.
/T	When your programs start getting large, use this option to prevent Turbo Pascal from loading TURBO.TPL into memory. Use TPUMOVER to extract all the standard units you need. Turbo Pascal will access these standard units by way of disk instead of memory.
/W*nn*	Use this option to change the window heap size. The default size is 32K, the minimum is 24K, and the maximum is 64K.
/X	Use this option to prevent Turbo Pascal from using expanded memory.

Examples

1. To start Turbo Pascal, load a program called MYFILE.PAS into the Turbo Pascal editor, and use a previously defined configuration file, type the following at the DOS prompt:

   `C:\TURBO MYFILE /CMyFile.TP`

   You can type the options in any order, as well as use upper-case or lowercase characters.

2. To start Turbo Pascal on an LCD laptop without color, you might make Turbo Pascal more readable by starting it with

   `C:\TURBO /L`

   The preceding line starts Turbo Pascal on a laptop computer with an LCD screen.

The Turbo Pascal Screen

Figure 2.3 shows the parts of the Turbo Pascal screen. From this screen you create, modify, and execute Turbo Pascal programs. After you start the Turbo Pascal program, press Esc to clear any copyright message. You see the Turbo Pascal screen. If you have a mouse, move it around on your desk so that you can see the mouse cursor.

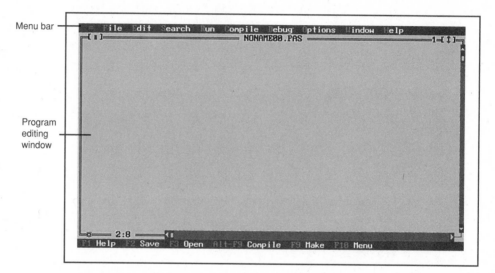

Figure 2.3. The parts of the Turbo Pascal screen.

Using the Mouse

You use the mouse to move around the screen quickly. Before mouse devices became common, users had to press the arrow keys continuously to move the cursor from one location to another. Now they can move the cursor by rolling the mouse across the desktop and clicking the cursor at the desired position.

continues

Throughout this book, you are asked to perform certain actions with the mouse. These require moving the mouse and using a mouse button. Press only the left button except when you need to get help. To get help with the mouse, press the right button.

When you are asked to *click* the mouse button, press and immediately release it. You might click the mouse button to select an item from a menu or to move the text cursor around the screen. Sometimes you click the mouse button after moving the mouse cursor over a *Yes* or *No* answer in response to a question.

Double-clicking the mouse button means pressing the mouse button twice in rapid succession. You can double-click the mouse to select a single line of text.

When you are asked to *drag* the mouse, press and hold the mouse button without letting up, and move the mouse cursor across the screen. Usually the area where you drag the mouse is highlighted on-screen, so you can see the path the mouse leaves. When you are finished marking the path, release the mouse button. This is one way to select several lines from a Turbo Pascal program so that you can move or erase them.

You will discover several more screen elements as you continue to use Turbo Pascal. These elements are discussed in later sections of this book.

The most important part of the screen is the *program editing window*, in which you work with Turbo Pascal programs. The window acts like a word processor's document-editing area. You can move the cursor with the arrow keys or mouse and make any necessary changes to the text.

The *menu bar* at the top of the screen makes using Turbo Pascal easy. Turbo Pascal programmers select only what they need from the menu bar.

Throughout this book, you learn many uses for the Turbo Pascal screen. For now, familiarize yourself with the names of the different parts of the screen. The rest of the book refers to these names.

Selecting from
Turbo Pascal's Menus

How do you know what to order when you dine at a new restaurant? You choose from a menu. Restaurant owners know that people who eat in their restaurants have not memorized everything the restaurant serves. In the same way, the authors of Turbo Pascal understood that users don't want to memorize the commands that control Turbo Pascal. They would rather look at a list of possible commands and select the desired one.

The Turbo Pascal menu bar displays ≡, **F**ile, **E**dit, **S**earch, **R**un, **C**ompile, **D**ebug, **O**ptions, **W**indow, and **H**elp. You can select these items from the Turbo Pascal screen by pressing Alt and the high-lighted menu option letter, pressing F10 to access the menu bar and using the arrow keys, or clicking a menu option. These menu options are not commands, but are instead headings for additional pull-down menus. These items are called *pull-down menus* because of their resemblance to a window shade being pulled down. For example, Figure 2.4 shows what happens if you select the File pull-down menu.

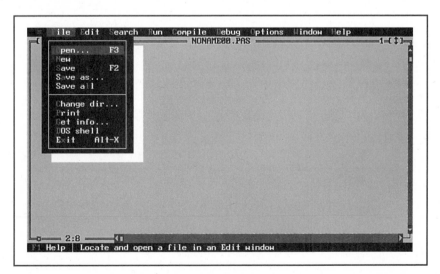

Figure 2.4. Viewing the complete File pull-down menu.

When you want to see any of the menus, you can use either the mouse or the keyboard. To display a pull-down menu with the mouse, move the mouse cursor over a menu bar item and click (see the sidebar "Using the Mouse"). If you click each of the rest of the words on the menu bar, you will see the remaining pull-down menus in succession.

Displaying a pull-down menu from the keyboard is just as easy as displaying it with the mouse. Press the Alt key followed by the first letter of the menu you want to see. For example, to display the Edit pull-down menu, press Alt–E.

If you change your mind, you can press Esc to remove a displayed menu. You are, in effect, escaping from the command you started.

> **TIP:** To display a menu, mouse users sometimes prefer the keyboard's Alt–*key* combination to clicking the mouse. Because your hands are already on the keyboard, pressing Alt–S for Search might be faster than pointing with the mouse and clicking.

Choosing an Option

When you display a pull-down menu, you must tell Turbo Pascal which command on the menu's list to perform. For example, the File pull-down menu lists several commands. You can request the command you want in one of three ways:

◆ Clicking with the mouse

◆ Pointing with the keyboard arrow keys

◆ Pressing the command's highlighted letter

For example, to request the New command, mouse users move the mouse cursor until it sits anywhere on the word New. One click of the mouse chooses the New command. Keyboard users press the down arrow until the New command is highlighted. Pressing the Enter key carries out the command. Keyboard users can also use a shortcut: simply typing the highlighted letter (called a *hot key* or *mnemonic key*) of the command they want. By pressing the *N* key, the keyboard user executes the **N**ew command. You can use either uppercase or lowercase letters to select any command.

If you begin to select from a menu but then change your mind, press Esc to close the menu and return to the program editing window. Mouse users only need to click the mouse outside the pull-down menu area to close the menu.

> **TIP:** The best way to learn how to choose items from Turbo Pascal's pull-down menus is to experiment. As long as you don't save anything to disk, you can't harm existing Turbo Pascal program files or data.

Sometimes commands appear in gray and are not as readable as others. For example, Figure 2.5 shows the Edit pull-down menu. Notice that most of the options on the menu are in gray and have no highlighted letter. You can't choose any of these commands. Turbo Pascal displays these commands so that you remember where they are when you need them. These commands return to their normal colors as they become available for operation in your Turbo Pascal session.

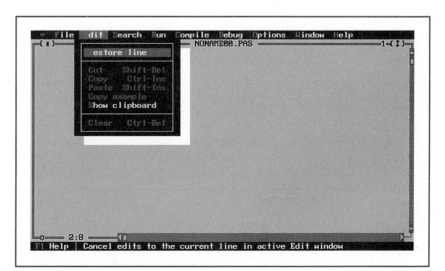

Figure 2.5. The Edit pull-down menu.

Using Menu Shortcut Keys

After using Turbo Pascal for a while, you become familiar with the commands on the pull-down menus. Despite the ease of using Turbo Pascal menus, there is a faster way to select some of these commands. Turbo Pascal's *shortcut keys* (also called *accelerator keys*) are easier to use than the menus, regardless of whether you use a mouse or a keyboard.

Many of the function keys execute menu commands when you press them. Table 2.2 lists these shortcuts. For example, to choose **W**indow | User screen, you could display the Window pull-down menu and then select User screen. On the **W**indow | User screen menu option, however, Alt–F5 is listed to the right. The listing to the right of an option is the shortcut key for that menu option. Instead of going through the menu steps, you can press Alt–F5 and immediately run the User screen command. You will understand the function of each of these shortcut keys as you learn more about Turbo Pascal.

Table 2.2. Turbo Pascal menu shortcut keys.

Key	Menu Command
F1	Help
F1	Help on help
F2	File	Save
F3	File	Open
F4	Run	Go to cursor
F5	Window	Zoom
F6	Window	Next
F7	Run	Trace into
F8	Run	Step over
F9	Compile	Make
F10	Menu Bar
Ctrl–Del	Edit	Clear (erase selected text)

Key	Menu Command
Ctrl–Ins	Edit I Copy to Clipboard
Ctrl–F1	Help I Topic search
Ctrl–F2	Run I Program reset
Ctrl–F3	Window I Call stack
Ctrl–F4	Debug I Evaluate/modify
Ctrl–F5	Window I Size/Move
Ctrl–F7	Debug I Watches I Add watch
Ctrl–F8	Debug I Toggle breakpoint
Ctrl–F9	Run I Run
Shift–Del	Edit I Cut
Shift–F1	Help I Index
Shift–F6	Window I Previous
Alt–Spacebar	≡ (Systems menu)
Alt–0	Window I List
Alt–F1	Help I Previous topic
Alt–F3	Window I Close
Alt–F5	Window I User screen
Alt–F9	Compile I Compile
Alt–X	File I Exit (quit Turbo Pascal)
Shift–Ins	Edit I Paste from clipboard

Using Dialog Boxes

Not all menu commands execute when you select them. Some are followed by an ellipsis (...), such as the File I Open... command. If you choose one of these commands, a *dialog box* opens in the middle of the screen. You must type more information before Turbo Pascal can carry out the command.

This extra information might be a number, a word, a filename, or the selection of one option from several. Sometimes, a dialog box requires a combination of several things from you.

In addition to the ellipsis, some menu commands are followed by a solid right arrow (→), such as Options | Environment. If you choose one of these commands, a submenu is displayed below the selected menu option. For example, press Alt–O to select the Options menu. Press E to select Environment.

Figure 2.6 shows the Options | Environment | Colors... dialog box. This is a good time to practice using a dialog box and changing Turbo Pascal's screen colors at the same time (assuming you have a color monitor). Select Colors... from the Environment menu (which is under the Options menu). Under Group, select Editor. Now press Tab to go to the Item window (or click inside the Item window). Select Normal text.

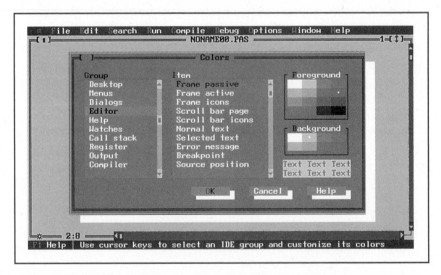

Figure 2.6. The Options|Environment|Colors... dialog box.

The Foreground option enables you to change the color of the characters on-screen, whereas the Background option enables you to change the color of the screen behind the characters.

Now, move to the Foreground color chart by pressing Tab or by clicking the color chart with the mouse. (This is how you move between sections of a dialog box.) Use the arrow keys to highlight the foreground color you prefer or click the desired color.

When you finish with the Foreground box, Tab to the Background color chart and select a background color or click the desired color. Press Enter to select OK or click the OK button. The text and screen of your Turbo Pascal programs now appear in the colors you selected. You can change the colors at any time. To save your changes in a configuration file, select Options | Save options. The standard name for the configuration file is TURBO.TP.

Notice the shaded bars to the right and bottom of the Editor window. These are the *scroll bars*. They show the relative position of the selected item in a list. The scroll bars are helpful if you have a mouse. When you point to the down arrow on a scroll bar and click the mouse, the editor scrolls upward. Conversely, clicking the up arrow of a scroll bar scrolls the editor downward. This is faster than using the arrow keys to scroll.

To see another type of dialog box, press Alt–O to select the Options Menu. Press E to select Environment again. Press E to select the Editor... option. Wherever you see brackets to the left of a dialog box choice, you can only toggle that choice on or off. An x in the brackets turns the option on, and a blank turns the option off. For example, to turn off Create backup files, press the Spacebar (or press hot key, **f**) to remove the x you see. Mouse users can click with the left mouse button. Conversely, pressing the Spacebar at the empty brackets of a dialog box choice marks that choice with the x.

The Tab size option illustrates the last type of dialog box. You can set the number of spaces that each Tab keystroke moves the cursor when you are writing Turbo Pascal programs. The default (the setting automatically used unless you specify otherwise) is eight spaces. You can replace the default by moving to the 8 and typing another number. If you leave the dialog box and start typing a Turbo Pascal program, the Tab key moves the cursor the number of spaces you requested every time you press that key.

> **TIP:** Setting the Tab Stops to three spaces usually is sufficient. Too many Tab spaces can force programs to pour over the right side of the screen. This book's Turbo Pascal program listings use 3 as the Tab Stop setting.

When you are finished with a dialog box, press Enter or click OK to implement your new dialog box selections. If you change your mind, even after changing the options in the dialog box, you can press Esc or click Cancel to close the dialog box and return to the original options. Clicking Help displays a help screen that explains everything you can do in the current dialog box. More of Turbo Pascal's online Help feature is explained in the next section.

Getting Help

When using Turbo Pascal, you can get help at any time by pressing F1. Help explains virtually every aspect of Turbo Pascal and the IDE. The Turbo Pascal Help system gives several kinds of help. Depending on your request, Turbo Pascal helps you with whatever you need, and even offers example programs that you can paste into your own programs.

For example, if you want help on the Search menu, highlight the Search menu and press F1 (see Figure 2.7). Mouse users can click Search with the right button.

The Help Menu

Figure 2.8 shows the Help pull-down menu. You can access the Topic command from the Help menu (although pressing Ctrl–F1 is easier).

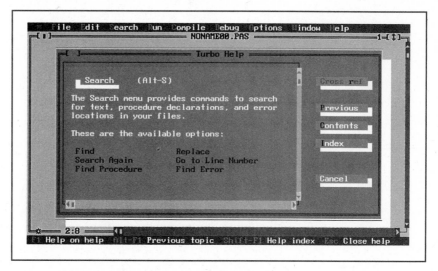

Figure 2.7. Getting help with the Help system.

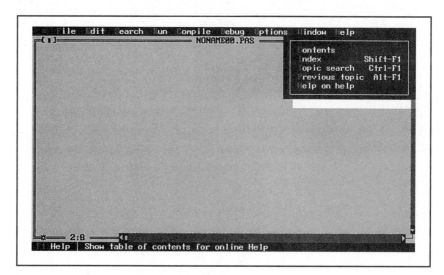

Figure 2.8. The Help pull-down menu.

The Help Table of Contents

Selecting **Help** | **Contents** displays the screen shown in Figure 2.9. The Contents screen displays help on various parts of Turbo Pascal by subject: How to Use Help, Menus and Hot Keys, Editor Commands, and a list of miscellaneous topics.

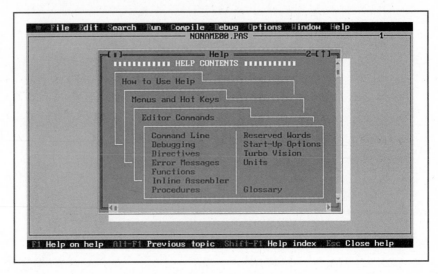

Figure 2.9. The Help table of contents.

The Help Index

Choosing **Help** | **Index** displays an extensive list of words and symbols used in Turbo Pascal. At this point, most of the topics probably make little sense to you. As you learn more about the Turbo Pascal programming language, however, you will understand these topics better. As shown in Figure 2.10, only a few of the topics fit on-screen at one time.

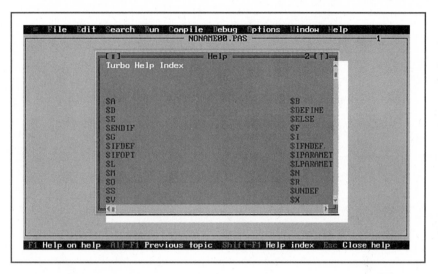

Figure 2.10. The Help index.

The index is more than just a list of topics. You can click (or use the arrow keys and press Enter) any topic in the list. A detailed explanation for that topic appears—often with sample Turbo Pascal program sections. As with all help screens, pressing Esc exits the help system.

Topic Search Help

When you become familiar with Turbo Pascal, the *context-sensitive help* feature will relieve some of your programming frustration. Whenever you request context-sensitive help by pressing Ctrl–F1 or choosing Help | Topic search, Turbo Pascal "looks" at what you are doing and provides you help with your problem. For example, if you are working on the Turbo Pascal WRITELN statement and the cursor is resting over the word WRITELN, when you press Ctrl–F1, Turbo Pascal displays help on the WRITELN command.

Previous Topic Help

This is a handy option when you need to quickly review a help screen you viewed previously. Using the shortcut combination Alt–F1, you can view up to 20 previous screens.

Help on Help

The Turbo Pascal online help system is so complete that it even provides help about using Help. The Help on help option explains the many ways to get help from Turbo Pascal. Selecting **Help** on help produces the screen shown in Figure 2.11. You can press the up-arrow key, the down-arrow key, the Page Up key, or the Page Down key to scroll through the text on-screen. Mouse users can click the scroll bar to scroll the text. You might find it helpful to press F5 (Window I Zoom) so that you can use the whole screen to view the Help window.

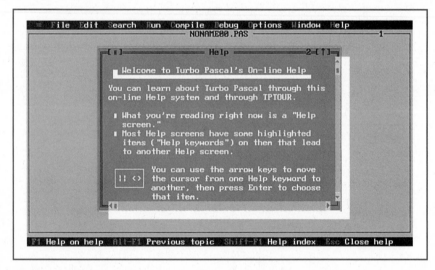

Figure 2.11. Help on help.

The System Menu (≡)

Selecting ≡ displays a submenu. When you select About..., a dialog box appears in the center of the screen that shows the version number of Turbo Pascal you are using. This is helpful if you call Borland for support and need to supply the version number of Turbo Pascal. Pressing Enter, Esc, or clicking OK removes the dialog box from the screen and returns you to the program editing window.

Quitting Turbo Pascal

When you finish your Turbo Pascal session, you can exit and return to DOS by choosing File | Exit (Alt–X). It is important to exit to DOS before turning off your computer because you might lose some of your work if you do not. If you made changes to a Turbo Pascal program and you try to exit to DOS without saving those changes to disk, Turbo Pascal displays the warning message dialog box shown in Figure 2.12.

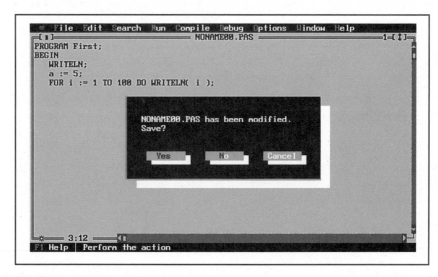

Figure 2.12. The Turbo Pascal warning message to save a file.

If you choose **Yes**, Turbo Pascal prompts you for a filename under which to save the file. Choosing **No** instructs Turbo Pascal that you want to exit to DOS without saving the file, although the latest changes are not recorded. Cancel instructs Turbo Pascal to return to the program editing window.

Summary

This chapter introduced you to Turbo Pascal's Integrated Development Environment (IDE). You learned how to start Turbo Pascal, use the menus, request online help, and exit the program. With its intuitive interface, Turbo Pascal makes working easy, whether you have a mouse or a keyboard.

This chapter prepares you for Chapter 3, "What Is a Program?," in which you learn the mechanics of programming, how to use the Turbo Pascal editor, and what you need to know to run your first Turbo Pascal program.

Review Questions

Answers to the Review Questions appear in Appendix B.

1. How would you start Turbo Pascal so that file ARTY.PAS would appear in an editor window?

2. Which part of the Turbo Pascal screen retains the program as you type it?

3. What are the differences among clicking, double-clicking, and dragging your mouse?

4. Do you need to remember command names so that Turbo Pascal can execute them? Why or why not?

5. What key do you press to access the menu bar?

6. What does *context-sensitive help* mean?

7. Why should you exit Turbo Pascal and return to DOS before turning off your computer?

8. What are two ways to get help in Turbo Pascal?

9. What key do you use to delete the character to the left of the cursor?

    A. F1

    B. Esc

    C. Backspace

    D. Right arrow

10. What are command-line options used for?

11. What are the keyboard shortcut keys used for?

What Is a Program?

Programming computers has been described by different people at different times as rewarding, challenging, easy, difficult, fast, and slow. Programming is a combination of all these descriptions. Programming your computer takes time, but you can have fun along the way, especially with help from Turbo Pascal. Writing more advanced programs takes time and can be frustrating, but when a complex program works well, the feeling is gratifying.

This chapter describes the concept of programming, from a program's inception to its execution on the PC. The most difficult part of programming is breaking the problem into logical steps that the computer can carry out. In this chapter, you will type and execute your first Turbo Pascal program.

This chapter covers the following topics:

- ◆ Understanding programming
- ◆ Running the programs included with Turbo Pascal
- ◆ Designing a program
- ◆ Using the Turbo Pascal editor
- ◆ Typing and running your first Turbo Pascal program

After completing this chapter, you will be ready for Chapter 4, which explains how to manage your Turbo Pascal program files.

Computer Programs

Program: A collection of instructions that directs the computer to perform certain tasks.

Before you can make Turbo Pascal work for you, you need to write a Turbo Pascal program. So far, you have seen the word *program* used several times in this book. Now is a good time to define a program as a group of instructions that makes the computer do things.

Keep in mind that computers are machines. They are not smart. In fact, they are quite the opposite. Computers cannot do anything until you provide them with detailed instructions. When you use your computer for word processing, the word processor is a program that someone wrote (in a language such as Turbo Pascal) telling the computer exactly how to behave when you type words.

If you ever have followed a recipe, you are familiar with the concept of programming. A recipe is just a program (a set of instructions) telling the cook how to make a certain dish. A good recipe gives these instructions in the proper order, completely describes how to cook the dish, and makes no assumptions that the cook knows anything about the dish in advance.

If you want your computer to help with your budget, keep track of names and addresses, or compute gas mileage for your travels, you must provide a program that tells the computer how to do those things. You can supply that program to your computer in two different ways: buy a program written by somebody else that performs the job you want, or write the program yourself.

Writing the program yourself is a big advantage for many applications because the program does exactly what you want it to do. If you buy one that is already written, you must adapt your needs to the needs of the program's designers. That's where Turbo Pascal comes into the picture. With Turbo Pascal (and a little study), you can direct your computer to perform any task.

Because computers are machines that do not think, the instructions you write in Turbo Pascal are detailed. You cannot assume that the computer understands what to do if the instruction is not in your program.

After you write a Turbo Pascal program, you then must *run*, or *execute*, it. Otherwise, your computer doesn't know that you want it to follow the instructions in the program. Just as a cook must follow a recipe's instructions before a dish is made, your computer must execute the program's instructions before it can accomplish what you want.

Borland supplies several Turbo Pascal sample programs. To better understand the process of running a program's instructions, take some time (and have some fun) running these Turbo Pascal programs. The next section explains the process.

Running the Borland Turbo Pascal Example Programs

Borland includes several programs that you can load into Turbo Pascal and run immediately. As explained in Chapter 1, "Welcome to Turbo Pascal," your computer must transfer programs from the disk to RAM before your CPU can execute the program's instructions. Before learning more about how to write your own programs, become familiar with what Turbo Pascal does by looking at the sample programs.

Table 3.1 describes two Borland Turbo Pascal programs and their disk filenames. The filenames are important, because without them Turbo Pascal doesn't know which program you want to run. (You can run only one program at a time.)

Table 3.1. Borland Turbo Pascal sample programs.

Filename	Description
ARTY.PAS	A computer version of a kaleidoscope.
BGIDEMO.PAS	A program that illustrates graphics features.

Notice that all Turbo Pascal filenames end in the extension .PAS. When you save a Turbo Pascal program to disk and Turbo Pascal prompts you for a filename, the editor assumes the .PAS extension without requiring you to type it.

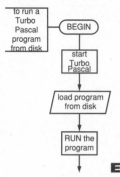

To run a Turbo Pascal program that is stored on disk, you must

1. Start Turbo Pascal.

2. Load the program into Turbo Pascal's program editing window.

3. Run the program.

Example

You can run the program by selecting from the menus. For example, run the ARTY.PAS program using the following steps:

1. Start Turbo Pascal by typing TURBO at the DOS prompt.

2. Select **O**pen... from the **F**ile pull-down menu. You see the Open a File dialog box as shown in Figure 3.1. Assuming you have installed Turbo Pascal on drive c: and in directory \TP, type c:\TP\BGI\ARTY and press Enter. (If you installed Turbo Pascal on a different drive or in different directories, you need to use your settings. When I refer to c:\TP\BGI in later sections, you should use your settings instead.)

   These two sample programs require a monitor that can display graphics.

3. After a brief pause, the program editing window is filled with the ARTY.PAS program from the disk. The program's filename appears in the center of the bar above the program editing area. If this is the first time you have seen a Turbo Pascal program, you might want to look through it to familiarize yourself with a large Turbo Pascal program.

4. Before you can run this program, you need to make two adjustments. First, edit one line in the program so that it will know where to find some graphics tools. Press Alt–S to select the **S**earch menu. From the pull-down menu, select the **G**o to line number... option. In the dialog box, type 194 for the line number and press Enter. The cursor should now

appear on the line starting with InitGraph. Change
InitGraph(GraphDriver, GraphMode, ''); to
InitGraph(GraphDriver, GraphMode, 'C:\TP\BGI');. (For the
BGIDemo program, go to line number 82 to make a similar
change.)

Now for the second change. Edit the IDE so that it can find
the graph file, GRAPH.TPU. Press Alt–O to select **O**ptions.
In the pull-down menu, press D to select **D**irectories. Press
Tab twice to move to the Unit Directories field. Then type
C:\TP\BGI and press Enter.

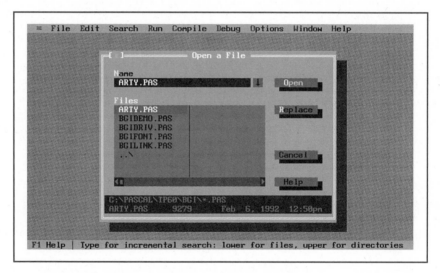

Figure 3.1. Selecting from the Open a File dialog box.

5. Select **R**un from the **R**un pull-down menu, or press Ctrl–F9.
   The program displays patterns and their mirror images.
   Figure 3.2 shows a sample session. When you are finished
   with the program, press Esc to quit.

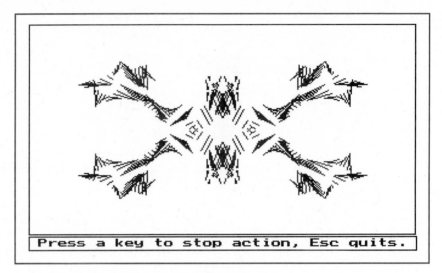

Figure 3.2. The ARTY.PAS game during play.

Stopping a Turbo Pascal Program

Most Turbo Pascal programs offer you a chance to quit when the program arrives at a logical stopping place. Sometimes, however, you might want to stop a Turbo Pascal program in the middle of its execution.

Stopping a Turbo Pascal program while it is in progress is simple. When you press Ctrl–Break, the program stops and the program editing window reappears. You then can load another program, select **R**un (Ctrl–F9), or exit to DOS.

Using Ctrl–Break

With some programs, you may not want the user to stop the program with Ctrl–Break. For example, this may cause some problems in the program disk files. At the start of your program, you can include the statement `CheckBreak := FALSE;`. The program now ignores Ctrl–Break.

> **The Program and Its Output**
>
> While programming, remember the difference between the program and its output. Your program contains the instructions that you write with Turbo Pascal. Only after you run the program does Turbo Pascal follow your instructions.
>
> Throughout this book, you will see a program listing (the Turbo Pascal instructions in the program) followed by the results that occur when you run the program. The results are the output of the program. They go to an *output device* such as a screen, a printer, or a disk file.

Output Device: Where the results of a computer program go—usually a screen, a printer, or a disk file.

Program Design

Design your programs before you type them.

You must plan your programs before you type them. When building houses, a carpenter doesn't pick up a hammer and nails and start building. A carpenter first finds out what the owner of the house wants, draws up the plans, orders the materials, gathers the workers, and *then* starts hammering the nails.

The hardest part of writing a program is breaking it into logical steps that the computer can follow. Learning the language is a requirement; however, the language is not the only thing to consider. Learning the formal program-writing procedure makes your programming job easier. To write a program you should:

1. Define the problem to be solved with the computer.

2. Design the output of the program (what the user sees).

3. Break the problem into logical steps to achieve the solution.

4. Write the program (this is where Turbo Pascal comes into play).

5. Test the program to ensure that it performs as expected.

As you can see, the actual typing of the program occurs toward the end of the programming process. You must plan how to tell a computer to perform certain tasks.

Your computer can perform instructions only in a step-by-step fashion. You must assume that your computer has no previous knowledge of the problem and that you must supply the computer with that knowledge. That is what good recipes do: a recipe for baking a cake that simply states, "Bake the cake" wouldn't be of much use because it assumes entirely too much from the cook. Even if the recipe is written in a step-by-step manner, you must ensure that the steps are in sequence (by planning in advance). Putting the ingredients in the oven before stirring them wouldn't be prudent.

This book follows the same step-by-step process that a computer program and a good recipe should follow. Before you see a program, this book shows you the thought process behind it. This book tells you the goals of the program, breaks them into logical steps, and then shows the written program.

Designing the program in advance makes the entire program structure more accurate and saves you from changing it much. A builder knows that a room is much harder to add after the house is built than before. When you don't plan properly and don't map out every step of your program, creating the final working program takes longer. Making major changes to a program is more difficult if you have already written it than if you make changes in the design stage.

Developing programs using these five steps becomes more important as you write longer and more complicated programs. Throughout this book, you will see tips for program design. Now, you can jump into Turbo Pascal and see what it's like to type and run your own program.

Using the Program Editor

Turbo Pascal's program editor is like a word processor. You can type a program, change it, move parts of it around, and erase pieces of it. You execute most of these functions from the menu bar, so you don't need to remember command names.

Typing a Program

Turbo Pascal programs appear in the large program editor window as you type them. After typing the program's instructions, you should run the program to witness the results and fix any problems that might arise. Before worrying about Turbo Pascal's instructions, type a program in the program editing window. The most important thing to understand is how to move the cursor. Keep the following helpful hints in mind:

♦ The cursor shows you where the next character you type will appear.

♦ Press Enter after each line in the program.

♦ The Backspace key moves the cursor to the left and erases as it moves.

♦ Use the arrow keys, Page Up, and Page Down to move the cursor left, right, up, and down the screen one character or one screen at a time.

♦ If you leave out a letter, word, or phrase, move the cursor to the place where you want to insert the missing text. Type the missing text. The rest of the line moves over to the right so that there is room for the inserted characters. The cursor turns into a block cursor if you press Insert. Pressing the Insert key toggles between the *insert* mode and the *overtype* mode. The overtype mode replaces letters on-screen as you type. When in overtype mode, the cursor changes to a solid blinking block.

♦ If you type an extra letter, word, or phrase, move the cursor over the extra text and press Delete. The rest of the line moves to the left to fill the gap left by the deleted text.

♦ If the program occupies more than one screen, the program editing window scrolls upward to make room for the new text. If you want to see the text that has scrolled off the screen, press the up-arrow, press Page Up, or click the top of the scroll bar with the mouse. Pressing the down-arrow, pressing Page Down, or clicking the bottom of the scroll bar moves the bottom portion of the text back into view.

Later in this chapter, Table 3.2 gives a more detailed list of editing commands.

> **TIP:** Many of Turbo Pascal's shortcut keys, such as the cursor movement keystrokes, are the same as the ones used in the WordStar word processing program.

Example

Type the following program in your program editing window. This program occupies less than one screen, so the program won't scroll. Don't worry about understanding the program. The rest of this book focuses on the Turbo Pascal language. For now, just practice using the program editor. If an editor window is not currently open, select File | New to open a new editor window.

```
PROGRAM MyFirstTPProgram;
USES Crt;
BEGIN

   { My first Turbo Pascal program }
   { This program displays a message on the screen }

   CLRSCR;
   WRITELN('Hello!  I am your computer.');
   WRITELN;
   WRITELN('Press a key to clear the screen...');
   REPEAT UNTIL KEYPRESSED;  { Wait for a keystroke }
   CLRSCR;
END.  {MyFirstTPProgram}
```

After you type the program, your screen should resemble the one in Figure 3.3. Make sure you type the program exactly as it appears here. Turbo Pascal does not care whether you type in uppercase or lowercase characters.

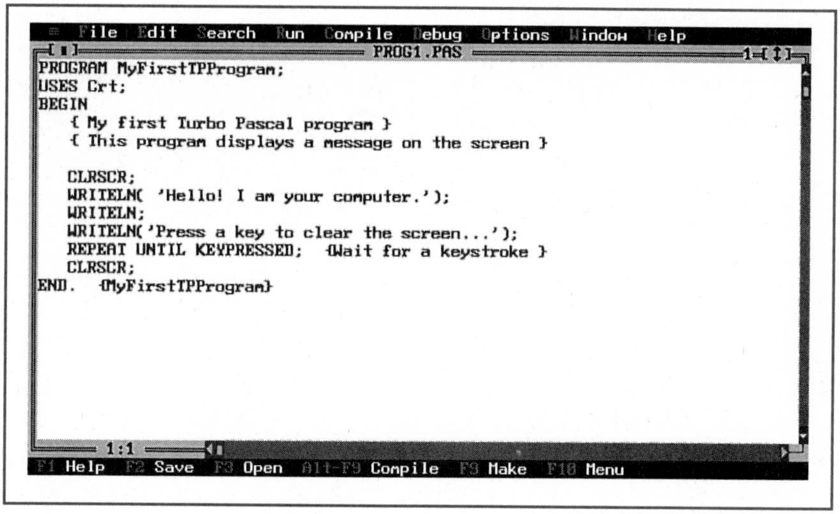

```
 = File Edit Search Run Compile Debug Options Window Help
[■]                          PROG1.PAS                          1=[↕]
PROGRAM MyFirstTPProgram;
USES Crt;
BEGIN
    { My first Turbo Pascal program }
    { This program displays a message on the screen }

    CLRSCR;
    WRITELN( 'Hello! I am your computer.');
    WRITELN;
    WRITELN('Press a key to clear the screen...');
    REPEAT UNTIL KEYPRESSED;   {Wait for a keystroke }
    CLRSCR;
END.   {MyFirstTPProgram}




    1:1
F1 Help  F2 Save  F3 Open  Alt-F9 Compile  F9 Make  F10 Menu
```

Figure 3.3. The program editing window after you type your first Turbo Pascal program.

You can see the results of this program by running it, just as you ran the ARTY.PAS program earlier. Select **R**un from the **R**un pull-down menu. Your screen will clear and you should see the output of the program.

If Errors Occur

Because you are typing instructions for a machine, you must be accurate. If you misspell a word, leave out a single quotation mark, or make any other mistake, Turbo Pascal informs you with a message in the top line of the editor's window (see Figure 3.4). Turbo Pascal highlights the word or line in the program where the application first spotted the error. The most common error is a *syntax error*, which usually means you've misspelled a word or forgotten a semicolon.

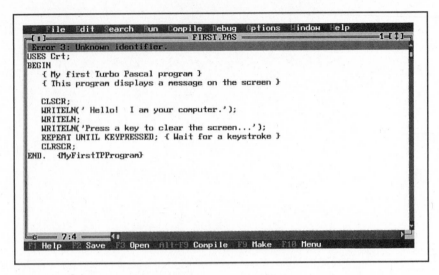

Figure 3.4. An error message from the compiler.

If an error message occurs, you can press Esc to return to the program editor and fix the problem. If you don't understand the error, press F1 for an explanation of what the error message means.

Getting the Bugs Out

One of the first computers, which was owned by the military, would not print some important data one day. After programmers spent many hours trying to find the solution within the program, a lady named *Grace Hopper* decided to check the printer.

She found a small moth lodged between two wires. When she removed the moth, the printer began working perfectly (although the moth didn't have as much luck).

Rear Admiral Grace Hopper retired from the Navy in 1986. At the time of her death in early 1992, she was a consultant to the Digital Equipment Corp. Although she is responsible for developing many important computer concepts (she is the author of the original COBOL language), she might be known best for discovering the first computer *bug*.

> Because a bug was discovered as the culprit, errors in computer programs are known as computer bugs. When you test a program, you might have to *debug* it—remove the bugs, or errors—by fixing your typing errors and changing the logic so that the program does exactly what you want.

This sample program illustrates the difference between the program and its output. You must type the program (or load it from disk) and then run the program to see its output.

Clear this program from memory by pressing Alt–F3. Select **No** when Turbo Pascal asks whether you want to save the file to disk.

Working with a Longer Program

For more practice using the program editor, type the following program. This program prompts for your name and displays it around the screen. As with the last program, do not worry about the language, but concentrate instead on using the program editor. Later in the book, as you get used to the program editor, you can concentrate on the language.

```
PROGRAM ShowName;
USES Crt;
CONST Width     = 14;
      EraseName = '              ';
VAR   i:          INTEGER;
      Row:        INTEGER;
      Col:        INTEGER;
      FirstName: STRING[10]; {use only first 10 chars of name}
BEGIN
   CLRSCR;
   WRITE('What is your first name? ');
   READLN(FirstName);
   CLRSCR;

       { Show the name randomly on the screen }
   FOR i := 1 TO 15 DO
      BEGIN
         Row := RANDOM(24) + 1;
```

```
        Col := RANDOM(81-LENGTH(FirstName)) + 1;
        GOTOXY(Col,Row);
        WRITE(FirstName);
        DELAY(500);          {show name for 1/2 second}
        GOTOXY(Col,Row);
        WRITE(EraseName);   {erase name by writing blanks over it}
    END;  {for}
  CLRSCR;

      { Show name in columns }
  FOR Row := 1 TO 24 DO
    BEGIN
        GOTOXY(1,Row);
        FOR Col := 1 TO 5 DO WRITE(FirstName:Width);
    END;  {for}
  DELAY(1000);
  CLRSCR;
      { Show message in the middle of the screen }
  GOTOXY(30,12);
  WRITE('That''s all, ',FirstName);
  READLN;
END.  {ShowName}
```

As the text scrolls, practice using the arrow keys (if you use the keyboard) and the scroll bar (if you use a mouse). When you finish typing the program, select **R**un | **R**un (Ctrl–F9) to see the results of the program. When you see the "That's all" message, press Enter to return to the editor. Press F2 to save your work as SHOWNAME.PAS.

Advanced Editing

Typing, scrolling, inserting, and deleting are all the tools you need to write and modify Turbo Pascal programs. Even beginners can master some advanced editing features with a little practice. You can work with *blocks* of text instead of individual characters. You can move or copy those blocks of text throughout your program. You can set up to 10 *bookmarks* that, as with regular books, help you find your way back to certain places within a long program. You also can view your program from two different windows, which enables you to see two different parts of your program at the same time.

Working with Blocks of Text

Before moving or copying a block of text, you must *select* (or mark) it. As you select text, Turbo Pascal highlights it so that you always know which text you are marking. The previous example displayed your name randomly around the screen, and then displayed it in five columns on-screen. If you want to reverse that order by displaying the columns first, you can delete the last half of the program and type this piece into the first half; however, that requires much typing. By selecting the text that displays the columns first, you can move the entire block of text with only a few keystrokes.

Example

To help you practice working with blocks of text, the following example shows you how to rearrange the screen displaying program.

To select the section of text that begins with the blank line before { Show name in columns }, move the cursor to this blank line. Hold down the Shift key and press the down-arrow key until the line with CLRSCR is highlighted (see Figure 3.5).

```
≡ File  Edit  Search  Run  Compile  Debug  Options  Window  Help
[•]                           SHOWNAME.PAS                      2[↕]
     Col:         INTEGER;
     FirstName: STRING[10];  {use only first 10 chars of name}
BEGIN
   CLRSCR;
   WRITE('What is your first name? ');
   READLN(FirstName);
   CLRSCR;

        { Show the name randomly on the screen }
   FOR i := 1 TO 15 DO
      BEGIN
         Row := RANDOM(24) + 1;
         Col := RANDOM(81-LENGTH(FirstName)) + 1;
         GOTOXY(Col,Row);
         WRITE(FirstName);
         DELAY(500);              {show name for 1/2 second}
         GOTOXY(Col,Row);
         WRITE(EraseName);     {erase name by writing blanks over it}
      END;   {for}
   CLRSCR;

  27:1         ◀▮
F1 Help  F2 Save  F3 Open  Alt-F9 Compile  F9 Make  F10 Menu
```

Figure 3.5. Selecting a block of text.

To move the text, you must delete and copy it to Turbo Pascal's *Clipboard*. The Clipboard is a section of memory reserved for blocks of text. The Clipboard holds only one block of text at a time. You cannot copy or delete more than one block of text to the Clipboard. The Clipboard is the in-between location for blocks of text. Now that you have selected the text, display the **E**dit pull-down menu. The menu shows the commands that work on Clipboard text. (These and other commands appear in Table 3.2 at the end of the chapter.)

Delete (**C**ut) the selected text from the program by selecting **C**ut (Shift–Delete). The entire block of text disappears from the program and goes to the Clipboard. Move the cursor until it rests on the blank line before { Show the name randomly on the screen } early in the program. Select Edit | **P**aste (Shift–Insert). Turbo Pascal places the Clipboard text back into the program. When you select **P**aste, this command always inserts the Clipboard text at the location of the cursor.

Run the program again to see the new order of the output.

> **TIP:** The block of text is still in the Clipboard, although you pasted it into your program. You can paste multiple copies of the block in several different places within the same program using Clipboard. This saves you from typing the same thing more than once. If you do not want the text moved from its original spot when you first move it to the Clipboard, select Edit | **C**opy (Ctrl–Insert), instead of Edit–Cut.

If you want to remove a block of selected text completely without destroying the contents of the Clipboard, select Edit | **C**lear (Ctrl–Delete). This removes the selected text from the program. The program closes up to fill the gap left by the deleted text.

Clear this program from memory by pressing Alt–F3. Select **No** when Turbo Pascal asks whether you want to save the changes to disk.

Using Blocks of Help Code

After mastering more of Turbo Pascal, you can begin to use the online help feature. The examples supplied for each command can be more helpful than the descriptions of the commands. If you spot a Turbo Pascal command in the online help program that is used in the same way that you want to use it, you can select and copy text from the help screen directly to your program. This is faster than retyping the example.

Example

Display the Help screen for the WRITELN statement. To do this, press Shift–F1 to select the Help Index. When the index appears, press **W** to scroll to the topics starting with the letter *W*. Press **R** to scroll to the topics starting with *WR*. Click the WRITELN statement (keyboard users can use Tab to move the cursor there and press Enter) to see the help text for the WRITELN statement.

Press Page Down once. You see a sample Turbo Pascal program that uses the WRITELN statement. You do not have to understand anything about this program now. Select all the lines of the program as though it were a block of text in your own program editing window (see Figure 3.6).

After you select the entire program, select **Edit | Copy** to copy the program to the Clipboard. Press Esc to exit online help. Press F3 to open a file, and call the file TEST. Now select **Edit | Paste**. The entire program from Help is copied to your program editing window.

```
 ≡   File  Edit  Search  Run  Compile  Debug  Options  Window  Help

  ┌[■]────────────────── Help ─────────────1═[↑]┐
  │ var                                          │
  │   s : String;                                │
  │ begin                                        │
  │   Write('Enter a line of text: ');           │
  │   ReadLn(s);                                 │
  │   WriteLn('You typed: ',s);                  │
  │   WriteLn('Hit <Enter> to exit');            │
  │   ReadLn;                                     │
  │ end.                                          │
  │                                               │
  │ ◄█                                         ▓► │
  └───────────────────────────────────────────────┘

 F1 Help on help  Alt-F1 Previous topic  Shift-F1 Help index  Esc Close help
```

Figure 3.6. Selecting Help's WRITELN statement program code.

Using Bookmarks

In programs that are several screens long, you might want to mark a line or two with bookmarks. Marking lines enables you to edit other parts of the program and then jump back to any of the bookmarks quickly, without having to scroll the entire program to find them.

> **NOTE:** You can set a maximum of 10 bookmarks in a program.

To set a bookmark, follow these steps:

1. Using the scrolling keys, move the cursor to the position where you want to place the bookmark.

2. Press Ctrl–K, followed by a number 0 through 9. Each number represents a different bookmark. Nothing on-screen will let you know the bookmark was set.

To move the cursor to any bookmark you have set, press Ctrl–Q followed by the number of the bookmark you want.

Window Editing

By using the Turbo Pascal windowing feature, you can view different parts of your program at the same time. By creating two windows, you essentially create two program editing windows, one on top of the other. Figure 3.7 shows the ShowName program displayed in two windows. Notice that the first few lines are in the top window and the last few are in the bottom window. In an extremely long program, having two windows enables you to see two different (but related) parts of a program at the same time.

```
≡ File  Edit  Search  Run  Compile  Debug  Options  Window  Help
┌──────────────────────── SHOWNAME.PAS ──────────────────────2──┐
│PROGRAM ShowName;                                               │
│USES Crt;                                                       │
│CONST Width    = 14;                                            │
│      EraseName = '           ';                                │
│VAR   i:          INTEGER;                                      │
│      Row:        INTEGER;                                      │
│      Col:        INTEGER;                                      │
│      FirstName: STRING[10]; {use only first 10 chars of name}  │
│BEGIN                                                           │
┌─[■]──────────────────── SHOWNAME.PAS ────────────────1═[↑]─┐
│        FOR Col := 1 TO 5 DO WRITE(FirstName:Width);           │
│      END;   {for}                                             │
│  DELAY(1000);                                                 │
│  CLRSCR;                                                      │
│                                                               │
│        { Show message in the middle of the screen }           │
│  GOTOXY(30,12);                                               │
│  WRITE('That''s all, ',FirstName);                            │
│  READLN;                                                      │
│END.   {ShowName}                                              │
│─*── 41:17 ──◀■                                               │
F1 Help  F2 Save  F3 Open  Alt-F9 Compile  F9 Make  F10 Menu
```

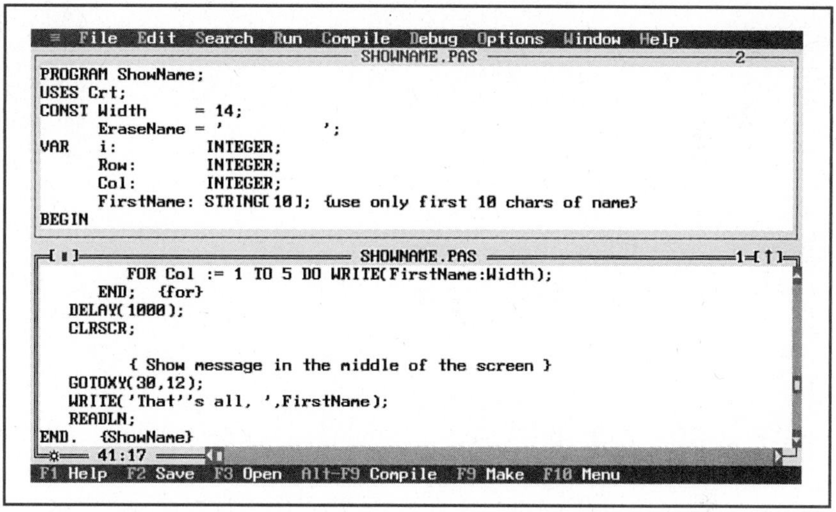

Figure 3.7. Viewing two editing windows at the same time.

You can open as many edit windows as your system's memory can handle. The following example illustrates how to create two edit windows for the same file. However, you can open different files as well.

Example

To create the two windows in Figure 3.7, press F3 to open one edit window. Type ShowName as the filename. Press F3 again and type ShowName again. Two edit windows are now open. Press Alt–W to select the **W**indow menu. Press T to select **T**ile. The window is now split horizontally into two windows. You can scroll the two windows independently of each other. To move the cursor to the other window, press F6. You can close the second window by pressing F6 to move the cursor to the second window, and by pressing Alt–F3 to close it.

Even when you are using several windows, only one Clipboard still exists. When you copy or cut text to the Clipboard from one window, you can move the cursor to the other window and insert that same Clipboard text there.

If you want to see more of the text in one of the windows, but you still want the split screen, press F5 to zoom out the current window (the window where the cursor is) so that it fills the entire program editing area as if it were the only active window. Pressing F5 again zooms the window back to its original size so that the split screen appears again.

By pressing Shift–F5, you can use the arrow keys to zoom the current window one row or column at a time. This enables you to fine-tune the size of each window.

Table 3.2 shows a complete list of editing commands. For your convenience, this table is also included in the inside front and back covers of this book.

Table 3.2. The Turbo Pascal editing keys.

Description	Keystroke	WordStar Equivalent
Cursor Movement		
Character left	Left arrow	Ctrl–S
Character right	Right arrow	Ctrl–D
To one word left	Ctrl–Left arrow	Ctrl–A
To one word right	Ctrl–Right arrow	Ctrl–F

Description	Keystroke	WordStar Equivalent
One line up	Up arrow	Ctrl–E
One line down	Down arrow	Ctrl–X
Beginning of line	Home	Ctrl–Q, S
Start of next line	Enter	
End of line	End	Ctrl–Q, D
Top of window	Ctrl–Home	Ctrl–Q, E
Bottom of window	Ctrl–End	Ctrl–Q, X
Top of document	Ctrl–PgUp	Ctrl–Q, R
Bottom of document	Ctrl–PgDn	Ctrl–Q, C
Beginning of block	Ctrl–Q, B	
End of block	Ctrl–Q, K	
Last cursor position	Ctrl–Q, P	
Insert and overstrike	Insert	Ctrl–V

Text-Scrolling Keys

One line up	Up arrow	Ctrl–E
One line down	Down arrow	Ctrl–X
One page up	Page Up	Ctrl–R
One page down	Page Down	Ctrl–C

Text-Selection Keys

Character left	Shift–Left arrow	
Character right	Shift–Right arrow	
Word left	Shift–Ctrl–Left arrow	
Word right	Shift–Ctrl–Right arrow	Ctrl KT
Current line	Shift–Down arrow	

continues

Table 3.2. Continued.

Description	Keystroke	WordStar Equivalent
Line above	Shift–Up arrow	
Start text selection	Ctrl–KB	
End text selection	Ctrl–KK	
Read block from disk	Ctrl–K, R	
Write block to disk	Ctrl–K, W	
Hide/display block	Ctrl–K, H	
Print block	Ctrl–K, P	
Indent block	Ctrl–K, I	
Unindent block	Ctrl–K, U	

To Insert, Copy, and Delete

Copy selected text without clipboard	Ctrl–K, C	
Move selected text without clipboard	Ctrl–K, V	
Copy selected text to the Clipboard	Ctrl–Ins	
Delete selected text and copy it to the Clipboard	Shift–Del	
Delete the current line and copy it to the Clipboard	Ctrl–Y	
Delete to end of line and copy it to the Clipboard	Ctrl–Q, y	
Paste the contents of the Clipboard	Shift–Ins	
Insert a blank line before the cursor position	End, Enter	
Insert a blank line before the cursor position	Home, Ctrl–N	

Description	Keystroke	WordStar Equivalent
Insert special characters	Ctrl–P, Ctrl–key	
Delete one character to the left of the cursor	Backspace	Ctrl–H
Delete one character at the cursor	Del	Ctrl–G
Delete the rest of the word the cursor is on	Ctrl–T	
Delete selected text	Ctrl–Delete	Ctrl–K, Y

Bookmark Keys

Set up to 10 bookmarks	Ctrl–K, 0-9	
Go to a specific bookmark	Ctrl–Q, 0-9	

Window Commands

Resize active window	Ctrl–F5	
Zoom in or out of the active window	F5	
Move to next window	F6	
Move to previous window	Shift–F6	

Miscellaneous

Pair matching	Ctrl–Q, [Ctrl–Q,]	
Repeat last command	Ctrl–L	
Restore error message	Ctrl–Q, W	
Restore line	Ctrl–Q, L	
Search	Ctrl–Q, F	
Search and Replace	Ctrl–Q, A	

Summary

After reading this chapter, you should understand the steps necessary to write a Turbo Pascal program. You know that advanced planning makes writing programs much easier and that the program's instructions produce output only after you run the program.

You also have the tools you need to type the program with the Turbo Pascal editor. The editor is as powerful as some word processors. Now that you know how to type programs in Turbo Pascal, it is time to look at Chapter 4, "Working with Your Program File," to examine how to save your programs to disk so that you can reuse them without typing them again.

Review Questions

Answers to the Review Questions appear in Appendix B.

1. What is a program?

2. What are the two ways to obtain the program you want?

3. True or False: Computers can think.

4. What is the difference between a program and its resulting output?

5. Which part of the IDE do you use to type Turbo Pascal programs into the computer?

6. What filename extension do all Turbo Pascal programs have?

7. Why is typing the program one of the last steps in the programming process?

8. True or False: You can use the left-arrow and Backspace keys interchangeably.

9. What do you call the area of memory in which you temporarily store blocks of text?

10. What is the maximum number of bookmarks you can put into a Turbo Pascal program?

Working with Your Program File

In the last chapter, you learned how to enter and edit a Turbo Pascal program. After you type the program, you want to save it to disk for future use. You need to understand the File menu's options for saving and loading Turbo Pascal programs from a disk. Before you learn the language elements, it helps to see the format of a Turbo Pascal program and how to search and replace text in your program. This chapter introduces the following concepts:

♦ Loading saved program files into the program editor

♦ Saving Turbo Pascal program files to disk

♦ Erasing a program from memory

♦ Printing a program on the printer

♦ Understanding the format of a Turbo Pascal program

♦ Searching for text in a Turbo Pascal program

♦ Replacing text in a Turbo Pascal program

This chapter finishes Part I, "Introduction to Turbo Pascal." When you master the concepts in this chapter, you will be ready to begin your journey into Turbo Pascal programming.

Loading Program Files from the Disk

In Chapter 3, you ran the ARTY.PAS program by loading it from the disk to memory. The File | Open... command loads program files, which is a process that will become second nature to you. Remember that a program you type is erased when you turn off the computer unless you save that program to a nonvolatile disk, such as a floppy disk or a hard disk.

Figure 4.1 shows the Open a File dialog box. You can type a filename in the Name box or select one from the list in the Files box. Remember that Tab takes you between the parts of a dialog box, and so does clicking with the mouse. When you finish entering the file information in the dialog box, press Enter or click OK.

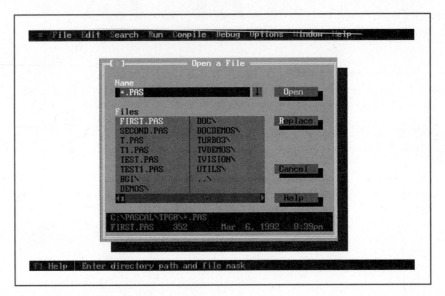

Figure 4.1. The Open a File dialog box.

Sometimes you may not want to save a program. For example, you may want to just test an idea. In this case, press Alt–F to display the File menu, and press N to select New. Turbo Pascal opens a file with a standard name of NONAME00.PAS.

In the IDE, the editor can hold as many programs or source files in memory as will fit in your system's memory. If you attempt to close (Alt–F3) a source file in memory and have not saved the source file, Turbo Pascal reminds you to save the file.

Saving Programs to Disk

Say you conduct your test on a file opened with **New**, and you decide to save this file after all. Press Alt–F to display the **F**ile menu. Press the *a* key to select the **S**ave as... option. Turbo Pascal will prompt you to type a name for the file. Figure 4.2 shows the Save File As dialog box.

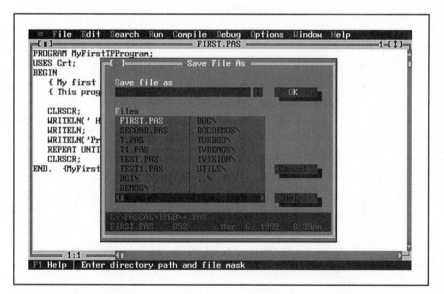

Figure 4.2. The Save File As dialog box.

When you save a file, you must choose a filename. You need only to type one to eight characters and Turbo Pascal will automatically append .PAS to the filename. You can type a new filename, or you can type the name of a file that already exists. If you choose the latter, Turbo Pascal prompts you to verify if you want to overwrite the existing file with the program in memory.

The filename can contain letters, numbers, the underscore character (_), and a few other special characters such as the exclamation point (!) and the pound sign (#).

> **TIP:** Many special characters cannot be included in a filename. It isn't easy to remember which characters you can and cannot use, so it's best to stay away from all special characters except letters, numbers, and the underscore. Use the underscore as a separating character, as in ACT_PAY.PAS, because you cannot put spaces in a filename.

The File | Save (F2) command saves the current program to disk under the most recent filename. For instance, if you load a file called MYFILE.PAS from disk and then make changes to it, File | Save saves it under the name MYFILE.PAS. This process is quicker than selecting File | Save as... and typing or selecting the same name it was saved under. If you previously used File | Save as... but are still working on the program, File | Save saves the program under the same previous name.

While working on a long program, you would be wise to save a program often (about every 10 minutes) in case of a power failure. Otherwise, you can recover only what is on the disk—not what was in memory when the power went out. You might consider also saving to a diskette periodically to guard against hard disk failure.

Erasing the Program Editing Window

Sometimes you will want to clear the program editing window without saving the program on which you are working. To start over with a clear program editing window, press Alt–F3 to close the current window. Turbo Pascal warns that you have not saved the program and gives you a chance to do so with the dialog box shown in Figure 4.3. You can select No to tell Turbo Pascal that you intend to erase the program without saving it first. The screen's program editing window also clears.

Figure 4.3. A dialog box warning that you have not saved the program.

Printing a Program

Sometimes you will want to send your program to the printer. Having a printout helps when you are working with a large program because it is easier to look for errors on paper than on-screen. The printout is also a safe backup copy (called a *hard copy*) for the program in case the disk file is erased.

If you want just to print a block of a program, position the cursor at the beginning of the block and press Ctrl–KB. Move the cursor to the end of the block and press Ctrl–KK. This highlights the text. (Or, you can hold down a Shift key and press the Down arrow key to select text.) When the printer is ready, press Ctrl–KP to print the block.

NOTE: To print your complete program, select the File | Print command. Make sure your printer is on and is loaded with paper before accepting this dialog box.

> **CAUTION:** You will receive a Device access error if you attempt to print to a printer that is turned off or is out of paper. If this occurs, correct the problem and press Enter to try again.

Writing a Turbo Pascal Program

Before learning the Turbo Pascal language, recall that a program is a set of instructions that tells the computer what to do and provides the steps in which to do it. You write a program to solve a problem.

Turbo Pascal programs execute one instruction after the other in top-to-bottom order. To override an order, you can *branch* to another part of the program using certain Turbo Pascal commands. The Turbo Pascal instructions are for the computer and must be precise.

Spacing in Programs

Turbo Pascal programs, however, can be typed *free-form*, meaning that you can add spacing and blank lines to make the program more readable. For example, Figure 4.4 shows the short program you typed in Chapter 3, with no spacing or blank lines. Your computer does not care about blank lines and spacing. You include them to break up the program so that it is more readable to you, the programmer.

Figure 4.5 illustrates the program with spacing and blank lines. Although all this may be cryptic to you now, you can see how Turbo Pascal's free-form style is a nice feature. Remember also that when you run the program, the computer looks at the first instruction and runs it first, followed by the second one, and so on. Spaces and blank lines, called *white space*, are completely ignored.

As you write your Turbo Pascal programs, remember the difference between Figure 4.4 and Figure 4.5 and use as much spacing and as many blank lines as you want. Notice that white space is not required in a Turbo Pascal line (except for one space between words), although the line is more readable if you put spaces between symbols and numbers as well.

```
 ═ File  Edit  Search  Run  Compile  Debug  Options  Window  Help
┌[■]═══════════════════════ SECOND.PAS ═══════════════════════1═[↕]─┐
│USES Crt;                                                          │
│CONST Width=14;                                                    │
│VAR i:INTEGER;                                                     │
│Row:INTEGER;                                                       │
│Col:INTEGER;                                                       │
│FirstName:STRING[10];                                             │
│EraseName:STRING[10];                                             │
│BEGIN                                                             │
│CLRSCR;                                                           │
│WRITE('What is your first name? ');                               │
│READLN(FirstName);                                                │
│CLRSCR;                                                           │
│{Print the name randomly on the screen}                           │
│FOR i:=1 TO 15 DO                                                 │
│BEGIN                                                            │
│Row:=TRUNC(RANDOM(24))+1;                                         │
│Col:=TRUNC(Random(81-LENGTH(FirstName)))+1;                       │
│GOTOXY(Col,Row);                                                  │
│WRITE(FirstName);                                                 │
│DELAY(500);                                                      │
│GOTOXY(Col,Row);                                                  │
└─●── 14:8 ═══◄▮─────────────────────────────────────────────────►─┘
 F1 Help  F2 Save  F3 Open  Alt-F9 Compile  F9 Make  F10 Menu
```

Figure 4.4. A program with no extra spaces or blank lines.

Example

To put all this together, type the program in Figure 4.5 in your Turbo Pascal program editing window (if it's not still there from the last chapter). Save the program to disk under the filename FIRST.PAS by selecting File | Save as... and typing the filename into the dialog box.

Print the program after you type and save it. Before printing with File | Print, make sure your printer is on and has paper. After the program has printed, erase your program editing window by pressing Alt–F3. Your program is now on disk (but not on your screen or in memory) in case you want to load it again later.

```
 =  File  Edit  Search  Run  Compile  Debug  Options  Window  Help
─[■]────────────────────── SECOND.PAS ──────────────────────1─[↑]─
USES Crt;
CONST Width = 14;
VAR    i:          INTEGER;
       Row:        INTEGER;
       Col:        INTEGER;
       FirstName: STRING[10];
       EraseName: STRING[10];
BEGIN
   CLRSCR;
   WRITE('What is your first name? ');
   READLN(FirstName);
   CLRSCR;

   {Print the name randomly on the screen}
   FOR i := 1 TO 15 DO
      BEGIN
         Row := TRUNC(RANDOM(24)) + 1;
         Col := TRUNC(Random(81 - LENGTH(FirstName))) + 1;
         GOTOXY(Col,Row);
         WRITE(FirstName);
         DELAY(500);
─────── 1:1 ════════◄▒───────────────────────────────────────────►
 F1 Help  F2 Save  F3 Open  Alt-F9 Compile  F9 Make  F10 Menu
```

Figure 4.5. A more readable program with spaces and blank lines.

Searching for Text in Your Programs

Turbo Pascal provides a helpful menu command typically found on word processors. It is the Find option from the Search pull-down menu. The Search | Find command searches for any character, word, or phrase in your Turbo Pascal program's editing window.

The Search menu is helpful when you work with long programs. When you edit a short, 10-line program, you can visually find text almost as easily as you can using the Search command. Most programs, however, especially those used in many business applications, span many screens of text. If you need to find the line that a specific command or phrase is on, the Search command makes it easy.

When you display the Search pull-down menu, you see six options: Find..., Replace..., Search again, Go to line number...,

Find procedure..., and Find **error**.... Suppose you want to find the following command (you will learn about the WRITE command in a later chapter):

```
WRITE('Please enter the amount: ');
```

To find this command line, display the **S**earch menu and select **F**ind... to display the dialog box shown in Figure 4.6. Next to the Text to find message, type enough of the line you are looking for so that Turbo Pascal can distinguish it from the rest of the program's lines. For instance, any of the following values for the Text to find prompt would find this command line if it were in your program:

```
WRITE('Please enter the amount: ');
('Please enter the amount: ');
```

Notice that it really doesn't matter which part of the line you search for. You can search for text at the beginning, middle, or end of the line. You must realize, however, that if there is another line anywhere in the program that contains matching text, Turbo Pascal finds the first match, whether or not it is the line you really want. You don't need to match the uppercase and lowercase letters in the line unless you tab (or point with the mouse) to **C**ase sensitive and select it by pressing the space bar (or clicking with the mouse). Typically, you shouldn't waste time matching uppercase and lowercase characters unless it is critical for finding the right item.

Select the **W**hole words only option if you want to search for a full word. For example, to find the line shown earlier, you could search for *am*, but you would probably find lines other than the one for which you were looking. For instance, if you searched for the letters *am*, Turbo Pascal would find the following lines:

```
WRITELN(LST,'The extra amount, ',ExtraAmt, ' is zero.');
TitleStr := "American Anthem";
```

If you don't want to find words that contain the letters *am*, but only those lines that contain the word *am*, you must select **W**hole words only.

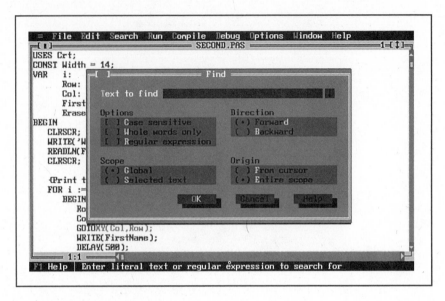

Figure 4.6. The Find dialog box.

When you finish answering the prompts in the Find dialog box, Turbo Pascal hunts for the first line containing the matching text. If Turbo Pascal does not find a match, it displays a dialog box with a Search string not found message. If it finds a match, however, it scrolls the screen to the line and highlights the matching text. You can then edit the text or press Ctrl–L (the shortcut key for the Search again command) to look for the next line that contains the same match.

Replacing Text in Your Programs

After mastering the Search | Find... command, you will find it easy to replace text in your programs. Suppose you printed a customer's last name as *MacMasters* throughout several lines of the program, but you discovered later that the name is correctly spelled *McMasters*. You could use the cursor-movement keys to scroll through the text and change each occurrence of the error; however, Turbo Pascal does the work for you with the Search | Replace... menu option. If you select Search | **R**eplace..., you see the dialog box in Figure 4.7.

Figure 4.7. The Replace dialog box.

Type the text you want changed after the **T**ext to find prompt, and type the change you want Turbo Pascal to make after the **N**ew text prompt. For this example, you would type *MacMasters* after **T**ext to find, and *McMasters* after **N**ew text.

The **C**ase sensitive and **W**hole words only options work as they did with the **F**ind... command. There are two new options at the bottom of the **R**eplace dialog box. If you select **P**rompt on replace, Turbo Pascal finds the text and asks your permission before changing it. This is a safeguard in case you do not want to change every match. If you select Change **a**ll, Turbo Pascal quickly finds every match and changes each one.

Summary

This is a short chapter, but it prepares you for managing program files and searching and replacing text within those program files. You are now ready to write programs from scratch by starting Part II, "Primary Turbo Pascal Language Elements."

Review Questions

Answers to the Review Questions appear in Appendix B.

1. What menu command loads a Turbo Pascal program file from disk to memory?

2. Why is it important to save your Turbo Pascal programs to disk?

3. How many letters can you use for the part of a filename to the left of the dot?

4. True or False: State whether the following are valid filenames for Turbo Pascal programs.

   A. PGM 1.PAS

   B. EMPLOYEES.PAS

   C. PAYROLL.PAS

5. How many source files can be open in the IDE's editor at the same time?

6. True or False: Erasing the program editing window with Alt–F3 erases the program from disk as well.

7. What does the term *free-form* mean?

8. Why is it a good idea to save your programs every few minutes as you enter them?

Part II

Primary Turbo Pascal Language Elements

5

Understanding Numeric Variables and Constants

To understand data processing with Turbo Pascal, you must understand how Turbo Pascal creates, stores, and manipulates data. This chapter covers the following topics:

♦ Variables and constants

♦ The naming and use of numeric variables

♦ The types of numeric variables

♦ The assignment statement

♦ The types of numeric constants

♦ The WRITELN and CLRSCR statements

You have mastered the Turbo Pascal screen, and you can use the IDE to manage your source files. By the end of this chapter, you will be able to write your own Turbo Pascal programs. You will also have fun seeing how easy it is.

Turbo Pascal Data

A Turbo Pascal program takes data and processes it into meaningful results. You have seen a few programs. Within those programs are statements and data.

Variable: Data that can change as a program runs.

Constant: Data that remains the same as a program runs.

The data consists of *variables* and *constants*. As the name implies, a variable is data that can change as the program runs. A constant is data that remains the same during a program run. In real life, a variable might be your age or your salary. Both increase over time (if you're lucky). A constant might be your first name or your Social Security number, which remain with you throughout your life.

This chapter focuses on numeric variables and constants. If you are not a "numbers person," don't worry. Working with numbers is the computer's job. You just need to understand how to tell the computer what you want it to do.

Variables

A variable is like a box inside your computer that holds something. That something can be a number, a special character, a word, a sentence, or an entire paragraph of text. You can designate as many variables as your program requires to hold changing data.

Because you are responsible for creating your own variables, you must understand each of the possible characteristics of variables so that you can choose one that fits the data. These characteristics stipulate that:

◆ Each variable has a name.

◆ Each variable has a type.

◆ Each variable holds your specified value.

To help you understand these characteristics, the following sections explain each of them.

Variable Names

Because you can include many variables in one program, you must assign a name to each variable so that you can keep track of them. Variable names are unique, like house addresses. If two variables had the same name, Turbo Pascal wouldn't know which variable you wanted when you requested the name.

Variable names can be as short as one letter, to a maximum of 63 characters. Variable names must begin with a letter of the alphabet or an underscore; after the first character, however, they can contain letters, numbers, or an underscore.

> **TIP:** You cannot use spaces in a variable name.

The following variable names are valid:

```
Salary

Aug91Sales

I

index

AGE
```

You can use uppercase or lowercase letters in a variable name. `Sales`, `SALES`, and `sales` all refer to the same variable. Variables cannot have the same name as a Turbo Pascal procedure or function. Appendix C lists all Turbo Pascal procedure and function names so that you can avoid using them when you name variables. You will learn more about procedures and functions later in Chapters 22 and 23.

The following variable names are invalid:

```
81-SALES

Aug91+Sales

MY AGE
```

> **Use Meaningful Variable Names**
>
> Although you can call a variable any name that complies with the naming rules (as long as it is not being used by another variable in the program), you should always use meaningful variable names. Give your variables names that describe the values they hold.
>
> For example, keeping track of total payroll in a variable called TotalPayroll is much more descriptive than using the variable name XYZ34. Although both names are valid, TotalPayroll is easier to remember, and later you will know what the variable holds just by looking at its name.

Variable Types

Numeric variables can hold two different types of numbers, *integers* and *real numbers*. For example, when a variable holds an integer, Turbo Pascal assumes that no decimal point or fractional part (the part to the right of the decimal point) exists for the variable's value. Table 5.1 lists the different integer types that Turbo Pascal recognizes.

Table 5.1. Turbo Pascal integer variable types.

Type	Examples	Minimum	Maximum
SHORTINT	–10, 0, 43	–128	127
INTEGER	12, 0, –21843	–32768	32767
LONGINT	32768, 99876	–2147483648	2147483647
BYTE	1, 100	0	255
WORD	7, 60000	0	65535

Basically, an integer is a number without a decimal place (its content is a whole number). Although the category name integer is the same as the second type, INTEGER, in the previous list, this will not be a problem. The difference is clear from the context. Whereas integer (no capital letters) refers to all types, INTEGER refers to the second type in Table 5.1.

Real numbers contain decimal points and a fractional part to the right of the decimal. REAL variables can accurately keep 11 to 12 significant digits, and EXTENDED variables can accurately keep 19 to 20 significant digits. Table 5.2 lists the different real types that Turbo Pascal recognizes.

Table 5.2. Turbo Pascal real variable types.

Type	Examples	Minimum	Maximum
REAL	0.01, −3.59	2.9×10^{-39}	1.7×10^{38}
SINGLE	2976.67	1.5×10^{-45}	3.4×10^{38}
DOUBLE	83544972.8	5.0×10^{-324}	1.7×10^{308}
EXTENDED	7628295234917.387	3.4×10^{-4932}	1.1×10^{4932}
COMP	39447285949.22	$-2^{63}+1$	$2^{63}-1$

The category name real is the same as the first type, REAL, in the previous list. Whereas real (no capital letters) refers to all types, REAL refers to the first type in Table 5.2.

For example, if you want to store a distance in miles between two cities in a variable called Distance, you might declare the variable as either a REAL or an INTEGER. If you want the mileage stored to the nearest tenth of a mile, declare Distance as a REAL.

NOTE: If you assign an integer constant to a real variable, Turbo Pascal converts that integer to a real number. It does not work the other way. If you try to assign a real constant to an integer variable, the compiler displays Error 26: Type mismatch.

You might wonder why it is important to have so many types. After all, a number is just a number. It turns out that the type of variable can influence the efficiency of your programs; however, it's not as difficult to use as it might appear at first. Tables 5.1 and 5.2 list the minimum and maximum values each variable type can hold. A variable can't hold just any value; it can hold only values that fall within its own type and range of values. You cannot, for instance, designate a number larger than 32,767 as a variable that is defined as an INTEGER. Only LONGINTS and WORDS can hold numbers larger than 32,767. Most of the time, INTEGERS and REALS are sufficient. If you are working with very large or very small numbers or are doing scientific work, however, you might need the extra precision that the other types of numbers give you.

All variables used in this book are INTEGER or REAL unless otherwise noted. The real types SINGLE, DOUBLE, EXTENDED, and COMP all require either a numeric coprocessor or the emulation of one. If you want to experiment with these types, you need to include a special compiler directive, {$N+, E+}, at the top of your program, or you can change the IDE. At **O**ptions | **C**ompiler..., turn on 8087/80827 and Emulation. If your system has a math coprocessor, this directive will allow your program to use it. If your system does not have a math coprocessor, this directive also allows your program to emulate one.

> **NOTE:** The variables mentioned in this chapter are all *numeric* and hold only numbers. In later chapters, this book discusses how to hold other types of data in variables.

The Lengths of Data

Because EXTENDED variables can hold such large numbers, you might be tempted to declare all variables as EXTENDED. At first glance, this seems like a good solution because you wouldn't have to worry whether your variables were large enough to hold the data. This isn't prudent, however, because your programs slow down considerably when you use EXTENDED variables (unless your system has a math coprocessor).

Ten bytes of memory are required to store an EXTENDED variable, as opposed to six for REAL variables, four for LONGINTS, and only two for regular INTEGERS. Therefore, when you don't need the extra precision, you use more memory than necessary.

This extra memory usage takes extra CPU time. Every time you use an EXTENDED variable when a REAL variable or an INTEGER would do, Turbo Pascal must retrieve 10 bytes of memory—two to five times as much as the other types. Therefore, be conscious of your data lengths and variable requirements and don't use an EXTENDED variable when an INTEGER or REAL is sufficient.

The Assignment of Values to Variables

Now that you know about variables, you're probably wondering how to put values in them. You do so with the assignment statement. The format of the assignment statement is

```
variable := expression;
```

assign value of expression to variable

Assigning values to variables is common in Turbo Pascal programs. The *variable* is any valid variable name you create. The colon and equal sign (:=) are required and must appear after the variable name. The *expression* is a constant, variable, or combination of constants, variables, and operators that equate to a value. (You learn more about expressions in Chapter 6.) Because a variable contains a value, you can assign variables to each other. Turbo Pascal uses a semicolon to act as a separator between statements. Because another Turbo Pascal statement usually follows an assignment statement, end the line with a semicolon.

> **TIP:** Think of the colon–equal sign combination as a left-pointing arrow. Loosely, the colon–equal sign means you want to take the number, variable, or expression on the right side of the colon–equal sign and put it into the variable on the left side of the colon–equal sign.
>
> *variable ← number, variable,* or *expression*

Examples

1. If you want to keep track of your current age, salary, and dependents, you can store these values in three variables and include them in your program. These values might change later in the program, for example, when the program calculates a pay increase for you.

   Good variable names might be Age, Salary, and Dependents. To assign values to these three variables, your program should look something like this:

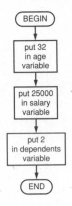

```
PROGRAM PersonalInfo1;

VAR Age:        BYTE;
    Salary:     REAL;
    Dependents: BYTE;

BEGIN
    Age        := 32;
    Salary     := 25000;
    Dependents := 2;
END.  {PersonalInfo1}
```

To be formal, start all Turbo Pascal programs with the PROGRAM statement and a name for your program.

Notice how all the variables are declared in one VAR section. This is part of Turbo Pascal's built-in structure. Not only does it help you ensure that the variables are defined with the appropriate type, but it also helps others who read your programs.

Another part of the structure is the BEGIN-END pair. This pair identifies the main part of your program. All Turbo Pascal programs contain this.

You don't need to put a decimal point in the Salary value because Turbo Pascal converts integer constants to real numbers for real variables.

Don't put commas in values you assign to variables. The following statement is invalid:

```
Salary := 25,000;     { an invalid assignment statement }
```

2. To practice assigning one variable to another, suppose you stored your tax rate in a variable earlier in the program and decide to use this tax rate for your spouse's tax rate as well. After declaring SpouseTaxRate in a VAR section, you can assign the variable as follows:

```
SpouseTaxRate := TaxRate;
```

The value you assigned to TaxRate would be copied at this point in the program to the variable named SpouseTaxRate. The value in TaxRate is still there after this line finishes.

3. Remember that a variable can hold only one number at a time. Therefore, you cannot put two values in the same variable. For example, the following program assigns Mileage one value, assigns Gallons a value, and then reassigns Mileage another value. Because a variable holds only one value at a time, the new value for Mileage replaces the original value in the third line.

```
VAR Mileage: REAL;
    Gallons: REAL;
BEGIN
    Mileage := 100;
    Gallons := 20;
    Mileage := 150; { value of 100 has been replaced }
    ⋮
```

The ability to change variables is important, but this example stretches it. No good reason exists for putting the value 100 in Mileage when you don't use Mileage for anything before you put another value into it two lines later. When you display and use variables for more powerful programs, you can see that sometimes it makes more sense to overwrite a variable after using its previous value for something else.

> **Remember to Initialize Variables**
>
> Turbo Pascal does not put values in variables for you. Always assign a value to each variable.

4. When you need to assign a real value that is between 0 and 1, you must use a leading zero. To assign .40 to a real variable, TaxRate, write

   ```
   TaxRate := 0.40;
   ```

NOTE: Leading zeros are required for real values between 0 and 1.

Using Turbo Pascal Constants

Unlike a variable, a *constant* does not change. Numbers are always constant. The number 7 always has the value of 7, and you cannot change it. You can change a variable, however, by putting another value into it.

Numeric constants can be positive or negative. Numeric constants also have ranges. It is important for you to be aware of those ranges. Unlike variables, however, Turbo Pascal interprets the constants in your programs and makes a good judgment on how to store them.

NOTE: Do not put commas in constants when you put them in your programs.

When you declare variables, you declare them in a VAR section. Similarly, when you declare constants, declare them in a CONST section.

Example

You may want to write a program where you analyze some students' results for different grade levels. Using constants can help document your program.

```
PROGRAM StudentResults;

CONST Grade9  =  9;
      Grade10 = 10;
      Grade11 = 11;
      Grade12 = 12;

BEGIN
:
END.  {StudentResults}
```

Notice that you do not use the colon–equal sign (:=) with a constant declaration. Just use the equal sign.

Scientific Notation

You might find it easier to use scientific notation when typing extremely small or large numbers. *Scientific notation* is a shortcut method of representing numbers of extreme values. Many people program in Turbo Pascal for years without using scientific notation. By understanding it, however, you can be more comfortable with many language reference manuals, and you won't be surprised if Turbo Pascal displays a number on your screen in scientific notation.

It is easiest to learn scientific notation by looking at a few examples. Basically, you can represent any number in scientific notation, but this representation usually is limited to extremely large or extremely small numbers. All scientific notation numbers are real number constants. Table 5.3 shows some scientific notation numbers, their equivalents, and their types.

Table 5.3. Looking at scientific notation numbers.

Scientific Notation	Equivalent	Type
3.08E+12	3,080,000,000,000	Single
−9.7587E+04	−97,587	Single
+5.164e−4	0.0005164	Double
−4.6545E−9	−0.0000000046545	Double
1.654E+402	1.654×10^{402}	Extended

Scientific notation numbers contain a letter *E* or *e*. Positive scientific notation numbers begin with a plus sign or have no sign at all. Negative scientific numbers begin with a minus sign.

To figure out the rest, take the portion of the number at the left and multiply it by 10 raised to the number on the right. Thus, +2.164E+3 means to take 2.164 and multiply it by 1,000 (1,000 is 10 raised to the third power, or 10^3) to get 2,164. Also, −5.432e−2 is negative 5.432 times 0.01 (10 raised to the −2 power, or 10^{-2}), or −0.05432.

Another way to look at it is to move the decimal point to the right or to the left a certain number of spaces. For example, to read 2.164E+3, move the decimal point to the right three spaces. The positive number after E means move the decimal to the right. As a result, you get 2,164. To read −5.432e−2, move the decimal to the left because the number following the e is negative. Move it two spaces to get −0.05432.

Examples

1. Light travels 186,000 miles per second. To store 186,000 as a variable in real scientific notation, type:

```
LightSpeed := 1.86E+5;
```

When you use Turbo Pascal to perform calculations, the application might choose to output a calculated value in scientific notation, although the calculations used numbers that were not in scientific notation.

2. The sun is 93,000,000 miles from the Earth. (You're learning space trivia while practicing programming.) The moon is only about 238,000 miles from the earth. To store these two distances in scientific notation, you can code them as follows:

```
SunDist  := 9.3E+7;
MoonDist := 2.38E+5;
```

Hexadecimal Constants

You can express Turbo Pascal integer constants in the *hexadecimal* (base 16) numbering system. This is helpful if you want to access internal memory locations in other advanced Turbo Pascal programs.

To express a constant in hexadecimal, add the prefix $ to the number. Any valid hexadecimal constant can follow the prefix. For instance, 32 is a decimal (base 10) integer constant, but $20 is that same hexadecimal constant. $CD3 is the hexadecimal representation for 3,283. You can type either uppercase or lowercase letters in the hexadecimal constant. For instance, $FF00 is the same as $ff00.

If you do not add a $, Turbo Pascal assumes the constant is decimal.

For more information about hexadecimal numbers, refer to Appendix D, "Memory Addressing, Binary, and Hexadecimal Review."

Viewing Output

Now that you understand variables and constants, you need to know how to look at that data on-screen. This section introduces one of the most important statements in the Turbo Pascal language, WRITELN.

The WRITELN **Statement**

The WRITELN statement takes whatever is to its right and sends it to the screen. The first format of the WRITELN statement you should understand is

```
WRITELN( expression );
```

The expression you display can be a variable, a constant, or a combination of variables, constants, and operators. If you use a variable name as the expression, WRITELN displays the contents of that variable on-screen. If you place a constant after WRITELN, that constant is displayed. WRITELN is a complex statement with more options, but for now, you should learn just this fundamental format.

If you place WRITELN on a line by itself, Turbo Pascal displays a blank line. This is a good way to separate lines of screen output from each other.

Examples

1. You can display the three variables you typed in an earlier example (Age, Salary, and Dependents) by adding three WRITELN statements after you initialize them. For example:

```
PROGRAM PersonalInfo2;

VAR Age:        BYTE;
    Salary:     REAL;
    Dependents: BYTE;

BEGIN
    Age        := 32;
    Salary     := 25000;
    Dependents := 2;

    WRITELN( Age );
    WRITELN( Salary );
    WRITELN( Dependents );
END.   {PersonalInfo2}
```

Notice the blank line before the group of WRITELN statements that separates them from the variable assignments. The blank line is not required, but it helps break the program into logical parts. If you type this program into the Turbo Pascal editor and run it (with **R**un I **R**un), you see the output:

```
32
 2.50000000000000E+0004
2
```

Notice that Turbo Pascal displays each of the variables' values on a separate line. Because you did not tell Turbo Pascal how to format the REAL variable, Salary, it displayed the results in scientific notation. I discuss formatting real numbers in Chapter 10, "Producing Better Output."

2. The order of statements in a program is up to the programmer. As long as your program follows a logical order and produces the output you desire, you decide how to order the statements. You can rewrite the last program as follows:

```
PROGRAM PersonalInfo3;

VAR Age:        BYTE;
    Salary:     REAL;
    Dependents: BYTE;

BEGIN
   Age := 32;
   WRITELN( Age );

   Salary := 25000;
   WRITELN( Salary );

   Dependents := 2;
   WRITELN( Dependents );
END.   {PersonalInfo3}
```

Again, the blank lines are optional. You might want to review the Turbo Pascal editor by changing the program to match the previous one and then running it. You can see that the results from both runs are the same.

3. You can also place constants to the right of a WRITELN statement. These numbers appear on-screen exactly as you type them. For example, Turbo Pascal displays the first three odd numbers followed by the first three even numbers when you type and run the following program. The odd numbers are stored in declared constants, and the even numbers are displayed as literal constants.

```
PROGRAM Odds;

CONST Odd1 = 3;
      Odd2 = 5;
      Odd3 = 7;

BEGIN
    WRITELN( Odd1 );
    WRITELN( Odd2 );
    WRITELN( Odd3 );
    WRITELN( 2 );
    WRITELN( 4 );
    WRITELN( 6 );
END.  {Odds}
```

In the CONST section, three separate lines declared the three constants. This program produces six lines of output:

```
3
5
7
2
4
6
```

4. If you want blank lines between lines of output, use blank WRITELN statements, as the following program shows:

```
PROGRAM Evens;

BEGIN
    WRITELN( 2 );
    WRITELN;
```

```
    WRITELN( 4 );
    WRITELN;

    WRITELN( 6 );
    WRITELN;
    WRITELN( 8 );
    WRITELN;
    WRITELN( 10 );
END.   {Evens}
```

When you run this program, you see the following output:

```
2

4

6

8

10
```

Notice that the blank line in the middle of the program did not add an extra blank line to the output; there is still only one blank line between the numbers when you run the program. You put blank lines in a program to separate lines of the program's listing. The program's output is affected only by WRITELN statements.

Clearing the Screen

If you have been running the examples so far in this chapter, you might notice an annoying problem with the output: the results of the previous output are still on-screen when you run another Turbo Pascal program. To eliminate this, use the CLRSCR statement in your programs.

The CLRSCR Statement

CLRSCR is an easy statement. Whenever Turbo Pascal runs a program and gets to a line with CLRSCR, it erases the output screen. The format for the CLRSCR statement is

CLRSCR

erase
the screen

Most Turbo Pascal programmers use CLRSCR as the first line of every program to clear the screen when the program runs. This eliminates output from previous runs of the program, so the current program starts with a fresh screen.

Turbo Pascal stores CLRSCR in a separate file called a *unit*. We discuss units in Chapter 25. For now, include the following after the PROGRAM statement when you want to use CLRSCR:

USES Crt;

Example

To clear the screen before displaying any results, insert a CLRSCR statement, as in this example:

```
PROGRAM PersonalInfo4;
USES Crt;

VAR Age:        BYTE;
    Salary:     REAL;
    Dependents: BYTE;

BEGIN
   CLRSCR;

   Age := 32;
   WRITELN( age );

   Salary := 25000;
   WRITELN( salary );

   Dependents := 2;
   WRITELN( Dependents );
END.   {PersonalInfo4}
```

If you run this program several times in succession, your screen clears before each run.

You can place the CLRSCR statement anywhere in a program. Many programs contain several CLRSCR statements. Whenever you need the program to erase the screen, insert a CLRSCR statement.

The BEGIN and END Statements

All Turbo Pascal programs have a main section that some refer to as the *main program block*. This section is always blocked with a BEGIN-END pair. A period follows the END statment. This marks the end of a Turbo Pascal program. This way, people who read the program listing know they are at the end of the program. Consequently, they won't worry about the possibility of a missing page.

> **NOTE:** A BEGIN statement is always paired with an END statement.

Summary

Congratulations. You now are writing Turbo Pascal programs. In this chapter, you learned about variables and constants, which are the fundamental building blocks for the rest of Turbo Pascal.

Now, you are ready to learn how to document your programs and make them more readable. You can expand your knowledge of the WRITELN statement by adding more options to it, such as displaying more than one value on the same line.

You also have seen some of Pascal's structure that you read about in Chapter 1. You can include a PROGRAM statement to give your program a title. All variables are declared together in a VAR section; all constants are declared together in a CONST section. The main program block is identified by a BEGIN-END pair.

Review Questions

Answers to the Review Questions appear in Appendix B.

1. What are the two parts of a Turbo Pascal program?

2. What is a variable?

3. Which of the following variable names are valid?

   ```
   81QTR   QTR-1-SALES   data file   DataFile
   ```

4. True or False: A variable can be any of three types of integers: INTEGER, SINGLE integer, or DOUBLE integer.

5. True or False: A variable can be any of five types of real numbers: REAL, SINGLE, DOUBLE, EXTENDED, or COMP.

6. How many values can a variable hold at the same time?

7. What statement writes output to the screen?

8. What statement erases the screen?

9. What are the regular number equivalents of the following scientific notation numbers? What are their types?

   ```
   -3.0E+2   4.541e+12   1.9E-03
   ```

10. Rewrite the following numbers in scientific notation format:

    ```
    15   -0.000043   -54,543   531234.9
    ```

Review Exercises

1. Write a program that stores your shoe size, weight (you can fib), and height in three variables.

2. Write a program that clears the screen and then displays the temperature on-screen. (You might have to look at a thermometer or the Weather Channel to get the temperature.)

3. Write a program that clears the screen and stores your two favorite television channels in two variables and displays them.

4. Write a program that stores and displays each type of integer variable you have learned about in this chapter. Make up any valid variable names you want. Because you know five types, you should have five variables.

5. Write a program that stores the following scientific notation numbers in three variables and then displays them to a blank screen.

```
-3.43E-9   +5.43345E+20   +5.43345E-20
```

6

Comments and Additional WRITELN Options

Now that you understand programs and data, it's time to expand on those fundamentals by exploring ways to improve your programs and their output. This chapter covers the following topics:

♦ Understanding program comments

♦ Displaying string constants

♦ Displaying more than one value on a line

♦ Displaying data in right-justified columns

♦ Printing to the printer

By mastering these new concepts and statements, you can write longer programs that do more than store and display values.

Program Comments

Comments tell you, in plain English, what a program is doing.

As you know, a program provides instructions for the computer to read and interpret. Often, you must make changes to a program that you wrote some time ago or that someone else wrote. You won't always remember, or know, what a specific part of a program does. Program comments can help you remember and understand what each section of a particular program is doing.

A *comment* is descriptive text that is written in plain English and placed next to code in a program. Although the computer completely ignores them, comments can make the code more understandable to humans. Comments are typically enclosed in braces:

```
{ any message you choose }
```

You can insert as many comments in your program as you want. Many programmers scatter comments throughout a program. The computer completely ignores comments—they produce no output, store no variables, and hold no constants. If you do not enclose comments in braces, Turbo Pascal thinks you are typing incorrect program statements.

TIP: When you include comments, double-check that each brace has a match. If a brace is missing, the compiler likely will try to interpret your comments as statements, and strange errors may appear. To verify that each brace has a match, position the cursor under a brace (left or right). Hold down the Ctrl and Q keys and tap either the left or right bracket key ([ ]). The editor moves the cursor to the matching brace. If the cursor does not move, the brace does not have a match.

Example

If a computer completely ignores comments, you probably wonder why you should bother to use them. Comments are there for people to use so that they can better understand programs. For example, a Turbo Pascal program that produces a fancy colored box with flashing lights around it and your name inside (like a marquee) can be quite involved. Before those statements you might put a comment such as:

```
{ The next few lines draw a colorful fancy boxed name }
```

This comment does not tell Turbo Pascal to do anything, but it makes the next few lines of code more understandable to you and others. This statement explains in English exactly what the program is going to do.

Comments are often used to insert the programmer's name at the top of a program. In a large company with several programmers, it's helpful to know who to contact if you need assistance when you change a programmer's original code. Remember, because the name is written as a comment it won't display when you run the program. It does, however, serve as a reference for anyone looking at the program's listing.

Additionally, you can insert the program name in an early comment. For example,

```
{ Programmer: Pat Johnston, Filename: PAYROL81.PAS }
```

tells who the programmer is and what the program's filename is on disk. When looking through many printed program listings, you can find the filename in the comment at the top of the program and, using the program editor, quickly load the one you want. Throughout this book, programs have comments that include possible filenames under which you can store the programs. The names have the format Cxname, in which C stands for "Chapter," x is the chapter number, and name is a short phrase to identify the program. For example, C6STR1.PAS is a program from Chapter 6, and C10PAY1.PAS is from Chapter 10.

An Alternative to Braces

Turbo Pascal supplies an alternative form for specifying comments. Instead of typing { }, you can type (* *). Having two styles of delimiters is handy, because you cannot nest two sets of delimiters that are the same style.

Examples

1. You cannot type

```
{ This is a comment. { This is a nested comment. } }
```

When the compiler reads the preceding line, it first interprets the left brace ({). It now ignores everything until it gets to a right brace (}). The first right brace it sees is associated with the nested comment. The compiler displays a *Syntax Error* message because it cannot interpret the last right brace.

Similarly, you cannot type

```
(* This is a comment. (* This is a nested comment. *) *)
```

To correctly nest the preceding example, you would type

```
{ This is a comment. (* This is a nested comment. *) }
```

or, you could type

```
(* This is a comment. { This is a nested comment. } *)
```

2. You can put comments anywhere you want. Suppose you wanted to put comments in the personal information program from the last chapter. The following example shows one way to insert comments into that program.

```
{ Filename: C6CMNT1.PAS }


{
  This program puts a few values in variables
  and then displays those values to the screen.
}

PROGRAM DemoComments1;
USES Crt;

VAR Age:        BYTE;
    Salary:     REAL;
    Dependents: BYTE;

BEGIN
   CLRSCR;
   Age         := 32;            { Stores the age }
```

```
    Salary     := 25000;        { Yearly salary }
    Dependents := 2;            { Number of dependents }

            { Display the results }

    WRITELN( Age );
    WRITELN( Salary );
    WRITELN( Dependents );
END.   {DemoComments1}
```

Because a Turbo Pascal program can contain blank lines, you don't have to use a comment to separate sections of the program. Pressing Enter to add an extra blank line is permissible.

With comments that extend over several lines, some programmers like to put the left brace on a separate line and the matching right brace on the line following the comment. In long programs, the right brace is sometimes difficult to spot, and this method makes the comment easier to identify.

When you use a comment to explain a particular statement, you usually place the comment to the right of the statement. Starting all such comments in the same column helps make larger programs more readable.

When you use a comment to explain several statements (such as { Display the results } in the above program), you can indent it so that the comment does not line up with the code. When you are concentrating on reading the code, the comment does not distract you.

3. The program statements in the preceding example are explained later in this chapter. For now, just concentrate on how to use comments. To run the program, press Ctrl-F9. Press Alt-F5 to view the output screen.

4. The C6CMNT1.PAS program in example #2 can be used to demonstrate one way you can use nested comments. Suppose you want to verify that the program displays Age correctly. Use (* *) to mask out the statements relating to Salary and Dependents. Programmers often refer to this

technique as commenting out a section of code. After verifying Age, you can comment out just Dependents. This is a common "divide and conquer" way to test your program.

```
{ Filename: C6CMNT2.PAS }


{
  This program puts a few values in variables,
  and then displays those values to the screen.
}

PROGRAM DemoComments2;
USES Crt;

VAR Age:        BYTE;
    Salary:     REAL;
    Dependents: BYTE;

BEGIN
   CLRSCR;
   Age := 32;              { Stores the age }
(*
   Salary := 25000:        { Yearly salary }
   Dependents := 2;        { Number of dependents }
*)


        { Display the results }

   WRITELN( Age );
(*
   WRITELN( Salary );
   WRITELN( Dependents );
*)
END.   {DemoComments2}
```

Use Helpful Comments

Although a program without comments can be difficult to understand, you should use only helpful comments. Comments explain what the program code is doing. The following comment, therefore, is not helpful:

```
{ Put the value 3 into the variable called NumKids }
NumKids := 3;
```

Although the previous comment techically is correct, it does not explain why the value 3 is placed in the statement. Consider the following improved example:

```
{ Save the number of kids for dependent calculations }
NumKids := 3;
```

This comment provides a better clue as to how the program's next statement is used. Someone trying to figure out the program would appreciate the second comment more than the first.

This was a simple example. Many Turbo Pascal statements do not require comments. For example, including a comment to explain CLRSCR would be useless because there is no ambiguity about what is going on; the screen is cleared.

Put comments in your programs as you write them. You are most familiar with your program logic when you are typing your program in the editor. Some programmer's do not include comments in their programs until after they are entirely written. As a result, some comments never are included, or the programmer makes a half-hearted attempt to include them later.

The remainder of the examples in this book include comments that explain how statements are being used in their respective programs.

More with WRITELN

After reading the previous chapter, you should understand the following features of the WRITELN statement:

- ◆ WRITELN displays on-screen output.

- ◆ WRITELN displays any constant enclosed in WRITELN's parentheses.

- ◆ WRITELN displays the contents of any variable enclosed in WRITELN's parentheses.

WRITELN can do many other things. To write more helpful programs, learn how to access more of WRITELN's options.

Displaying String Constants

In Turbo Pascal, a *string constant* is one or more groups of characters inside single quotation marks (' '). Here are five string constants:

```
'This is a string constant.'
'ABC 123 $#@ --- +=][ x'
'X'
'Turbo Pascal is fun!'
'123.45'
```

Notice that even one character, when it is inside single quotation marks, is a string constant. (String constants are sometimes called *string literals*.) The only member of this list you might find questionable is the string '123.45'.

'123.45' fulfills the definition of a string constant: one or more characters enclosed within single quotation marks. '123.45' is not a number, a numeric constant, or a variable. Single quotation marks always designate string constants. You cannot use '123.45' in mathematical calculations because Turbo Pascal does not view it as a number.

String constants are helpful for displaying names, titles, addresses, and messages on-screen and for printing them on the printer. When you want your Turbo Pascal program to display a title or a word, enclose it inside the parentheses after the word WRITELN.

Examples

1. To display the name and address of Widgets, Inc. on-screen, put the following section of code in the program:

```
{ Filename: C6TITLE.PAS }

{ Displays a company's name and address on-screen. }
```

```pascal
PROGRAM Title;
USES Crt;

BEGIN
   CLRSCR;
   WRITELN( 'Widgets, Inc.');
   WRITELN( '307 E. Midway');
   WRITELN( 'Jackson, MI    03882');
END.  {Title}
```

After running this program, your screen should look like this:

```
Widgets, Inc.
307 E. Midway
Jackson, MI    03882
```

2. The primary reason for using string constants is to label your output. Earlier, when you ran the personal information program (PROGRAM DemoComments1), three numbers appeared on-screen. Anyone who did not write the program might not know what each number meant. You can modify the program to describe its output, as in:

```pascal
{ Filename: C6STR1.PAS }

{
  This program puts a few values in variables
 and then displays those values and labels to the screen.
}

PROGRAM DemoStringConstants;
USES Crt;

VAR Age:       BYTE;
    Salary:    REAL;
    Dependents: BYTE;

BEGIN
   CLRSCR;
   Age        := 32;        { Stores the age }
```

```
Salary     := 25000;     { Yearly salary }
Dependents := 2;         { Number of dependents }

       { Display the results }

WRITELN( 'Age' );
WRITELN( Age );
WRITELN( 'Salary' );
WRITELN( Salary:8:2 );
WRITELN( 'Dependents' );
WRITELN( Dependents );
END.   {DemoStringConstants}
```

The output of this program should look like this:

```
Age
32
Salary
25000.00
Dependents
2
```

Look closely at the previous six lines. The word "Age" is displayed followed by the value of the variable Age, because in the program you displayed the string constant 'Age' followed by the variable Age. The same is true for the other WRITELN statements. (In the fourth WRITELN statement, the :8:2 formats the REAL variable, Salary. This will be explained later in this chapter.)

The preceding program (PROGRAM DemoStringConstants) illustrates why single quotation marks are required around string constants. Without them, the previous example's program would not know when to display the word "Age" and when to display the contents of the variable Age.

NOTE: Whenever you display string constants, everything inside the single quotation marks appears on-screen exactly as it is written in the program. This includes any spaces you typed between the quotation marks.

The following four WRITELN statements all produce different output because the data inside the single quotation marks is different.

```
WRITELN( 'The Amount is ', amt );
WRITELN( 'The Amount is   ', amt );
WRITELN( 'The  Amount is', amt );
WRITELN( 'T h e   A m o u n t   i s', amt);
```

3. To display "Sales for Margo's Region," you would probably write:

```
WRITELN('Sales for Margo's Region');   {does not work}
```

The compiler interprets the first single quotation mark properly. However, when the compiler encounters the apostrophe in "Margo's," it interprets this as the end of the string. To solve this problem, use two adjacent single quotation marks. This tells the compiler that a single quotation mark is being used as part of the text. To correct the preceding example, write

```
WRITELN('Sales for Margo''s Region');   {this works}
```

NOTE: To display an apostrophe inside a string, type two adjacent single quotation marks.

Displaying More Than One Value on a Line

You now know several ways to use WRITELN, but this statement can do more. The WRITELN statements you have seen so far displayed one value per line (a numeric constant, a variable, or a string constant). You also can display several values on a line in one statement. When displaying more than one value on a line, you must separate each value with a comma.

WRITELN **with Commas**

To display two or more values next to each other, separate them with a comma in the WRITELN statement. When you use the comma, the format of WRITELN looks like this:

```
WRITELN( value1,value2[,value3][,value#]...);
```

In other words, if you put more than one value (these values can be variables or constants or a combination of both) after WRITELN and separate them with commas, Turbo Pascal displays those values adjacently instead of on separate lines.

WRITELN **with Formatting**

To display more than one value separated by several spaces, you might want to use some special formatting options. You can right-justify the output by using a colon to control the width of the value. This is also helpful in a WRITELN statement when you want to display columns of output. For example, to display two column headers as right-justified in columns 20 characters wide, type

```
WRITELN('Column Header 1':20, 'Column Header 2':20);
```

If you are displaying real values, you can control the number of decimal places (the number of digits to the right of the decimal point) by using an additional colon. For example, to display two previously declared real values to two decimal places in columns 20 characters wide, type

```
WRITELN(Col1Value:20:2, Col2Value:20:2);
```

In other words, when you put more than one value (variables, constants, or a combination of both) after WRITELN and separate them with commas, Turbo Pascal displays those values and separates them according to the numbers after the colons.

Examples

1. You can change the C6STR1.PAS program to use the screen more efficiently by displaying the values of each variable

after its description. The following program produces a more readable output screen:

```
{ Filename: C6FORM1.PAS }

{
  This program puts a few values in variables
  and then displays those values to the screen
  for better-looking output.
}

PROGRAM DemoFormatting;
USES Crt;

VAR Age:        BYTE;
    Salary:     REAL;
    Dependents: BYTE;

BEGIN
    CLRSCR;
    Age        := 32;              { Stores the age }
    Salary     := 25000;          { Yearly salary }
    Dependents := 2;              { Number of dependents }

              { Display the results }

    WRITELN( 'The age is ',Age );
    WRITELN;
    WRITELN( 'The salary is ',Salary:8:2);
    WRITELN;
    WRITELN( 'The number of dependents is ', Dependents);
END.  {DemoFormatting}
```

Figure 6.1 illustrates the screen output produced by the preceding program. This example illustrates one way of displaying numbers. Notice that a space appears before each variable. This is the space at the end of the string and before the variable. Without this space, the end of the string would bump up against the value of the variable.

```
The age is 32

The salary is 25000.00

The number of dependents is 2
```

Figure 6.1. **Improving the output.**

Notice the formatting for the display of `salary`. When used with real numbers, the number after the first colon specifies the total number of spaces (including the decimal point). The number after the second colon specifies the total number of digits to display after the decimal point.

2. Turbo Pascal knows that every number is either positive or negative. When Turbo Pascal displays a negative number, it displays the negative sign in front of the number. Turbo Pascal must display the negative sign to indicate to you that the number is negative. It does not, however, display a plus sign in front of a positive number.

To see another example, run the following program. It displays three string constants, three negative numbers, and three positive numbers separated by commas and using colons to format the data into columns.

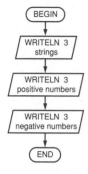

```
{ Filename: C6WRITLN.PAS }


{
  This program displays three sets of values showing
  how Turbo Pascal handles the spacing between them.
}

PROGRAM DemoWriteln;
USES Crt;

CONST CWid = 10;                        {column width}

BEGIN
   CLRSCR;

          { Three string constants }
      WRITELN( 'Books':CWid, 'Movies':CWid, 'Theatre':CWid);

          { Three positive numbers }
      WRITELN( 123:CWid,        456:CWid,        789:CWid);

          { Three negative numbers }
     WRITELN( -123:CWid,       -456:CWid,       -789:CWid);
END.   {DemoWriteln}
```

When you run this program, you should see the screen shown in Figure 6.2. This example illustrates how Turbo Pascal displays right-justified data.

If you don't want to use a colon to format and you want to display three string constants with a space between them, you would code WRITELN in the following way:

```
WRITELN( 'Books ', 'Movies ', 'Theatre');
```

To ensure that the space is displayed, you must insert the space inside the quotation marks of the string constant. The space after the comma does not affect the output but makes the line more readable.

```
Books    Movies   Theatre
 123        456       789
-123       -456      -789
```

Figure 6.2. Right-justifying values by using a colon.

3. So far, every WRITELN statement has started the output on a new line because Turbo Pascal automatically sends a carriage return-line feed sequence after each WRITELN.

If you do not want the carriage return-line feed sequence, you can use the WRITE statement instead. With this statement, the output continues on the same line until the right side of the screen is reached or the next WRITELN is encountered. For example, the following short section of code displays all three names on the same line:

```
{ Filename: C6WRITE.PAS }


{

    The program builds an output line of three names.
    First, the last name uses a WRITELN to position the
    cursor on the next line. Second, all three names
    are displayed with WRITE followed by WRITELN.
}

PROGRAM DemoWrite;
```

```
USES Crt;

BEGIN
    CLRSCR;
    WRITE( 'Heath ');
    WRITE( 'Jarrod ');
    WRITELN( 'Nick');

    WRITE( 'Heath ');
    WRITE( 'Jarrod ');
    WRITE( 'Nick');
    WRITELN;
END.   {DemoWrite}
```

The output of this program should look like this:

```
Heath Jarrod Nick
Heath Jarrod Nick
```

Because the string constants in the first two WRITE statements each have a space following the name, the names are separated by spaces when they display.

At first, you might think you will never use WRITE. After all, you can accomplish the same output with the following statement:

```
WRITELN( 'Heath ','Jarrod ','Nick');
```

As you do more programming in Turbo Pascal, however, you might want to *build* your output line. That is, you might want to display some of the line, make some computations, and then finish displaying the rest of the line. This means that you can keep everything on the same line with WRITE statements, and then use WRITELN to position the cursor on the next line. As illustrated in the preceding example, you can use WRITELN with the last item to display on the line, or you can use WRITELN by itself after displaying all items with WRITE.

4. The following program illustrates the use of the comma and colon with WRITELN values. The three lines display the animals' names in four columns. Although the names are different lengths, the formatting tells Turbo Pascal to insert

leading spaces until the length of the name plus the leading spaces matches the column width. This process right-justifies each name.

```
{ Filename: C6COMMA.PAS }


{
  Uses the comma between displayed values.
}

PROGRAM DemoCommas;
USES Crt;

CONST CWid = 15;                        {column width}

BEGIN
   CLRSCR;
   WRITELN('Lion':CWid,'Whale':CWid,'Monkey':CWid,'Fish':CWid );
   WRITELN('Alligator':CWid,'Bat':CWid,'Seal':CWid,'Tiger':CWid );
   WRITELN('Dog':CWid,'Lizard':CWid,'Cat':CWid,'Bear':CWid );
END.   {DemoCommas}
```

Figure 6.3 shows the output for the preceding program. Only string constants are displayed in this example, but you can also display variables and numeric constants.

Displaying Spaces

Besides right-justifing a string or numeric value, you also can generate an exact number of spaces. For example, to display five spaces, type:

```
WRITELN(' ':5);
```

Or, to make your program more readable, declare a constant, Spc, as a single space:

```
      Lion          Whale        Monkey         Fish
 Alligator            Bat          Seal        Tiger
       Dog         Lizard           Cat         Bear
```

Figure 6.3. Displaying string constants in columns.

```
CONST Spc = ' ';
BEGIN
   WRITELN(Spc:5);
   ⋮
```

Using these two ideas together provides a way of building a table with right-justified data and a fixed number of spaces between columns.

Examples

1. The following program displays animal names in columns ten spaces wide. Five spaces separate each column.

```
{ Filename: C6RJ1.PAS }

{
  Uses Spc:n to put spaces between displayed values.
}

PROGRAM RightJustify1;
USES Crt;
```

```
CONST CWid = 10;                        { width of column }
      BWid =  5;                        { width between columns }
      Spc  = ' ';

BEGIN
  CLRSCR;
  WRITELN( 'Lion':CWid,       Spc:BWid, 'Whale':CWid,  Spc:BWid,
           'Monkey':CWid,     Spc:BWid, 'Fish':CWid);
  WRITELN( 'Alligator':CWid, Spc:BWid, 'Bat':CWid,     Spc:BWid,
           'Seal':CWid,       Spc:BWid, 'Tiger':CWid);
  WRITELN( 'Dog':CWid,        Spc:BWid, 'Lizard':CWid, Spc:BWid,
           'Cat':CWid,        Spc:BWid, 'Bear':CWid);
END.   {RightJustify1}
```

You don't have to include the spaces before the Spc constant
in the preceding WRITELN statements, but the spaces make the
program more readable. Figure 6.4 shows the result of
running this program.

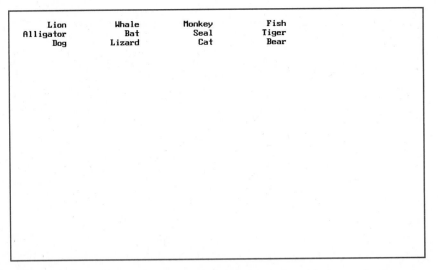

Figure 6.4. The result of using the Spc constant to add spaces between
columns.

> **TIP**: When you need to split a WRITELN statement into more than one line, split the line after a comma. Do not split a string. If you accidently split a string, the compiler gives this error message:
>
> `Error 8: String constant exceeds line.`

2. The right-justify option is especially helpful for tables of data. Although words and values don't always occupy the same width on-screen (Alligator is longer than Dog), you might want the data to display in the same column.

   The following program displays a list of names and addresses on-screen.

```
{ Filename: C6RJ2.PAS }

{ Uses right-justification to display a name and address
  report. }

PROGRAM RightJustify2;
USES Crt;

CONST Spc = ' ';
      nw  = 20;                      { name width }
      aw  = 23;                      { address width }
      cw  = 12;                      { city width }
      sw  =  9;                      { state width }
      zw  = 11;                      { zip code width }

BEGIN
   CLRSCR;
        { Display underlined report titles }
   WRITELN( Spc:71, 'Zip');
   WRITELN( 'Name':nw, 'Address':aw,
           'City':cw,'State':sw, 'Code':zw);

   WRITELN( '----':nw, '-------':aw,
           '----':cw,'----':sw, '----':zw);

        { Display the data values }
```

```
        WRITELN( 'Michael Stapp':nw,     '6104 E. 6th':aw,
                'Tulsa':cw, '   Okla.':sw, '74135':zw);
    WRITELN( 'Jayne M. Wiseman':nw, 'Elm and Broadway':aw,
                'Cleveland':cw,'Ohio':sw,   '19332':zw);

    WRITELN( 'Lou Horn':nw,          '12 East Sheridan Ave.':aw,
                'Carmel':cw, 'Indi.':sw, '46332':zw);

    WRITELN( 'Luke Ben Tanner':nw, '5706 S. Indianapolis':aw,
                'Salem':cw, 'Mass.':sw,  '23337':zw);
END.  {RightJustify2}
```

In this example, the constant (for example, nw) after the colon defines the column width size. Notice that a WRITELN statement was required to display the heading Zip on a line by itself so that it sits on top of Code in the next line.

The dashes help underline each title and separate the title from the data. Figure 6.5 shows the output from the preceding program.

```
                                                  Zip
              Name              Address     City    State    Code
              ----              -------     ----    -----    ----
     Michael Stapp          6104 E. 6th    Tulsa    Okla.    74135
   Jayne M. Wiseman    Elm and Broadway  Cleveland  Ohio     19332
         Lou Horn   12 East Sheridan Ave.   Carmel   Indi.    46332
   Luke Ben Tanner    5706 S. Indianapolis   Salem   Mass.    23337
```

Figure 6.5. **Displaying a report with titles using the** WRITELN **option.**

Printing to Paper

You have made much progress toward producing attractive, good-looking output. Displaying to the screen, however, is not always the best method. For a permanent copy, send the output to the printer. Printing with the printer is easy to do. Again, you use the WRITELN statement.

Printing with the WRITELN Statement

If you want to display This is a test on-screen, you write:

```
WRITELN('This is a test');
```

This is a shortcut for:

```
WRITELN(OUTPUT,'This is a test');
```

The reserved word OUTPUT normally sends all output to the screen. To send the test string to the printer, use the reserved word LST.

```
WRITELN(LST,'This is a test');
```

Any program that uses WRITELN statements can be redirected to the printer by substituting a WRITELN(LST,...); for each WRITELN(...) statement. Turbo Pascal needs an additional unit, Printer, to actually send the data to the printer. Include the following statement after the PROGRAM statement:

```
USES Printer;
```

NOTE: To send data to the printer, be sure to include both a WRITELN(LST,...); and a USES Printer; statement.

Example

The following program is identical to C6RJ1.PAS, which displayed the animal names on-screen. All the WRITELN(...) statements in the original program, however, are changed to WRITELN(LST,...) statements. CLRSCR still clears the screen, but it does nothing to the printer.

```
{ Filename: C6PRNT1.PAS }

{ All output goes to the printer. }

PROGRAM Print1;
USES Crt, Printer;

CONST c1 = 10;                    { column 1 width }
      c2 = 15;                    { column 2 width }
      c3 = 15;                    { column 3 width }
      c4 = 15;                    { column 4 width }

BEGIN
   CLRSCR;
   WRITELN(LST, 'Lion':c1,'Whale':c2,'Monkey':c3,'Fish':c4);
   WRITELN(LST, 'Alligator':c1,'Bat':c2,'Seal':c3,'Tiger':c4);
   WRITELN(LST, 'Dog':c1,'Lizard':c2,'Cat':c3, 'Bear':c4);
END.   {Print1}
```

If your printer isn't on or doesn't have paper, the following error message appears:

```
Device fault
```

Correct the problem and r un the program again if you receive this message.

Summary

In this chapter, you learned to document your programs by adding comments. You discovered that it's important to provide a comment documenting the program's filename and author. It's also important to scatter comments throughout the program that describe (in plain English) the program's logic. As you write longer programs, comments become even more important.

This chapter illustrated many ways to display values with the WRITELN statement. You now can send multiple values, variables, and string constants to the screen or printer. Chapter 7, "Turbo Pascal's Math Operators," discusses the math operators in Turbo Pascal and illustrates how Turbo Pascal can do calculations for you.

Review Questions

Answers to Review Questions appear in Appendix B.

1. What are the two ways to write a comment?

2. What does the computer do when it finds a comment?

3. True or False: The following section of a program puts a 4 in the variable called R, a 5 in ME, and a 6 in S.

```
R  := 4;
ME := 5;
{S := 6;}
```

4. True or False: WRITELN sends output to the screen.

5. What character does Turbo Pascal use to separate statements?

6. To print data to the printer, what two things must you include in your program?

7. True or False: Comments using only braces may be nested.

8. What does the following WRITELN statement do?

```
WRITELN(LST,' ':20,'Computer');
```

9. What does the following WRITELN statement print?

```
WRITELN(LST,'Month':8, 'Day':4,'Year':5);
```

10. How would you display Hello in column 28?

11. How would you display Bob's Sales?

12. What is the output of the following program?

```
BEGIN
   { ------------------ }
   {    SECRET AGENTS   }
   { ------------------ }
   WRITELN( 86 );
   WRITELN( ' and');
   WRITELN( 99 );
   WRITELN( ' are secret agents.');
END.
```

Review Exercises

1. Write a program to store your shoe size, weight, and height in three different variables. Display the values with their corresponding descriptions on three separate lines. Then, display the values next to each other on the same line. Use appropriate comments to document the program.

2. Modify the previous program to display your weight in column 15, your height in column 25, and your shoe size in column 35.

3. Write a program that prints (to the printer) the names and phone numbers of your three best friends. Add appropriate comments to document the program. Make sure you print nicely underlined titles over the names and phone numbers. The report's columns should line up.

4. Look in your newspaper's financial section and find a table of figures. Try to duplicate the table on your screen or printer. Make sure the columns of data line up neatly under appropriate headings. Try to match the newspaper as closely as possible. The newspaper's characters are not always the same size, so you might have to guess and not use the same number of spaces the paper uses. The more displaying you

do (practicing all three ways of aligning columns), the faster you can produce any screen output required by any program you ever want to write.

5. Find and correct the six errors in the following program excerpt:

```
{ This program displays payroll information }
Pay := 2,102.32;
Dependents := 3;
TaxRate = .35      { This is the percentage tax rate }
WRITELN;
WRITELN( 'The pay is: ', Pay);
WRITELN( 'The number of dependents is: '; Dependents);
CLRSCR;
WRITELN( 'The tax rate percentage is:', TaxRate);
```

6. You can use the WRITELN(LST,...); statement to print pictures to the printer. Use a series of WRITELN statements to produce the following house and rocket:

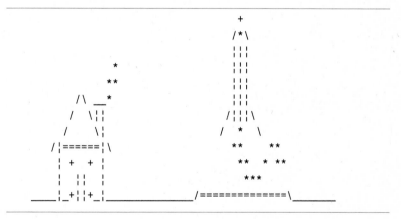

Turbo Pascal's Math Operators

If you are dreading this chapter because you do not like math, relax. Turbo Pascal does all your math for you. It is a misconception that you must be good at math to program computers. The computer follows your instructions and does all the calculating for you. This chapter explains how Turbo Pascal computes by introducing

- ♦ Turbo Pascal math operators

- ♦ The order of operators

- ♦ How to store the results of calculations in variables

- ♦ How to display the results of calculations

Many people who dislike math actually enjoy learning how the computer does the calculations. After learning the operators and a few simple ways Turbo Pascal uses them, you can feel comfortable putting calculations in your programs. Computers can perform math operations many times faster than people can.

The Math Operators

A *math operator* is a symbol used for addition, subtraction, multiplication, division, or other calculations. The operators are similar to the ones you use when you do arithmetic. Table 7.1 lists every Turbo Pascal operator and its meaning.

Table 7.1. The Turbo Pascal math operators and their meanings.

Symbol	Meaning
*	Multiplication
/	Division
+	Addition
-	Subtraction
DIV	Integer division
MOD	Modulus

The Four Primary Operators

The four primary Turbo Pascal operators, *, /, +, and -, operate in the way you are used to. Multiplication, division, addition, and subtraction produce the same results as when you do these math functions with a calculator. Table 7.2 contains four samples that illustrate each of these simple operators.

Table 7.2. The results of calculations done with the primary operators.

Formula	Result
4 * 2	8
95 / 2	47.5
80 – 15	65
12 + 9	21

For multiplication you must use the asterisk rather than *x*, as you normally write it by hand. You cannot use an *x* because Turbo Pascal would confuse it with a variable called x; Turbo Pascal would not know whether you wanted to multiply or use the value of x.

You can use the addition and subtraction operators by themselves to indicate a positive or negative number. In this case, they are called *unary* operators because the operator works on only one number rather than two. (The unary addition operator is optional; Turbo Pascal assumes a positive value unless you tell it otherwise.) For instance, you can assign a variable a positive or negative number or assign it a positive or negative variable by using the unary plus or minus, such as:

```
a := -25;
b := +25;
c := -a;
d := +b;
```

Math Inside the Computer

Internally, your computer can perform addition only. This seems strange because people use computers for all kinds of powerful mathematical solutions. Addition, however, is all your computer needs to know.

At the binary level, your computer can add two binary numbers. Your computer has no problem with adding 6 + 7. To subtract 6 from 7, however, your computer has to use *modified addition*.

To subtract 6 from 7, your computer actually adds a negative 6 to 7. When your program stores the result of 7 - 6 in a variable, your computer interprets it as 7 + -6. The result is 1.

Your computer can add positive and negative numbers (the negative of a number is called the *two's complement*). These two things are all the computer requires to simulate subtraction.

Multiplication is simply repeated addition. Therefore, 6 * 7 is interpreted as 6 added to itself seven times, or 6 + 6 + 6 + 6 + 6 + 6 + 6.

continues

Division is repeated subtraction. When you calculate 42 / 6, the computer repeatedly subtracts 6 from 42 until it gets to zero and then adds the number of times it did that. This becomes 42 - 6 - 6 - 6 - 6 - 6 - 6 - 6 = 0. Reaching 0 takes seven subtractions of 6 (or actually the addition of seven negative 6s). Thus, the result of 42 / 6 is 7. Depending on the numbers, division does not always result in an even number. If the repeated subtraction would result in a negative number, there is a remainder.

When your computer is able to add and simulate subtraction, multiplication, and division, it has the tools required for every other math function as well.

Integer Division and Modulus

The two remaining operators, DIV (integer division), and MOD (modulus, or integer remainder), might be new to you. They are as easy to use as the four operators you saw in the previous section.

Use integer division to produce the integer (or whole number) result of a division. Integer division always produces an integer result and discards any remainder. You must put integers on both sides of the DIV operator. This is another example of Pascal's structure. If you use DIV, then you must use integers. If you try to use real numbers with DIV, Turbo Pascal gives you a compiler error (Operand types do not match operator). When you see the term integer in this chapter, remember that it can be type BYTE, INTEGER, LONGINT, SHORTINT, or WORD. Table 7.3 shows the results of some sample integer division programs.

Table 7.3. Integer division results.

Formula	Result
8 DIV 2	4
9 DIV 2	4
95 DIV 2	47

The MOD operator produces the *modulus,* or integer remainder, of division. The numbers on both sides of the MOD operator must be integers. Table 7.4 shows the results of some simple MOD operations.

Table 7.4. MOD operation results.

Formula	Result
8 MOD 2	0
8 MOD 3	2
15 MOD 7	1

When displaying reports to the screen, for example, you may need to know the number of complete pages and the number of lines on the last page. If your report can print 50 lines per page and you have a total of 260 lines, you can use DIV and MOD to determine these numbers, as shown in the following example:

```
VAR TotalLines: INTEGER;
    PageLines:  INTEGER;
    FullPages:  INTEGER;
    LastPage:   INTEGER;
BEGIN
  :
  TotalLines := 260;
  PageLines  :=  50;
  FullPages  := TotalLines DIV PageLines;
  LastPage   := TotalLines MOD PageLines;
  :
END.
```

The Assignment of Formulas to Variables

Most of your programs use variables to store the results of these calculations. You already have seen how to assign values and variables to other variables. The true power of variables appears when you assign results of formulas to them.

Examples

1. The following program illustrates a payroll computation. The program assigns the hours worked, the pay per hour (the `rate`), and the tax rate to three variables. It then creates three new variables (`grosspay`, `taxes`, and `netpay`) from calculations using the three original variables.

```
{ Filename: C7PAY1.PAS }

{ Computes three payroll variables. }

PROGRAM Pay1;
USES Crt;

CONST HoursWorked = 40;              { Total hours worked }
      Rate        = 7.80;            { Pay per hour }
      TaxRate     = 0.40;            { Tax rate percentage }

      GrossPay    = HoursWorked * Rate;
      Taxes       = TaxRate * GrossPay;
      NetPay      = GrossPay - Taxes;

BEGIN
   CLRSCR;

           { Display the results }

   WRITELN( 'The Gross Pay is ', GrossPay:8:2 );
   WRITELN( 'The Taxes are ', Taxes:8:2 );
   WRITELN( 'The Net Pay is ', NetPay:8:2 );
END.  {Pay1}
```

The C7PAY1.PAS program displays the following results:

```
The Gross Pay is    312.00
The taxes are    124.80
The Net Pay is    187.20
```

In the first output line there are three spaces before the gross pay of 312.00. The first space is from the trailing space in the string literal. The remaining two spaces are a result of formatting with 8:2. The 2 specifies two decimal places. 312.00 requires a total of six columns. Because the formatting specified a total of eight columns, Turbo Pascal inserts two leading spaces.

2. The following program takes the value in the variable Inches and converts it to feet.

```
{ Filename: C7IN2FT.PAS }

{ Converts inches to feet. }

PROGRAM ConvertInchesToFeet;
USES Crt;

VAR    Feet:   REAL;
       Inches: REAL;

BEGIN
   CLRSCR;
   Inches := 72.0;
   Feet   := Inches / 12.0;
   WRITELN( 'The number of feet in ',Inches:5:1,
            ' are ',Feet:5:1 );
END.
```

The Order of Operators

Knowing the meaning of the math operators is the first of two steps toward understanding Turbo Pascal calculations. You also must understand the _order of operators_. The order of operators (sometimes called the _hierarchy of operators_ or _operator precedence_) determines exactly how Turbo Pascal computes formulas. The order of operators is exactly the same as that used in high school algebra. To see how the order of operators works, try to determine the result of the following calculation:

```
2 + 3 * 2
```

Many people would say the answer is 10. However, 10 is correct only if you interpret the formula from left to right. But what if you calculated the multiplication first? If you took the value of 3 * 2, got an answer of 6, and then added the 2 to it, you would end up with the answer 8. That is the answer Turbo Pascal would compute.

Turbo Pascal performs any multiplication and division first. If there are several multiplications and divisions in a formula, it computes them from left to right. Then it performs addition and subtraction. Table 7.5 shows the Turbo Pascal order of operators.

Table 7.5. The order of operators.

Order	Operator
1	Unary addition and subtraction
2	Multiplication, division, integer division, integer remainder (*, /, DIV, MOD)
3	Addition, subtraction (+, -)

Examples

1. It is easy to follow Turbo Pascal's order of operators if you follow the intermediate results one at a time. The two complex calculations in Figure 7.1 show you how to do this.

2. Looking back at Table 7.5, notice that multiplication, division, DIV (integer division), and MOD (modulus) are on the same level. This implies that there is no hierarchy on that level. If more than one of these operators appears in a calculation, Turbo Pascal performs the math from left to right. The same is true of addition and subtraction; the leftmost operation is performed first.

Figure 7.2 shows an example of left-to-right division and multiplication.

Because the division appears to the left of the multiplication (and because division and multiplication are on the same level), the division is computed first.

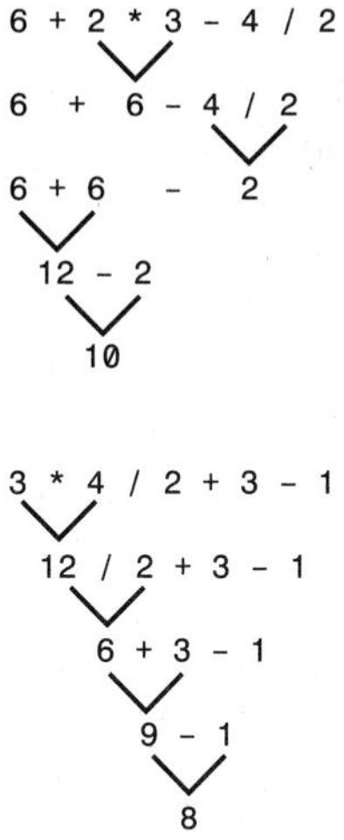

```
6 + 2 * 3 - 4 / 2
      \/
6  +  6  - 4 / 2
         \/
6 + 6    -   2
  \/
12 - 2
   \/
   10
```

```
3 * 4 / 2 + 3 - 1
\/
12 / 2 + 3 - 1
   \/
   6 + 3 - 1
     \/
     9 - 1
       \/
       8
```

Figure 7.1. Two complex calculations showing how to follow Turbo Pascal's order of operators.

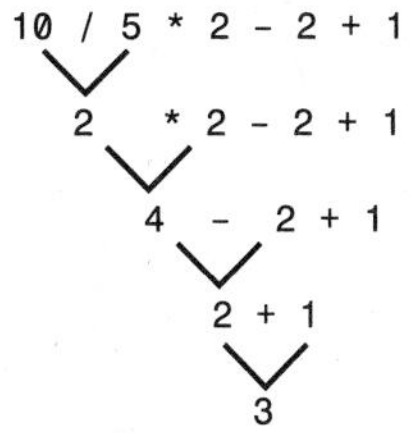

```
10 / 5 * 2 - 2 + 1
  \/
2    * 2 - 2 + 1
  \/
  4   - 2 + 1
    \/
    2 + 1
      \/
      3
```

Figure 7.2. Operators on the same precedence level calculate from left to right.

It is important to understand the order of operators so that you know how to structure your calculations. Now that you have mastered operator order, you can see how to use parentheses to override that order.

Parentheses

If you want to override the order of operators, put parentheses in the calculation. In other words, anything in parentheses, whether it is addition, subtraction, division, or whatever, always is calculated before the rest of the line. The remaining calculations are performed in the normal order.

> **TIP:** If there are expressions with parentheses inside other parentheses, such as ((5 + 2) - 7 + (8 + 9 - (5 + 2))), calculate the innermost expression first. As with comment delimiters, you can use the editor to find matching parentheses. Position the cursor under a parenthesis (left or right). Hold down the Ctrl and Q keys and tap the left or right bracket key ([ ]). The editor moves the cursor to the matching parenthesis. If the cursor does not move, the parenthesis does not have a match.

The formula 2 + 3 * 2 produced an 8 because multiplication is performed before addition. If you add parentheses around the addition, as in (2 + 3) * 2, the answer becomes 10.

Examples

1. The calculations in Figure 7.3 illustrate how parentheses override the regular order of operators. These are the same three formulas shown in Figure 7.2, except their calculations are different because the parentheses override the order of operators.

2. The following program produces an incorrect result, although it looks as though it should work. See whether you can spot the error.

```
{ Filename: C7AVG1.PAS }

{ Attempts to compute the average of three grades }

PROGRAM Average1;
```

```
VAR Grade1: INTEGER;
    Grade2: INTEGER;
    Grade3: INTEGER;

BEGIN
    Grade1 := 86;
    Grade2 := 98;
    Grade3 := 72;

    Avg := Grade1 + Grade2 + Grade3 / 3;
    WRITELN( 'The average is ', Avg:5:2);
END.  {Average1}
```

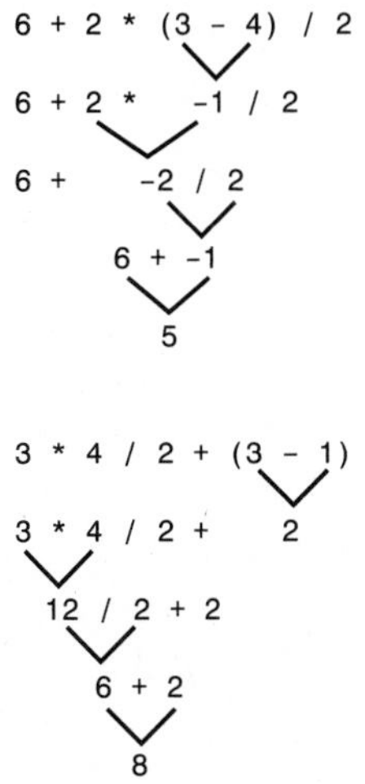

```
6 + 2 * (3 - 4) / 2
6 + 2 *   -1 / 2
6 +    -2 / 2
         6 + -1
           5


3 * 4 / 2 + (3 - 1)
3 * 4 / 2 +    2
12 / 2 + 2
       6 + 2
         8
```

Figure 7.3. Overriding the order of operators with parentheses.

The problem is that division is performed first. Therefore, the third grade is divided by three, and then the other two grades are added to that result. To fix the problem, you have to add one set of parentheses, as shown in the following code:

```
{ Filename: C7AVG2.PAS }

{ Fix the Computation of the average of three grades }

PROGRAM Average2;

VAR Grade1: INTEGER;
    Grade2: INTEGER;
    Grade3: INTEGER;

BEGIN
    Grade1 := 86;
    Grade2 := 98;
    Grade3 := 72;

    Avg := (Grade1 + Grade2 + Grade3) / 3;
    WRITELN( 'The average is ', Avg:5:2);
END.  {Average2}
```

TIP: Use plenty of parentheses in your programs to make the order of operators clearer, even if you don't override the order of operators. The parentheses make the calculations easier to understand if you modify the program later.

Displaying Calculations

You have seen how WRITELN displays and prints variables and constants. This statement also can display and print the values of expressions. As long as the expression results in a valid constant, you can put the expression to the right of WRITELN.

Do not use WRITELN with the assignment statement. The following WRITELN statement is invalid:

```
WRITELN( Sales := 'are the sales' );        { invalid }
```

Running this line in a program would result in a syntax error. WRITELN requires an expression to the right of WRITELN. The colon-equal sign is reserved for the assignment statement. You would first have to assign a value to Sales and then display that value, as in the following program:

```
PROGRAM Sales;

VAR Sales: REAL;

BEGIN
   Sales := 18750.43;
   WRITELN( Sales:8:2, ' are the sales.' );
END.  {Sales}
```

Examples

1. You can compute and display payroll amounts at the same time. The following program, a rewritten version of C7PAY1.PAS, displays the results of the three payroll expressions without storing the results in variables.

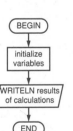

```
{ Filename: C7PAY2.PAS }

{ Computes and displays three payroll values. }

PROGRAM Pay2;
USES Crt;

CONST HoursWorked = 40;        { Total hours worked }
      Rate       = 7.80;       { Pay per hour }
      TaxRate    = 0.40;       { Tax rate percentage }

BEGIN
   CLRSCR;
   WRITELN( 'Gross Pay is ', HoursWorked * Rate:8:2 );
   WRITELN( 'Taxes are ', TaxRate * HoursWorked * Rate:8:2 );
   WRITELN( 'Net Pay is ',((HoursWorked * Rate) -
            (HoursWorked * Rate * TaxRate)):8:2);
END.  {Pay2}
```

This program results in

```
Gross Pay is   312.00
Taxes are   124.80
Net Pay is   187.20
```

Notice that the results are identical to the output of the original program C7PAY1.PAS, although the programs are very different.

This program is not necessarily better than the original, but it does illustrate that you can display variables, constants, and expressions. Notice that not all the parentheses are required in the last expression, but they make the meaning of the formula clearer: You must compute the gross pay before subtracting the taxes.

Although this program is shorter than C7PAY1.PAS, a shorter program is not always better. A more readable program is generally the best kind. Being able to store the three values lets you use them later in the program without recalculating their results. The last expression is much less complicated if you first calculate and store the GrossPay and Taxes, as you did in the original program.

Shorter Is Not Always Better

If you program computers for the company you work for, it is much more important to write programs that are easy to understand than programs that are short or include a tricky calculation.

Maintainability is the computer industry's word for the ability to change and update programs that were written in a simple style. The business world is changing rapidly, and the programs that companies have used for years must be updated to reflect the changing environment. Businesses do not always have the resources to write programs from scratch, so they must modify the ones they have.

Years ago, when computer hardware was much more expensive and when computer memories were much smaller, it was important to write small programs, despite the problems these programs caused when they had to be changed. These problems were aggravated when the original programmers left and someone else had to step in and modify the code.

Companies are realizing the importance of spending time to write programs that are easy to modify and that do not rely on tricks or "quick and dirty" routines that are hard to follow. You are a much more valuable programmer if you write clean programs with ample white space, plentiful comments, and straightforward code. Put parentheses around formulas if doing so makes them clearer, and use variables for storing results in case you require the same answer later in the program. Break long calculations into several smaller ones.

2. You can write simple programs to illustrate the operators in Turbo Pascal. Suppose you want to write a tutorial program that shows how each operator works. The following program computes and displays the results of simple calculations using each operator.

```
{ Filename: C7OPRTR.PAS }

{ This program shows the result of each operator. }

PROGRAM DemoOperators;
USES Crt;

CONST Num1 = 7;                { The constants to compute with }
      Num2 = 4;

BEGIN
   CLRSCR;
   WRITELN( Num1,' - ',Num2,'   is ', Num1-Num2 );
   WRITELN( Num1,' + ',Num2,'   is ', Num1+Num2 );
   WRITELN( Num1,' * ',Num2,'   is ', Num1*Num2 );
```

```
      WRITELN( Num1,' / ',Num2,'   is ', (Num1/Num2):5:2 );
      WRITELN( Num1,' DIV ',Num2,' is ', Num1 DIV Num2 );
      WRITELN( Num1,' MOD ',Num2,' is ', Num1 MOD Num2 );
END.  {DemoOperators}
```

The preceding program displays the following results:

```
7 - 4   is 3
7 + 4   is 11
7 * 4   is 28
7 / 4   is 1.75
7 DIV 4 is 1
7 MOD 4 is 3
```

Summary

Now, you can perform almost any math function you'll ever need. By understanding the order of operators, you know how to structure your formulas so that Turbo Pascal computes the answers the way you prefer them. You can always override the order of operators by using parentheses.

There is much more to computers than math. The next chapter shows how you can store letters, words, and sentences in variables, and thus store names and addresses. When you learn how to store character string data in variables, you will have mastered most of the data types of Turbo Pascal and you will be ready to process that data with more powerful Turbo Pascal commands.

Review Questions

Answers to Review Questions appear in Appendix B.

1. What are the results of the following expressions?

A. 1 + 2 * 4 / 2

B. (1 + 2) * 4 / 2

C. 1 + 2 * (4 / 2)

2. What are the results of the following expressions?

   A. `9 DIV 2 + 1`

   B. `(1 + (10 - (2 + 2)))`

3. What output does the following program produce?

```
PROGRAM TestOutput;

VAR a: BYTE;
    b: BYTE;

BEGIN
    a := 6;
    b := 10;
    WRITELN( 'a:5, b:5' );
    WRITELN( a:5, b:5 );
END.
```

4. Convert each of the formulas in Figure 7.4 to its Turbo Pascal assignment equivalent.

$$a = \frac{3+3}{4+4}$$

$$x = (a-b) * (a-c)^2$$

$$f = \frac{a^{1/2}}{b}$$

$$d = \frac{(8-x^2)}{(x-9)} - \frac{(4*2-1)}{x^3}$$

Figure 7.4. Formulas to be converted to Turbo Pascal assignment equivalents.

5. Write a line of code that displays the area of a circle with a radius of 4. Pi is equal to 3.14159 on the screen. (The area of a circle is equal to Pi * radius^2.)

6. Write a WRITELN statement that displays only the remainder of 100 / 4.

Review Exercises

1. Write a program that displays each of the first eight even numbers. Use comments to include your name at the top of the program. Clear the screen before displaying anything. Display string constants that describe each answer. The first two lines of your output should look like this:

```
The first even number is 2
The second even number is 4
```

2. Change C7PAY1.PAS so it computes and displays a bonus of 15 percent of the gross pay. Don't take taxes out of the bonus. After displaying the four variables, GrossPay, Taxes, Bonus, and NetPay, print a paycheck to the printer. Add string constants so the check includes the name of the payee. Print your name as the payor at the bottom of the check.

> **TIP:** Use WRITELN for the screen prompts and WRITELN(LST,...) for the check. Be sure to include Printer on the USES line.

3. Store the weights and ages of three people in variables. Display a table (with titles) of the weights and ages. At the bottom of the table display the average of the weights and ages, and their totals.

4. Assume that a video store employee works 50 hours in a pay period. The employee is paid $4.50 for the first 40 hours. She receives time-and-a-half pay (1.5 times the regular pay rate) for the first five hours over 40. She receives double-time pay for hours over 45. Assuming a 28 percent tax rate, write a program that displays her gross pay, taxes, and net pay to the screen. Label each amount with appropriate titles (using string constants), and add appropriate comments in the program.

String Variables

Chapter 5, "Understanding Numeric Variables and Constants," explained how to use string constants. Without string constants you would not be able to display messages to the screen or printer. You are now ready to see how to store string data in variables. A *string variable* can hold string data, just as integer variables hold integers and real variables hold real numbers. By storing strings of characters in variables, you can change the strings. This is useful if you have to keep track of names and addresses; when a person moves to another city, simply change the string variable containing that person's city.

Learning about string variables completes Section II of this book. After this chapter, you will know almost everything there is to know about the fundamental data types and variables in Turbo Pascal. Part III, "Input and Output," shows you how to manipulate, control, and process this data into meaningful results.

This chapter introduces the following topics:

♦ Creating string variables

♦ Displaying string variables

♦ String concatenation

♦ Ensuring proper types with variables

♦ A summary of advanced string uses

By storing string data in string variables, you have to type your string data only once, even if you must display it several times. After storing the string data in a string variable, you simply display the string variable from then on.

Creating String Variables

If computers worked only with numbers, they would be little more than calculators. True data processing occurs when you can process any type of data, including character string data. String variables can hold any character, word, or phrase your PC can produce.

Turbo Pascal stores string data a little differently than integers or reals. Strings have two parts: 1) the number of characters in the string, and 2) the actual characters of the string. With the storing of integers and reals you used an analogy of a box inside the computer. With the storing of strings, think of a series of adjacent boxes. The first box stores the number of characters in the string and is called the *length byte*. The remaining boxes store the characters of the string—one character per box.

String variables can hold strings as long as 255 characters. This should be more than ample for most applications.

Naming String Variables

As with numeric variables, it is up to you to give names to your string variables. String variable names follow the same naming rules as numeric variables (must begin with a letter or underscore, cannot contain spaces, and so on). The following are valid string variable names:

```
_MyName     month     CustomerCity     X     address
```

To store a name, an address, or any other character, word, or phrase in a variable, create a name for the variable and declare it. There are two ways to declare a string variable. If you declare a string variable as type STRING, you reserve memory for 255 characters plus the length byte, for a total of 256 bytes. For short programs, this will not cause any problems. However, for longer programs with many string variables, you could run out of memory. To minimize memory usage, declare the string variable with the maximum length you will need. After STRING, add the number of bytes in brackets, such as STRING[9].

As with string constants, Turbo Pascal does not recognize the variable as numeric just because you put a string of numbers in a string variable. When you declare the variable as a string type, this informs Turbo Pascal that no math is to be done with the variable's data, so Turbo Pascal looks at the string of numbers only as individual characters and not as one number.

Examples

1. If you want to keep track of a customer's name, address, city, state, ZIP code, and age in variables, you might create the following variable names:

```
VAR CustName:    STRING[30];
    CustAddress: STRING[50];
    CustCity:    STRING[30];
    CustState:   STRING[14];
    CustZip:     STRING[10];
    CustAge:     BYTE;
```

Notice the customer's age is numeric, so it is stored in a numeric variable. You should store data in numeric variables only if you might do math with it. This generally excludes data such as phone numbers, Social Security numbers, customer numbers, and so on. For instance, although ZIP codes consist of numbers, you never add or subtract ZIP codes. They are best stored in string variables. You might use CustAge in an average age calculation, so it is best to leave it in a numeric variable.

2. If you want to keep track of an employee's salary, age, name, employee number, and number of dependents, you might use the following variable names:

```
VAR EmpSalary:     REAL;
    EmpAge:        BYTE;
    EmpName:       STRING[30];
    EmpNumber:     STRING[6];
    EmpDependents: BYTE;
```

Only the name and employee number should be stored in string variables. The salary should be stored in a numeric variable; use a REAL variable here. The age is stored in a BYTE variable, and the number of dependents also is stored in a BYTE variable.

Storing Data in String Variables

You put data in string variables with the assignment statement just as you do with numeric data and variables. You can put either a string constant or another string variable in a string variable with an assignment. The format of the string assignment statement is

```
VarName := 'Some string';
```

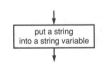

or

```
VarName1 := VarName2;
```

Each variable (*VarName*, *VarName1*, and *VarName2*) can be any valid string variable name. Any string constant or another string variable name can follow the colon–equal sign.

Notice that if you put a string constant in a string variable name, you must enclose the string constant in single quotation marks. The single quotation marks are not stored in the string; only the data between the single quotation marks is.

You can put an empty string, called a *null string*, in a string variable by putting two single quotation marks with no space between them after the equal sign. For instance, the assignment statement

```
E := '';
```

puts an empty string, with zero length, in the string variable named E. Turbo Pascal does not initialize the strings of any string variables before you use them. You might want to start with a null string if you build strings one character at a time—such as receiving data sequentially from a modem.

Examples

1. Appendix E, "The Complete Application," contains a complete sample application that manages a book inventory for a library, collector, or bookstore. Throughout this text you see portions of the book management program in examples.

    To keep track of a book's title, author, and edition, you might store the data in three string variables as follows:

    ```
    BookTitle   := 'In Pursuit of Life';
    BookAuthor  := 'Francis Scott Key';
    BookEdition := '2nd';
    ```

2. You can assign a string variable's value to another string variable, as the second line in the next example shows.

    ```
    EmpLastName    := 'Payton';
    SpouseLastName := EmpLastName;
    ```

Displaying String Variables

To display the data stored inside a string variable, put the string variable after WRITELN, just as you did for numeric variables. You can combine numeric variables, string variables, string constants, and commas in WRITELN statements if the output warrants it.

> **TIP:** If you have to display a string several times in a program, it is easiest to declare that string as a constant (CONST) and then display the string constant name. For instance, if you have to display your company's full legal name at the top of several checks and reports, declare the name as a constant, such as `CompName`, and display `CompName` to keep from having to type (and risk mistyping) the entire company name throughout the program.

Separating Spaces

When displaying a string variable next to another string variable, Turbo Pascal does not automatically display a separating space between them. Therefore, if you have to display a text description before a string variable, be sure to add a space inside the text's closing single quotation mark, as shown in the following line:

```
WRITELN( 'The highest-paid executive is: ', MaxExe );
```

You have to include a separating space surrounded by two single quotation marks if you want to display two string variables next to each other. If you store the names of three automobile makers in three string variables and want to display them, you would want to display them separated by a space, as in

```
WRITELN( Auto1, ' ', Auto2, ' ', Auto3 );
```

This would place a blank space between the names of the automobile makers, as in

```
GM Ford Chrysler
```

Otherwise, you receive run-on string output, like

```
GMFordChrysler
```

which is harder to read.

Examples

1. The following program stores and displays the three book-related string variables mentioned in a previous example.

```
{ Filename: C8BKSTR1.PAS }

{ Stores and displays three book-related variables. }

PROGRAM ShowStrings1;

CONST BookTitle   = 'In Pursuit of Life';
      BookAuthor  = 'Francis Scott Key';
      BookEdition = '2nd';

          { Now, display them to the screen }

BEGIN
   CLRSCR;
   WRITELN( BookTitle );
   WRITELN( BookAuthor );
   WRITELN( BookEdition );
END.  {ShowStrings1}
```

2. You know by now that displaying the contents of variables without first describing them produces confusing output. To improve on the previous program, you could add a header and descriptive titles, and right-justify the data so that it begins in the same column, as the following program shows:

```
{ Filename: C8BKSTR2.PAS }

{ Stores and displays book-related variables with a title. }

PROGRAM ShowStrings2;

CONST BookTitle   = 'In Pursuit of Life';
      BookAuthor  = 'Francis Scott Key';
      BookEdition = '2nd';
      TitleRJ     = 25;            { right justify title }
      DataRJ      = 20;            { right justify data }

          { Now, display them to the screen }
```

```
BEGIN

        { Display a title }

    CLRSCR;
    WRITELN( 'Book Listing':TitleRJ );
    WRITELN( '---- -------':TitleRJ );
    WRITELN;                            { Display two }
    WRITELN;                            { blank lines }

        { Now, display the book data to the screen }

    WRITELN( 'The book''s title is:   ',   BookTitle:DataRJ );
    WRITELN( 'The book''s author is: ',   BookAuthor:DataRJ );
    WRITELN( 'The book''s edition is: ', BookEdition:DataRJ );
END.  {ShowStrings2}
```

Figure 8.1 shows the screen output from this program. Although the descriptions are three different lengths, the book's data is right-justified.

```
            Book Listing
            ---- -------


The book's title is:     In Pursuit of Life
The book's author is:     Francis Scott Key
The book's edition is:              2nd
```

Figure 8.1. Results of displaying the strings with descriptions.

If you want the book data to go to the printer rather than the screen, change the WRITELN(...) statements to WRITELN(LST,...) statements.

3. The following program adapts the payroll example programs shown in earlier chapters to print a paycheck. Before running the program, be sure your printer is on and has paper in it.

```
{ Filename: C8PAY.PAS }

{ Computes and prints a payroll check. }

PROGRAM PayCheck;
USES Printer;

CONST Spc        = ' ';
      EmpName     = 'Larry Payton';
      PayDate     = '01/09/92';
      HoursWorked = 40;              { Total hours worked }
      Rate        = 7.50;           { Pay per hour }
      TaxRate     = 0.40;           { Tax rate percentage }


         { Compute the pay }


      GrossPay = HoursWorked * Rate;
      Taxes    = TaxRate * GrossPay;
      NetPay   = GrossPay - Taxes;

BEGIN


         { Print the results in the format of a check }

   WRITELN(LST, Spc:40,'Date: ', PayDate );
   WRITELN(LST);                        { Print a blank line }
   WRITELN(LST, 'Pay to the Order of: ', EmpName );
   WRITELN(LST);
   WRITELN(LST, 'Pay the full amount of: $',GrossPay:10:2 );
   WRITELN(LST, Spc:25,'----------' ); { Underline the amount }
```

```
    WRITELN(LST);
    WRITELN(LST, Spc:40,'----------------------' );
    WRITELN(LST, Spc:40,'Dan Chambers, Treasurer' );
END.   {PayCheck}
```

Figure 8.2 shows the result of running this program. (Granted, this check does not have the amount written out in words as well as numbers.) You are learning some of the different ways to print string variables and numeric data together in the same program.

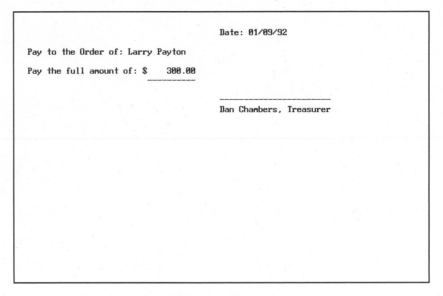

Figure 8.2. The check printed to the printer.

At this point you might think it would be easier to type the check in a typewriter than to write the program to compute and print it. Do not despair. You are learning the solid groundwork required to make Turbo Pascal do your tedious work for you. As you learn more of the language, writing the program becomes much faster than typing the data by hand, especially when you are using large data files.

String Concatenation

You cannot perform math on string variables, even if they contain numbers. You can, however, perform another type of operation on string variables: *concatenation*. Concatenation is attaching one string to the end of another or combining two or more strings into a longer string. You can concatenate string variables, string constants, or a combination of both and assign the concatenated strings to a string variable.

The string concatenation operator is the plus sign. Because of its context, Turbo Pascal knows not to confuse the concatenation symbol with the addition symbol; if it sees string data on either side of the plus sign, it knows to concatenate the strings. For example, to concatenate two string variables and assign the result to a third string variable, type

```
Str3 := Str1 + Str2;
```

Turbo Pascal also has the CONCAT statement that does the same thing as the plus sign. To use CONCAT, include the strings to be concatenated in parentheses, such as

```
Str3 := CONCAT(Str1, Str2);
```

Most programmers use the plus sign because it is easier to use.

> **CAUTION:** You can concatenate as many strings (variables and constants) as you like, as long as you do not exceed Turbo Pascal's string variable limit of 255 characters.

Examples

1. If you store an employee's first name in one string variable and his last name in a second string variable, you can display his full name by displaying the two string variables next to each other, as the following example shows:

```
FirstName := 'Bill';
LastName  := 'Cole';
WRITELN( FirstName,' ',LastName );
```

The problem with displaying the two variables is that you always have to display both of them together with a separating space between them. It would be easier to concatenate the two names into another string variable, as shown in the following code:

```
FirstName := 'Bill';
LastName  := 'Cole';
FullName  := FirstName + ' ' + LastName;
WRITELN( FullName );
```

The extra space is a string constant you concatenate between the two strings. If you didn't include it, the names would run together.

Running this short section of code produces

```
Bill Cole
```

on the screen.

This might seem like extra typing because you have to include the line that concatenates the two variables. Nevertheless, this process makes displaying the full name much easier later in the program, especially if you have to display it several times.

2. If you want to display the previous example's full name with the last name first, you can do so by concatenating a comma between the names, as in

```
FirstName := 'Bill';
LastName  := 'Cole';
FullName  := LastName + ', ' + FirstName;
WRITELN( FullName );
```

Running this section of code produces

```
Cole, Bill
```

on your screen. The space after the comma is there because it was concatenated in the string constant that contained the comma in the third line of code.

3. The book management database program in Appendix E saves the book data in a file specified by the user. If you do not type a file extension, the program automatically concatenates one to the filename you typed, in code similar to the following code:

```
FileName := UserFileName + '.DAT';
```

You then could append a disk drive name, which is stored in another string variable, as follows:

```
FileName := DiskDrive + FileName;
```

Notice that you are adding to the length of the string variable on the left side of the colon–equal sign.

Do Not Mix Types

You have seen many examples of programs using each of these variables and constants:

♦ INTEGER

♦ REAL

♦ STRING

You must be careful when you use the assignment statement. Never put string data in a numeric variable or numeric data in a string variable (see following CAUTION box).

> **CAUTION:** In an assignment statement, always be sure both sides of the colon–equal sign contain compatible types of data and variables.

For instance, the example below shows several assignment statements. You have seen many like them. There is nothing wrong with them because the variable on the left side of the colon–equal sign has a type compatible with the expression, variable, or constant on the right side. Be sure you understand why the statements in this example are valid before reading on.

```
PROGRAM Assignments;

VAR Distance2: INTEGER;
    Distance:  INTEGER;
    Diff:      REAL;
    Salary:    REAL;
    Length:    REAL;
    Range:     REAL;
    MonthPay:  REAL;
    Name1:     STRING;
    Name2:     STRING;
    FullName:  STRING[30];
    FirstName: STRING[15];
    LastName:  STRING[15];

BEGIN
    Distance  := 175;
    Distance2 := Distance;
    Diff      := Distance DIV 2;
    Salary    := 45023.92;
    Length    := Range;
    MonthPay  := Salary / 12.0;
    Name1     := 'Margo';
    Name2     := Name1;
    FullName  := FirstName + LastName;
END.  {Assignments}
```

These assignment statements are arbitrary assignment statements that have a compatible type of variable, constant, or expression on both sides of the colon–equal sign.

If you follow some precautions, you can mix certain types of numeric data types in the same expression. Typically, you can assign a smaller variable type to a larger one. For example, you can assign an INTEGER to a REAL variable. Turbo Pascal converts the INTEGER to a REAL when it assigns the INTEGER to the variable. In a like manner, you can assign a REAL number, variable, or expression to an EXTENDED real variable without any loss of accuracy.

Table 8.1 is very different. It shows many combinations of assignments that do not work because the type on one side of the colon–equal sign does not match the type on the other side.

```
VAR Greet:   STRING;
    Salary:  REAL;
    AvgAge:  REAL;
    Weight:  INTEGER;
    Pounds:  REAL;
    Kilos:   REAL;
    Month:   BYTE;
    MonthName:    STRING;
```

Table 8.1. Invalid assignment statements with nonmatching types.

Assignment	Problem Description
Greet := hello;	No quotation marks around 'hello'.
Salary := '43234.54';	Do not put string constants in numeric variables.
AvgAge := '100' / 2;	You cannot perform math with string constants.
Weight := Pounds + Kilos;	You cannot put a real number in an integer.
Month := MonthName;	You cannot put a string variable in a numeric variable.

If you attempt to mix strings and numeric variables in an assignment statement, you receive a *type mismatch* error like the one in Figure 8.3.

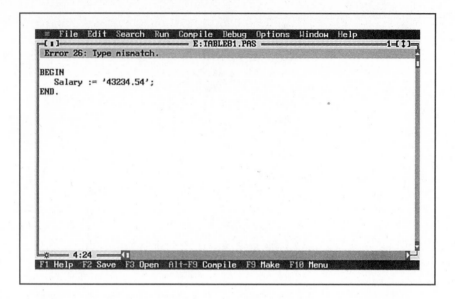

```
 =  File  Edit  Search  Run  Compile  Debug  Options  Window  Help
[■]                          E:TABLE81.PAS                        1-[↑]
 Error 26: Type mismatch.

BEGIN
    Salary := '43234.54';
END.





                                                                      ▒


    ═ 4:24 ═══◄■                                                         ►
 F1 Help  F2 Save  F3 Open  Alt-F9 Compile  F9 Make  F10 Menu
```

Figure 8.3. The error that occurs when you mix types in an assignment statement.

Other String Features

You can perform many more operations on string variables and string constants than on non-string variables and constants. Storing and displaying them are only the first steps in learning about Turbo Pascal strings. Future chapters address the string functions enabling you to move, copy, and delete parts of a string variable while keeping the remaining characters intact.

Throughout the rest of this book, you will learn additional string features and see how to tackle their advanced programming requirements.

Summary

This chapter showed you the basics for working with string variables. By storing strings in variables, you can display and change them throughout a program. You also can concatenate them to build longer string variables.

This chapter concludes Part II, "Primary Turbo Pascal Language Elements." You have learned how to store and display the different types of Turbo Pascal variables and constants, although most of the displaying has been limited. The next section shows you ways to display color on your screen, and how to input data to your programs from the keyboard.

Review Questions

Answers to the Review Questions appear in Appendix B.

1. How many characters of data can a string variable hold?

2. What is the string concatenation operator?

3. How would you concatenate two strings without the concatenation operator?

4. What is the length byte of a string?

5. Given the following descriptions, which of the following assignment statements are valid?

```
VAR f:        STRING[4];
    g:        BYTE;
    h:        STRING[10];
    Name:     STRING[30];
    LastName: STRING[30];
    EmpName:  STRING[20];
    FirstName: STRING[30];
```

A. f := g + h;

B. Name := 'Michael';

C. LastName := 'Harrison';

D. EmpName := FirstName + LastName;

6. True or False: When calculating payroll taxes, the following statement would work:

```
Taxes := GrossPay * '40';
```

7. Write a statement to display `City` and `State` with a comma and space between them.

8. Given the assignment statement

   ```
   Filename := 'AugSales';
   ```

   how would you, in one statement, add the disk drive `c:\` to the front oef the file name, and the extension `.DAT` to the end of it?

Review Exercises

1. Write a program to store your first, middle, and last names in three string variables. Display the names on the screen and print them to the printer with appropriate descriptions.

2. Modify the program in the preceding exercise to display your name in reverse order, with your last name first. Display the names in the following ways: next to each other and in separate columns.

3. Write a program to store your first, middle, and last name in three separate string variables. Concatenate them so that they are stored in one string variable called `FullName`. Be sure there is at least one space between the three names when you concatenate them. Display `FullName` on-screen after clearing it first.

4. Change the C8PAY.PAS payroll program presented earlier in this chapter. Print a string of asterisks around the check to mark the check's border. Change the name on the check so that the check pays to you. Give yourself a raise by increasing the hourly rate.

Part III

Input and Output

Inputting Values

You now should understand data and variables in Turbo Pascal. You have seen several methods for outputting data with the WRITELN statement. Nevertheless, you have not seen one critical part of programming: inputting data to your programs.

Every program you have seen so far in this book has had no data input. All data you worked with was assigned to variables or constants within the program. This way is not the best way, however, to get the data your programs process; you rarely know what the data will be when you write your programs. The data values are known only when a user runs the programs.

To give you a sampling of some ways to get input in Turbo Pascal, this chapter introduces:

♦ The READLN statement

♦ The READ statement

This chapter shows you ways to program the complete data-processing cycle: *input → process → output*. Starting with this chapter, the programs you write work on different data depending on what the *user* (the person who runs the program) types at the keyboard.

The READLN **Statement**

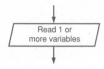

Here is the READLN statement in its simplest form:

```
READLN( var1 [, var2][, var3][, ..., varN] );
```

READLN is placed on a line by itself and is followed by one or more variables, each separated by commas. The main purpose of READLN is to get one or more values from the person at the keyboard.

When your program reaches the READLN statement, it waits for the user to type one or more values. If one variable follows READLN, the program expects only one value. If more than one variable follows READLN, the user must type values separated by spaces until each of the variables is filled. Pressing Enter after typing values in response to READLN informs Turbo Pascal that the user is finished typing values into the READLN variables.

Using READLN **to Fill Variables with Values**

There is a major difference between READLN and the assignment statements you have seen. Both fill variables with values. An assignment statement, however, assigns specific values to variables *at programming time.* When you run a program with assignment statements, you know from the program listing exactly what values go in the variables because you wrote the program to store those values there. The results are the same every time you run the program, because the same values go in the same variables.

When you write programs that use READLN, you have no idea what values go in the READLN variables, because their values are not known until the program is run (called *runtime*). This makes for more flexible programs that a variety of people can use. Every time the user runs the program, different results are output depending on what the user types for the READLN variable or variables.

Examples

1. Here is a program that computes a 7 percent sales tax and allows the user to input the sales data:

```
{ Filename: C9SLSTX.PAS }

PROGRAM SalesTax1;
USES Crt;

CONST TaxRate = 0.07;                { Leading 0 required }

VAR   TotalSales: REAL;
      SalesTax:   REAL;              { Sales tax }

BEGIN
   CLRSCR;
   READLN( TotalSales );             { user inputs total sales }
   SalesTax := TotalSales * TaxRate; { Calculate sales tax }

         { Display the results }
   WRITELN( 'The sales tax on', TotalSales:8:2, ' is: ',
            sTax:5:2 );
   WRITELN( 'Bringing the total needed to: ',
            (TotalSales + sTax):8:2);
END. {SalesTax1}
```

NOTE: Turbo Pascal requires a leading 0 for a real number less than 1.

When you run this program, the screen clears and Turbo Pascal waits for you to type a value. This value is stored in TotalSales when you type it. You always must press Enter when you finish typing values for READLN. If you make a mistake while typing, use the Backspace key to erase. Or, if you want to start fresh, press Esc.

To use the Turbo Pascal procedure CLRSCR, you need the USES Crt statement. CLRSCR is in unit Crt. Units are discussed in Chapter 25.

The program then computes the sales tax, displays the tax, and displays the total for the sale, including the sales tax.

> **TIP:** Although the program name is optional, Turbo Pascal considers it an identifier and verifies that it is not duplicated in any remaining identifiers. If you see the message Error 4: Duplicate Identifier, check that no identifier matches the program name.

Sometimes your WRITELN statements will be very long. It usually is best to break them at a comma. If you have a string that is very long, you might have to break the string into parts and concatenate them in the WRITELN statement. For an example, refer to the third WRITELN in Review Question 8 at the end of this chapter.

2. Suppose that you want to write a program which computes the average of three numbers. In Chapter 7, "Turbo Pascal's Language Operators," you saw a program that used the assignment statement to store three numbers and display their average.

A much more helpful program first would ask the person running the program which three numbers to average. Then the program would display the average of those three numbers. The following code does that:

```
{ Filename: C9AVG1.PAS }

PROGRAM Average1;
USES Crt;

VAR Num1: REAL;
    Num2: REAL;
    Num3: REAL;
    Avg:  REAL;
```

```
BEGIN
   CLRSCR;
   READLN( Num1, Num2, Num3 );        { User inputs 3 numbers }
   Avg := (Num1 + Num2 + Num3) / 3;    { Calculate average }
   WRITELN( 'The average of your three numbers is: ',
            Avg:8:2);
END. {Average1}
```

When you run this program, the screen clears and Turbo Pascal waits for you to type three values, each separated by a space. After you type three values and press Enter, the program continues from the READLN statement, calculates the average, and displays the results. If you run this program and enter these three numbers,

```
19  43  56
```

you will see the following output:

```
The average of your three numbers is:    39.33
```

NOTE: If your program has the USES Crt statement and if the user needs to type data for a READLN with more than one variable, the user should separate values with a space and should not use a comma.

3. The following program asks the user to type a name in two separate variables. The program then displays the name as it would appear in a phone book: the last name, a comma, and then the first name.

```
{ Filename: C9PHONE1.PAS }

{
  User inputs name and program displays it
  to the screen as it would appear in a phone book.
}
```

```
PROGRAM PhoneBook1;
USES Crt;

VAR FirstName: STRING[30];
    LastName:  STRING[30];

BEGIN
   CLRSCR;
   READLN( FirstName );
   READLN( LastName );

   WRITELN( 'In a phone book, your name would look like this:' );
   WRITELN( LastName, ', ', FirstName );
END. {PhoneBook1}
```

The following output shows the result of running this program. Run it yourself and see the results on your screen. Run it a second time and type a completely different pair of names. See how READLN makes the output of your program change, although the actual program does not change.

```
George
Harris
In a phone book, your name would look like this:
Harris, George
```

This example illustrates another aspect of READLN. You can input any value to any kind of variable, even string variables, as long as the values you type at the keyboard match the type of variable listed after READLN. If you combine the two READLN statements into one, as in the READLN statement

```
READLN( FirstName, LastName );
```

you would have to type both names separated by a space, because that is the format of this particular READLN.

CAUTION: Your keyboard input values must match in number and type the variables that follow the READLN statement.

Improving the Use of READLN

The preceding programs have flaws. These flaws are not exactly program bugs, but the programs contain logic not appropriate for users. The problem is that when users run the programs, they have no idea what kind or how many values to type.

You always should *prompt* users for values they must type in response to READLN. Display a message telling the users exactly what they should type.

The following examples build on previous examples to illustrate the importance of using prompts before READLN statements.

Examples

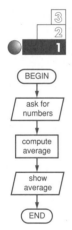

1. The following program is a rewritten version of the program that averages three numbers. The addition of a WRITELN statement greatly improves the program.

```
{ Filename: C9AVG2.PAS }

PROGRAM Average2;
USES Crt;

VAR Num1: REAL;
    Num2: REAL;
    Num3: REAL;
    Avg:  REAL;

BEGIN
   CLRSCR;
         { Prompt user at kbd }
   WRITELN( 'Please type three numbers, separated by spaces' );

   READLN( Num1, Num2, Num3 );       { User inputs 3 numbers }
   Avg := (Num1 + Num2 + Num3) / 3;  { Calculate average }
         { Display the results }
   WRITELN( 'The average of your three numbers is: ', Avg:8:2 );
END. {Average2}
```

The following output shows what will appear on your
screen if you run this program. Notice that the users know
exactly what to type. There is no ambiguity and little chance
that they will type input in the wrong format.

```
Please type three numbers, separated by spaces
42  67  94
The average of your three numbers is:    67.67
```

Some programmers prefer to display an example READLN
response to further ensure that the user knows exactly
what to type. You can do this by adding a second WRITELN
statement.

```
WRITELN( 'Please type three numbers, separated by spaces' );
WRITELN( '(for example, 4 25 70), and press Enter when done.' );
```

2. The following program adds prompts to the phone book
listing. The program also prompts for the address and
telephone number. Without the prompts, the user has no
idea what to type next.

```
{ Filename: C9PHONE2.PAS }

{
  User inputs phone book info and displays
    it to the screen as it would appear in a phone book.
}

PROGRAM PhoneBook2;
USES Crt;

VAR FirstName: STRING[30];
    LastName:  STRING[30];
    Address:   STRING[50];
    Phone:     STRING[12];

BEGIN
    CLRSCR;
    WRITELN( 'Please type your first name' );
```

```
    READLN( FirstName );

    WRITELN( 'Please type your last name' );
    READLN( LastName );

    WRITELN( 'Please type your address' );
    READLN( Address );

    WRITELN( 'Please type your telephone number' );
    READLN( Phone );

    WRITELN( 'In a phone book, your listing would look like: ' );
    WRITELN( LastName, ', ', FirstName, ' ',
             Address,'.....', Phone );
END. {PhoneBook2}
```

Figure 9.1 shows a result of running this program.

```
Please type your first name
Mary
Please type your last name
Carter
Please type your address
3234 East Maple Dr.
Please type your telephone number
555-6543
In a phone book, your listing would look like:
Carter, Mary 3234 East Maple Dr......555-6543
```

Figure 9.1. Prompting for the phone book information.

When you use WRITELN to display the prompt, Turbo Pascal generates a carriage return-line feed and displays the next line. The user then types the value on the new line. Rather than display a prompt on one line and type values on the next line, users might find it more natural to type the value just after the prompt. The Turbo Pascal WRITE statement does not generate a carriage return–line feed. When you use WRITE to display a prompt, be sure to leave an extra space at the end of the prompt. Otherwise, the value the user types will be right next to the prompt.

3. Consider the following child's addition program. Notice how you can ask a question directly and the question marks fall where they would fall naturally—at the end of the question.

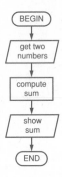

```
{ Filename: C9MATH1.PAS }


{  Program to help children with simple addition. }


{ Prompt child for two values, after displaying a title message. }

PROGRAM Math1;
USES Crt;

VAR Num1: INTEGER;
    Num2: INTEGER;
    Ans:  INTEGER;

BEGIN
   CLRSCR;
   WRITELN( '*** Math Practice ***' );
   WRITELN;                            { Display blank line }
   WRITELN;
                                       { Leave space after "?" }
   WRITE( 'What is the first number? ' );
   READLN( Num1 );

   WRITE( 'What is the second number? ' );
   READLN( Num2 );

   Ans := Num1 + Num2;                 { Compute answer }
```

```
     WRITELN;
     WRITELN( 'Press Enter when you want to see the answer...' );

     READLN;                        { Give child a chance }
     WRITELN;                       { Display blank line }
     WRITELN( Num1, ' plus ', Num2, ' is: ', Ans);
     WRITELN;
     WRITELN( 'I hope you got it right!' );
END. {Math1}
```

Figure 9.2 shows the result of running this addition program. Using WRITE and READLN, the program's questions are smoother and sound more appropriate. When you use READLN without any variables, Turbo Pascal waits for an Enter key to be pressed.

```
*** Math Practice ***

What is the first number? 6
What is the second number? 3

Press Enter when you want to see the answer...


6 plus 3 is: 9

I hope you got it right!
```

Figure 9.2. Running the addition program with improved prompts.

> **TIP:** When you run a program from the IDE, Turbo Pascal immediately returns to the editor. To view the results of your program, press Alt–F5 to view the User Screen.
>
> Or, insert a READLN as the last statement in your program before END. This statement causes Turbo Pascal to wait until you press the Enter key.

4. The book management program in Appendix E gets its initial book data from the user at the keyboard. By properly prompting for each value, the program gets correct data, as the following code fragment shows:

```
          { Section of book data input routine }
WRITE( 'What is the book''s title? ');
READLN( BookTitle );
WRITE( 'What is the book''s author? ');
READLN( Author );
WRITE( 'What is the publication date? ');
READLN( PubDate );
WRITE( 'What edition is it (1, 2, 3, etc.)? ');
READLN( Edition );
```

Notice that the first two prompts have two single quotation marks inside the prompt to display an apostrophe. Also, the last prompt explains how to type the book edition. If the user types a value such as 2nd, an error occurs because a numeric variable (Edition) cannot hold the last two characters of 2nd.

5. The following program asks the user for a book title and displays the title on-screen.

```
{ Filename: C9BOOKT1.PAS }

{ User inputs a book title and program displays it on the
  screen. }

PROGRAM BookTitle1;
USES Crt, Printer;
```

```
VAR BookTitle: STRING[50];

BEGIN
   CLRSCR;
   WRITELN( 'Type a book''s title.');
   WRITELN;
   WRITE( 'What is the name of the book? ');
   READLN( BookTitle );
   WRITELN;
   WRITELN( 'The title you typed is: ', BookTitle );
END. {BookTitle1}
```

Notice that only one string variable, BookTitle, is read, and only one is displayed. Because BookTitle is declared as type STRING, you can type any punctuation.

Figure 9.3 shows a sample run.

```
Type a book's title.

What is the name of the book? "To Err, To Live"

The title you typed is: "To Err, To Live"
```

Figure 9.3. Entering a comma as part of a READLN value.

6. The following program requests three city-and-state combinations. Figure 9.4 shows the results of running the program and entering the three cities. Notice that only three variables are entered, but that more than three words are entered. Be

sure to study the input values to see exactly how the city-state combinations are entered in three different variables.

```
{ Filename: C9CITST1.PAS }

{  User inputs 3 city-state pairs in a single READLN
    statement. }

PROGRAM CityStatePairs1;
USES Crt;

VAR CityState1: STRING[50];
    CityState2: STRING[50];
    CityState3: STRING[50];

BEGIN
   CLRSCR;
   WRITELN( 'Please type three city and state pairs.' );
   WRITE('City, State 1: ');
   READLN( CityState1 );
   WRITE('City, State 2: ');
   READLN( CityState2 );
   WRITE('City, State 3: ');
   READLN( CityState3 );

   WRITELN( 'You typed the following:');
   WRITELN( CityState1, CityState2:25, CityState3:25 );
END. {CityState1}
```

Matching the READLN Variables

This chapter has stressed the need for good prompts for your READLN statements. There is a one-to-one correlation between the number and types of your READLN variables and the values you type at the keyboard. Nevertheless, sometimes a user will not enter enough values, enter too many values, or enter the wrong type of values for the variables being read.

Suppose that your program requires the user to type three values. If the READLN statement looks like

```
READLN( num1, num2, num3 );
```

but the user enters only two numbers, Turbo Pascal realizes that there are not enough values typed for the READLN statement. The program does not display an error message, however; it just keeps waiting for you to type the third value.

```
Please type three city and state pairs.
City, State 1: Joplin, MO
City, State 2: New York, NY
City, State 3: San Diego, CA
You typed the following:
Joplin, MO              New York, NY              San Diego, CA
```

Figure 9.4. Entering city-state pairs in individual variables.

If the user types too many values for the variables specified, the extra values are ignored. If the user enters values with the wrong type, a runtime error occurs and the program halts. This error most commonly occurs when the user types a string value for a numeric variable. In this case, Turbo Pascal generates runtime error 106, Invalid numeric format (assuming that the compiler directive I/O Checking is On).

You will learn in later chapters how to avoid runtime errors and awkward input techniques.

TIP: In requesting input, it usually is better to use a separate WRITE and READLN combination for each value.

Example

The book-management program in Appendix E requests much book information. By using the appropriate combination of WRITE and READLN statements and displaying blank lines, you can create your own data-entry input screens with titles and prompts that make you feel as though you are entering data on a blank form or an index card, as you might do with a manual book-file system.

The following program illustrates the beginnings of such an input data-entry screen.

```
{ Filename: C9DATENT.PAS }


{
  Program that builds a data-entry screen as the
  user enters data for a book management system.
  Displays a title at the top of the screen.
}

PROGRAM DataEntry;
USES Crt, Printer;

CONST Spc = ' ';

VAR BookTitle: STRING[30];
    Author:    STRING[30];
    Edition:   STRING[2];
    Price:     STRING[8];
    PubDate:   STRING[8];
    Notes:     STRING[126];

BEGIN
  CLRSCR;
  WRITELN( Spc:15, '*** Book Data-Entry Screen ***' );
  WRITELN( Spc:15, '    --------------------' );
  WRITELN;                              { Display blank line }
  WRITELN;

  WRITE( 'Book title? ');               { Request the data }
  READLN( BookTitle );
  WRITELN;
```

BEGIN

get book
info

get notes

show book
info

END

```
    WRITE( 'Author? ' );
    READLN( Author );
    WRITELN;

    WRITE( 'Edition? ' );
    READLN( Edition );
    WRITE( 'Price? ' );
    READLN( Price );
    WRITE( 'Date of Publication? ' );
    READLN( PubDate );
    WRITELN;

    WRITE( 'Type any notes here -> ' );
    READLN( Notes );
    WRITELN;
    WRITELN;
         { Print results when user is ready }
    WRITELN( 'Press Enter to print book data on printer' );
    READLN;

    WRITELN(LST, Spc:20, '*** Book Data ***' );
    WRITELN(LST, Spc:20, '    ---------' );
    WRITELN(LST);
    WRITELN(LST);
    WRITELN(LST, 'Title: ', BookTitle );
    WRITELN(LST);
    WRITELN(LST, 'Author: ', Author );
    WRITELN(LST);
    WRITELN(LST, 'Edition: ',Edition,'  Price: ',Price,
                 'Publication date: ',PubDate );
    WRITELN(LST);
    WRITELN(LST, 'Notes: ', Notes );
END. {DataEntry}
```

This program is the longest one you have seen so far in this book. It is only the first step toward inputting data in ways the user best understands. Figure 9.5 shows a sample run.

```
                    *** Book Data-Entry Screen ***
                    -------------------------------

Book title? It's not Friday, but It'll Do!

Author? Billy Bob

Edition? 4th
Price? 3.95
Date of Publication? 1987

Type any notes here -> This is one of Billy Bob's classics. It is a signed, and
limited edition!
```

Figure 9.5. Building a book data-entry screen.

Data-Entry Fields

Each input value in a data-entry form is called a *field*. The preceding program has six fields: title, author, edition, price, publication date, and notes.

When you write programs that require much input, consider building data-entry forms such as the one in the preceding example. Later chapters in the book show you how to generate even better forms with colors and lines around them.

Make data-entry screens look like forms you would see on paper. This adds to the *user-friendliness* of a program.

A program is *user-friendly* if it makes the user comfortable and simulates what the user is already familiar with. The term "user-friendly" has been overused during these past few boom years of computers; nevertheless, always keep the user in mind when you design your programs. Keep input screens simple, add blank space so that screens do not appear too "busy," and prompt the user for data in a logical order.

READ **and Cursor Control**

One last option is available when you want to control data entry. If you use READ rather than READLN, the cursor remains on the same line as the input prompt. For example, the format for the READ statement is

```
READ( var1 [, var2][, var3][,..., varN] );
```

With READ, Turbo Pascal keeps the cursor where it is located after the user inputs the data. In other words, if you answer this WRITE and READLN statement:

```
WRITE( 'What is your name? ');
READLN( FullName );
```

by typing Steve Austin and pressing Enter, Turbo Pascal places the cursor on the next line. Subsequent WRITE and READLN statements begin on the next line. If you use READ instead, as in

```
WRITE( 'What is your name? ');
READ( FullName );
```

subsequent WRITE and READLN statements begin immediately after the *n* in *Steve Austin*. This usually is very awkward. This book uses WRITE and READLN.

Summary

In this chapter you learned to write a program that can accept input from the keyboard. Before reading this chapter, you had to assign values to variables when you wrote the program. The variables can be filled in by prompting the users for values when the users run the program. Depending on the required data, you can use READLN, READ, or a combination of both.

This chapter has focused on input; the next chapter, however, builds on your knowledge of output. You will learn commands that produce color, move the cursor, and display numeric data exactly the way you want it displayed.

Review Questions

Answers to the Review Questions appear in Appendix B.

1. What are two Turbo Pascal statements that accept input from the keyboard?

2. Why is the prompt message important when you use READ or READLN?

3. True or False: You can enter more than one variable value with READLN.

4. To input a value on the same line as a prompt, what statement should you use for the prompt?

5. Name two ways to assign a value to a variable.

6. What is usually the last character of a prompt displayed with a WRITE statement?

7. What is incorrect in the following statement?

```
READLN( Var1; Var2);
```

8. How would you rewrite the following code so that each variable has its own prompt?

```
WRITELN( '*** Miles Per Gallon ***' );
WRITELN;
WRITELN(' Type the mileage driven and gallons of fuel used' +
        ' since your last fill-up?');
READLN( Miles, Gallons );
```

9. What error message appears if you type a string value for a numeric variable?

Review Exercises

1. Write a line of code that prompts users for their name and weight, stores the name and weight in appropriate variables, and keeps the cursor on the same line.

2. Assume that you are a college professor needing to average grades for ten students. Write a program that prompts you for ten different grades and then displays an average of them.

3. Modify the program in the preceding grade-averaging exercise to ask for each student's name as well as the student's class grade. Print the grade list to the printer, with each student's name and grade in two columns. At the bottom of the report, print the average of the grades. (*Hint*: Store the 10 names and 10 grades in different variables, such as Name1, Grade1, Name2, Grade2, and so on.) This program is easy, but it takes almost 30 lines of code, plus appropriate comments. Later, you will learn ways to streamline this program.

4. Write a program that prompts the user for the number of hours worked, the hourly rate, and the tax rate, and then displays the taxes and net pay.

5. Write a program to prompt the user for a full name, hours worked, hourly rate, and tax rate. Compute the taxes and net pay, and print a "check" to the user on the printer.

6. Modify the child's math program shown earlier in this chapter so that the child can practice subtraction, multiplication, and division after finishing the addition.

Producing Better Output

This chapter shows you ways to add pizazz to your program's output. Turbo Pascal gives you many tools in addition to WRITELN that improve the appearance of your program's output. For instance, programs with color screens appeal to users. Another way to improve your output's appearance is to format numerical output so that two decimal places always appear, which is great for displaying dollars and cents.

To give you a sampling of some ways to get better output from Turbo Pascal, this chapter introduces

♦ The WRITELN statement with formatting

♦ The SOUND and NOSOUND statements

♦ The ASCII table and the CHR function

♦ The CHAR type

♦ Displaying color

♦ The GOTO statement

♦ The GOTOXY statement

After learning the material in this chapter, you will be able to display much more appealing output. Several of the later chapters include programs that use many of these powerful output statements.

The WRITELN Statement with Formatting

You already have seen some ways to use formatting with a WRITELN statement by using a field width (see Chapter 6, "Comments and Additional WRITELN Options"). To right-justify an integer value, i, in a column 20 characters wide, use

```
WRITELN( i:20 );
```

show formatted results

To right-justify a real value, r, in a column 20 characters wide and show two decimal places, use

```
WRITELN( r:20:2 );
```

To right-justify a string value, s, in a column 20 characters wide, use

```
WRITELN( s:20 );
```

The following sections review these ideas and expand on them.

Examples

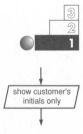

show customer's initials only

1. Assume that a customer's first and last names are stored in two string variables called FirstName and LastName. You can display the customer's initials with this statement:

   ```
   WRITELN( FirstName[1], LastName[1] );
   ```

   You can display periods after each initial with

   ```
   WRITELN(  FirstName[1], '.', LastName[1], '.' );
   ```

   If you want a space between the complete first and last names, you have to add one:

   ```
   WRITELN( FirstName,' ', LastName );
   ```

2. Sometimes it improves readability to use constants, as the following example shows:

```
CONST Period = '.';

WRITELN( FirstName[1], Period, LastName[1], Period );
```

3. Assume that you are displaying the customer's first and last names on mailing labels. You don't have room to display a long name. Therefore, you can limit the customer's first name to eight characters, regardless of how many characters are in the name, with the following statements:

```
USES Printer;
CONST Spc = ' ';
VAR   FNLabel: STRING[8];
      LNLabel: STRING[8];
BEGIN
      .                    { get first and last names somehow }
      .
      .
   FNLabel := FirstName;
   LNLabel := LastName;
                     { use LST to print on mailing labels }
   WRITELN(LST, FNLabel, Spc, LNLabel);
      .
      .
      .
END.
```

The Spc causes the program to print a blank between the two names. Without the Spc, the two names are printed next to each other.

4. If you want to display an apostrophe inside a string, use two single quotation marks with no intervening spaces.

```
WRITELN( 'The customer''s bill is: ' );
```

Displaying Numbers with WRITELN

The formatting for real constants and variables is more specific than for strings and integers. You rarely want real numbers to be displayed exactly as they appear in memory because they might contain more decimal places than you want displayed. You probably want control over the number of spaces the number can use and the number of decimal places.

If Turbo Pascal cannot fit the number inside your designated field width, it automatically expands the field width as needed. You can take advantage of this capability by using a field width of 1. Turbo Pascal will add the minimum number of places needed, and your output will look neater. For example, the following two lines are identical except for the formatting.

```
WRITELN( 'The sale amount is $',Sale:8:2 );
WRITELN( 'The sale amount is $',Sale:1:2 );
```

If Sale has a value of 123.45 in the first WRITELN statement, Turbo Pascal inserts two blank spaces for a total of 8 columns. In the second WRITELN, Turbo Pascal recognizes that 123.45 requires a minimum of 6 columns and therefore uses Sale:6:2—even though the WRITELN statement has Sale:1:2.

```
The sale amount is $  123.45
The sale amount is $123.45
```

If the field width is wider than needed, Turbo Pascal adds blanks to the left side of the number.

> **TIP:** If you specify the number of decimal places as 0, Turbo Pascal rounds a real number up to the nearest integer.

Example

The next program is a rewrite of the payroll programs you have seen throughout this book. You can display each dollar amount with a dollar sign and two decimal places.

```pascal
{ Filename: C10PAY1.PAS }

{ Computes and displays payroll data. }

PROGRAM Payroll1;
USES Crt;

CONST Spc = ' ';
VAR   EmpName:     STRING[30];
      PayDate:     STRING[8];
      HoursWorked: REAL;
      Rate:        REAL;
      TaxRate:     REAL;
      GrossPay:    REAL;
      Taxes:       REAL;
      NetPay:      REAL;
BEGIN
        { Initialize variables }
   EmpName      := 'Larry Payton';
   PayDate      := '01/09/92';
   HoursWorked := 40;                  { Total hours worked }
   Rate         := 7.5;               { Pay per hour }
   TaxRate      := 0.40;              { Tax rate % }

        { Compute the pay }
   GrossPay := HoursWorked * Rate;
   Taxes    := TaxRate * GrossPay;
   NetPay   := GrossPay - Taxes;
        { Display results }
   CLRSCR;
   WRITELN( 'As of: ', PayDate );
                                       { Usually break WRITELN }
                                       { at a comma }
   WRITELN( Spc:5, EmpName, ' worked ', HoursWorked:1:1,
          ' hours' );
   WRITELN( Spc:10, 'and got paid $', GrossPay:1:2 );
```

```
    WRITELN( Spc:10, 'After taxes of: $', Taxes:1:2 );
    WRITELN( Spc:10, 'his take-home pay was: $', NetPay:1:2 );
END. {Payroll1}
```

The following output shows the result of running this program. There is much to this program's simple-looking output; by mastering it, you are well on your way to understanding formatted output and Turbo Pascal.

```
As of: 01/09/92
    Larry Payton worked 40.0 hours
        and got paid $300.00
        After taxes of: $120.00
        his take-home pay was: $180.00
```

show spacing
in output

Although extra blanks could have been used in the strings, it is more convenient to use Spc:5 and Spc:10 to indent.

Displaying the date does not require any formatting, because there are no fixed decimal points to worry about. Because HoursWorked was declared as REAL, you have to format the number to avoid scientific notation. The last three lines of the program display dollar amounts, so they require formatting. The program displays HoursWorked to one decimal place, and the dollar amounts to two decimal places.

A field width of 1 is used deliberately for the field width of all the reals. Turbo Pascal decides how many spaces to use. This allows the $ in the string part to be displayed next to the dollar amount. Unfortunately, if the dollar amounts are larger than $999.99, Turbo Pascal does not add commas automatically.

Using SOUND and NOSOUND

use the
PC's speaker

The SOUND and NOSOUND commands are fun commands that use the system unit's speaker. SOUND causes the speaker to emit a specified frequency. NOSOUND turns off the speaker. The format of the SOUND command is

SOUND(*Frequency*);

SOUND's only parameter specifies the frequency in hertz (Hz). Although most people can hear frequencies from about 20 Hz to 20,000 Hz, most PC speakers can handle a range of about 20 Hz to 7,000 Hz. For the musically inclined, here are some common notes with the corresponding Hz in parentheses: C (262), D (294), E (330), F (349), G(392), A (440), and B (494).

You can use SOUND (or several SOUNDs and NOSOUNDs together) to warn the user, to signal the user for input, to tell the user that an operation is finished, or to play a short tune. Because the speaker continues to emit a frequency until a NOSOUND is used, always be sure to use NOSOUND whenever you use SOUND. To control how long the speaker should emit a frequency, use the DELAY statement. The format of the DELAY statement is

```
DELAY( Time );
```

DELAY also has only one parameter. The *Time* parameter is measured in milliseconds.

The format of the NOSOUND command is just

```
NOSOUND;
```

SOUND, DELAY, and NOSOUND all are in the Crt unit. In your program, include USES Crt as a statement.

> **TIP:** Do not overuse SOUND. Users get tired of hearing the signal too often.

Examples

1. To have the speaker emit a frequency of 500 Hz (hertz) for one second, use the following:

```
SOUND( 500 );                          { 500 Hz }
DELAY( 1000 );                         { 1000 milliseconds }
NOSOUND;                               { don't forget this! }
```

2. If you want to send output to the printer, make LST the first
WRITELN parameter. Your program should include Printer also
in the USES statement. Before printing is to begin, you might
also warn the user to check the printer for ample paper. If the
printer is not ready, you will see the message Error 160: Device
write fault.

The following code is a rewritten version of the preceding
program with output going to the printer.

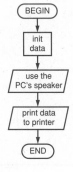

```
{ FileName C10PAY2.PAS }


PROGRAM Payroll2;
USES Crt, Printer;

CONST Spc = ' ';
VAR    EmpName:      STRING[30];
       PayDate:      STRING[8];
       HoursWorked:  REAL;
       Rate:         REAL;
       TaxRate:      REAL;
       GrossPay:     REAL;
       Taxes:        REAL;
       NetPay:       REAL;
BEGIN
                                           { Initialize variables }
    EmpName      := 'Larry Payton';
    PayDate      := '01/09/92';
    HoursWorked  := 40;                    { Total hours worked }
    Rate         := 7.5;                   { Pay per hour }
    TaxRate      := 0.4;                   { Tax rate % }
    GrossPay     := HoursWorked * Rate;
    Taxes        := TaxRate * GrossPay;
    NetPay       := GrossPay - Taxes;

                                           { Display results }
    SOUND( 700 );                          { Get user's attention }
    DELAY( 500 );                          { Sound for 1/2 second }
    NOSOUND;
    CLRSCR;
    WRITELN( 'Press Enter when the printer is ready' );
    READLN;                                { Pause until user
                                             presses Enter }
```

```
    WRITELN(LST, 'As of: ', PayDate );
    WRITELN(LST, Spc:5, EmpName, ' worked ', HoursWorked:1:1,
            ' hours' );
    WRITELN(LST, Spc:10, 'and got paid $', GrossPay:1:2 );
    WRITELN(LST, Spc:10, 'After taxes of: $', Taxes:1:2 );
    WRITELN(LST, Spc:10, 'his take-home pay was: $',
            NetPay:1:2 );
END. {Payroll2}
```

Displaying Special Characters

You know how to display and store characters that are on the keyboard. You can type string constants and store them in string variables, and you can display string constants (or string variables) on-screen and print them on the printer. You also might want to type several more characters that do not appear on the keyboard. They include characters from various countries, math symbols, line-drawing characters, and more.

Your computer uses a table that includes every character your computer can represent. This table is called the *ASCII table*. The complete ASCII (pronounced *as-kee*) table is in Appendix A. Turn to Appendix A and glance at the table. You see many special characters, only some of which are on the keyboard.

Your computer internally represents these ASCII characters by their ASCII numbers. A different number is assigned to each character. These number assignments were designed arbitrarily to be similar to the Morse code table. A unique number represents each character.

When you press a letter on the keyboard, your keyboard does not send that character to the computer. Rather, it sends the ASCII-number equivalent of that character. Your computer stores that number. When you see characters on the screen or printer, your screen or printer has converted to its character representation the number sent to it by the computer.

ASCII Representations

Your computer stores characters in binary format. There are 256 ASCII codes (0 to 255). The numbers 0 through 255 are represented in 8 bits (00000000 through 11111111), with a bit being a 1 or a 0. (*Bits* comes from the term *BInary digiTS*.)

Eight bits make a byte. Because you can represent every possible PC character in 8 bits, only 8 bits are required in order to represent a byte or a character. This is the intrinsic reason that a byte is the same thing as a character. In Chapter 1, "Welcome to Turbo Pascal," you learned that if your computer has 640K of RAM, it has 640K bytes, or 640K characters, of memory. It takes a total of 8 bits (1 byte) to represent a character from the ASCII table.

By having the ASCII table available, you can display any character by referring to its ASCII number. For instance, the capital letter *A* is number 65. The lowercase *a* is 96. A space is ASCII 32 (to your computer, the space is a character, just as the other characters are).

Because you can type letters, numbers, and some special characters on your keyboard, the ASCII table is not needed much for these. You cannot, however, under normal circumstances use the keyboard to type the Spanish Ñ or the cent sign (¢). You need a way to tell Turbo Pascal to display these special characters that do not appear on the keyboard. You do this with the CHR function.

The format of CHR is

```
CHR( ASCII number )
```

The ASCII number can be a numeric constant or a numeric variable. CHR is a *function*. Chapter 20, "Numeric Functions," and Chapter 21, "String and CHAR Functions," are devoted exclusively to functions. You can begin to use string and numeric functions without understanding their intricacies.

You do not use CHR by itself. It is combined with other state-ments. If you combine CHR with WRITELN, the character matching the ASCII number in the parentheses is displayed. The following state-ment displays an up arrow on the screen:

```
WRITELN( CHR(24) );
```

Without the CHR(24), you could not type the up arrow from a key on the keyboard. Pressing the up-arrow key controls the cursor by moving it upward; it does not display an up arrow.

You can use the CHR function also to store special characters in string variables. The concatenation operator (+) lets you insert a special character inside another string and store the complete string in a variable, as in

```
Message := 'One-half is ' + CHR(171) +
           ' and one-fourth is ' + CHR(172);
```

If you then display Message on the screen, you see this result:

```
One-half is 1/2 and one-fourth is 1/4
```

The first 31 ASCII codes represent *nonprinting* characters. Nonprinting characters cause an action to be performed, rather than characters to be produced. For instance, ASCII 7 is the *bell* character. If you type

```
WRITELN( CHR(7) );
```

the computer's speaker beeps. If you have a dot-matrix printer, however, you can cause your printer to beep by sending it an ASCII 7, as in

```
WRITELN(LST, CHR(7) );
```

You can cause a dot-matrix printer to *form feed* (ASCII 12) by sending it the form-feed ASCII code

```
WRITELN( CHR(12) );
```

This code ensures that the next WRITELN begins printing at the top of the page. If the preceding program leaves the print head in the middle of the page, printing CHR(12) ejects the rest of the page so that the next WRITELN begins at the top of the next page. Conversely, if your program has been printing several lines of text to the printer, one of the last things you can do is print a CHR(12) to eject the page on which you were working. The next program then begins printing on a fresh piece of paper.

The higher ASCII codes are line-drawing characters. With practice, you can combine them to form shapes and boxes that enclose text on the screen or printer.

Example

You can use the ASCII table to produce some uncommon characters.

```
{ Filename: C10ASC1.PAS }

{ Program that illustrates displaying of special characters. }

PROGRAM Ascii1;
USES Crt;
CONST w = 5;
BEGIN
   CLRSCR;
   WRITELN( 'Some common Greek characters are:' );
   WRITELN( CHR(224):w, CHR(225):w, CHR(226):w,
            CHR(227):w, CHR(228):w );
END. {Ascii1}
```

The output of this program is shown in Figure 10.1.

The CHAR Type

Until now, the examples have used only integer and real data types. Sometimes you might want to store a character value. For example, you might want to know whether a user responded with a Y or N character. Turbo Pascal provides the CHAR data type to store character data. The ASCII table in Appendix A represents a list of all possible characters you can use with CHAR. Each character uses one byte.

The CHAR data type is similar to a type declaration of STRING[1]. A STRING[1] type, however, uses two bytes—one byte holds the length of the string and the other holds the character.

```
Some common Greek characters are:
    ∝   ß   Γ   π   Σ
```

Figure 10.1. Using the ASCII table to display special characters.

Examples

This declaration is used for the following examples:

```
VAR Ch: CHAR;
```

1. There are several options for representing a CHAR value. Like strings, you can use single quotation marks. To assign an uppercase *A* to Ch, write:

   ```
   Ch := 'A';
   ```

   This is the same as

   ```
   Ch := CHR(65);
   ```

2. You can also use the ASCII number from Appendix A. Just precede the number with the number symbol (#). To assign an uppercase *A* to Ch, write:

   ```
   Ch := #65;
   ```

3. ASCII numbers from 0 to 31 also can be represented by the caret symbol (^) combined with the character associated with a particular ASCII number, plus 64. For example, ASCII 0 is ^@ (0 + 64 = 64, the ASCII number for @—the "at" sign), ASCII 1 is ^A (1 + 64 = 65, the ASCII number for A), ASCII 7 is ^G, ASCII 26 is ^Z, and ASCII 31 is ^_.

4. With the editor, it sometimes is convenient to display extended ASCII characters (those with ASCII numbers 128 and above) as a symbol rather than using CHR. For example, to display the solid block symbol (#219), type

```
WRITELN( CHR(219) );
```

or

```
WRITELN( #219 );
```

To display #219 as a symbol, begin the statement by typing

```
WRITELN('
```

Now, hold down the Alt key and use the numeric keypad to type *219*. (The Num Lock key can be either enabled or disabled when you access these ASCII characters.) When you release the Alt key, the editor displays a solid block. Complete the above WRITELN statement by typing a closing single quotation mark, right parenthesis, and semicolon. When you finish, you should see

```
WRITELN('■');
```

Displaying Color

If you have a color monitor, you can add colors to your output with the TEXTCOLOR and TEXTBACKGROUND statements. The format of the TEXTCOLOR statement is

```
TEXTCOLOR( Foreground Color );
```

set screen colors for future output

The Foreground Color is usually a number from 0 to 15 that represents the color of the characters on-screen. To produce special effects, you can use the numbers from 16 to 255. Special effects include hidden characters, blinking, and all combinations of foreground and background colors.

The format of the TEXTBACKGROUND statement is similar:

```
TEXTBACKGROUND( Background Color );
```

The *Background Color* is a number from 0 to 7 that represents the color of the screen behind the characters. (In this book, the foreground color is black and the background is white.)

The TEXTCOLOR statement does not affect any text on-screen that was displayed before the TEXTCOLOR statement. TEXTCOLOR affects only future WRITELN (or WRITE) statements.

Table 10.1 shows the predefined colors and their corresponding Turbo Pascal names.

Table 10.1. Color constants defined in the Crt unit.

Number	Name	Number	Name
0	BLACK	8*	DARKGRAY
1	BLUE	9*	LIGHTBLUE
2	GREEN	10*	LIGHTGREEN
3	CYAN	11*	LIGHTCYAN
4	RED	12*	LIGHTRED
5	MAGENTA	13*	LIGHTMAGENTA
6	BROWN	14*	YELLOW
7	LIGHTGRAY	15*	WHITE
		128	BLINK

* Denotes foreground only.

If you add 128 to a color number, the characters blink in the color of that number. For example, setting the foreground color to 140 (12 + 128):

```
TEXTCOLOR( 140 );
```

produces blinking light red text with the next WRITELN statement. Instead of using 128, you can use the Turbo Pascal constant BLINK to improve readability of your code:

```
TEXTCOLOR( LIGHTRED + BLINK );
```

TIP: Do not overuse colors. Too many colors make the screen look too "busy" and not as readable.

Although monochrome (one foreground color) monitors do not produce colors, you can specify special screen attributes (such as underlining and blinking) on monochrome monitors. Not all monochrome monitors display the same. Table 10.2 lists some results common to most monochrome monitors:

Table 10.2. The result of using TEXTCOLOR on a monochrome monitor.

Color	Result
1	Underlined
7	Normal
9	Highlighted and underlined
15	Highlighted
119	Reverse video
240	Blinking reverse video

If the foreground and background numbers are the same, Turbo Pascal displays the text, but you cannot see it.

Example

To illustrate the effects of different color combinations, the following program displays several lines of text, each with a different color. This program illustrates the TEXTCOLOR and TEXTBACKGROUND statements well but shows you that too much color is too much to look at for normal applications.

```
{ Filename: C10COLOR.PAS }

{ Displays several lines of text in different colors. }

PROGRAM Colors1;
USES Crt;

BEGIN
   CLRSCR;
   TEXTCOLOR( WHITE );
   TEXTBACKGROUND( BLUE );
   WRITELN( 'Bright white characters on blue' );
   TEXTCOLOR( BLUE );
   TEXTBACKGROUND( LIGHTGRAY );
   WRITELN( 'Blue characters on white' );
   TEXTCOLOR( RED );
   TEXTBACKGROUND( GREEN );
   WRITELN( 'Red characters on green' );
   TEXTCOLOR( YELLOW + BLINK );
   TEXTBACKGROUND( GREEN );
   WRITELN( 'Blinking yellow characters on green' );
   TEXTCOLOR( LIGHTMAGENTA );
   TEXTBACKGROUND( BLACK );
   WRITELN( 'Light magenta on black' );
END. {Colors1}
```

> **TIP:** To "paint" the screen a certain background color, use
>
> ```
> TEXTCOLOR(LIGHTGRAY);
> TEXTBACKGROUND(BG);
> CLRSCR;
> ```
>
> where *BG* is a background color from 0 to 7. Specifying TEXTCOLOR makes sure the cursor doesn't disappear.

The GOTO **Statement**

The next few examples require more program control than you have seen in this book. The GOTO statement provides that extra control. GOTO enables your program to jump to a different location in the program code. Each program you have seen executes sequentially; the statements execute one line after another, in a sequential order. GOTO lets you override that default execution. With GOTO, you can make the last line (or any other line) in the program execute before execution normally would get there. GOTO lets you execute the same line (or lines) repeatedly.

The format of the GOTO statement is

```
GOTO statement label
```

You have not seen statement labels in the Turbo Pascal programs presented so far, because none of the programs required them. Statement labels usually are optional, although if you have a GOTO you must include a statement label in your program. Labels must be declared as variables and constants.

Each of the four lines of code following the LABEL declaration has a statement label. These four lines are not a program, but rather are individual lines that might be included in a program. Notice that statement labels go to the left of their lines. Separate statement labels from the rest of the line with a colon. Name nonnumeric labels according to the same rules you would use to name variables. (See Chapter 5, "Understanding Numeric Variables and Constants," for a review of naming variables and other identifiers.)

```
LABEL Pay, Again, 20, SetColor;          { declare labels }
   Pay: WRITELN( 'Place checks in the printer' );
   Again: WRITELN( 'What is the next employee''s name ', EmpName );
   20: CLRSCR;
   SetColor: TEXTCOLOR( WHITE );
```

Statement labels are not intended to replace comments, although the labels should reflect the code that follows. Statement labels give GOTO statements a place to go. When your program gets to the GOTO, it branches to the statement labeled by the statement label. The program then continues to execute sequentially until the next GOTO changes the order again (or until the program ends).

> ### Use GOTOs Judiciously
>
> GOTO is not a good programming statement if it is overused. Programmers, especially beginners, tend to include too many GOTOs in a program. If a program branches all over the place, it is difficult to follow. Some people call programs with GOTOs *spaghetti code.*
>
> Using one or two GOTOs here and there is not necessarily a bad practice. Usually, however, you can substitute better, more thought-out code. To eliminate GOTOs and write programs with more structure, you must learn a few more control concepts. The next few chapters in this book address alternatives to GOTO, namely loops, subroutines, procedures, and functions.
>
> For now, become familiar with GOTO so that you can continue to build on your knowledge of Turbo Pascal.

Examples

1. The following program has a problem that is the direct result of the GOTO. This program, however, is one of the best illustrations of the GOTO statement. The program consists of an *endless loop* (sometimes called an *infinite loop*). The first three lines after the comments execute. Then the fourth line (the

GOTO) causes execution to loop back to the beginning and repeat the first three lines. The program continues to loop until the user presses the Ctrl–Break key combination.

```
{  Filename: C10GOTO1.PAS }


{
  Program to show use of GOTO.
  (This program ends only when user presses CTRL-BREAK.
}
PROGRAM GoTo1;
USES Crt;
LABEL Again;
CONST Spc = ' ';

BEGIN
   CLRSCR;
 Again: WRITELN( 'This message' );
   WRITELN( Spc:14, 'keeps repeating' );
   WRITELN( Spc:30, 'over and over' );
   GOTO Again;                        { Repeat continuously }
END. {GoTo1}
```

Notice that the statement label has a colon to separate it from the rest of the line but that you never put the colon on the label at the GOTO statement that branches to it.

Figure 10.2 shows the result of running this program. To stop the program, press Ctrl–Break.

2. The following poorly written program is the epitome of spaghetti code. Nevertheless, do your best to follow it and understand its output. By understanding the flow of the output, you hone your understanding of GOTO. You will appreciate that the rest of this book uses GOTO only when it is required to make the program clearer.

```
{ Filename: C10GOTO2.PAS }

{ Program demonstrates overuse of GOTO. }
PROGRAM GoTo2;
USES Crt;
```

```
LABEL Here, First, Final, There;

BEGIN
   CLRSCR;
   GOTO Here;
   First:
   WRITELN( 'A' );
   GOTO Final;
   There:
   WRITELN( 'B' );
   GOTO First;
   Here:
   WRITELN( 'C' );
   GOTO There;
   Final:
END. {GoTo2}
```

```
This message
            keeps repeating
                           over and over
This message
            keeps repeating
                           over and over
This message
            keeps repeating
                           over and over
This message
            keeps repeating
                           over and over
This message
            keeps repeating
                           over and over
This message
            keeps repeating
                           over and over
This message
            keeps repeating
                           over and over
```

Figure 10.2. **A repeating displaying program.**

At first glance, this program seems to display the first three letters of the alphabet; however, the GOTOs make them display in reverse order: C B A. Although the program is not a well-designed program, indenting the lines that don't have statement labels would make it more readable.

3. This indention would let you quickly distinguish the statement labels from the rest of the code, as you can see from the following program.

```
{ Filename: C10GOTO3.PAS }


{
  Program demonstrates overuse of GOTO.
  (Indentions separate labels from the other statements.)
}
PROGRAM GoTo3;
USES Crt;
LABEL Here, First, Final, There;

BEGIN
    CLRSCR;
    GOTO Here;

  First:
    WRITELN( 'A' );
    GOTO Final;
  There:
    WRITELN( 'B' );
    GOTO First;
  Here:
    WRITELN( 'C' );
    GOTO There;
  Final:
END. {GoTo3}
```

This program's listing is slightly easier to follow than the preceding program's listing, although the programs do the same thing. The rest of the programs in this book that use statement labels use indentions also.

The GOTO warning is worth repeating: Use GOTO sparingly and only when its use makes the program more readable and maintainable. Usually, there are better commands you can use.

The GOTOXY **Statement**

The screen is divided into 25 rows and 80 columns. Use the GOTOXY statement to place the cursor at the screen position where you want to display characters. The format of GOTOXY is

```
GOTOXY( Column, Row );
```

Column must be a number from 1 to 80. Row has to be a number from 1 to 25. GOTOXY places the cursor at the column and row you specify. The next WRITELN (or WRITE) statement begins displaying at the cursor's new location. If you use an invalid number for the column or row, Turbo Pascal ignores the GOTOXY statement.

Example

The following program displays Turbo Pascal in four different locations on-screen after setting the colors:

```
{ Filename: C10LOC1.PAS }

{ Displays Turbo Pascal in four screen locations. }
PROGRAM Location1;
USES Crt;

BEGIN
   TEXTCOLOR( WHITE );
   TEXTBACKGROUND( BLUE );                  { white on blue }
   CLRSCR;
   GOTOXY( 60, 22 );
   WRITE( 'Turbo Pascal' );
   GOTOXY( 5, 2 );
   WRITE( 'Turbo Pascal' );
   GOTOXY( 25, 17 );
```

```
        WRITE( 'Turbo Pascal' );
        GOTOXY( 40, 3 );
        WRITE( 'Turbo Pascal' );
END. {Location1}
```

Figure 10.3 shows the result of this program. Notice that the column and row numbers of the GOTOXY statements placed the message at the specified locations.

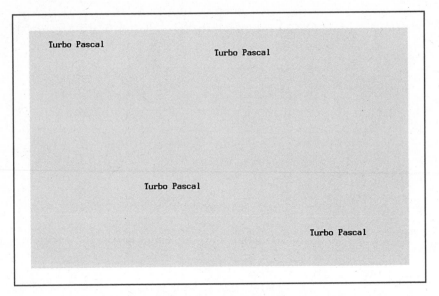

Figure 10.3. Displaying at four different places on the screen.

TIP: When you use GOTOXY, you often want to use WRITE rather than WRITELN. This avoids unexpected carriage return-line feeds.

Summary

Although the WRITELN command is easy to understand, it has more options than any command you have seen so far in this book. WRITELN lets you format your output of strings and numbers so that screens and displayed results look the way you want them to look. Combining WRITELN with TEXTCOLOR, TEXTBACKGROUND, SOUND, NOSOUND, the ASCII table, and the CHR function lets you control your screen and produce eye-catching displays. By using GOTO judiciously, you can repeat sections of your code.

One problem with using GOTO is its inability to stop. GOTO is an *unconditional branching* instruction that always occurs. To better control GOTO, Chapter 11 introduces a fundamental concept in every computer programming language: comparing data. By learning ways to test for certain results, you can begin to limit the use of GOTO as you learn more powerful ways to program in Turbo Pascal.

Review Questions

Answers to the Review Questions appear in Appendix B.

1. How would you right-justify an integer in the first 20 columns on the screen?

2. True or False: You can use either a numeric variable or a numeric constant to format a numeric value.

3. What are the ASCII numbers for the following characters?

   M $ £   z

4. The GOTO statement causes the computer to execute:

   A. The next statement in sequence.

   B. The next READLN statement.

   C. The statement having the label that follows the GOTO.

   D. The last WRITELN statement in the program.

5. What happens if you use 0 as the number of decimal places when you format a real value?

6. What happens if the number you want to format is larger than the field width?

7. How does GOTO change the order in which a program normally would execute statements?

8. True or False: The following two statements do exactly the same thing:

```
WRITELN( CHR(7));
WRITELN(LST, CHR(7) );
```

9. What colors and attributes are set by the following statements?

```
TEXTCOLOR( 141 );
TEXTBACKGROUND( 5 );
```

10. What output is produced by the following GOTOXY statement?

```
GOTOXY( 40, 12 );
```

11. What are three ways to make the computer's speaker beep?

Review Exercises

1. Write a program that prompts for three test grades (with READLN) to be put into three variables. Compute the average of the grades. Display the average on-screen with two decimal places.

2. Write a program to ask for the user's favorite month. Change the screen colors, clear the screen, and use GOTOXY and WRITELN to display the month's first three letters on-screen in five different places.

3. Write a program that asks the user for an ASCII number from 32 to 255. (ASCII codes lower than 31 cannot be displayed.) Display the ASCII character that matches the number the user entered. Continue to ask the user for the number until the user presses Ctrl–Break.

4. Produce a report showing the user's business expenses. Ask for a description of each expense and the dollar amount, one expense at a time. After displaying an appropriate title at the top of the paper, display down the page the expenses and their descriptions. Make sure that you display them with dollar signs and two decimal places. Because of the user's

accounting requirement, all negative amounts (prior expenses that were reimbursed) should have *trailing* negative signs. (Because a GOTO is required to keep asking the user for the next expense, the user can stop the program only by pressing Ctrl–Break.) Prompt the user to press Ctrl–Break when she wants to stop.

5. Rewrite the program that draws the picture in Review Exercise 6 in Chapter 6, "Comments and Additional WRITELN Options." Use as many of the line-drawing characters from the ASCII table as possible in place of the dashes and plus signs used previously. Use GOTOXY to move the cursor. Make the computer beep to get the user's attention when the drawing is complete.

Comparing Data

Believe it or not, not every statement in your Turbo Pascal programs should execute every time you run the program. Your programs operate on data. They are known as *data-driven* programs. In other words, the data should dictate what the program does. For example, you would not want the computer to print a paycheck every pay period for every employee who works for you; some of them might have taken a leave of absence, or some might be on a sales commission and might not have made a sale during that pay period. Printing paychecks for no money would be ridiculous. You want the computer to print checks to only the employees who have pay coming to them.

This chapter shows you how to create data-driven programs. These programs do not execute the same way every time you run them. Rather, they look at the constants and variables in the program and operate based on what they find. This might sound difficult, but it is straightforward and intuitive.

This chapter shows you ways to compare data and run programs according to those comparisons. It introduces

♦ Comparison operators

♦ IF-THEN logic

♦ String comparisons

♦ Compound logical operators

♦ The complete order of operators

♦ The BOOLEAN type

Comparison Operators

In addition to the math operators you learned about earlier, there are operators, called *relational operators*, you use for data comparison. Relational operators compare data; they tell how two variables or constants relate to each other. They tell you whether two variables are equal or not equal, or which one is less than or more than the other. Table 11.1 lists each relational operator and its description.

Table 11.1. The relational operators.

Operator	Description
=	Equal to
>	Greater than
<	Less than
>=	Greater than or equal to
<=	Less than or equal to
<>	Not equal to

These six operators form the foundation of comparing data in Turbo Pascal. They always appear with two constants, variables, or expressions, or a combination of the three, on each side. Many of these relational operators might be familiar to you already. You should learn how to use them as well as you know how to use the +, -, *, and / mathematical operators.

Examples

1. Assume that a program initializes four variables as follows:

   ```
   A := 5;
   B := 10;
   C := 15;
   D := 5;
   ```

   The following statements are true:

A is equal to D	A = D
B is less than C	B < C
C is greater than A	C > A
B is greater than or equal to A	B >= A
D is less than or equal to B	D <= B
B is not equal to C	B <> C

   These statements are not Turbo Pascal statements but rather are statements of relational fact about the values in the variables. Relational logic is not difficult. Relational logic always produces a true or false result. Each of the preceding statements is true.

2. Assuming the values in the preceding example's four variables, each of the following statements about the values is false:

   ```
   A = B
   B > C
   D < A
   D > A
   A <> D
   B >= C
   C <= B
   ```

   You should study these statements to see why each is false. Because A and D are equal to the same value (5), neither is greater than or less than the other.

   You deal with relational logic in everyday life. Think of the following statements you might make:

"The generic butter costs less than the name brand."

"My child is younger than Johnny."

"Our salaries are equal."

"The dogs are not the same age."

Each of these statements can be only true or false. No other outcome is possible.

Watch the Signs!

Many people say that they are not "math-inclined" or "logical," and you might be one of them. As mentioned earlier, you do not have to be good in math to be a good computer programmer. You should not be frightened by the term *relational logic*; you just read that you use relational logic everyday. Nevertheless, some people see relational operators and get confused about their meaning.

The two primary relational operators, less than (<) and greater than (>), are easy to remember. You might have been taught which is which in school but forgotten them. Their symbols tell you exactly what each one means.

The arrow of the < or > points to the smaller of the two values. Notice that in the true examples (in Example 1) the small part of the operator, or the point of the < and >, always points to the smaller number. The large, open part of the operator points to the larger value.

The relation is false if the arrow points in the wrong direction. In other words, 4 > 9 is false because the small part of the operator is pointing to the 9. In English, "4 *is greater than 9*" is false because 4 is less than 9.

EXAMPLE

The IF **Statement**

You incorporate relational operators in Turbo Pascal programs with the IF statement. IF (sometimes referred to as an *IF-THEN statement*) is a *decision statement*. It tests a relationship using the relational operators and makes a decision about which statement to execute next based on the result of that decision.

IF has several formats. The first one is

```
IF condition THEN Turbo Pascal statement
```

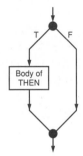

IF is the first Turbo Pascal statement you have seen with two keywords: IF and THEN. The condition is any relational comparison. You saw several relational comparisons earlier, such as A=B, C<D, and so on. The Turbo Pascal statement is any possible Turbo Pascal statement, such as WRITELN. That statement executes only if the condition is true. If the condition is false, Turbo Pascal ignores the statement and simply executes the next physical statement in the program following the IF.

The condition following the IF is often called a *boolean expression*, in honor of George Boole, a 19th century English mathematician who did some of the original work on symbolic logic.

As with relational logic, you use IF logic in everyday life. Consider the following:

"If the day is warm, then I will go swimming."

"If I make enough money, then we will build a new house."

"If the light is green, then go."

"If the light is red, then stop."

Each of these statements is *conditional*. That is, if and only if the condition is true do you complete the statement.

Examples

1. The following is a valid Turbo Pascal IF statement:

```
IF Sales > 5000 THEN WRITELN('You earned a bonus');
```

Assuming that this statement is part of a Turbo Pascal program, the value inside the variable Sales determines what happens next. If Sales contains more than 5000, the next statement that executes is the WRITELN. If Sales is 5000 or less, however, the WRITELN is ignored, and the line following the IF executes.

It usually is helpful to enclose the relational test in parentheses. The parentheses make the IF more readable. You can rewrite the preceding line as follows:

```
IF (Sales > 5000) THEN WRITELN('You earned a bonus');
```

Using the parentheses does not change the meaning of the statement, but it does help you spot the relational test more easily.

2. The following IF statement is another example of how you can compare a variable to a constant:

```
IF (Age < 21) THEN WRITELN('Person is a minor');
```

If the value in Age is less than 21, the WRITELN executes next. You do not have to include the THEN on the same line as the IF. For example, the above IF statement could be written as:

```
IF (Age < 21)
   THEN WRITELN('Person is a minor');
```

3. In this example, two variables are compared:

```
IF (Balance > LowBalance) THEN WRITELN('You have extra funds');
```

If Balance is greater than LowBalance, the WRITELN is executed. You can compare two variables (as in this example), a variable to a constant (as in the preceding example), a constant to a constant (although it rarely is done), or an expression in place of any variable or constant.

4. These examples illustrate how to use expressions in an IF statement:

```
IF (Pay * TaxRate < Minimum) THEN WRITELN('You need a pay raise');
IF (i/j = q*6) THEN WRITELN('Number is valid');
```

You can make expressions such as these much more readable by using parentheses around them, although parentheses are not required. Here is a rewrite of these two IF statements with ample parentheses:

```
IF ((Pay * TaxRate) < Minimum) THEN WRITELN('You need a pay raise');
IF ((i/j) = (q*6)) THEN WRITELN('Number is valid');
```

String Comparisons

In addition to comparing numeric data with the IF, you can use the IF to compare character string data. This capability is useful for alphabetizing, testing answers, comparing names, and much more.

In comparing string data, you always should refer to the ASCII table in Appendix A to see how characters relate to each other. Sometimes the ASCII table is known as the *collating* sequence of Turbo Pascal; it tells the order of characters.

You know that A comes before B. Therefore, it is true that A is less than B. The ASCII numbers determine the order of the characters. The ASCII table is handy also when you are comparing nonalphabetic data. For instance, the ASCII table shows that a question mark is greater than an exclamation point. You can see also that lowercase letters are higher than uppercase letters. Therefore, an uppercase *P* is less than the lowercase *p*.

When Turbo Pascal compares more than one character at a time, it scans each character of each string being compared until it finds a difference. For instance, *Adam* and *Adam* are exactly equal. *Jody* is less than *Judy*, however, because the *o* is less than the *u* according to the ASCII table. Also, a longer string such as *Shopping* is greater than *Shop* because of the extra characters.

TIP: An empty string, called a *null string*, is always less than any other string except another null string. A null string can occur when you press Enter in response to a `READLN(value);` without typing a value.

Examples

1. All the following string comparisons are true. If you are unsure about some of them, check the ASCII table in Appendix A to see for yourself why they compare to true.

```
'abcdef' > 'ABCDEF'
'Yes!' < 'Yes?'
'Computers are fun!' = 'Computers are fun!'
'PC' <> 'pc'
'Books, Books, Books' >= 'Books, Books'
```

Notice that the strings always have single quotation marks around them. This is consistent with the string constants you have seen so far.

2. You can use string comparisons to determine whether users type correct passwords. After typing a password, compare it to an internal password to check its validity.

   This program requests a password. It then checks the entered password against one stored in a variable. If the passwords match, the program displays a secret message. If they do not match, the program halts. Only when a correct password is entered does the secret message appear.

```
{ Filename: C11PASS1.PAS }

{
  Program to prompt for a password and
  check it against an internal one.
}
```

```
PROGRAM Password1;
USES Crt;

CONST StoredPass = 'XYZ123';
VAR   UserPass: STRING[10];

BEGIN
   TEXTCOLOR( WHITE );
   TEXTBACKGROUND( BLUE );
   CLRSCR;
   WRITE( 'What is the password? ');
   TEXTCOLOR( BLUE );                  { Blue on blue to hide }
                                       { the user input. }
   READLN( UserPass );
   TEXTCOLOR( WHITE );                 { Restore color }

   IF (UserPass = StoredPass)
      THEN WRITELN( 'The cash safe is behind the picture of
                    the ship.' );
END.  {Password1}
```

If users know the password, they see the secret message. (Be sure to type uppercase letters.) Of course, users can press Ctrl–Break to stop the program and look at the listing to find the password and secret message. After learning how programs work with data files, you will see how to *encrypt* the passwords so that users cannot find them as easily.

Password routines are good for front-end sections of programs with confidential data, such as payroll or banking systems.

Intelligent Passwords

Throughout your use of computers, you will have to choose passwords. Please take this responsibility seriously. Computer crime is serious and illegal.

continues

You should change your password every few weeks. This keeps someone from using it for long if they do determine it. Do not write down your password, and do not make it so long that you forget it.

Make up passwords that are not English words, even though they might be more difficult to remember. Foreign words and letter-number combinations make good passwords. Passwords such as X1Y2Z6, Giorno, and MY912AB are good candidates.

Compound Logical Operators

There might be times when you need to test more than one set of variables. You can combine more than one relational test into a *compound relational test* by using these logical operators:

AND   OR   XOR   NOT

These operators might not seem typical. The operators you have learned about so far have been symbols, such as +, <, >, and *. These logical operators are operators of Turbo Pascal, however, and they go between two or more relational tests.

Tables 11.2, 11.3, 11.4, and 11.5 show how each of the logical operators works. These tables are called *truth tables* because they show how to achieve true results from an IF test that uses them. Take a minute to study the tables.

Table 11.2. The AND truth table: both sides must be true.

True AND True	= True
True AND False	= False
False AND True	= False
False AND False	= False

Table 11.3. The OR truth table: one side or the other must be true.

True OR True = True

True OR False = True

False OR True = True

False OR False = False

Table 11.4. The XOR truth table: one side or the other—but not both—must be true.

True XOR True = False

True XOR False = True

False XOR True = True

False XOR False = False

Table 11.5. The NOT truth table: causes an opposite relation.

NOT True = False

NOT False = True

Examples

1. The true or false on each side of the operator represents a relational IF test. For instance, the following valid IF tests use logical operators (sometimes called *compound relational operators*):

A must be less than B, and C must be greater than D for the next statement to execute.

```
IF ((A < B) AND (C > D))
   THEN Delta := 5*(B-A) + 7*(C-D);
```

The Sales *must be more than* 5000 *or the* HrsWorked *must be more than* 80 *before the next statement executes.*

```
IF ((Sales > 5000) OR (HrsWorked > 80))
   THEN Bonus := 100;
```

The variable called bit2 *must be equal to* 0 *or* bit3 *must not be equal to* 1 *before* Error *is displayed. If they both are true, however, the test fails (because XOR is used), the* WRITELN *is ignored, and the next instruction in sequence executes.*

```
If ((bit2 = 0) XOR (bit3 <> 1)) THEN WRITELN( 'Error' );
```

If the Sales *are not less than* 2500, *the* Bonus *is initialized.*

```
IF (NOT (Sales < 2500)) THEN Bonus := 500;
```

This line illustrates an important programming tip: Use NOT sparingly. (As some people wisely state: Do not use NOT, or your programs will not be NOT(unclear).) It would be much clearer to rewrite this example and turn it into a positive relational test, as in

```
IF (Sales >= 2500) THEN Bonus := 500;
```

Notice that the overall format of the IF statement is retained, but the relational test has been changed to use positive logic.

TIP: Instead of using the negative logic expression on the left, use the equivalent positive logic expression on the right:

```
NOT (A < B)            A >= B
NOT (A > B)            A <= B
NOT (A <= B)           A > B
NOT (A >= B)           A < B
```

You can even have three or more, as in

```
IF ((A = B) AND (D = F) OR (L = m) XOR (K <> 2)) THEN ...
```

This example is a little too much. Good programming practice dictates using only two relational tests inside one IF. If you need to combine more than two, use more than one IF statement.

As with other relational operators, you use these in everyday conversation, as in these examples:

"If my pay is high *and* my vacation time is long, we can go to Italy this summer."

"If you take the trash out *or* clean your room, you can watch television tonight."

"I can go to the grocery *or* go to the flower shop, *but not both*."

The first two examples are straightforward. The last example illustrates the XOR operator. Notice from the XOR truth table that one side of the XOR or the other side of the XOR can be true for the final result to be true, but not both sides. This is known as the *exclusive or* operator, and sometimes is called the *mutually exclusive* operator. Many times you are faced with two choices, but you can do only one or the other; you do not have the time or resources to do both.

Internal Truths

The true or false results of relational tests occur internally at the bit level. For example, look at the following IF test:

```
IF (A = 6) THEN ...
```

To determine the truth of the relation (A = 6), the computer takes a binary 6, or 00000110, and compares it bit-by-bit to the variable A. If A contains 7, a binary 00000111, the result of the equal test is false because the right bit (always called the *least-significant bit*) is different.

2. The following program gets three numbers from the user. Regardless of the order in which the user types the numbers, the program displays the smallest and the largest of the three. The program uses several compound IF statements.

```
{ Filename: C11MNMAX.PAS }

{ Program to display largest and smallest of three input values }
PROGRAM MinMax1;
USES Crt;
CONST Max = ' is highest';
      Min = ' is smallest';

BEGIN
    CLRSCR;
    WRITE( 'Please type 3 different numbers, ');
    WRITELN( 'and separate them with spaces' );
    READLN( num1, num2, num3 );

            { Test for highest }
    IF ((num1 > num2) AND (num1 > num3)) THEN WRITELN(num1,Max);
    IF ((num2 > num1) AND (num2 > num3)) THEN WRITELN(num2,Max);
    IF ((num3 > num1) AND (num3 > num2)) THEN WRITELN(num3,Max);

            { Test for smallest }
    IF ((num1 < num2) AND (num1 < num3)) THEN WRITELN(num1,Min);
    IF ((num2 < num1) AND (num2 < num3)) THEN WRITELN(num2,Min);
    IF ((num3 < num1) AND (num3 < num2)) THEN WRITELN(num3,Min);
END.  {MinMax1}
```

Future chapters show you even better ways to produce results such as these.

The Complete Order of Operators

The order of math operators in Chapter 5, "Understanding Numeric Variables and Constants," did not include the relational operators you are learning about in this chapter. You should be familiar with the entire order, presented in Table 11.6. As you can see, math operators take precedence over relational operators, and parentheses override any of these defaults.

Table 11.6. The entire order of operators.

Order	Operator
1	()
2	NOT, Unary +, Unary -
3	*, /, DIV, MOD, AND
4	Binary +, Binary -, OR, XOR
5	=, <, >, <=, >=, <>

You might wonder why the relational and logical operators are included. The following statement helps show why:

```
IF (Sales < MinSal * 2 AND YrsEmp > 10 * Sub) ...
```

Without the complete order of operators, it would be impossible to determine how such a statement would execute. Using the operator order and extra parentheses, you want this IF statement to execute as follows:

```
IF ((Sales < (MinSal * 2)) AND (YrsEmp > (10 * Sub))) ...
```

This statement still is confusing, but it is less confusing than the preceding statement. The two multiplication operations are performed first, followed by the relations < and >. The AND is performed last because all the other operators are included in parentheses.

To avoid such problems, use ample parentheses, even if you want the actions to be performed in the default order. In addition, do not combine too many expressions inside one IF relational test.

> **TIP:** When you have a lot of nested parentheses, you can use the editor to verify that you have matching pairs. Position the cursor under either the left or right parenthesis. Hold down the Ctrl and Q keys (Ctrl–Q) and press either the left or right bracket key ([or]). The editor moves the cursor to the matching parenthesis. If there is no matching parenthesis, the cursor does not move. You can use this tip to find matching comment braces also.

The BOOLEAN Type

In addition to integer, real, and CHAR data types, Turbo Pascal has also a BOOLEAN data type. A BOOLEAN data type can be either true or false. With this new data type, you can store the result of a boolean expression. BOOLEAN variables can help break up long, complicated IF statements.

Examples

1. Rather than use:

```
IF ((Sales < (MinSal * 2)) AND (YrsEmp > (10 * Sub))) ...
```

you could write

```
VAR SalesChk:   BOOLEAN;
    ServiceChk: BOOLEAN;
BEGIN
    SalesChk   := Sales < (MinSal * 2);
    ServiceChk := YrsEmp > (10 * Sub);
    IF (SalesChk AND ServiceChk) ...
```

2. When you use a BOOLEAN variable or constant in a WRITELN (or WRITE) statement, Turbo Pascal displays TRUE or FALSE.

```
VAR GoodCh: BOOLEAN;
BEGIN
   GoodCh := FALSE;
   WRITELN( 'GoodCh = ',GoodCh);
   ⋮
```

In this example, you see GoodCh = FALSE.

Summary

This chapter showed you how to compare data. By testing constants and variables, your program can behave differently depending on its input data. Computers should be data-driven. When programmers write programs, they do not know what data will be entered. Therefore, programmers should write the programs to execute certain statements conditionally depending on the data given.

This chapter is the basis of many programs you will write. Programs that test results and conditionally execute accordingly make computers flexible by enabling them to react to given data.

Review Questions

Answers to the Review Questions appear in Appendix B.

1. Please state whether these relational tests are true or false.

   A. 4 >= 5

   B. 4 >= 4

   C. 165 = 165

   D. 0 <> 25

2. True or False: Turbo Pascal is fun displays on-screen when the following statement is executed:

   ```
   IF (54 <= 50) THEN WRITELN( 'Turbo Pascal is fun' );
   ```

3. Using the ASCII table, please state whether these string relational tests are true or false.

   A. 'Que' < 'QUE'

   B. '' < '0'

   C. '?' > '}'

   D. 'yES' < 'Yes'

4. What is the result of executing the following program lines?

```
N1 := 0;
N1 := N1 + 5;
```

   A. The value of N1 is 0.

   B. The value of N1 is 6.

   C. The value of N1 is 5.

   D. The value of N1 cannot be determined.

5. The following compound relational tests compare true and false values. Determine whether each of them is True or False.

   A. NOT (TRUE OR FALSE)

   B. (TRUE AND FALSE) AND (FALSE XOR TRUE)

   C. NOT (TRUE XOR TRUE)

   D. TRUE OR (FALSE AND FALSE) OR FALSE

Review Exercises

1. Write a program that asks for the user's age. If the age is under 21, display the following message:

   `Have a lemonade!`

2. Write a program that generates your own XOR truth table.

3. Write a payroll program that asks for the weekly hours worked and the pay per hour. Compute the pay, and assume that the firm pays regular pay (*rate * hours worked*) for all hours less than or equal to 40, time and a half (1.5) for any hours more than 40 and less than 50, and double pay for any hours 50 or more. Run the program several times, and try different values for the hours worked to ensure that the calculations are correct. Your program probably will have at least two or three IF statements to handle the various types of overtime pay. Do not worry about taxes or other deductions.

Part IV

Control Statements

The FOR Loop

The repetitive capability of the computer makes it a good tool for processing large amounts of information. The GOTO statement provides one method of repeating a group of statements, but you have seen that endless loops can occur if you don't use GOTO with care. GOTO can also make programs difficult to follow. For these reasons, there are better ways to repeat sections of your programs than to use GOTO statements.

LOOP: A repeated, circular execution of one or more statements.

The FOR statement offers a way to repeat sections of your program conditionally. It creates a *loop*, which is the repeated circular execution of one or more statements. The FOR loop is a control structure that repeats a section of code a certain number of times. When that number is reached, execution continues to the next statement in sequence. This chapter focuses on the FOR loop construct by introducing

♦ The FOR statement with TO

♦ Counters and totals

♦ The FOR Statement with DOWNTO

♦ Nested FOR loops

♦ Enumerated types

The FOR loop is just one of several ways to loop through sections of code. Chapter 13, "The WHILE Loop," and Chapter 14, "The REPEAT Loop," introduce additional looping commands.

The FOR **Statement with** TO

The format of this FOR statement is

```
FOR index := start TO last DO
   BEGIN
      statement1;
      statement2;
      .
      .
      .
   END;  {for}
```

So far, you have seen a BEGIN-END pair used only to block off the main program section. When more than one statement is associated with a FOR loop, you also use a BEGIN-END pair to block off the associated statements. The BEGIN-END pair and associated statements often are referred to as a *compound statement*. The statements between the BEGIN-END pair are called the *body* of the loop. The body of the loop repeats a certain number of times. The programmer controls the number of times the loop repeats.

If the FOR loop has only one statement, the BEGIN-END pair is optional.

index is a numeric variable that you supply. This variable is important to the FOR loop. It helps control the body of the loop. *index* is initialized to the value of *start* before the first iteration of the loop. The *start* value typically is 1, but it can be any numeric value (or variable) you specify. Every time the body of the loop repeats, *index* increments by 1.

The value of *last* is a number (or variable) that controls the end of the looping process. When *index* is equal to or greater than *last*, Turbo Pascal does not repeat the loop, but rather continues at the next statement following the FOR loop.

If *index* is less than *last*, Turbo Pascal increments *index* by 1, and the body of the loop repeats again.

If *start* initially is greater than *last*, then the loop does not execute.

The Concept of FOR Loops

You use the concept of FOR loops in your daily life. Whenever you have to repeat a certain procedure a specified number of times, the procedure is a good candidate for a computerized FOR loop.

To further illustrate the concept of a FOR loop, suppose that you are putting 10 new shutters on your house.

For each shutter, you must complete the following steps:
Move the ladder to the location of the next shutter.
Take a shutter, a hammer, and nails up the ladder.
Nail the shutter to the side of the house.
Climb down the ladder.

You must perform each of these four steps exactly 10 times, because you have 10 shutters. After 10 times, you don't put up another shutter because the job is finished. You are looping through a procedure that has four steps. These four steps are the body of the loop. It certainly is not an endless loop, because you have a fixed number of shutters; you run out of shutters after 10.

For a less physical example that might be more easily computerized, suppose you must complete a tax return for each of your three teenage children. (If you have three teenage children, you probably need more than a computer to help you get through the day!)

For each child, you must complete the following steps:
Add the total income.
Add the total deductions.
Complete a tax return.
Put it in an envelope.
Mail it.

You must repeat this procedure two more times.

Notice that the sentence introducing these steps began like this: "For each child...." This phrase signals a structure similar to the FOR loop.

Example

The following counting program gives you a glimpse of the FOR loop's capabilities. Before reading the description of its contents, look at the program and the output that follows. The results speak for themselves and illustrate the FOR loop well.

```
{ Filename: C12FOR1.PAS }

PROGRAM ForLoop1;
USES Crt;
VAR i: INTEGER;
BEGIN
   CLRSCR;
   FOR i := 1 TO 10 DO WRITELN( i );
END.  {ForLoop1}
```

Here is the output for the preceding program.

```
1
2
3
4
5
6
7
8
9
10
```

Counters and Totals

Associated with loops are two powerful concepts: *counters* and *totals*. Computers do not think, but they do lightning-fast calculations, and they do not get bored. This makes them perfect for counting and adding totals.

ALGORITHM:
Step-by-step
instructions for
solving a problem.

There are no commands inside Turbo Pascal to count occurrences or total a list of numbers; however, you can write these routines yourself. Almost every program in use today has some sort of counter or totaling *algorithm*, or a combination of both.

Counting with Turbo Pascal

Counting is important for many applications. You might want to know how many customers you have. You might want to know how many people scored over a certain average in a class. You might want to count how many checks you wrote last month with your computerized checkbook system.

To begin developing a Turbo Pascal routine to count occurrences, think of how you count in your own mind. When you add the total number of something (such as the stamps in your stamp collection or the number of wedding invitations you have sent), you follow this procedure:

Start at 0 and add 1 for each item you are counting. When you finish, you have the total number (the total count) of the items.

In the following program the heart of the counting process is the following statement:

```
LCCnt := LCCnt + 1;
```

In algebra, this statement would not be valid because nothing is ever equal to itself plus 1. In Turbo Pascal, however, the colon–equal sign means assignment; the right side of the colon–equal sign is computed, 1 is added to whatever is in LCCnt at the time, and that value is stored back in LCCnt, in effect replacing the old value of LCCnt.

When you count with Turbo Pascal, put 0 in a variable and add 1 to it every time you process another data value.

Example

Using a counter, you can keep track of certain occurrences. The following program counts the number of lowercase characters that a user types.

```
{ Filename: C12CNT1.PAS }

{ Program to count lower case characters. }

PROGRAM Counter1;
```

```
USES Crt;

VAR    LCCnt: INTEGER;              { number of lowercase chars }
       i:     INTEGER;              { FOR loop index }
       Ch:    CHAR;                 { char typed by user }

BEGIN
   CLRSCR;
   LCCnt := 0;                      { Init counter to 0 }
   WRITELN( 'Type any character and press Enter');
   FOR i := 1 TO 10 DO
      BEGIN
         WRITE( 'Character ',i,' = ');
         READLN(Ch);
         IF (Ch >= 'a') AND (Ch <= 'z')
            THEN INC(LCCnt);
      END; {for}
   WRITELN( 'Number of lowercase characters typed = ',LCCnt);
END.  {Counter1}
```

Figure 12.1. shows the output from this program.

```
Type any character and press Enter
Character 1 = a
Character 2 = b
Character 3 = c
Character 4 = Z
Character 5 = X
Character 6 = Y
Character 7 = 5
Character 8 = 3
Character 9 = q
Character 10 = ?
Number of lowercase characters typed = 4
```

Figure 12.1. Illustrating how to use a counter.

TIP: Because incrementing a variable is so common, Turbo Pascal has another statement called INC. INC executes very fast. Rather than

```
i := i + 1;
```

use

```
INC(i);
```

If you need to increment by a number other than 1, use

```
INC(i,n);
```

where *n* is some integer.

Similarly, use

```
DEC(i)
```

for

```
i := i - 1
```

To decrement by a number other than 1, use

```
DEC(i,n);
```

Producing Totals

Writing a routine to add values is as easy as counting. Rather than add 1 to the counter variable, you add a value to the total variable. For instance, if you want to find the total dollar amount of checks you wrote in December, start at 0 (nothing) and add to that each check written in December. Rather than build a count, you build a total.

When you want Turbo Pascal to add values, initialize a total variable to 0 and add each value to the total until you have gone through all the values.

Examples

1. Suppose that you want to write a program to add your grades for a class you are taking. The teacher has informed you that if you earn more than 450 points, you will receive an A.

   The following program asks you to type the number of grades to be added. This value will be used in a FOR loop to prompt you for each grade. The program displays a Congratulations message if you receive an A.

```
{ Filename: C12GRAD1.PAS }


{ Adds grades and determines whether an A was made }
PROGRAM Grades1;
USES Crt;

VAR TotalGrade: INTEGER;
    Grade:      INTEGER;
    MaxGrades:  INTEGER;
    i:          INTEGER;

BEGIN
    TotalGrade := 0;                    { Init total variable }
    TEXTCOLOR( WHITE );
    TEXTBACKGROUND( BLUE );             { White on blue }
    CLRSCR;

    WRITE( 'How many grades do you wish to add? ' );
    READLN( MaxGrades );
    FOR i := 1 TO MaxGrades DO
       BEGIN
          WRITE( 'What is your grade? ' );
          READLN( Grade );
          INC(TotalGrade, Grade );      { Add to total }
       END;  {for}
    WRITELN( 'You made a total of ', TotalGrade, ' points.' );
    IF (TotalGrade >= 450) THEN WRITELN( '** You made an A!!' );
END.   {Grades1}
```

2. The following program adds the numbers from 100 to
200 using a FOR loop. This example shows how adding a
start value other than 1 starts the loop with a larger index
variable.

```
{ FileName: C12FOR3.PAS }

PROGRAM ForLoop3;
VAR Total: INTEGER;
    i:      INTEGER;
BEGIN
   Total := 0;
   FOR i := 100 TO 200 DO              { Loop goes 100, 101, }
                                       { 102, ..., 200 }

      INC(Total,i);                    { Bump Total by i }
   WRITELN( 'The total is ', Total ); { Not part of loop }
END.   {ForLoop3}
```

Although the FOR loop adds the numbers 100 through 200,
the body of the loop in both programs executes only 101
times. The starting value is 100, not 1 as in preceding
examples.

Notice how the body of the FOR loop is indented. Indenting is
a good habit to develop; it makes the beginning and end of
the loop easier to find. The indentation has no effect on the
loop's execution.

> **TIP:** If you need to indent (or un-indent) a block of code, the
> editor provides a handy tool. First select the code you want
> to move. Then hold down the Ctrl and K keys and press I
> (Ctrl–K–I) to shift the block to the right. Similarly, press
> Ctrl–K–U to shift the block to the left.

3. Unfortunately, Turbo Pascal does not have a STEP option
with which you can specify how much the index should
increment. The increment is always 1. If a loop depends on
an increment greater than 1, you must use another variable
to handle it.

The following program displays the even numbers from 1 to 20. It then displays the odd numbers from 1 to 20. The variable Num is used to keep track of the numbers to be displayed.

```
{ Filename: C12EVOD1.PAS }

{ Prints the first few odd and even numbers. }
PROGRAM EvensAndOdds;
USES Crt;
VAR Num: INTEGER;
    i:   INTEGER;

BEGIN
   CLRSCR;
   WRITELN( 'Even numbers 20 and below' );
   Num := 2;
   FOR i := 1 TO 10 DO
      BEGIN
         WRITELN( Num );
         INC(Num,2);
      END;  {for}
   WRITELN;
   WRITELN( 'Odd numbers below 20' );
   Num := 1;
   FOR i := 1 TO 10 DO
      BEGIN
         WRITELN( num );
         INC(Num,2);
      END;  {for}
END.  {EvensAndOdds}
```

The first section's *last* value is 10 rather than 20. If it were 20, you would get the first 20 even numbers. Two loops are in this program. The body of each consists of a WRITELN statement and a statement that calculates the next number.

The CLRSCR and the first WRITELN are not part of either loop. If they were, the screen would clear and the title would print before each number printed. The following is the output from running this program.

```
Even numbers 20 and below
2
4
6
8
10
12
14
16
18
20

Odd numbers below 20
1
3
5
7
9
11
13
15
17
19
```

Other FOR Options

Always let Turbo Pascal manage the index. Although you can change the index, this makes for some awful debugging sessions. It sounds complicated, and it is.

TIP: *Never* change the index within the body of a FOR loop. Let the FOR loop take care of it.

Example

The following program does nothing except show how the FOR loop *index* can be changed in the body of the loop. Trace the result of the program, shown following the program, to see how the results generate. The program is difficult to follow, so be cautious about changing any *index* in the body of the loop.

```
{ Filename: C12FORVR.PAS }

{ Program that changes the FOR loop control variables }
PROGRAM Control1;
USES Crt;
VAR StartVar: INTEGER;
    EndVar:   INTEGER;
    i:        INTEGER;
BEGIN
   StartVar := 15;
   EndVar   := 30;
   CLRSCR;
   FOR i := StartVar TO EndVar DO
     BEGIN
       WRITELN( i );
       INC(i);
     END;  {for}
END.   {Control1}
```

Here is the output from the program.

```
15
17
19
21
23
25
27
29
```

The programming task dictates whether you use variables or constants or a mixture of both. This program does not have any "real world" application. If you were asking the user how many checks to process or how many grades to average, however, you would want to use variables in the FOR statement so that it loops only as many times as the user requests.

> **NOTE:** Turbo Pascal looks at the *start* and *end* values only once. Because the FOR loop acts as though the original values are in effect, there is never a need to change *start* or *end*.

The FOR **Statement with** DOWNTO

The format of this FOR statement is

```
FOR index := start DOWNTO end DO
    BEGIN
        statement1;
        statement2;
          .
          .
          .
    END;   {for}
```

If the FOR loop has only one statement, the BEGIN-END pair is optional. Every time the body of the loop repeats, the *index* variable decrements by 1. If the *index* variable is greater than the *end* variable, Turbo Pascal decrements the *index* variable by 1, and the body of the loop repeats again.

If the *start* value initially is less than the *end* value, then the loop does not execute.

Example

To display the first ten numbers in reverse order, use:

```
FOR i := 1xDOWNTO 1 DO WRITELN( i );
```

Nested FOR **Loops**

NESTED LOOP: A loop within a loop.

Any Turbo Pascal statement can go inside the body of a FOR loop—even another FOR loop. When you put a loop within a loop, you create *nested loops*. The clock in a sporting event works like a nested loop. The clock at a football game counts down from 15 minutes to 0 minutes for each of four quarters. One loop is a countdown from 15 to 0 (for each minute). That loop is nested within another loop that counts from 1 to 4 (for each of the four quarters).

Any program that needs to repeat a loop more than once is a good candidate for a nested loop. Figure 12.2 shows the outlines of two nested loops. You can think of the inside loop as looping "faster" than the outside loop. In the example on the left, the FOR loop that counts from 1 to 5 is the inside loop. It loops fastest because the variable inner goes from 1 to 5 before the outside loop, the variable outer, finishes its first iteration. The outside loop does not repeat until the inside loop completes. When the outside loop finally iterates a second time, the inside loop starts over again.

```
FOR Outer := 1 To 10 DO          FOR Outer := 1 To 10 DO
   BEGIN                            BEGIN
     :                                :
     FOR Inner := 1 To 5 DO           FOR Inner1 := 1 To 5 DO
        BEGIN                            BEGIN
          :                                :
        END; {inner for}               END; {inner1 for}
     :                                :
END; {outer for}                     FOR Inner2 := 1 To 5 DO
                                        BEGIN
                                          :
                                        END; {inner2 for}
                                     :
                                  END; {outer for}
```

Figure 12.2. The outlines of two nested loops.

In the example on the right, two loops within an outside loop are illustrated. Both of these inner loops execute in their entirety before the outside loop finishes its first iteration. When the outside loop starts its second iteration, the two inside loops repeat again.

Notice the order of the END statements in each example. The inside loop *always* finishes, and therefore its END must come before the outside loop's END statement.

> **NOTE:** To sum up nested loops, follow this rule of thumb: In nested loops, the END statement should match the BEGIN of the FOR loop. The inside loop (or loops) then has a chance to complete before the outside loop's next iteration.

Nested loops become important later when you use them for array and matrix processing, described later in Chapter 17, "An Introduction to Arrays," and Chapter 18, "Multidimensional Arrays."

Examples

1. The following program contains a loop within a loop—a nested loop.

   The inside loop counts and displays the numbers 1 to 5. The outside loop counts from 1 to 3. Therefore, the inside loop repeats in its entirety three times. In other words, this program displays the values 1 to 5, and does so three times.

```
{ Filename: C12NEST1.PAS }

{ Displays numbers from 1 to 5 three times using a nested
loop. }
PROGRAM Nested1;
USES Crt;
VAR Times: INTEGER;
    Num:   INTEGER;

BEGIN
   CLRSCR;
   FOR Times := 1 TO 3 DO                  { Outside loop }
      BEGIN
         FOR Num := 1 TO 5 DO              { Inside loop }
            WRITELN( num );
         WRITELN;
      END;  {for}
END.  {Nested1}
```

Notice that the inside loop that prints from 1 to 5 repeats three times. The following output shows the result of running this program. The indention also maintains the standard for FOR loops; every statement in each loop is indented three spaces. Because the inside loop is indented already, its body is indented three more spaces.

```
1
2
3
4
5

1
2
3
4
5

1
2
3
4
5
```

2. In this example, the outside loop's index variable changes each time through the loop. If one of the inside loop's control variables is the outside loop's index variable, you see an effect such as that shown in the following program.

```
{ Filename: C12NEST2.PAS }

{ Inside loop controlled by outer loop's index variable. }
PROGRAM Nested2;
USES Crt;
VAR Inner: INTEGER;
    Outer: INTEGER;

BEGIN
   CLRSCR;
   FOR Outer := 5 DOWNTO 1 DO
```

```
      BEGIN
         FOR Inner := 1 TO Outer DO WRITE( Inner:4 );
         WRITELN;
      END;  {for}
  END.  {Nested2}
```

The output from this program follows. The inside loop repeats five times (as Outer counts down from 5 to 1) and prints the numbers from 5 to 1.

```
1  2  3  4  5
1  2  3  4
1  2  3
1  2
1
```

Table 12.1 shows the two variables being traced through the program. Sometimes you must "play computer" when you are learning a new concept such as nested loops. By executing one line at a time and recording each variable's contents, you produce a table such as Table 12.1.

Table 12.1. Tracing output of C12NEST2.PAS.

Value of Outer	Value of Inner
5	1
5	2
5	3
5	4
5	5
4	1
4	2
4	3
4	4

continues

Table 12.1. Continued.

Value of Outer	Value of Inner
3	1
3	2
3	3
2	1
2	2
1	1

A Tip for Mathematicians

The FOR statement is similar to the mathematical summation symbol. When you write programs to simulate the summation symbol, the FOR statement is an excellent candidate. A nested FOR statement is good for double summations.

For example, the summation

$$\sum_{i = 1}^{i = 30} (i \ / \ (i * 2))$$

can be rewritten as:

```
Total := 0;
FOR i := 1 TO 30 DO
    Total := Total + (i DIV (i * 2))
```

Enumerated Types

To improve the readability of your program, Turbo Pascal provides the *enumerated type*. You get to name the data type and define all valid values. The name you chose goes in the TYPE section.

All defined values are listed in parentheses and separated by commas. An enumerated type can have as many as 256 values.

To use an enumerated type, declare a variable in the VAR section with the name you specified in the TYPE section. Enumerated types can be used in FOR loops in place of the *start* and *last* variables, making the FOR loop more closely represent what it is counting.

Examples

1. Here are some sample enumerated types:

```
Directions = ( North, South, East, West );
KeyType    = ( F1, F2, F3, F4, F9 ,F10 );
Compass    = ( North, NorthEast, East, SouthEast,
               South, SouthWest, West, NorthWest );
Fruit      = ( Apple, Banana, Orange );
Days       = ( Sunday,   Monday, Tuesday, Wednesday,
               Thursday, Friday, Saturday);
Months     = ( January,   February, March,     April,
               May,       June,     July,      August,
               September, October,  November, December );
Seasons    = ( Spring, Summer, Autumn, Winter );
Colors     = ( Red, White, Blue );
```

2. You often use an enumerated type in a FOR loop.

```
  .
  .
  .
TYPE Directions = ( North, South, East, West );
VAR Dir: Directions;

BEGIN
  .
  .
  .
FOR Dir := North TO West DO
   BEGIN
      IF Dir = North THEN WRITELN( 'Going North' );
      IF Dir = South THEN WRITELN( 'Going South' );
```

```
              IF Dir = East  THEN WRITELN( 'Going East' );
              IF Dir = West  THEN WRITELN( 'Going West' );
          END;  {for}
```

.

.

.

3. Unfortunately, you cannot include one of your enumerated types in a WRITELN statement.

```
VAR Color: Colors;
BEGIN
   Color := Red;
   WRITELN( 'The color is ', Color );    { can't do this }
```

.

.

.

When you compile this code, you see the following message,

```
Error 64: Cannot Read or Write variables of this type.
```

Summary

This chapter has taught you how to control loops. As opposed to the tendency of GOTO loops to get out of hand, the FOR loop enables you to control the number of iterations made. All FOR loops contain two parts: starting and ending values.

Several other types of loops are possible in Turbo Pascal. Chapter 13 shows you yet another way to control a loop: the WHILE loop. Chapter 14 introduces the REPEAT loop.

Review Questions

Answers to the Review Questions appear in Appendix B.

1. What is a loop?

2. What is a nested loop?

3. Which loop "moves fastest": the inner loop or the outer loop?

4. What is the output from the following program?

   ```
   FOR i := 10 DOWNTO 1 DO WRITELN( i );
   ```

5. True or False: A FOR loop is good to use when you know in advance exactly how many iterations a loop requires.

6. What happens when the *index* variable becomes larger than the *last* variable in a FOR statement?

7. True or False: The following program contains a valid nested loop:

   ```
   FOR i := 1 TO 10 DO
      FOR j := 1 TO 5 DO
         WRITELN( i, j );
   ```

8. What is the output of the following program?

   ```
   StartVal := 1;
   EndVal   := 5;

   FOR i := StartVal TO EndVal DO
      BEGIN
         WRITELN( i );
         DEC(EndVal);
      END;  {for}
   ```

Review Exercises

1. Write a program that prints the numbers from 1 to 15 on the screen. Use a FOR loop to control the printing.

2. Write a program to print the values from 15 to 1 on the screen. Use a FOR loop to control the printing.

3. Write a program that uses a FOR loop to print every odd number from 1 to 100.

4. Write a program that asks users for their age. Use a FOR loop to print Happy Birthday! for every year of the age.

5. Change the program in the preceding exercise to ask users whether they want to see the message again. (Some people don't like to be reminded of their birthday.)

6. Write a program that uses a FOR loop to print the ASCII characters from 32 to 255 on the screen. *Hint:* Use the CHR function with the FOR loop's *index* variable inside the CHR's parentheses.

7. Using the ASCII table in Appendix A and the CHR function, write a program to print the following output using a nested FOR loop:

```
A
AB
ABC
ABCD
ABCDE
```

Hint: The outside loop should loop from 1 to 5. The inside loop's *start* variable should be 65 (the value of ASCII A).

The WHILE Loop

The FOR loop is only one way to control a loop. Although a FOR loop works well for loops that must execute a specific number of times, the WHILE loop lets your program execute a loop as long as a certain BOOLEAN condition is true.

This chapter shows you how to program a loop by introducing the WHILE loop. The chapter is relatively short; when you understand the nature of loops, understanding WHILE loops is easy.

Using the WHILE Loop

The WHILE statement encloses a repeating loop, just as the FOR loop does. Unlike the FOR loop, however, the WHILE loop is controlled by a BOOLEAN condition and not by a specified number of iterations.

The format of WHILE is

```
WHILE BOOLEAN condition is true DO
    BEGIN
        statement1;
        statement2;
        ⋮
        END;   {while}
```

When more than one statement is associated with a WHILE loop, use a BEGIN-END pair to block the associated statements. If the WHILE loop has only one statement, the BEGIN-END pair is optional. Because the BEGIN and END statements enclose a loop, indent the body of the loop as you did with the FOR loop. As you probably noticed in the last chapter, a comment after the END helps identify the BEGIN-END block.

The body of the WHILE loop executes repeatedly as long as the BOOLEAN condition is true.

The BOOLEAN condition can include any relational or compound BOOLEAN condition. You can use the same types of tests you used with the IF statement. As long as the BOOLEAN condition is true, the WHILE loop repeats (the body of the loop executes).

This statement implies that the body of the loop *must* modify one of the variables being tested in the BOOLEAN condition; otherwise, the loop will repeat indefinitely. Also, the loop does not execute even one time if the BOOLEAN condition is false. In Chapter 14, "The REPEAT Loop," you see a loop that always executes at least one time. As with most statements, examples should help clarify the WHILE loop considerably.

Examples

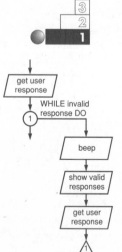

1. The following program checks the user's input to make sure that Y or N was entered. WHILE loops repeat as long as the BOOLEAN condition is true.

```
{ Filename: C13WHIL1.PAS }


{
   Input routine used to ensure that user types a correct
response.
   This routine might be part of a larger program.
}
PROGRAM WhileLoop1;
USES Crt;
VAR Ans: CHAR;                              { answer typed by user }

BEGIN
   CLRSCR;
   WRITE( 'Do you want to continue? (Y/N) ');
   READLN( Ans );
   WHILE ((UPCASE(Ans) <> 'Y') AND (UPCASE(Ans) <> 'N')) DO
```

```
BEGIN
   WRITELN( #7 );                    { beep }
   WRITELN( 'You must type Y or N' );
   WRITELN;
   WRITE( 'Do you want to continue? (Y/N) ' );
   READLN( Ans );
END;  {while}
END.  {WhileLoop1}
```

Notice there are two WRITE-READLN statements that do the same thing. The initial WRITE-READLN statements outside the WHILE loop must be done to get an answer that the WHILE loop can check for. If the user types something other than Y or N, the program prints an error message, asks for another answer, and loops back to check the answer again.

The WHILE loop tests for the BOOLEAN condition at the top of the loop. That is why the loop might never execute; if the test is initially false, the loop does not execute even once. The following code shows the output from this program. The program repeats indefinitely until the BOOLEAN condition is false (until the user types either Y, y, N, or n).

```
Do you want to continue? (Y/N) h

You must type Y or N

Do you want to continue? (Y/N) q

You must type Y or N

Do you want to continue? (Y/N) y
```

This example introduces another Turbo Pascal function, UPCASE. UPCASE requires one parameter of type CHAR. For example, if the parameter is *t*, then UPCASE(t) converts it to uppercase and returns T. If the character is already uppercase, the function does nothing. Table 13.1 illustrates use of the UPCASE function.

Table 13.1. UPCASE **function examples.**

Original Parameter	UPCASE (Parameter)
a	A
d	D
E	E
G	G
9	9
&	&

If you did not use UPCASE in the above example, you would have had to check for Y, y, N, and n as possible valid user responses. With UPCASE, you can simplify the BOOLEAN condition. Without UPCASE, you would have to write:

```
WHILE ((Ans <> 'Y') AND (Ans <> 'N') AND
       (Ans <> 'y') AND (Ans <> 'n')) DO
```

Because the WHILE executes until the condition is false, it is known as an *indeterminate loop* because you do not know in advance how many cycles of the loop will be made (unlike the FOR loop).

2. The following code fragment is an example of how *not* to use a WHILE loop. See whether you can find the problem.

```
A := 10;
B := 20;
WHILE (A > 5) DO
   BEGIN
      WRITELN( A, B );
      B := B - 1;
   END;   {while}
```

This WHILE loop is an endless loop. At least one of the statements inside the WHILE statement must change the control variable or the condition will always be true and the WHILE will always loop. Because A does not change inside the WHILE loop, the program never ends without the user's Ctrl–Break intervention.

3. In getting input from users, it often is wise to perform *data validation* on the values they type. If users enter bad values (for instance, a negative number when the input cannot be negative), you can inform them of the problem and ask them to reenter the input.

Not all data can be validated, but most of it can be checked to see that it's reasonable. For example, if you write a record-keeping program to track each student's name, address, age, and other pertinent data, you can check to see whether the given age falls within a reasonable range. If the user enters 213 for the age, you know that the value is incorrect. If the user enters -4 for the age, you know that the input value also is incorrect. If the student is 21 and types 22, however, your program has no way of knowing whether the age is correct, because 22 falls within a reasonable range.

The following program section is a routine that requests an age and checks to make sure that it is less than 100 and more than 14. This test certainly is not foolproof, because the user still can enter an incorrect age. The program can, however, detect an unreasonable age.

```
{ Filename: C13AGE1.PAS }


{ Program that helps ensure that age values are reasonable }
PROGRAM Age1;
USES Crt;
VAR   Age: INTEGER;                      { age typed by user }

BEGIN
   CLRSCR;
   WRITE( 'What is the student''s age? ' );
   READLN( Age );
   WHILE NOT ((Age > 14) AND (Age < 100)) DO
      BEGIN
         WRITELN( #7 );
         WRITELN( '*** The age must be between 14 and 100 ***' );
```

```
            WRITELN( 'Try again...' );
            WRITELN;
            WRITE( 'What is the student''s age? ' );
            READLN( Age );
         END;  {while}
      WRITELN( 'You typed a valid age.' );
   END.  {Age1}
```

This routine can be a section of a longer program. This program uses WRITELN statements to warn users that they have entered an incorrect age.

If the entered age is less than 14, users get an error message. The same is true if the age is too large (over 100). The program continues to beep and warn users about the incorrect age until they enter a more reasonable age.

Here is the output of the previous program:

```
What is the student's age? 2

*** The age must be between 14 and 100 ***
Try again.

What is the student's age? 24
You typed a valid age.
```

4. When your program checks for valid data-entry values, you can sometimes use the SET type. Rather than use complicated BOOLEAN conditions, you simply list the valid answers in brackets. A set in Turbo Pascal differs from a math set in three respects:

A Turbo Pascal set can have a maximum of 256 members.

A Turbo Pascal set requires that all set members be of the same *ordinal type.*

A Turbo Pascal set has a maximum size of 32 bytes.

Turbo Pascal uses bits to save the members of a set. Because there is a maximum of 256 members in a set, the maximum size for a set is 256 divided by 8 bits per byte— or 32 bytes.

NOTE: An ordinal type consists of values that may be ordered in a finite list. This means it must be a *simple type*. Simple types include all integer types, BOOLEAN, CHAR, and enumerated types. For example, type BYTE consists of numbers from 0 to 255. There is a definite order and the type has a definite list of possible values. The definition for the BOOLEAN type is (FALSE, TRUE). In contrast, reals and strings are not simple types.

TIP: Because of the 32-byte size limit for sets, avoid using sets of numbers. For example, if you want to test if a number, Num, is in a range from 0 to 255, you cannot use IF Num IN [0..255]. When Turbo Pascal attempts to build this set, only the first 32 bytes are used. This means that only numbers 0 to 31 fit in the set. If Num is greater than 31, the results will be unpredictable because Turbo Pascal will be using whatever happens to be in memory past the set. Also, you cannot have a set such as [1.2, 1.3, 1.4] or ['company', 'client', 'city', 'state', 'zip'] because the set elements are not simple types.

Here is the first example rewritten to show how to use sets:

```
{ Filename: C13WHIL2.PAS }


{
  Input routine used to ensure that user types a correct
response.
  This routine might be part of a larger program.
}
PROGRAM WhileLoop2;
USES Crt;
VAR Ans: CHAR;                         { answer typed by user }

BEGIN
   CLRSCR;
   WRITE( 'Do you want to continue? (Y/N) ');
   READLN( Ans );
   WHILE NOT (Ans IN ['Y','N','y','n']) DO
```

```
    BEGIN
       WRITELN( #7 );                     { beep }
       WRITELN( 'You must type Y or N' );
       WRITELN;
       WRITE( 'Do you want to continue? (Y/N) ' );
       READLN( Ans );
    END;   {while}
END.   {WhileLoop2}
```

The valid responses are listed inside brackets: ['Y','N','y','n']. IN is used to check whether the user response is in the set. When you use NOT with a set, be sure to use parentheses to surround the complete SET statement. You cannot use

```
WHILE Ans NOT IN ['Y','N','y','n'] DO       { wrong! }
```

Alternatively, to illustrate positive logic, the example could have used

```
WHILE Ans IN ['A'..'M','O'..'W','Z','a'..'m','o'..'w','z'] DO
```

Notice how you can use two dots to define a subrange of a set. To reduce the size of the above set, use:

```
WHILE UPCASE(Ans) IN ['A'..'M','O'..'W','Z'] DO
```

5. The following program is a "poor man's word processor." It accepts lines of input from the keyboard and sends that input to the printer. You can use this simple text-to-printer program to turn your computer into a typewriter.

The program keeps looping for another line until TextLine is the null string (''). TextLine becomes the null string when the user presses Enter without typing anything.

```
{  Filename: C13TYPE.PAS }

{
  Program that loops to get input lines and sends
  them to the printer.
}
PROGRAM TypeWriter;
USES Crt, Printer;
```

```
VAR TextLine: STRING[80];              { line typed by user }

BEGIN
    CLRSCR;
    WRITELN( 'Typewriter program.' );
    WRITELN( '(Make sure your printer is on and has paper.)' );
    WRITELN( 'To Quit, press Enter with no text' );
    WRITELN( 'Please type your text' );
    WRITE( '? ' );
    READLN( TextLine );
    WHILE (TextLine <> '') DO
        BEGIN
            WRITELN(LST, TextLine );
            WRITE( '? ' );
            READLN( TextLine );
        END;   {while}
END.   {TypeWriter}
```

6. A mathematician once found an easy way to approximate the square root of any number. Subtract from any number the odd numbers (1, 3, 5, and so on) in succession. When you reach 0 or less, the square root is the number of subtractions it took to reach 0.

For example, to find the square root of 49, start subtracting odd numbers until you reach (or go past) 0, as in

$49 - 1 = 48$

$48 - 3 = 45$

$45 - 5 = 40$

$40 - 7 = 33$

$33 - 9 = 24$

$24 - 11 = 13$

$13 - 13 = 0$

You have to subtract the first seven odd numbers to find the square root of 49. It is 7.

The following program computes the root of the number specified, using this odd-number subtraction method. Notice the program's use of the WHILE loop to count through the odd numbers as it subtracts.

```
{ Filename: C13SQRT.PAS }

{
  Program to approximate square root by subtracting
  consecutive odd numbers.
}
PROGRAM SquareRoot;
USES Crt;

VAR Count:   INTEGER;          { Count odd numbers used }
    OddNum:  INTEGER;          { Odd numbers }
    Num:     INTEGER;          { User's number }
    NumSave: INTEGER;          { Save copy of Num }

BEGIN
  Count   := 0;
  OddNum  := 1;                { First odd number }
  CLRSCR;
  WRITE( 'What number do you want the square root of? ');
  READ( Num );
  NumSave := Num;              { Save copy - Num
                                  modified later }
  WHILE (Num > 0) DO
    BEGIN
        DEC(Num,OddNum);        { Subtract odd number }
        INC(OddNum,2);          { Get next odd number }
        INC(Count);             { Count odd numbers used }
    END;  {while}               { Quit when reach zero }
  IF (Num < 0) THEN DEC(Count); { Went 1 too far if < 0 }
  WRITELN( 'The square root of ', NumSave,
           ' is approximately ', Count );
END.  {SquareRoot}
```

When you have a loop that is performing various calculations, you usually want the loop to execute as fast as possible. INC and DEC are designed especially for fast, tight loops.

```
DEC(Num,OddNum); is faster than  Num := Num - OddNum;
INC(OddNum,2);   is faster than  OddNum := OddNum + 2;
INC(Count)       is faster than  Count := Count + 1;
```

Because DEC(Count) is outside the WHILE loop, using DEC(Count) instead of Count := Count - 1; does not significantly improve execution speed.

Summary

This chapter showed you how to use the WHILE loop. If you do not know the exact number of times a loop needs to execute, a WHILE loop might be the correct structure to use. It's an advantage to use the WHILE loop over the FOR loop when the loop might not need to execute. A WHILE loop continues to execute as long as a certain condition is true. When that condition no longer is true, the WHILE loop stops.

Review Questions

Answers to the Review Questions appear in Appendix B.

1. True or False: More than one statement can appear in the body of a WHILE loop.

2. True or False: The body of a WHILE loop always executes at least once.

3. What Turbo Pascal statements are especially useful in loops doing calculations?

4. How does the test of a WHILE loop differ from that of a FOR loop?

5. How many times does the body of the following loop execute?

```
A := 10;
WHILE (A > 5) DO WRITELN( 'Careful!' );
```

6. What is the output of the following program?

```
A := 10;
WRITELN( 'Here''s the loop:' );
WHILE (A < 10) DO WRITELN( 'Turbo Pascal' );
```

Exercises

1. Write a program with a WHILE loop that prints the numbers from 10 to 20 with a blank line between each number.

2. Write a program to ask the user for a number between 1 and 10. Have the program prompt the user by making the program beep the desired number of times. For example, to prompt for the number 3, beep three times and wait for the user to type 3.

3. Write a program using WHILE that prints the ASCII characters from number 65 through 90 (these are the uppercase letters from A through Z). Immediately following that loop, print the characters backward using a WHILE loop.

4. Use a WHILE loop to produce the following pattern of letters:

```
A
AB
ABC
ABCD
ABCDE
```

The REPEAT Loop

The FOR and WHILE loops are two ways to control a loop. If you know that the loop must execute a specific number of times, the FOR loop is the best loop to use. If the number of times the loop must execute is indeterminate and the loop might not need to execute at all, the WHILE loop is the appropriate loop to use.

If the number of times the loop must execute is indeterminate but you know that the loop must execute at least once, then the REPEAT loop is the loop to use.

This chapter shows you how to program the REPEAT loop.

After completing this chapter, you will know every command Turbo Pascal offers to control the execution of a loop.

> The body of a REPEAT loop always executes at least once.

Using the REPEAT Loop

The format of the REPEAT is

REPEAT UNTIL test is true

```
REPEAT
    statement1;
    statement2;
        ⋮
UNTIL BOOLEAN condition is true;
```

Although the REPEAT loop is similar to the WHILE loop, they have three main differences:

◆ The REPEAT loop has the BOOLEAN condition occur at the *bottom* of the loop. This ensures that the body of the loop executes at least once. The WHILE loop has the BOOLEAN condition at the top of the loop.

◆ The body of the REPEAT loop continues to execute as long as the BOOLEAN condition is false. A WHILE loop keeps looping as long as the BOOLEAN condition is true.

◆ Because the REPEAT loop always has a matching UNTIL statement, there is no need to use a BEGIN-END pair.

As with the WHILE loop, the body of the REPEAT loop *must* modify one of the variables being tested in the BOOLEAN condition; otherwise, the loop repeats indefinitely. The BOOLEAN condition can include any relational or compound BOOLEAN condition. You can use the same types of tests you used with the IF statement.

Because REPEAT executes until the test is true, it is known also as an *indeterminate loop* because you do not know in advance how many cycles of the loop will be made (similar to the WHILE loop).

You can put one or more statements between REPEAT and UNTIL. Because REPEAT and UNTIL enclose a loop, indent the body of the loop, as you did with the FOR and WHILE loops.

Checking at the bottom of the loop has its advantages at times. The following examples illustrate the REPEAT loop.

Examples

1. The REPEAT loop lets you make a little clearer the input-checking routine that was shown in Chapter 13, "The WHILE loop." Because the body of the loop always executes at least once, you need only one pair of WRITE-READLN statements to accomplish the same thing.

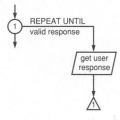

```
{ Filename: C14REP1.PAS }


{
   Input routine used to ensure that user types a correct
response.
   This routine might be part of a larger program.
}
PROGRAM GetInput;
USES Crt;

VAR Ans: CHAR;                              { answer typed by user }

BEGIN
   CLRSCR;
   REPEAT
      WRITE( 'Do you want to continue? (Y/N) ' );
      READLN( Ans );
   UNTIL Ans IN ['Y','N','y','n'];
   :
END.  {GetInput}
```

The READLN is not required before the loop starts because it is
the second statement in the loop and always executes at least
once. This gives the user a chance to enter the answer. If the
answer to the prompt is either Y or N (or y or n), the BOOLEAN
condition is satisfied (at the bottom of the loop), and the rest
of the program continues from there.

2. The following program is a brief example of using a
   decrementing counter.

```
{ Filename: C14CTDN.PAS }


{ Program to count down to a blast-off using REPEAT }
PROGRAM BlastOff;
USES Crt;
VAR Count: INTEGER;

BEGIN
   CLRSCR;
   Count := 10;                              { Begin the count... }
```

```
REPEAT
    WRITELN( Count );
    DEC(Count);
UNTIL (Count <= 0);                    { Do not loop past 1 }
    WRITELN( '*** Blast off! ***' );
END.  {BlastOff}
```

Here is the output from the preceding program.

```
10
9
8
7
6
5
4
3
2
1
*** Blast off! ***
```

3. The following program is an example of how *not* to use a
   REPEAT loop. See whether you can find the problem.

```
A := 1;
B := 20;
REPEAT
    WRITELN( A, B );
    DEC(B);
UNTIL (A > 5);
```

This REPEAT loop is an endless loop. At least one of the statements inside the loop must change the control variable;
otherwise, the condition will always be true and the REPEAT
will always loop. Because A does not change inside the REPEAT
loop, the program never ends without the user's Ctrl–Break
intervention.

4. In addition to READ and READLN, Turbo Pascal also has the
   READKEY statement. With READKEY you have control over most
   keystrokes that a user would type. READKEY is a function and
   returns a character.

```
{ Filename: C14GSTR.PAS }

{
   Illustrates how to get a user's input on a character-by-
   character basis.
}
PROGRAM GetString;
USES Crt;
CONST Null     = '';                    { Null string }
      EnterKey = #13;                   { Carriage-return value }
                                        { from ASCII table }
VAR   Ch:      CHAR;                     { character typed by user }
      UserStr: STRING[80];              { user's resulting string }
BEGIN
   CLRSCR;
   WRITELN( 'Type some characters and then press Enter.' );
   UserStr := Null;
   REPEAT
      Ch := READKEY;
      IF Ch <> EnterKey
         THEN BEGIN
                 WRITE( Ch );
                 UserStr := UserStr + Ch;
              END;
   UNTIL (Ch = EnterKey);
   WRITELN;
   WRITELN( 'You typed: ',UserStr);
END.  {GetString}
```

This program checks for only the regular keys. It does not
check for function keys and combinations of keys. Notice
that you must be careful not to add the final carriage return
(Enter) value to the user's string. When the user presses
Enter, that keystroke should signal the end of the string—not
become part of the string.

This example also illustrates a good application of WRITE. The
program needs WRITE or WRITELN to show what you type. If
you used WRITELN, you would get one character per line. With
WRITE, the characters stay on the same line and Turbo Pascal
automatically adjusts the cursor for you.

5. The following program requests a list of numbers. As the list of numbers is input, the program adds them to a total and counts them. When the user enters a 0, the program computes the final total and average. The 0 is not part of the list. It signals the end of input.

```
{ Filename: C14Add1.PAS }


{
  Program that accepts a list of numbers and shows the
  total and average.
}
PROGRAM Adder;
USES Crt;
VAR Total: INTEGER;          { running total }
    Count: INTEGER;          { # of numbers typed by user }
    Num:   INTEGER;          { number typed by user }

BEGIN
    Total := 0;                      { Init variables }
    Count := 0;
                                     { Get input until get 0 }
    CLRSCR;
    REPEAT
       WRITE( 'What is your number (0 will end the input)? ' );
       READLN( Num );
       INC(Total,Num);
       IF Num <> 0 THEN INC(Count);   { Don't count 0 }
    UNTIL (Num = 0);
                                     { Control gets here }
                                     { when last number = 0 }

    WRITELN;
    WRITELN( 'The total is ', Total );
    WRITELN( 'The average is ', (Total / Count):1:2);
END.  {Adder}
```

Notice that the program works even if 0 is entered as the first number. The WRITE statement also informs the user of the way to end the input. Because an average often is not an integer, the program shows the result as a real number with formatting to two decimal places. Figure 14.1 shows a sample run of the program.

```
What is your number (0 will end the input)? 45
What is your number (0 will end the input)? 43
What is your number (0 will end the input)? 22
What is your number (0 will end the input)? 56
What is your number (0 will end the input)? 76
What is your number (0 will end the input)? 5
What is your number (0 will end the input)? 0

The total is 247
The average is 41.17
```

Figure 14.1. Using a REPEAT to obtain user input.

The use of FOR, WHILE, or REPEAT loops to process data values is up to you. Which one you choose depends on which one best suits the application. The more comfortable you are with your code, the cleaner it will be, and the easier it will be to maintain in the future.

Summary

This chapter showed you how to use the REPEAT loop. If you do not know the exact number of times that a loop needs to execute, a REPEAT loop might be the right structure to use. If you know that the loop must execute at least once, the REPEAT loop probably is a better choice than the WHILE loop.

Review Questions

Answers to the Review Questions appear in Appendix B.

1. True or False: More than one statement can appear in the body of a REPEAT loop.

2. Is the test at the top or the bottom of the following loops?

   A. REPEAT UNTIL

   B. WHILE

3. True or False: The body of a REPEAT loop always executes at least once.

4. How does the test of a REPEAT loop differ from that of a WHILE loop?

5. How many times does the body of this loop occur?

```
A := 0;
REPEAT
    WRITELN( 'Careful!' );
UNTIL (A > 5);
```

6. What is the output of the following program?

```
A := 10;
WRITELN( 'Here's the loop:' );
REPEAT
    WRITELN( 'Turbo Pascal' );
UNTIL (A <= 10);
```

Exercises

1. Write a program with a REPEAT loop that prints the letters *a* through *z*.

2. Write a program with a REPEAT to ask the user for a number from 1 to 10. When you get the number, make the program beep that many times.

3. Write a program using the REPEAT loop that prints the ASCII characters from number 65 to number 90 (these are the uppercase letters *A* through *Z*). Immediately following that loop, print the characters backward using another REPEAT loop.

4. Use a REPEAT loop to count the letters in the words of any sentence you type. Do not count spaces or apostrophes.

The IF-THEN-ELSE Statement

This chapter is one of the most important chapters in the book. It teaches you few new statements; however, it shows how you can build on the conditional IF statement to create truly well-written, structured programs. When you sit down to write a program, you should always think about how easy it should be to follow, how little it should jump from place to place, and how well-documented (with ample comments) it should be.

This chapter introduces you to the IF-THEN-ELSE statement. Here you learn how to create powerful, but readable, conditional logic that performs complicated decision-making with little effort from you or your program.

Styles Come and Go....

When PCs were first gaining popularity in the early 1980s, several magazines and books were written describing these new machines and how to program them. Memory and disk space were at a premium. Compared to today, RAM and disk memory were small and expensive.

continues

Programmers learned to make the most of the small memory by writing compact, tight code that did much in little space. Eventually, such programmers were praised for their wit and insight when magazines started offering prizes for *one-liners*, which are complete programs that do many things on one line.

Graphics screens, music, and math puzzles were programmed in a single line. Variable names were kept to single letters, and programmers avoided large constants for the sake of saving space.

Today, the tide has turned. Programmers have much more room in which to work. The short, quick, and tight one-liners have been replaced by well-documented programs with ample white space and better development. Programs are not constant. The world is forever changing, and programs must be modified to take advantage of those changes. To ensure your future as a programmer, stay away from one-liners and produce well-documented code that does its job well and clearly.

Using the IF-THEN-ELSE Statement

An IF-THEN statement can have an optional ELSE statement. This section introduces the ELSE statement by showing you the IF-THEN-ELSE compound statement in its simplest format:

```
IF BOOLEAN condition is true
     THEN BEGIN
               statement1;
               statement2;
                  ⋮
          END
     ELSE BEGIN
               statementa;
               statementb;
                  ⋮
          END;
```

BLOCK: One or more statements treated as though they are a single statement.

The first part of this statement is identical to the IF-THEN described in Chapter 11, "Comparing Data." Often you will want to perform several statements if the IF test is true. There also might be several statements you want performed if the ELSE portion is true. If more than one statement is associated with the THEN or with the ELSE, then the statements are blocked with a BEGIN-END pair. If only one statement is associated with the THEN or ELSE, then the BEGIN-END pair is optional.

In computer terminology, a *block* is generally one or more statements treated as though they are a single statement.

BOOLEAN condition = true, statement following THEN executes.

If the BOOLEAN condition is true, Turbo Pascal executes the statement or statements following THEN. If the BOOLEAN condition is false, however, Turbo Pascal executes instead the statement or statements following ELSE.

BOOLEAN condition = false, statement following ELSE executes.

The simple IF-THEN determines only what happens when the BOOLEAN condition is true. The IF-THEN-ELSE determines what happens if the BOOLEAN condition is true as well as what happens if the BOOLEAN condition is false. Regardless of the outcome, the statement following the IF-THEN-ELSE executes next.

> **NOTE:** If the BOOLEAN condition is true, the block of statements following THEN is performed.
>
> If the BOOLEAN condition is false, the block of statements following ELSE is performed.

The IF-THEN-ELSE statement enables you to create well-structured programs. All the statements associated with the true BOOLEAN condition are packaged together with the THEN part; all the statements associated with the false BOOLEAN condition are packaged together with the ELSE part.

> **NOTE:** Recall that Turbo Pascal uses the semicolon as a statement separator. IF-THEN-ELSE is one statement. This means that you put a semicolon after the ELSE part—not after the THEN. If you are using only IF-THEN, then you put the semicolon after the THEN part.

Examples

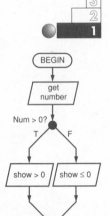

1. The following program asks the user for a number. It then displays a message indicating whether the number is greater than or less than 0, using the IF-THEN-ELSE statement.

```
{ Filename: C15IFEL1.PAS }


{
 Program demonstrates IF-THEN-ELSE by displaying
 whether an input value is greater than or less than 0.
}
PROGRAM Guess1;
USES Crt;
CONST MaxCount = 5;
VAR   Num:    INTEGER;          { number typed by user }
      NumCnt: INTEGER;          { # of numbers typed by user }

BEGIN
   CLRSCR;
   NumCnt := 0;
   REPEAT
     WRITE( 'What is your number? ' );
     READLN( Num );
     IF (Num > 0)
        THEN WRITELN( 'More than 0' )   { No semicolon here }
        ELSE WRITELN( 'Less or equal to 0' );
     INC(NumCnt);
     WRITELN;
   UNTIL ((NumCnt >= MaxCount) OR (Num = 0));
   WRITELN( 'Thanks for your time!' );
END.   {Guess1}
```

Because only one statement is associated with the THEN and also with the ELSE, there is no need to use a BEGIN-END pair. Notice that a semicolon comes after the ELSE part of the IF-THEN-ELSE and not after the THEN.

2. The following program is an improvement over some of the input routines you have seen so far. It uses the IF-THEN-ELSE to test the user's response to a yes or no question. You can

incorporate this program into your own programs just as the book-management database program in the back of the book does.

If the user answers the yes or no question with a Y or an N, the program completes normally. (You typically execute certain code depending on the answer.) If the user does not type a Y or an N, however, the program prompts for a correct response inside the block.

```
{ Filename: C15YN.PAS }


{ Checks the input using the IF-THEN-ELSE. }
PROGRAM YesNo;
USES Crt;
VAR Ans: CHAR;                            { answer typed by user }

BEGIN
    CLRSCR;
    REPEAT
        WRITE( 'What is your answer? (Y/N) ' );
        READLN( Ans );
        IF (UPCASE(Ans) IN ['Y','N'])    { Valid response? }
            THEN WRITELN( 'Thank you.' ) { Show thanks }
            ELSE BEGIN                    { Show problem }
                    WRITELN( #7 );
                    WRITELN;
                    WRITELN( 'You must enter a Y or an N!' );
                    WRITELN( 'Please try again...' );
                    WRITELN;
                END;
        WRITELN;
    UNTIL (UPCASE(Ans) IN ['Y','N']);
            { Rest of program would go here }
END.   {YesNo}
```

Figure 15.1 shows the result of running this program. The user takes a while to type an N or a Y. The program keeps looping until the user succeeds in typing a valid response.

```
What is your answer? (Y/N) s

You must enter a Y or an N!
Please try again...

What is your answer? (Y/N) 6

You must enter a Y or an N!
Please try again...

What is your answer? (Y/N) y
Thank you.
```

Figure 15.1. Validating data with the IF-THEN-ELSE.

The indention makes this program very readable without affecting the program's operation. Every time a new block begins, it is preceded by another set of three spaces.

3. The following program is an example of using string variables to display a message. The program asks for a name. If the name is in the list of club members, a message saying so is displayed. Otherwise, a message is displayed saying that the person is not a member.

The IF-THEN-ELSE helps build the message string as shown here:

```
{ Filename: C15CLUB.PAS }

{ Determines whether the input name is a member of the club. }
PROGRAM Club1;
USES Crt;

CONST ClubName1 = 'Johnson';      { Members' last names }
      ClubName2 = 'Smith';
      ClubName3 = 'Brown';
```

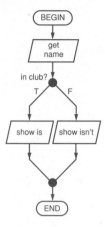

```
VAR   Msg:       STRING[5];      { show "is" or "isn't" }
      Message:   STRING[30];     { complete message to show }
      Person:    STRING[10];     { name typed by user }

BEGIN
   CLRSCR;
   WRITE( 'What is the person''s last name? ' );
   READLN( Person );
   IF ((Person = ClubName1) OR
       (Person = ClubName2) OR
       (Person = ClubName3))
      THEN Msg := 'is'            { No semicolon here }
      ELSE Msg := 'isn''t';
   Message := Person + ' ' + Msg + ' ' + 'in club.';
   WRITELN( Message );
END.   {Club1}
```

Notice how the message is built from the result of the
IF-THEN-ELSE. When you type a name, it must match exactly.
For example, if you type brown, the program responds that
brown isn't in club.

Because Turbo Pascal requires that sets consist of an *ordinal
type*, you cannot use strings in a set. For example, you cannot
define a set constant like this:

```
ClubList = ['Johnson','Smith','Brown'];  { not valid! }
```

4. The following routine can be used by the book management
   database application in Appendix E. The routine asks for an
   edition of the book and prints an appropriate message to a
   label on the printer.

```
{ Filename: C15BOOK.PAS }


{ Program to print a label for a book's edition. }
PROGRAM Book;
USES Crt, Printer;
VAR Ed: INTEGER;                          { edition }
```

```
BEGIN
   CLRSCR;
   WRITE( 'What is the book''s edition (1, 2, 3, ...) ' );
   READLN( Ed );

{ Print a label based on that number }
   IF (Ed = 1)
    THEN WRITELN(LST, '1st Edition' )
    ELSE IF (Ed = 2)
     THEN WRITELN(LST, '2nd Edition' )
     ELSE IF (Ed = 3)
      THEN WRITELN(LST, '3rd Edition' )
      ELSE IF (Ed = 4)
       THEN WRITELN(LST, '4th Edition' )
       ELSE IF (Ed = 5)
        THEN WRITELN(LST, '5th Edition' )
        ELSE WRITELN(LST, 'Older edition' );
END.  {Book}
```

This program helps to show that a long multiple-case IF can be confusing if it is overused. Rather than use three spaces for indenting, this program uses just one.

5. The following program uses GOTOXY, TEXTCOLOR, TEXTBACKGROUND, and the IF-THEN-ELSE to display a message on-screen in several colors and at several locations. The IF-THEN-ELSE controls the location of the cursor to keep it within the screen's boundaries.

```
{ Filename: C15SCRN.PAS }

{ Fancy screen displaying program. }
PROGRAM Fancy1;
USES Crt;
CONST Msg = 'Turbo Pascal';              { Message to show }
VAR Foregrnd:          BYTE;             { Foreground color }
    Backgrnd:          BYTE;             { Background color }
    Row:       BYTE;                     { Row to show message }
    Col:       BYTE;                     { Column to show message }

BEGIN
   Foregrnd  := LIGHTGRAY;
```

```
    Backgrnd  := BLACK;
    Row       := 1;
    Col       := 1;
    TEXTCOLOR( Foregrnd );
    TEXTBACKGROUND( Backgrnd );
    CLRSCR;                        {Paint screen BLACK}
    REPEAT
       GOTOXY( Col, Row );
       WRITELN( Msg );
                                   { Add 1 to col, row, Foregrnd, }
                                   { Backgrnd, unless they are }
                                   { out of bounds }

       IF (Row < 24)
          THEN INC(Row)
          ELSE Row := 1;
       IF (Col < 68)
          THEN INC(Col)
          ELSE Col := 1;
       IF (Foregrnd < WHITE)
          THEN INC(Foregrnd)
          ELSE Foregrnd := LIGHTGRAY;
       IF (Backgrnd < LIGHTGRAY)
          THEN INC(Backgrnd)
          ELSE Backgrnd := BLACK;
       TEXTCOLOR( Foregrnd );          { Next message color }
       TEXTBACKGROUND( Backgrnd );
    UNTIL KEYPRESSED;
END.  {Fancy}
```

This program knows that the screen has only 25 rows and 80 columns. It makes sure that the row and column being displayed do not go past these boundaries. As long as the row and column values are within this range, the program adds 1 to both of them to ensure that Turbo Pascal is displayed in a different location each time through the loop. The Msg constant, Turbo Pascal, has 12 characters. The program could use 69 (80–12+1) as the right-most column and Turbo Pascal would fit on the line. However, when using WRITELNS, displaying a character in column 80 causes the screen to automatically scroll up one line. To avoid this scrolling, the program uses column 68 instead of 69 as the right-most starting column. Figure 15.2 shows a sample run of this program.

IF-THEN-ELSE logic controls the row and column values, as well as the foreground and background colors.

You have probably seen demo programs that run until you press a key. You can do this in Turbo Pascal with the KEYPRESSED function. As soon as you press any key, KEYPRESSED returns true and the program stops.

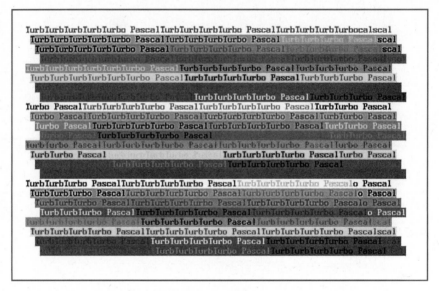

Figure 15.2. IF-THEN-ELSE in a REPEAT loop.

6. Suppose that you want to give an annual award to employees based on years of service to your company. You are giving a gold watch to those who have served more than 20 years, a paperweight to those with more than 10 years, and a pat on the back to everyone else.

One way to display these messages is with three separate IF-THEN statements. Here is one way:

```
{ Filename: C15SERV1.PAS }


{ Program to display a message depending on years of service. }
PROGRAM Service1;
USES Crt;
VAR Yrs: INTEGER;                     { years typed by user }

BEGIN
   CLRSCR;
   WRITE( 'How many years of service ' );
   READLN( Yrs );
   IF (Yrs > 20)
      THEN WRITELN( 'Give a gold watch' );

   IF ((Yrs > 10) AND (Yrs <= 20))
      THEN WRITELN( 'Give a paperweight' );

   IF (Yrs <= 10)
      THEN WRITELN( 'Give a pat on the back' );
END.   {Service1}
```

This program tests for the length of time and displays a matching message. There is no IF-THEN-ELSE, however, in this program. By rewriting the program to take advantage of this command, you can see that the readability is improved again, as shown here:

```
{ Filename: C15SERV2.PAS }

{
  Improved program to display a message
  depending on years of service using
  the IF-THEN-ELSE.
}
PROGRAM Service2;
USES Crt;
VAR Yrs: INTEGER;
BEGIN
   CLRSCR;
   WRITE( 'How many years of service ' );
   READLN( Yrs );
```

```
IF (Yrs > 20)
   THEN WRITELN( 'Give a gold watch' )
   ELSE IF ((Yrs > 10) AND (Yrs <= 20))
           THEN WRITELN( 'Give a paperweight' )
           ELSE WRITELN( 'Give a pat on the back' );
        END.  {Service2}
```

This program illustrates how another IF statement can be associated with the ELSE. Depending on the program requirements, you could have another IF statement associated with the THEN as well.

You probably should not rely on the IF-THEN-ELSE to take care of too many conditions, because having more than three or four conditions starts to get confusing again. (You can get into messy logic, such as *If this is true, and then if this is true, then do something, else if this is true do something, else if this is true do something,* and so on.) The CASE statement in Chapter 16 handles these types of multiple IF selections better than a long IF-THEN-ELSE.

7. When you mix IF-THEN and IF-THEN-ELSE statements, you should be careful to make sure that the ELSE matches the correct THEN. The ELSE always matches the last THEN.

   If you have an IF-THEN statement associated with the THEN, you might need to use a BEGIN-END pair because Turbo Pascal always matches an ELSE with the last THEN, as shown here:

```
Filename: C15IFEL2.PAS }

{ Show IF-THEN and IF-THEN-ELSE together. }
PROGRAM Match;
USES Crt;
VAR Num: INTEGER;

BEGIN
   CLRSCR;
   WRITE( 'Type a number ' );
```

```
      READLN( Num );
      IF Num < 10
         THEN BEGIN
                 IF Num = 5 THEN WRITELN( 'Num = 5' );
              END
         ELSE WRITELN( 'Num is 10 or more' );
      END.  {Match}
```

If you type 2, nothing happens. However, if you wrote the code using an IF-THEN-ELSE statement as:

```
IF Num < 10
   THEN IF Num = 5
           THEN WRITELN( 'Num = 5' )
   ELSE WRITELN( 'Num is 10 or more' );
```

If you type 2 this time, you get Num is 10 or more.

TIP: Sometimes you can make your code clearer by reversing the logic of the IF-THEN-ELSE statement. For example, if you reverse the preceding code fragment's logic, you get:

```
IF Num >= 10
  THEN WRITELN( 'Num is 10 or more' )
  ELSE IF Num = 5
     THEN WRITELN( 'Num = 5' );
```

Summary

You now have the tools to write powerful programming constructions. This chapter showed how you can use the ELSE statement, which gives the IF statement another option for its BOOLEAN condition.

Chapter 16 introduces the CASE statement, which adds readability to your multiple-decision IF statements.

Review Questions

Answers to the Review Questions appear in Appendix B.

1. True or False: If more than one statement is associated with THEN, you must use a BEGIN-END pair.

2. True or False: The THEN statement can never end with a semicolon.

3. Rewrite the following code using an IF-THEN-ELSE:

```
VAR Done: BOOLEAN;
    Num:  INTEGER;
BEGIN
  ⋮
Done := (Num = 0);
  ⋮
```

4. True or False: If a decision has more than one branch, an IF-THEN-ELSE can be used.

5. What does the following code fragment display as output?

```
a := 6;
IF (a > 6)
   THEN WRITELN( 'George' )
   ELSE IF (a = 6)
           THEN WRITELN( 'Henry' )
           ELSE IF (a < 6)
                   THEN WRITELN( 'James' )
```

6. What is wrong with the following code fragment?

```
IF Num < 100
   THEN WRITELN( 'Num is OK ');
   ELSE WRITELN( 'Num should be less than 100' );
```

Review Exercises

1. Write a program that uses an IF-THEN statement which asks for a number (*n*) and displays the square (*n* * *n*) and the cube (*n* * *n* * *n*) of the input number, as long as the number is greater than 1. Otherwise, do not display anything.

2. Ask the user for three test scores. Display the largest of the three scores.

3. Ask the user for two numbers. Display a message telling how the first number compares to the second. In other words, if the user types 5 and 7, the program displays

   `5 is less than 7.`

4. Ask the user for an employee's annual salary before taxes. Display the employee's salary and taxes. The taxes are 10 percent of the salary if the employee made less than $10,000, 15 percent if the employee earned between $10,000 and $20,000, and 20 percent if the employee earned more than $20,000.

5. Ask the user for three numbers. Display a message telling the user whether any two of the numbers add up to the third.

6. Write a program to ask users for their first and last names. Then give them a choice from the following selection:

   Display your first and last name on-screen.

   Print your first and last name on the printer.

   Display your name, last name first, on-screen.

   Print your name, last name first, on the printer.

   Ask the users which option they choose, and then give them a chance to input that option's value (1, 2, 3, or 4, for example). Depending on their response, perform that option. (This is called a *menu* program because it gives users a chance to order what they want, similar to ordering food from a restaurant menu.)

7. Write a simplified equivalent code fragment for the following:

```
IF Ch IN ['/',' ','.',';','?','!']
    THEN BEGIN
            EndWord := TRUE;
            IF Ch IN ['.','?','!']
                THEN EndSentence := TRUE
                ELSE EndSentence := FALSE;
        END
    ELSE EndWord := FALSE;
```

The CASE Statement

This chapter focuses on the CASE statement, which improves on the IF-THEN-ELSE statement by streamlining the "IF within an IF" construction.

This chapter introduces:

♦ The CASE statement

♦ The HALT statement

The CASE statement is similar to an IF that has multiple selections. If you have mastered the IF-THEN-ELSE statement, you should have little trouble with CASE. By learning the CASE statement, you will be able to write menus and multiple choice data-entry programs with ease.

Introducing CASE

This chapter develops the CASE statement by starting with a simple form and then adding options. The format of CASE is a little longer than the statements you have seen so far. The format of the CASE statement is

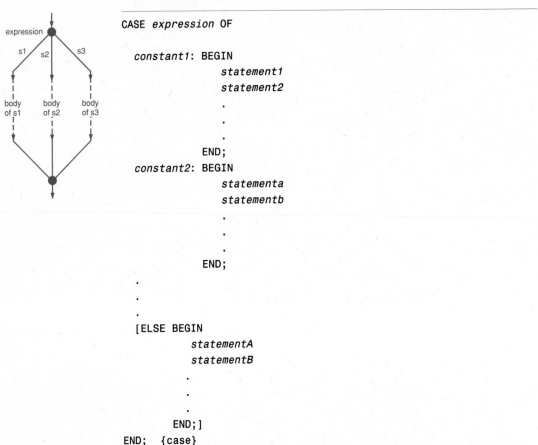

```
CASE expression OF

    constant1: BEGIN
                    statement1
                    statement2
                    .
                    .
                    .
               END;
    constant2: BEGIN
                    statementa
                    statementb
                    .
                    .
                    .
               END;
    .
    .
    .
    [ELSE BEGIN
             statementA
             statementB
             .
             .
             .
         END;]
END;   {case}
```

Your application determines the number of CASE constants that follow the CASE line. The *constants* must be an *ordinal type* and must be

◆ One constant

◆ Several constants separated by commas

◆ A subrange

All CASE *constants* must match the type of the CASE *expression*. All CASE *constants* must be constants also—variables are not allowed.

If you have more than one *statement* associated with a CASE constant, you must block them with a BEGIN-END pair. If you have only one *statement* associated with a CASE constant, the BEGIN-END pair is optional.

The use of CASE is easier than its format might lead you to believe. A CASE statement usually is easier to follow than an IF-THEN-ELSE.

Do not hesitate to use IF-THEN-ELSE, however. It is not a bad statement, nor is it difficult to follow. When the *BOOLEAN condition* that determines the choice is complex and contains many AND and OR operators, the IF is the better alternative. The CASE statement is preferred when there are multiple-choice possibilities based on one decision.

The following set of examples clarifies the CASE statement. They compare the CASE to the IF-THEN-ELSE.

Examples

1. Suppose you are writing a program to teach your child how to count. Your program should ask the child for a number from 1 to 5. The program then beeps that number of times.

   The program can assume that the child presses a number from 1 to 5. The following program uses the IF-THEN-ELSE to accomplish the counting program.

```
{ Filename: C16CNT1.PAS }

{ Get a number from the child (you may have to help) }

{ Beep a certain number of times. }
PROGRAM Count1;
USES Crt;
CONST B = #7 + ' ';              { Beep speaker and show space }

VAR Num: INTEGER;                { Number typed by user }
```

```
BEGIN
   CLRSCR;
   WRITE( 'Please type a number: ');
   READLN( Num );

   IF (Num = 1)
     THEN WRITE( B)
     ELSE IF (Num = 2)
             THEN WRITE( B,B )
             ELSE IF (Num = 3)
                     THEN WRITE( B,B,B )
                     ELSE IF (Num = 4)
                             THEN WRITE( B, B, B, B )
                             ELSE IF (Num = 5)
                                     THEN WRITE( B, B, B, B, B );
END.  {Count1}
```

Notice that if the child types anything other than 1 through 5, the program ignores the number. This program also illustrates the advantage of using a constant, B. If you decide later to use an ASCII character other than #7, you need to change only one statement.

The following program improves on the preceding one by substituting a CASE statement for the IF-THEN-ELSE.

```
{ Filename: C16CNT2.PAS }

{ Get a number from the child (you may have to help) }

{ Beep a certain number of times. }
PROGRAM Count2;
USES Crt;
CONST B = #7 + ' ';                { Beep speaker and show space }

VAR Num: INTEGER;                  { Number typed by user }
BEGIN
   CLRSCR;
   WRITE( 'Please type a number: ');
   READLN( Num );
   CASE Num OF
```

```
   1: WRITE( B );
   2: WRITE( B, B );
   3: WRITE( B, B, B );
   4: WRITE( B, B, B, B );
   5: WRITE( B, B, B, B , B );
  END;  {case}
END.  {Count2}
```

Notice how much easier this multiple-choice program is to follow. It is obvious that the value of the variable Num controls the execution. Only the CASE constant that matches Num executes. The indention helps separate the CASE constants from each other.

The CASE statement has another advantage: If none of the cases' constants match the input value, nothing happens. The program continues to the statement following END; {case} without performing any of the cases. If the child types a 7, therefore, nothing happens.

If there are duplicate case constants, Turbo Pascal executes only the first one it finds. After execution, Turbo Pascal jumps to the END part of the CASE. For example, you might have a case constant specifying a subrange and another case constant that specifies a value already included in the subrange:

```
CASE x OF
   1..10: WRITELN('x is between 1 and 10, inclusive');
   5:     WRITELN('x is 5');
END;  {case}
```

If the x in the above CASE has a value of 5, only the first WRITELN will execute. The second WRITELN never will be used.

2. If the child does not type a 1, 2, 3, 4, or 5, nothing happens in the preceding program. Here is the same program modified to take advantage of the CASE ELSE option. The CASE ELSE block of statements executes if none of the previous cases were true.

```
{ Filename: C16CNT3.PAS }

{ Get a number from the child (you may have to help) }

{ Beep a certain number of times. }
PROGRAM Count3;
USES Crt;
CONST B = #7 + ' ';                { Beep speaker and show space }

VAR Num: INTEGER;                  { Number typed by user }
BEGIN
    CLRSCR;
    WRITE( 'Please type a number: ');
    READLN( Num );
    CASE Num OF
      1: WRITE( B );
      2: WRITE( B, B );
      3: WRITE( B, B, B );
      4: WRITE( B, B, B, B );
      5: WRITE( B, B, B, B , B );
      ELSE WRITELN( 'You must type a number 1, 2, 3, 4, or 5!' );
    END;  {case}
END.  {Count3}
```

If the child types a number other than 1 through 5, the program requests that only 1 through 5 be typed.

3. Unfortunately, the expression that controls the CASE cannot be a string variable. The expression must evaluate to an ordinal value. In the following program, a department number must be typed rather than a department name.

```
{ Filename: C16DEPT.PAS }

{
  Display a meeting message to certain people.
  Their department determines the message displayed.
}

PROGRAM Dept1;
USES Crt;
VAR Dept: INTEGER;              { department typed by user }
```

```
BEGIN
   CLRSCR;
   WRITELN( '*** Message Center ***' );
   WRITELN;
   WRITE( 'What department are you in? (100 - 500) ' );
   READLN( Dept );
   CASE Dept OF
     100: WRITELN( 'Your meeting is at 9:00 this morning.' );
     200: WRITELN( 'Your meeting is at 10:00 this morning.' );
     300: WRITELN( 'You have no meetings this week.' );
     400: WRITELN( 'You have 2 meetings on Tuesday at 1 & 3.' );
     500: WRITELN( 'You have no meetings this week.' );
     ELSE WRITELN( 'I do not recognize your department.' );
   END;  {case}
END.   {Dept1}
```

The following code shows the result of running this program. It can be part of a larger program used by office employees to get messages. The employees must type their department number; otherwise, the message is not displayed. If an employee types a department number greater than 500, an error message is displayed.

```
*** Message Center ***

What department are you in? (100 - 500) 400
You have 2 meetings on Tuesday at 1 & 3.
```

4. The CASE is ideal for handling a menu. As mentioned in the exercises at the end of Chapter 15, "The IF-THEN-ELSE Statement," a menu is simply a selection of options the user can order the computer to perform. Rather than users having to remember many commands, they can look at a menu of choices that you display and select one of the choices from the menu. The book management program in Appendix E uses the CASE statement in all its menus.

The following program is an adaptation of the math tutorial program shown at the end of Chapter 7, "Turbo Pascal's Math Operators." It asks for two numbers and then asks users which type of math they want to perform. This program lets users check their math accuracy.

Although the program seems lengthy, most of it is made up of WRITELN statements. The CASE makes choosing from the menu straightforward.

```pascal
{ Filename: C16MATH1.PAS }

{ Program to practice math accuracy. }
PROGRAM Math1;
USES Crt;
CONST Delta = 0.000001;
VAR Num1:   REAL;                   { first number typed by user }
    Num2:   REAL;                   { second number typed by user }
    Choice: INTEGER;                { menu choice selected by user }

BEGIN
   TEXTCOLOR( WHITE );
   TEXTBACKGROUND( BLUE );          { white on blue }
   CLRSCR;
   WRITELN( '*** Math Practice ***' );
   WRITE( 'First number is ' );
   READLN( Num1 );
   WRITE( 'Second number is ' );
   READLN( Num2 );
   WRITELN;
   REPEAT
      WRITELN( 'Choose your option: ' );  { Display the menu }
      WRITELN( '1. Add ',      Num1:1:0, ' to ',   Num2:1:0 );
      WRITELN( '2. Subtract ', Num2:1:0, ' from ', Num1:1:0 );
      WRITELN( '3. Multiply ', Num1:1:0, ' and ',  Num2:1:0 );
      WRITELN( '4. Divide ',   Num1:1:0, ' by ',   Num2:1:0 );
      WRITELN;
      READLN( Choice );
   UNTIL ((Choice >= 1) AND (Choice <= 4));

   {
     Execute the appropriate math operation
     and display its result
   }
```

```
CASE Choice OF
   1: WRITELN( Num1:1:0,' plus ', Num2:1:0,' is ',
                (Num1 + Num2):1:0 );
   2: WRITELN( Num1:1:0,' minus ',Num2:1:0,' is ',
                (Num1 - Num2):1:0 );
   3: WRITELN( Num1:1:0,' times ',Num2:1:0,' is ',
                (Num1 * Num2):1:0 );
   4: IF ABS(Num2) < Delta
         THEN WRITELN( 'Cannot divide by 0' )
         ELSE WRITELN( Num1:1:0, ' divided by ', Num2:1:0,
                ' is ', (Num1 / Num2):1:1 );
   END;  {case}      { Done }

END.  {Math1}
```

Figure 16.1 shows a sample run of this program. The program is *bulletproof*, which means that all input is checked to ensure that it is within bounds (the user cannot cause the program to stop working by typing a strange value for the menu option, such as an 8). Because the program keeps looping until the user chooses a proper menu option (1 through 4), no CASE ELSE is required.

```
Please type two numbers, separated by a space
(For example, 8  5) and press ENTER
3 6

Choose your option:
1. Add 3 to 6
2. Subtract 6 from 3
3. Multiply 3 and 6
4. Divide 3 by 6

3
3 times 6 is 18
```

Figure 16.1. Using CASE to choose from a menu.

The program is simple, but it illustrates a concept you haven't seen before: the IF statement within a CASE statement. The IF takes care of a possible division by 0. The program uses the ABS function to compare the divisor with a very small number. The programmer usually determines how small Delta should be.

> **TIP:** When you work with real numbers, using a comparison is safer than checking for equality because of the way real numbers are stored in the computer. When you work with integers, it is safe to check for equality.

ABSOLUTE VALUE:
The positive
representation of a
positive or negative
number.

The ABS function returns the *absolute value* of its argument. The absolute value of a number is simply the positive representation of a positive or negative number. Use ABS when you want to look at the magnitude of a number without being concerned about whether it is positive or negative.

The Range of CASE Choices

Instead of comparing a CASE expression to a constant, you can test for a subrange of constant values. Also, you can test for an explicit list of multiple constants separated by commas. The format of this last CASE statement is

```
CASE expression OF
    constant1..constant2: BEGIN          { subrange }
                        statement1;
                        statement2;
                            .
                            .
                            .
                    END;
```

```
      constant1,constant2:  BEGIN                 { explicit list }
                              statementa;
                              statementb;
                                  .
                                  .
                                  .
                            END;
      .
      .
      .

  [ELSE BEGIN
          statementA;
          statementB;
              .
              .
              .
          END;]
END;
```

The `constant1..constant2` format of the CASE lets you specify a subrange of values that Turbo Pascal checks to determine which statements are to be executed. For example, if your program needs to check for lowercase characters, use

```
CASE Ch OF
   'a'..'z': BEGIN
                 .
                 .
                 .
             END;
   .
   .
   .
END;  {case}
```

The *constant1,constant2* format lets you specify specific values. For example, if your program needs to check for even numbers less than ten, use

```
CASE Num OF
  2,4,6,8: BEGIN
          .
          .
          .
        END;
      .
      .
      .
END;  {case}
```

Both of these formats are useful when possibilities are ordered sequentially and you want to perform certain actions if one of the sets of values is chosen.

With the subrange format, *constant1* must be lower numerically, or as determined by the ASCII table if it is character data, than *constant2*.

With the specific value format, you usually list the values in order. The following examples make this clear.

> **TIP:** Put the most likely case at the top of the CASE list. Turbo Pascal mandates no particular order, but this order improves your program's speed. If you are testing for cases 1 through 6 and the fifth case is the most likely, put it at the top of the list. The only CASE statement that must go last is the CASE ELSE.

Examples

1. This program tests for the user's age and displays an appropriate driving message. The program looks at a range of age values. Because ages of people are always sequential (that is, a person gets exactly one year older every birthday), using the CASE range is a good way to program this problem.

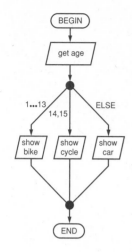

```
{ Filename: C16AGE1.PAS }


{ Program to tell legal vehicles based on age. }
PROGRAM Drive1;
USES Crt;


VAR Age: INTEGER;                    { age typed by user }
BEGIN
   CLRSCR;
   WRITE( 'How old are you? ' );
   READLN( Age );
   CASE Age OF
     1..13: WRITELN( 'You can only ride a bike' );
     14,15: WRITELN( 'You can ride a motorcycle' );
     ELSE   WRITELN( 'You can drive a car' );
   END;  {case}
END.  {Drive1}
```

1..13 illustrates a subrange. 14,15 illustrates explicit values.

2. The preceding program has one subtle bug. It seems to
   work, but if the user enters a bad age value, such as 0 or –43,
   the program tells the user to drive a car. This is not a good
   example of data validation. You can add a range check to
   display a message if the age is not valid, as the following
   program shows.

```
{ Filename: C16AGE2.PAS }


{ Program to tell legal vehicles based on age. }
PROGRAM Drive2;
USES Crt;


VAR Age: INTEGER;
BEGIN
   CLRSCR;
   REPEAT
     WRITE( 'How old are you? ' );
     READLN( Age );
     CASE Age OF
       1..13: WRITELN( 'You can only ride a bike' );
       14,15: WRITELN( 'You can ride a motorcycle' );
      16..99: WRITELN( 'You can drive a car');
```

325

```
      ELSE    WRITELN( 'Please type a number from 1 to 99' );
    END;  {case}
  UNTIL ((Age >= 1) AND (Age <= 99));
END.  {Drive2}
```

The range check ensures that everyone from age 16 to 99 will be told that they can drive a car. Any age *not* checked for, however, such as 0 and negative ages, triggers the CASE ELSE error message.

The HALT **Statement**

HALT quits execution of a program before the regular end of the program is reached.

The HALT statement can go anywhere in a program, and it immediately stops the execution of the program. When Turbo Pascal encounters a HALT statement, it quits execution of the current program.

Because HALT is unconditional, you usually see it as an option of the IF or CASE statements. A menu program is a good use of HALT. When you display a menu, give users an option to stop the program. If the users display the menu and then decide that they do not want to perform any of the options on it, they can choose the Quit option. The IF or CASE statement controlling the menu then can execute HALT without performing any of the other options.

Examples

1. Here is the math program with a menu that was presented earlier. This time, it has an extra option that lets the user quit the program without seeing any math performed.

```
{ Filename: C16MATH2.PAS }

{ Program to practice math accuracy. }
PROGRAM Math2;
USES Crt;
CONST Delta = 0.000001;
VAR   Num1:   REAL;           { first number typed by user }
      Num2:   REAL;           { second number typed by user }
      Choice: INTEGER;        { menu choice selected by user }
```

```
BEGIN
   TEXTCOLOR( WHITE );
   TEXTBACKGROUND( BLUE );            { white on blue }
   CLRSCR;
   WRITELN( '*** Math Practice ***' );
   WRITE( 'First number is ' );
   READLN( Num1 );
   WRITE( 'Second number is ' );
   READLN( Num2 );
   WRITELN;
   REPEAT
      WRITELN( 'Choose your option: ' );  { Display the menu }
      WRITELN( '1. Add ',       Num1:1:0, ' to ',   Num2:1:0 );
      WRITELN( '2. Subtract ', Num2:1:0, ' from ', Num1:1:0 );
      WRITELN( '3. Multiply ', Num1:1:0, ' and ',  Num2:1:0 );
      WRITELN( '4. Divide ',    Num1:1:0, ' by ',    Num2:1:0 );
      WRITELN( '5. Quit the program' );
      WRITELN;
      READLN( Choice );
   UNTIL ((Choice >= 1) AND (Choice <= 5));

   {
      Executes the appropriate math operation and
      displays its result
   }
   CASE Choice OF
      1: WRITELN( Num1:1:0,' plus ', Num2:1:0,' is ',
                  (Num1 + Num2):1:0 );
      2: WRITELN( Num1:1:0,' minus ',Num2:1:0,' is ',
                  (Num1 - Num2):1:0 );
      3: WRITELN( Num1:1:0,' times ',Num2:1:0,' is ',
                  (Num1 * Num2):1:0 );
      4: IF ABS(Num2) < Delta
            THEN WRITELN( 'Cannot divide by 0' )
            ELSE WRITELN( Num1:1:0, ' divided by ', Num2:1:0,
                        ' is ', (Num1 / Num2):1:1 );
      5: HALT;
   END;  {case}
END.  {Math2}
```

This example stretches the point a little because the program stops anyway immediately after doing any of the math. You can get an idea of how HALT works, however;it quits execution of a program before the regular end-of-program is reached. You can have more than one HALT in a program if several places require the capability to end execution depending on certain situations.

2. The program asks the user for a number and then displays the square of that number (the number raised to the second power) and the square root of the number (the number raised to the one-half power). Because negative numbers cannot have a square root (nothing multiplied by itself equals a negative number), the program does not display the square root of a negative number.

A REPEAT loop controls the flow so that users can keep seeing the program execute with different values. The program does, however, offer a chance to HALT. Notice that this HALT is conditional; the program stops only if the user requests that it stop.

```
{ Filename: C16SQRT.PAS }


{ Program that finds squares and roots of input values. }
PROGRAM SquareRoot1;
USES Crt;
VAR Num: REAL;
    Ans: CHAR;

BEGIN
   CLRSCR;
   WRITELN( 'Program that displays the square and '+
           'square root of any number' );
   REPEAT
      WRITE( 'What number would you like to use? ' );
      READLN( Num );
      IF Num >= 0
         THEN BEGIN
              WRITELN( Num:1:2, ' squared is ',
                       (Num * Num):1:2 );
              WRITELN( 'The root of ', Num:1:2, ' is ',
                       SQRT(Num):1:2 );
            END
```

```
        ELSE BEGIN              { Handles negative values }
              WRITELN( Num:1:2, ' squared is ',
                       (Num * Num):1:2 );
              WRITELN( 'There is no square root for ',
                       Num:1:2 );
           END;
     WRITELN;
     WRITE( 'Do you want to see another? (Y/N) ' );
     READLN( Ans );
     IF UPCASE(Ans) = 'N' THEN HALT;
   UNTIL FALSE;              { infinite loop }
END.   {SquareRoot1}
```

This example illustrates how you can purposely set up an infinite loop as long as you provide a means of escaping the loop. This example also shows a new Turbo Pascal function, SQRT. SQRT requires one parameter (integer or real) and returns the square root.

Summary

You have seen the CASE statement and all its related options. It can improve the readability of a complex IF-THEN-ELSE selection. The CASE statement is especially good when several outcomes are possible based on a certain choice. You also can use the HALT statement inside a CASE statement to enable the user to end a program earlier than its physical conclusion.

This chapter ends Part IV, "Control statements." Part V, "Data Structures," introduces advanced data types. Now that you can control the execution of your programs, you are ready to store more complex (but not complicated) data values in formats that will improve your ability to represent real-world data.

Review Questions

Answers to the Review Questions appear in Appendix B.

1. What statement sometimes can substitute for the IF-THEN-ELSE?

2. Which CASE option executes if none of the CASE conditions meets the CASE selector?

3. True or False: The HALT statement performs the same function as the EXIT statement.

4. True or False: CASE constants sometimes can have a different type than the type of the CASE expression.

5. True or False: The order of the CASE options has no bearing on the efficiency of your program.

6. Rewrite the following example, and replace the IF-THEN-ELSE with a CASE.

```
IF (Num = 1)
   THEN WRITELN( 'Alpha' )
   ELSE IF (Num = 2)
           THEN WRITELN( 'Beta' )
           ELSE IF (Num = 3)
                   THEN WRITELN( 'Gamma' )
                   ELSE WRITELN( 'Other' );
```

7. Rewrite the following example, and replace the IF-THEN-ELSE with a CASE.

```
IF Grade = 100
  THEN WRITELN('You got an A+')
  ELSE IF ((Grade >= 95) AND (Grade <= 99))
        THEN WRITELN('You got an A')
        ELSE IF ((Grade >= 88) AND (Grade <= 94))
              THEN WRITELN('You got a B')
              ELSE IF ((Grade >= 77) AND (Grade <= 87))
                    THEN WRITELN('You got a C')
                    ELSE IF ((Grade >= 70) AND (Grade <= 76))
                          THEN WRITELN('Yellow Alert: You got a D')
                          ELSE WRITELN('Red Alert: You got an F');
```

8. Rewrite the following example, and replace the IF-THEN-ELSE with a CASE.

```
IF (Sales > 5000)
   THEN Bonus := 50
   ELSE IF (Sales > 2500)
           THEN Bonus := 25
           ELSE Bonus := 0;
```

Review Exercises

1. Write a program using a CASE statement to ask users for their ages. Display a message saying You rarely worry about tomorrow if the age is less than 5, You often think you will live forever if the age is less than 21 but greater than 5, and, otherwise, one that says You are often amazed that you made it this far.

2. Write a program that your local cable-television company can use to compute charges. Here is how your cable company charges: If you live within 20 miles of the city limits, you pay $12 per month. If you live within 30 miles of the city limits, you pay $23 per month. You pay $34 per month if you live within 50 miles of the city limits.

3. Write a program that calculates parking fees for a multilevel parking garage. Ask whether the driver is in a car or a truck. Charge the driver $2 for the first hour, $3 for the second hour, and $5 for parking more than two hours. If the driver is in a truck, add an extra $1 to the total fee. (*Hint:* Use one CASE and an IF statement.)

4. Modify the parking problem to charge depending on the time of day the car is parked. If the car is parked before 8 a.m., charge the fees in the preceding exercise. If the car is parked after 8 a.m. and before 5 p.m., charge an extra usage fee of 50 cents. If the car is parked after 5 p.m., deduct 50

cents from the computed price. You will have to prompt the user for the starting time in a menu, as shown here:

A. From 12 midnight to 8 a.m.

B. From 8 a.m. to 5 p.m.

C. From 5 p.m. to 12 midnight

Part V

Data Structures

An Introduction to Arrays

This chapter begins a new approach to an old concept: storing data in variables. The difference is that you now will store data in *array* variables. An array is a list of variables, sometimes called a *table* of variables.

This chapter introduces

♦ Storing data in arrays

♦ The ARRAY statement

♦ Finding the highest and lowest values in an array

♦ Searching arrays for values

♦ Sorting arrays

♦ Advanced ARRAY subscripts

♦ The STRING connection

Conquering arrays is your next step toward understanding advanced uses of Turbo Pascal. This chapter's examples are some of the longest programs in this book. Arrays are not difficult, but their power enables them to be used with advanced programs.

What Is an Array?

ARRAY: A list of several variables with the same name.

An *array* is a list of more than one variable with the same name. Not every list of variables is an array. The following list of four variables is *not* an array:

```
Sales     Bonus92     FirstName     Ctr
```

These four variables do not declare an array because they each have different names. You might wonder how more than one variable can have the same name; this seems to violate the rules of variables. If two variables had the same name, how would Turbo Pascal know which one you wanted when you used the name of one of them?

Array variables are distinguished from each other by a *subscript*. A subscript is a number inside brackets that differentiates one *element* of an array from another. Elements are the individual variables in an array.

Before you read too much more about definitions, an illustration might help.

Good Array Candidates

Suppose you want to keep track of 35 people in your neighborhood association. You might want to track their names and their monthly dues. Their dues are fixed and are different for each person because the people joined the association at different times and bought houses with different prices.

Without arrays, you would have to store the 35 names in 35 different variables. You also would have to store in 35 different variables the amount each person pays in dues. Both of these factors would make for a complex and lengthy program. To enter the data, you would do something like this:

```
WRITE( 'What is the 1st family member''s name? ');
READLN( Family1 );
WRITE( 'What are their dues? ' );
READLN( Dues1 );
WRITE( 'What is the 2nd family member''s name? ' );
READLN( Family2 );
```

```
WRITE( 'What are their dues? ' );
READLN( Dues2 );
WRITE( 'What is the 3rd family member''s name? ' );
READLN( Family3 );
WRITE( 'What are their dues? ' );
READLN( Dues3 );
                    ⋮
WRITE( 'What is the 35th family member''s name? ' );
READLN( Family35 );
WRITE( 'What are their dues? ' );
READLN( Dues35 );
```

Every time you have to display a list of members, calculate average dues, or use any of this data, you must scan at least 35 different variable names. You would grow tired of doing this. For this reason, arrays were developed; it is too cumbersome for similar data to have different variable names. The time and typing required to process more than a handful of variables with different names is too much. Not only that, but imagine if the neighborhood grew to 500 residents!

Arrays let you store similar data, such as the neighborhood data, in one variable. In effect, each of the data values has the same name. You distinguish the values (the elements in the array) from each other by a numeric subscript. For instance, rather than use a different variable name (Family1, Dues1, Family2, Dues2, and so on), give the similar data the same variable name (Family and Dues) and differentiate the variables with subscripts, as shown in Table 17.1.

Table 17.1. Using arrays to store similar data.

Old Names	Array Names
Family1, Dues1	Family[1], Dues[1]
Family2, Dues2	Family[2], Dues[2]
Family3, Dues3	Family[3], Dues[3]
⋮	⋮ ⋮ ⋮ ⋮
Family35, Dues35	Family[35], Dues[35]

The number inside the brackets is the *subscript number* of the array. Subscript numbers are never part of an array name; they always are enclosed in brackets and serve to distinguish one array element from another.

How many arrays are listed in Table 17.1? If you said *two*, you are correct. Each array has 35 elements. How many elements are there in Table 17.1 in the Array Names column? There are 70 (35 Family elements and 35 Dues elements). The difference is very important when you consider how you can process them.

> **TIP:** Because the subscript number (the only thing that differentiates one array element from another) is not part of the array name, you can use a FOR loop or any other counter variable to input, process, and output all elements of arrays.

For instance, to input every family name and the family's dues into the two arrays, you do not need 140 statements as you did when each variable had a different name. You would need only *four* statements in a loop, as shown here:

initialize family
and dues arrays

```
FOR Ctr := 1 TO 35 DO
   BEGIN
      WRITE( 'What is the name of family member ',Ctr,'? ' );
      READLN( Family[Ctr] );
      WRITE( 'What are their dues? ' );
      READLN( Dues[Ctr] );
   END;  {for}
```

This is a major advantage. Notice that the FOR loop keeps incrementing Ctr throughout the data input. The first time through the loop, the user types a value in Family[1] and in Dues[1] (because Ctr is equal to 1). The loop then increments Ctr to 2, and the input process starts again for the next two variables. These four lines of code are much easier to write and maintain than were the previous 140 lines, and they do exactly the same thing: They use only two arrays of 35 elements rather than two groups of 35 different variable names.

> **NOTE:** You cannot use a FOR loop to process a group of differently named variables, even if the variables have names with numbers, such as Dues1, Dues2, and so on.

When you are working with a list of data with similar meanings, an array works best. Arrays make your input, process, and output routines much easier to write.

Using ARRAY to Set Up Arrays

Unlike when you use nonarray variables, you must tell Turbo Pascal that you are going to use a specific number of array elements. You use the ARRAY statement to do this. To reserve enough array elements for the 35 families, you define 35 string array elements called Family and 35 real array elements called Dues. Here is the format of the ARRAY statement:

```
ArrayName: ARRAY[range of elements] OF ElementType;
```

reserve memory for arrays

For example, to reserve space or allocate the Family and Dues arrays, you type the following:

```
TYPE FamilyName = STRING[30];
VAR  Family: ARRAY[1..35] OF FamilyName;
     Dues:   ARRAY[1..35] OF REAL;
```

FamilyName defines the type for each element. You do not have to define the element type separately. Because you often have to refer to the element definition (FamilyName), this practice is common. If you have no need to refer to FamilyName, you can write:

```
VAR Family: ARRAY[1..35] OF STRING[30];
```

> **NOTE:** You must remember the following rule: All array elements must be the same type (STRING, INTEGER, and so on). You must declare an array before using it.

Because each element in an array has the same type (and if the element type is a real or integer), you might see the elements being used in calculations, just as nonarray variables are, as in

```
Dues[5] := Dues[4] * 1.5;
```

If your program has several arrays of the same type, define the array type in the TYPE section. You still must declare the array itself in the VAR section. For example,

```
TYPE FamilyName = STRING[30];
     FamilyArray = ARRAY[1..35] OF FamilyName;
VAR  Family1: FamilyArray;
     Family2: FamilyArray;
```

When you declare a variable, Turbo Pascal stores the variable in an area of memory called the *data segment*. This applies to arrays as well. Turbo Pascal can use only one data segment, and the maximum size is 64K (65,535 bytes). Turbo Pascal uses some of the data segment to store variables associated with starting and ending your program. This affects the maximum number of elements that an array can have. For example, the following declarations show the maximum number of elements for some different element sizes:

```
USES Crt
VAR  i: WORD;      { subscript }
VAR  ByteArr: ARRAY[1..64842] OF BYTE;
```

or

```
IntArr:  ARRAY[1..32421] OF INTEGER;
```

or

```
StrArr:  ARRAY[1..4052] OF STRING[15];
```

Because each of the preceding arrays fills the data segment, your program can include only one of these arrays. With the last array, each element consists of 16 bytes—15 bytes of string data plus 1 byte for the length byte. These numbers illustrate maximum sizes. If your program requires such large arrays, you will need to study alternate data structures that use another area of memory called the *heap.* Although beyond the scope of this book, such alternate data structures include dynamically allocated arrays and linked lists.

> **TIP:** If you need more elements in an array than Turbo Pascal can give you, consider using two or more arrays. Be careful, however; you can easily fill the data segment and not have room to hold all your data. If your array is too big, Turbo Pascal will show this compile error: `Error 49: Data segment too large.`

To further illustrate the way an array works, suppose that you allocate (reserve space for) an eight-element array called Ages with the following ARRAY statement:

```
Ages: ARRAY[1..8] OF BYTE;
```

Its elements are numbered Ages[1] through Ages[8], as shown in Figure 17.1. (The numbers 1 through 8 are referred to also as array *indices.*) The values of each element are filled in when the program runs with READLN or assignment statements. (A third technique, *typed constants,* is introduced later in this chapter.)

> **NOTE:** Before using an array, you should initialize all elements to some value. Arrays with numerical types are often initialized to 0 or –1. Arrays with string types are often initialized to null strings.

Ages[1..8]

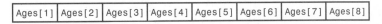

| Ages[1] | Ages[2] | Ages[3] | Ages[4] | Ages[5] | Ages[6] | Ages[7] | Ages[8] |

Figure 17.1. The eight elements and their subscripts in the Ages array.

Although the following examples show array elements being filled by WRITE, READLN, and typed constants, most programs get their input data from disk files. Because arrays can store large amounts of data, you don't want to have to type that data into the variables every time you run a program. Also, typed constants do not always suffice, either, because they are not good statements to use for extremely large amounts of data. For now, concentrate on the arrays and how they operate. In Chapter 27, "Sequential Disk Processing," you see how arrays can be initialized from data on a disk drive.

Arrays and Storage

Turbo Pascal wants to know the maximum number of array elements your program will use because it must reserve that many elements of memory in the data segment. Arrays can take up much memory. For instance, it takes more than 32,000 bytes of memory to hold the array created by the following ARRAY statement:

```
Measurements: ARRAY[1..4000] OF LONGINT;
```

Because array memory adds up fast, Turbo Pascal must ensure that there is enough memory to handle the highest array element your program will ever use. This is an advantage to programmers; Turbo Pascal does not wait until you have data in several array elements before it knows whether it has enough memory to store that data. If there is not enough room to create the array when it is allocated, Turbo Pascal tells you then (assuming that Range Checking is On).

Examples

1. Here is the full program that allocates two arrays for the neighborhood association's 35 family names and their dues. It prompts for input and then displays the names and dues. If you type this program, you might want to change the number of MaxFamily from 35 to 5 to avoid having to type so much input.

   Notice that the program can input and display all these names and dues with simple routines. The input and display routines both use a FOR loop. The method you use to control the loop is not critical. The important thing to see at this point is that you can input and display a large amount of data without having to write much code. The array subscripts make this possible.

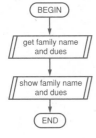

```
{ Filename: C17FAM1.PAS }


{ Program to gather and display 35 names and dues. }
PROGRAM Family1;
USES Crt;

CONST MaxFamily = 35;
      FamilyLen = 30;
TYPE  FamilyName = STRING[FamilyLen];
VAR   Family: ARRAY[1..MaxFamily] OF FamilyName;
      Dues:   ARRAY[1..MaxFamily] OF REAL;
      i:      INTEGER;                    { subscript }
BEGIN
         { Initialize arrays }
   FOR i := 1 TO MaxFamily DO
      BEGIN
         Family[i] := '';
         Dues[i]   := 0.0;
      END;  {for}
   CLRSCR;
   FOR i := 1 TO MaxFamily DO
      BEGIN
         WRITE( 'What is the name of family ',i,'? ' );
         READLN( Family[i] );
         WRITE( 'What are their dues? ' );
         READLN( Dues[i] );
      END;  {for}
   FOR i := 1 TO MaxFamily DO
      BEGIN
         WRITELN( 'Family ', i, ' is ', Family[i] );
         WRITELN( 'Their dues are ', Dues[i]:1:2 );
      END;  {for}
END.  {Family1}
```

Notice how the program uses a constant, MaxFamily, rather than 35 throughout the program. When a new family moves into the neighborhood, only the one line with `MaxFamily` must be changed.

This program is an example of *parallel arrays*. Two arrays are working side-by-side. Each element in each array corresponds to one in the other array.

2. The neighborhood association program is fine for illustration, but it works only if there are exactly 35 families. If the association grows, however, you must change the program.

Most programs, therefore, do not have a fixed limit like the preceding example does. Most programmers allocate more than enough array elements to handle the largest array they could ever need. The program then enables the user to control how many of those elements are used.

The following program is similar to the preceding one, except that it allocates 500 elements for each array. This allocation reserves more than enough array elements for the association. The user then inputs only the actual number (from 1 to 500 maximum). Notice that the program is flexible, allowing a variable number of members to be input and displayed each time it is run. It does have, however, an eventual limit, but that limit is reached only when there are 500 members.

```
{ Filename: C17FAM2.PAS }

{ Program to gather and display up to 500 names and dues. }
PROGRAM Family2;
USES Crt;
CONST MaxFamily = 500;
      FamilyLen =  30;
TYPE  FamilyName = STRING[FamilyLen];
VAR   Family: ARRAY[1..MaxFamily] OF FamilyName;
      Dues:    ARRAY[1..MaxFamily] OF REAL;
      i:       INTEGER;               { subscript }
      j:       INTEGER;
      Done:    BOOLEAN;
BEGIN
```

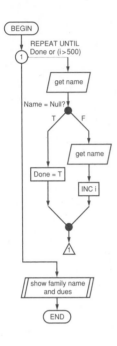

```
          { Initialize arrays }
FOR i := 1 TO MaxFamily DO
   BEGIN
      Family[i] := '';
      Dues[i]   := 0.0;
   END;  {for}
CLRSCR;
j := 1;                         { Init subscript to }
                                { start loop }
```

{

The following loop asks for family names and dues until the user presses Enter without typing a name. Whenever a null input is given (just an Enter keypress), the loop exits early with j holding the number input at that point.

}

```
Done := FALSE;
WRITELN( 'To quit, press Enter without typing a name.' );
REPEAT
   WRITE( 'Please type name for family ',j,': ' );
   READLN( Family[j] );
   IF (Family[j] = '')
      THEN Done := TRUE            { Trigger early exit }
      ELSE BEGIN
              WRITE( 'What are their dues? ');
              READLN( Dues[j] );
              INC(j);              { Bump subscript }
           END;
UNTIL (Done OR (j > MaxFamily));
WRITELN;

   { When last loop finishes, j holds actual number input }

FOR i := 1 TO (j - 1) DO          { Use j-1 since last INC }
                                  { bumped j for next read }
   BEGIN                          { Display input data }
      WRITELN( 'Family ', i, ' is ', Family[i] );
      WRITELN( 'Their dues are ', Dues[i]:1:2 );
   END;  {for}
END.  {Family2}
```

The output for the program follows:

```
To quit, press Enter without typing a name.
Please type name for family 1: Johnson
What are their dues? 18.55
Please type name for family 2: Underhill
What are their dues: 12.54
Please type name for family 3: Blackburn
What are their dues? 17.92
Please type name for family 4:

Family 1 is Johnson
Their dues are 18.55
Family 2 is Underhill
Their dues are 12.54
Family 3 is Blackburn
Their dues are 17.92
```

Only a few of the maximum 500 families are entered in the preceding code. The empty Enter keypress is a good way to trigger the early exit of the loop (by setting the BOOLEAN variable, Done, to be true). Just because 500 elements are reserved for each array does not mean that you must use all 500 of them. Notice that the REPEAT loop has two conditions. In addition to the Done variable, there is also a safety check to make sure that the user does not go past the maximum number of elements.

Allocating more than enough array elements is common, but don't go overboard. Too many allocated array elements could cause your computer to run out of memory.

TIP: Alternatively, if users are familiar with the data, you can ask them how many values they want to enter. You then loop until that value is reached. Because users rarely are familiar enough with their data to know how many values they will input, this method is not as common as the previous one, which enables the user to trigger the end of the input.

Introducing Typed Constants

TYPED CONSTANT:
a variable of a
declared type and
initial value.

Not all data is known when a programmer writes a program. The programmer knows in advance, however, such things as the names of the 12 months. Many Turbo Pascal programmers use *typed constants* to fill arrays with month names, days of the week, and so on. A typed constant is the same as an initialized variable.

Declare typed constants in the CONST section. With a regular constant, you just assign the value the constant should have. With a typed constant, you specify the type also. The format is

```
CONST Name: Type = SomeValue;
```

Here are some simple typed constants:

```
CONST Ctr:  INTEGER = 1;
CONST Done: BOOLEAN = TRUE;
```

Programmers often use typed constants to initialize short arrays. When you type the values for an array typed constant, you must be sure to match the number of elements in your list with the allocated size.

The following example illustrates how to declare an array typed constant to hold the days of the week. Because the array is declared with seven elements, there must be exactly seven elements listed in the typed constant.

Examples

1. The following program initializes day names into seven variables.

```
{ Filename: C17DAYS1.PAS }

PROGRAM Days1;
USES Crt;

TYPE  DayNames = ARRAY[1..7] OF STRING[9];
```

```
CONST Days: DayNames =
          ('Sunday',   'Monday', 'Tuesday', 'Wednesday',
           'Thursday', 'Friday', 'Saturday');

VAR   Ctr: INTEGER;

BEGIN
   CLRSCR;
   FOR Ctr := 1 TO 7 DO
      WRITELN( 'Day ', Ctr, ' is ', Days[Ctr] );
END.  {Days1}
```

2. The following program shows how you can use an array typed constant to convert a BYTE value (0 to 255) into hexadecimal. The nested REPEAT loop does some checking to make sure that the user types a value in the correct range. If you type a number out of range, the program ignores the number and prompts again for a number from 0 to 255. Type 0 to stop.

```
{ Filename: C17Hex1.PAS }

{ Converts number from 0 to 255 into hexadecimal. }

PROGRAM Hex1;
USES Crt;
CONST HexDigits: ARRAY[0..15] OF CHAR = '0123456789ABCDEF';
VAR   H16: BYTE;                      { hex sixteens' column }
      H1:  BYTE;                      { hex ones' column }
      Num: INTEGER;                   { number typed by user }
      OK:  BOOLEAN;                   { if valid number typed }
BEGIN
   CLRSCR;
   REPEAT
         { Do some error checking }
      REPEAT
         WRITE( 'Type a number from 0 to 255 ' );
         READLN( Num );
         OK := ((Num >= 0) AND (Num <= 255));
      UNTIL OK;
      IF Num <> 0
```

```
        THEN BEGIN
                H16 := Num DIV 16;
                H1  := Num MOD 16;
                WRITELN( 'Decimal number, ',Num,
                        ', converts to $', HexDigits[H16],
                        HexDigits[H1],' in hex.');
            END;
    UNTIL Num = 0;
    END.  {Hex1}
```

The following illustrates a sample run for this program:

```
Type a number from 0 to 255 255
Decimal number, 255, converts to $FF in hex.
Type a number from 0 to 255 100
Decimal number, 100, converts to $64 in hex.
Type a number from 0 to 255 16
Decimal number, 16, converts to $10 in hex.
Type a number from 0 to 255 43
Decimal number, 43, converts to $2B in hex.
Type a number from 0 to 255 256
Type a number from 0 to 255 0
```

Searching and Sorting Arrays

Arrays are one of the primary means by which data is stored in Turbo Pascal programs. As mentioned earlier, array data usually is read from a disk. Chapter 26 explains disk processing. For now, you should understand how to manipulate arrays so that you see the data exactly the way you want to see it.

In previous examples, you saw arrays displayed in the same order in which you entered the data. This is sometimes done, but it is not always the most appropriate method of looking at data. For instance, suppose that a high school uses Turbo Pascal programs for its enrollment. As each student enrolls, the clerk at the computer types the student's name. When the next student walks up, his or her name is entered, and so on, until the names of the entire student body are in the computer, stored in a string array.

What if the school wants a listing of each student's name in alphabetical order? You cannot write a FOR loop to display the elements from 1 to the total number of students; because the students did not enroll in alphabetical order, the list is out of sequence.

You need a method of putting arrays in a specific order, even if that order is not the same order in which the elements were entered. This is called *sorting* an array. When you sort an array, you put that array in a specific order, such as alphabetical order or numerical order. A dictionary is in sorted order, as is a telephone book.

If an array is ordered such that successive elements increase by some criteria, the array is in *ascending order*. For example, an array of lowercase characters ('a','b','c',...,'z') is in ascending order. If you reverse the order of an ascending array, the array is in *descending order.*

For instance, if you want to look at a list of all employees in descending salary order, the highest-paid employees are displayed first.

Before learning to sort, it is helpful to learn how to search an array for a value. This is a preliminary step in learning to sort. What if one of those students gets married and wants her record to reflect her name change? Neither the student nor the clerk knows under which element the student's name is stored. As the following section shows, however, the computer can search for the name.

Searching for Values

You do not need to know any new commands to search an array for a value. An IF statement and a FOR loop are all you need. To search an array for a value, simply compare each element in that array with the item you are looking for to see whether they match. If they do, you have found the value. If they do not, keep searching down the array. If you run out of array elements before finding the value, it is not in the array.

You can perform several different kinds of searches. You might need to find the highest or lowest value in a list (array) of numbers. This information is helpful when you have much data and want to know the extremes of the data (such as the highest and lowest sales region in your division).

The following example program illustrates one of these array-searching techniques. It displays the highest sales of a company's sales staff.

Example

To find the highest number in an array, you compare each element to the first one. If you find a higher value, it becomes the basis for the rest of the search, or until you find a still higher value. Continue until you reach the end of the array and you will have the highest value, as the following program shows.

```
{ Filename: C17HIGH.PAS }

{ Find the highest sales total in the data. }
PROGRAM High;
USES Crt;
CONST MaxSales = 6;                      { Reserve room for up to }
                                         { 6 sales values }
TYPE  SalesArray = ARRAY[1..MaxSales] OF INTEGER;
CONST Sales: SalesArray = ( 2900, 5400, 3429, 3744, 7678, 4585 );

VAR Ctr:       INTEGER;
    HighSales: INTEGER;

BEGIN
   CLRSCR;
   HighSales := Sales[1];    { Sales[1] has highest value so far }
   FOR Ctr := 2 TO MaxSales DO        { Compare others to it }
      IF Sales[Ctr] > HighSales       { Store current sales if }
         THEN HighSales := Sales[Ctr]; { it is higher than high }
                                       { sales so far }
   WRITELN( 'The highest sales total is ', HighSales );
END.  {High}
```

Notice that the IF statement needs no ELSE. This is because you must save the high-sales information only if you find a higher value than the one you are comparing. Finding the smallest value in an array is just as easy. However, make sure that you compare to see whether each succeeding array element is less than the lowest value found so far.

Sorting Arrays

Many times you need to sort one or more arrays. Suppose that from a list of names you write each name on a separate piece of paper and throw the pieces in the air. The steps you would take to alphabetize the names (shuffling and changing the order of the pieces of paper) would be similar to what your computer must do to put numbers or character data into a sorted form.

You should be able to see that the following does not exchange the values of a and b:

```
a := b;        { a and b are now the same }
b := a;        { Put b's value back in b ??? }
```

This exchange technique doesn't work because, in the first line, the value of a is replaced with b's value. When the first line finishes, both a and b contain the same value. The second line therefore cannot work.

To swap these variables, you type

```
tmp := a;
a   := b;
b   := tmp;
```

Using a temporary variable, tmp, with the same type as a and b enables you to exchange the values in the two variables.

There are several ways to sort arrays. These methods include the *bubble sort*, the *quick sort*, and the *shell sort*. The goal of each method is to compare each array element to another array element and swap them, if needed, to put them in order.

A discussion of the differences among these sorts is beyond the scope of this book; however, the bubble sort is one of the easiest sorting methods to follow. Values in an array are compared to each other, a pair at a time, and swapped if they are not in correct order. The lowest value eventually "floats" to the top of the list, like a bubble in a glass of water.

The following programs show the bubble sort in action.

Examples

1. The following program reads 10 random numbers into an array and displays them in sorted order.

```pascal
{ Filename: C17SORT1.PAS }

{ Sort and display a list of numbers. }
PROGRAM Sort1;
USES Crt;
CONST MaxNum = 10;
VAR   Number: ARRAY[1..MaxNum] OF INTEGER;
      Ctr1:   INTEGER;
      Ctr2:   INTEGER;
      tmp:    INTEGER;
BEGIN
   CLRSCR;
   RANDOMIZE;                       { Do not generate same }
                                    { random number each time }
                                    { program is run }
   WRITELN( 'Here are the unsorted numbers:' );
   FOR Ctr1 := 1 TO MaxNum DO
     BEGIN
        Number[Ctr1] := RANDOM(100);  { Get a random number }
                                      { from 0 to 99 }
        WRITE( Number[Ctr1]:4 );
     END;  {for}
   WRITELN;
          { Nested FOR loops implement bubble sort }
   FOR Ctr1 := 1 TO MaxNum DO
     FOR Ctr2 := Ctr1 TO MaxNum DO
        IF Number[Ctr1] > Number[Ctr2]
           THEN BEGIN         { swap Ctr1 and Ctr2 elements }
                   tmp         := Number[Ctr2];
                   Number[Ctr2] := Number[Ctr1];
                   Number[Ctr1] := tmp;
                END;
   WRITELN;
   WRITE( 'Press Enter to see the sorted numbers.' );
   READLN;
   WRITELN;
```

```
    WRITELN( 'Here are the sorted numbers:' );
    FOR Ctr1 := 1 TO MaxNum DO        { Proves numbers }
                                      { were sorted }

      WRITE( Number[Ctr1]:4 );
    WRITELN;
END.  {Sort1}
```

The following code shows the output from this program and demonstrates the bubble sort.

```
Here are the unsorted numbers:
   73  74  29  73  16  74  24  14  77   6


Press Enter to see the sorted numbers.


Here are the sorted numbers:
    6  14  16  24  29  73  73  74  74  77
```

> **TIP:** To sort in reverse order, from high to low, use a less than sign (<) in place of the greater than sign (>).

2. You can sort character data also. The computer uses the ASCII table to decide how the characters sort. The following program is similar to the first one in this section (C17SORT1.PAS), but it reads and sorts a list of people's names.

```
{ Filename: C17SORT2.PAS }

{ Sorts and displays a list of names. }
PROGRAM Sort2;
USES Crt;
CONST MaxNames   = 15;
      NameLen    = 25;
TYPE  NameString = STRING[NameLen];
      NameArray  = ARRAY[1..MaxNames] OF NameString;
CONST Names: NameArray =
              ('Jim',   'Larry',   'Julie', 'Kimberly', 'John',
               'Mark', 'Mary',     'Terry', 'Rhonda',   'Jane',
               'Adam', 'Richard', 'Hans',   'Ada',      'Robert');
```

```
VAR Ctr1: INTEGER;
    Ctr2: INTEGER;
    tmp:  NameString;     { temp var to swap array elements }

BEGIN
   CLRSCR;
   WRITELN( 'Here are the unsorted names:' );
   FOR Ctr1 := 1 TO MaxNames DO
      IF Ctr1 MOD 3 = 0
         THEN WRITELN( Names[Ctr1]:NameLen )
         ELSE WRITE( Names[Ctr1]:NameLen );

         { Nest FOR loops implement bubble sort }
   FOR Ctr1 := 1 TO MaxNames DO
      FOR Ctr2 := Ctr1 TO MaxNames DO
         IF Names[Ctr1] > Names[Ctr2]
            THEN BEGIN                   { swap names }
                   tmp         := Names[Ctr2];
                   Names[Ctr2] := Names[Ctr1];
                   Names[Ctr1] := tmp;
                 END;
   WRITELN;
   WRITE( 'Press Enter to see the sorted names.' );
   READLN;
   WRITELN;
   WRITELN( 'Here are the sorted names: ' );
   FOR Ctr1 := 1 TO MaxNames DO
      IF Ctr1 MOD 3 = 0
         THEN WRITELN( Names[Ctr1]:NameLen )
         ELSE WRITE( Names[Ctr1]:NameLen );
END.  {Sort2}
```

Notice that Ada sorts before Adam, as it should. Remember that the goal of a sort is to reorder the array, but not to change any of the array's contents. This program illustrates also how you can use the MOD function to control spacing.

Advanced ARRAY Options

The ARRAY statement has options to make the first subscript any number, even a negative number.

The first subscript must be less than the last subscript. The total number of elements reserved is computed as follows:

```
total := (last subscript - first subscript + 1)
```

Therefore, if the ARRAY statement looks like

```
Ara: ARRAY[4..10] OF INTEGER;
```

there are seven total elements (10 minus 4 plus 1), and they are

Ara[4]	Ara[5]	Ara[6]	Ara[7]
Ara[8]	Ara[9]	Ara[10]	

If the ARRAY statement reads

```
Scores: ARRAY[-45..-1] OF INTEGER;
```

there are 45 total subscripts (–1 minus –45 plus 1 is 45), and they are

Scores[-45]	Scores[-44]	Scores[-43]
⋮		
Scores[-3]	Scores[-2]	Scores[-1]

Although many of your arrays often use the subscript boundaries from the usual starting index of 1, there are times when using another starting index might be a little clearer. For example, suppose that you must write a Turbo Pascal program to keep track of the internal value of a bank's safety-deposit boxes. The bank's boxes are numbered 101 through 504. You can store the values in an array based at 1.

It is much easier, however, to reserve the storage for this array with the following ARRAY statement:

```
Boxes: ARRAY[101..504] OF REAL;
```

The subscripts then are very meaningful, and they make it easier to reference the value of a specific box.

In addition to using explicit numbers for the range of the array, you can use an enumerated type also. Enumerated types have the advantage of improving the readability of your program.

Examples

1. The following program illustrates how to set up an array using a meaningful index.

```
{ Filename: C17EMP1.PAS }


PROGRAM EmployeeNumbers;
USES Crt;
CONST MinEmpNum       = 1000;      { minimum employee number }
      MaxEmpNum       = 1010;
      MaxVacationDays = 5000;
TYPE  EmployeeRange   = MinEmpNum..MaxEmpNum;
      EmployeeArray   = ARRAY[EmployeeRange] OF INTEGER;
CONST Employee: EmployeeArray =
              (1000, 1001, 1002, 1003, 1004, 1005, 1006, 1007,
               1008, 1009, 1010);
VAR   Vacation: ARRAY[EmployeeRange] OF INTEGER;
      i:        INTEGER;                { subscript }
      GoodDays: BOOLEAN;               { Check input }
BEGIN
          { Initialize array }
    FOR i := MinEmpNum TO MaxEmpNum DO Vacation[i] := 0;
    CLRSCR;
    FOR i := MinEmpNum TO MaxEmpNum DO
       REPEAT
          GoodDays := FALSE;
          WRITE( 'Type number of vacation days for Employee ',
                  i,': ' );
          READLN( Vacation[i] );
          IF ((Vacation[i] >= 0) AND
             (Vacation[i] <= MaxVacationDays))
             THEN GoodDays := TRUE
             ELSE WRITELN( 'Please type a number from 0 to ',
                            MaxVacationDays );
```

```
    UNTIL GoodDays;
  WRITELN( 'Press Enter to view list of vacation days.');
  READLN;
  FOR i := MinEmpNum TO MaxEmpNum DO
    IF Vacation[i] = 1
      THEN WRITELN( 'Employee ',i,' has ',Vacation[i],
              ' vacation day.' )
      ELSE WRITELN( 'Employee ',i,' has ',Vacation[i],
              ' vacation days.' );
END.  {EmployeeNumbers}
```

Notice how a REPEAT UNTIL loop is used to block the statements for the FOR loop. Although the program could have used a BEGIN-END pair, it would be redundant. Also, the output was adjusted to display correctly day or days.

2. The following program illustrates how to use an enumerated type to index an array.

```
{ Filename: C17OCEAN.PAS }

PROGRAM Oceans1;
USES Crt;
TYPE  OceanTypes = (Atlantic,Indian,Pacific );
      OceanNameArray = ARRAY[OceanTypes] OF STRING[9];
      OceanSizeArray = ARRAY[OceanTypes] OF WORD;
CONST Oceans: OceanNameArray =
              ('Atlantic','Indian','Pacific');
      OceanSize: OceanSizeArray =
              (30246, 24442, 36200);
      Spc = ' ';
VAR   Ocean: OceanTypes;
BEGIN
   CLRSCR;
   WRITELN( '** Maximum Depth (in feet) of Major Oceans **' );
   WRITELN;
   FOR Ocean := Atlantic TO Pacific DO
      BEGIN
         WRITELN( Spc:13,Oceans[Ocean],' Ocean: ',
                  OceanSize[Ocean] );
```

```
        WRITELN;
      END;  {for}
  END.  {Oceans1}
```

The preceding code uses an enumerated type with an array. The output of this program follows.

```
** Maximum Depth (in feet) of Major Oceans **

          Atlantic Ocean: 30246

          Indian Ocean: 24442

          Pacific Ocean: 36200
```

Notice that an extra array, Oceans, is used to display the names because you cannot display enumerated types directly with a WRITELN statement. Using an enumerated type makes it easier to follow the code as opposed to something like this:

```
FOR OceanCtr := 1 TO 3 DO
```

The STRING Connection

You probably have noticed the similarity of arrays to strings. You can consider a string as an array of CHAR with two exceptions:

♦ Strings use index 0 to store the length byte of the string.

♦ Strings always start CHAR data at index 1.

When you declare a string variable, you usually specify the maximum length you will need. Earlier, when you defined FamilyName as type STRING[30], you were telling Turbo Pascal to use 31 bytes (don't forget the length byte) to store the string data. If the family name is Smith, Turbo Pascal still uses 31 bytes. The length byte is a CHAR value of 5, however. The data in STRING[6] through STRING[30] is undefined.

The following program illustrates how a string can be treated as an array. The last WRITELN shows how you usually display a string.

```
{ Filename C17STR1.PAS }

PROGRAM StrArray1;
USES Crt;

TYPE FamilyName = STRING[30];

VAR  Family: FamilyName;
     i:      INTEGER;
BEGIN
   CLRSCR;
   Family := 'Smith';
   WRITELN( 'The length byte is ',ORD(Family[0]) );
   FOR i := 1 TO LENGTH(Family) DO      { as an array of CHAR }
     WRITE( Family[i] );
   WRITELN;
   WRITELN( Family );                       { as a string variable }
END.  {StrArray1}
```

Notice that two Turbo Pascal functions are used. The first, ORD, converts the CHAR length byte to a number. The second, LENGTH, returns the current length of the string. The current length consists only of the number of characters in the string. It does not include the length byte.

Summary

This chapter covered a lot of ground. You learned about arrays, which are a more powerful way to store lists of data. By stepping through the array subscript, your program can quickly scan, display, sort, and calculate a list of values or names. You have the tools to sort lists of names and numbers, as well as search for values in a list.

After you have mastered this chapter, Chapter 18, "Multidimensional Arrays," is easy. That relatively short chapter shows how you can keep track of arrays in a different format, called a *multidimensional array*. Not all lists of data lend themselves to matrices, but you should be prepared for them when you do need them.

Review Questions

Answers to the Review Questions appear in Appendix B.

1. True or False: Arrays hold more than one variable with the same name.

2. How do Turbo Pascal programs tell one array element (value) from another if the elements have identical names?

3. Can array elements be different types?

4. True or False: All arrays must start with an index 1.

5. How many elements are reserved in the following ARRAY statement?

   ```
   Ara: ARRAY[0..78];
   ```

6. What compiler option should be set when you are using arrays?

7. How do you exchange the values of two variables?

8. How are FOR loops related to arrays?

9. How many elements are reserved in the following ARRAY statement?

   ```
   Staff: ARRAY[-18..4] OF INTEGER;
   ```

Review Exercises

1. Write a program to store six of your friends' names in a single string array. Use WRITE-READLN to initialize the arrays with the names. Display the names on-screen.

2. Modify the program in the preceding exercise, and display the names backward after using a typed constant to initialize the arrays.

3. Write a simple database program to track the names of a radio station's top 10 hits. After storing the array, display the songs in reverse order (to get the top 10 countdown).

4. Write a program that uses a typed constant to initialize an array that holds the names of the top 10 graduating seniors from a local high school. After reading in the values, ask the principal which number (1 through 10) he or she wants to see, and display that name.

5. Write a program that small-business owners can use to track their customers. Assign each customer a number, starting at 1001. When customers come in, store their last names in the element numbers that match their new customer numbers (the next unused array element). When the owner signals the end of the day by pressing Enter without entering a name, display a report of each customer's number and name information for that day. Make sure that you start the subscripts at 1001.

6. Change the program assigned in Exercise 5 to sort and display the report in alphabetical order by customer name. After each name, display the customer's account number as well (his or her corresponding subscript).

Multidimensional Arrays

Some data fits into lists such as those you read about in Chapter 17, "An Introduction to Arrays," whereas other data is better-suited to a table of information. This chapter expands on arrays. The preceding chapter introduced *single-dimensional* arrays, which have only one subscript. Single-dimensional arrays represent a list of values.

This chapter introduces arrays of more than one dimension, called multidimensional arrays. Multidimensional arrays, sometimes called *tables* or *matrices,* have rows and columns. This chapter explains the following concepts and procedures:

♦ Multidimensional arrays

♦ Putting data in multidimensional arrays

♦ Using nested FOR loops to process multidimensional arrays

If you understand single-dimensional arrays, you should have no trouble understanding arrays with more than one dimension.

What Multidimensional Arrays Are

MULTIDIMEN-
SIONAL ARRAY is
similar to a table of
values. It has "rows"
and "columns."

A *multidimensional array* is an array with more than one subscript. A single-dimensional array is a list of values; a multidimensional array simulates a table of values or multiple tables of values. The most commonly used table is a two-dimensional table (an array with two subscripts).

Suppose that a softball team wants to keep track of its players' hits. The team played 10 games, and 15 players are on the team. Table 18.1 shows the team's hit record.

Table 18.1. A softball team's hit record.

					Games					
Player Names	1	2	3	4	5	6	7	8	9	10
Adams	2	1	0	0	2	3	3	1	1	2
Berryhill	1	0	3	2	5	1	2	2	1	0
Downing	1	0	2	1	0	0	0	0	2	0
Edwards	0	3	6	4	6	4	5	3	6	3
Franks	2	2	3	2	1	0	2	3	1	0
Grady	1	3	2	0	1	5	2	1	2	1
Howard	3	1	1	1	2	0	1	0	4	3
Jones	2	2	1	2	4	1	0	7	1	0
Martin	5	4	5	1	1	0	2	4	1	5
Powers	2	2	3	1	0	2	1	3	1	2
Smith	1	1	2	1	3	4	1	0	3	2
Smithtown	1	0	1	2	1	0	3	4	1	2
Townsend	0	0	0	0	0	0	1	0	0	0
Ulmer	2	2	2	2	2	1	1	3	1	3
Williams	2	3	1	0	1	2	1	2	0	3

Do you see that the softball table is a two-dimensional table? It has rows (one of the dimensions) and columns (the second dimension). Therefore, you would call this a two-dimensional table with 15 rows and 10 columns. (Generally, the number of rows is specified first.)

Each row has a player's name, and each column has a game number associated with it, but these are not part of the data. The data consists only of 150 values (15 rows times 10 columns equals 150 data values). The data in a table, like the data in an array, always is the same type of data (in this case, every value is an integer). If the table contained names, it would be a string table, and so on.

The number of dimensions—two, in this case—corresponds to the dimensions in the physical world. The first dimension represents a line. The single-dimensional array is a line, or list, of values. Two dimensions represent both length and width. Two dimensions represent a flat surface; you write on a piece of paper in two dimensions. Three dimensions represent width, length, and depth; you have seen three-dimensional movies. The images have not only width and height, but also (seem to) have depth.

It is difficult to visualize more than three dimensions. You can, however, think of each dimension after three as another occurrence. In other words, a list of one player's season hit record can be stored in an array. The team's hit record (as shown previously) is two-dimensional. The league, made of up several team's hit records, represents a three-dimensional table. Each team (the depth of the table) has rows and columns of hit data. If there is more than one league, leagues can be considered another dimension.

Turbo Pascal has no limit on the number of dimensions, although "real world" data rarely requires more than two or three dimensions.

Allocating Multidimensional Arrays

Use the ARRAY statement to reserve multidimensional tables. Rather than put one value in the brackets, you put a range for each dimension in the table. The basic syntax of the ARRAY statement for multidimensional arrays is

```
ArrayName: ARRAY[row1..rowN, col1..colN, depth1..depthN, ...])
           OF ElementType;
```

For example, to reserve the team data from Table 18.1, you use the following ARRAY statement:

```
Teams: ARRAY[1..15, 1..10] OF INTEGER;
```

reserve array space for teams

This statement reserves a two-dimensional table with 150 elements. Each element's subscript looks like those in Figure 18.1.

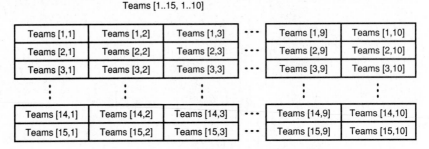

Teams [1..15, 1..10]

Teams [1,1]	Teams [1,2]	Teams [1,3]	•••	Teams [1,9]	Teams [1,10]
Teams [2,1]	Teams [2,2]	Teams [2,3]	•••	Teams [2,9]	Teams [2,10]
Teams [3,1]	Teams [3,2]	Teams [3,3]	•••	Teams [3,9]	Teams [3,10]
⋮	⋮	⋮		⋮	⋮
Teams [14,1]	Teams [14,2]	Teams [14,3]	•••	Teams [14,9]	Teams [14,10]
Teams [15,1]	Teams [15,2]	Teams [15,3]	•••	Teams [15,9]	Teams [15,10]

Figure 18.1. Subscripts for the softball team table.

If you need to track three teams, and each team has 15 players and plays 10 games, you can allocate the table as:

```
Teams: ARRAY[1..15, 1..10, 1..3] OF INTEGER;
```

This allocates three dimensions of the team table shown in Figure 18.1.

When you are allocating a table, always put the range for the rows first and the range for the columns second. It is up to you as the programmer to decide what data should go in the rows and what data should go in the columns.

The following statement allocates a three-dimensional table. The first dimension (the number of rows) subscripts from –5 to 6. The second dimension (the number of columns) subscripts from 200 to 300. The third dimension (the number of depth values, or the number of sets of rows and columns) is subscripted from 5 to 10.

```
Ara1: ARRAY[-5..6, 200..300, 5..10) OF INTEGER;
```

The number of elements in an array can add up quickly. Be careful not to reserve so many array elements that you run out of memory in which to store them. (From Chapter 17, you learned that arrays are stored in a section of memory called the Data Segment.) If you run out of memory, you receive the following error message:

```
Error 49: Data Segment too large.
```

Tables and FOR Loops

As the examples demonstrate, nested FOR loops are good candidates for looping through every element of a multidimensional table. For instance, the section of code

```
FOR Row := 1 TO 2 DO
    FOR Col := 1 TO 3 DO
        WRITELN( Row, Col );
```

produces the following output:

```
1    1
1    2
1    3
2    1
2    2
2    3
```

These are exactly the subscripts, in row order, for a two-row-by-three-column table that is allocated in

```
Table: ARRAY[1..2, 1..3] OF INTEGER;
```

Notice that there are as many FOR statements as there are dimensions in the ARRAY statement (two). The outside loop represents the first dimension (the rows), and the inside loop represents the second dimension (the columns).

You can use WRITE–READLN statements to fill a table, although this is rarely done. Multidimensional array data may come from typed constants, or more often, from data files from the disk. Regardless of which method stores values in multidimensional arrays, nested FOR loops are excellent control statements to step through the subscripts. The following examples illustrate how nested FOR loops work with multidimensional arrays.

Examples

1. The following statements reserve enough memory elements for a television station's shows for one week:

```
Shows: ARRAY[1..7, 1..48] OF STRING[30];
```

These statements reserve enough elements to hold seven days (the rows) of 30-minute shows. (Because there are 24 hours in a day, this table holds as many as 48 30-minute shows.)

Every element in a table is always the same type. In this case, each element is a string variable. Some of them can be initialized with the following assignment statements:

```
Shows[3, 12] := 'Sally's Shoreline';
Shows[1,  5] := 'Guessing Game Show';
Shows[7, 20] := 'As the Hospital Turns';
```

2. A computer company sells two sizes of disks: 3½-inch and 5¼-inch. Each disk comes in one of four capacities: single-sided double-density, double-sided double-density, single-sided high-density, and double-sided high-density.

The disk inventory is well-suited for a two-dimensional table. The company has determined that the disks have the following retail prices:

	Double Density		High Density	
	Single Sided	*Double Sided*	*Single Sided*	*Double Sided*
3½-inch	2.30	2.75	3.20	3.50
5¼-inch	1.75	2.10	2.60	2.95

The company wants to store the price of each disk in a table for easy access. The following program does that with assignment statements.

```
{ Filename: C18DISK1.PAS }


{ Assigns disk prices to a table. }
PROGRAM Disks1;
USES Crt;

VAR Disks: ARRAY[1..2, 1..4] OF REAL;
    Row:   INTEGER;
    Col:   INTEGER;

BEGIN
    Disks[1, 1] := 2.30;      { Row 1, Column 1 }
    Disks[1, 2] := 2.75;      { Row 1, Column 2 }
    Disks[1, 3] := 3.20;      { Row 1, Column 3 }
    Disks[1, 4] := 3.50;      { Row 1, Column 4 }
    Disks[2, 1] := 1.75;      { Row 2, Column 1 }
    Disks[2, 2] := 2.10;      { Row 2, Column 2 }
    Disks[2, 3] := 2.60;      { Row 2, Column 3 }
    Disks[2, 4] := 2.95;      { Row 2, Column 4 }

    CLRSCR;
    FOR Row := 1 TO 2 DO                   { Display the prices }
        FOR Col := 1 TO 4 DO
            WRITELN( Disks[Row, Col]:1:2 );
END.   {Disks1}
```

This program displays the disk pricing values, as shown in the following output.

```
2.30
2.75
3.20
3.50
1.75
2.10
2.60
2.95
```

The program displays the prices one line at a time without any descriptive titles. Although the output is not extremely helpful, it illustrates how you can use assignment statements to initialize a table, and how nested FOR loops can display the elements.

3. Filling table elements with values is cumbersome if you use assignment statements such as those shown previously. When a table has more than eight values (as most do), such assignment statements are especially difficult to follow.

Most tables therefore are filled with either typed constants or WRITE–READLN statements (or else they are filled from a disk file, as you will see later in Chapter 26, "Reading and Writing to Disk"). The following program fills the disk-inventory pricing table with typed constants.

```
{ Filename: C18DISK2.PAS }

{ Reads disk prices into a table. }

PROGRAM Disks2;
USES Crt;
CONST Disks: ARRAY[1..2,1..4] OF REAL =
               (( 2.30, 2.75, 3.20, 3.50 ),
                ( 1.75, 2.10, 2.60, 2.95 ));

VAR Row: INTEGER;
    Col: INTEGER;
```

```
BEGIN
   CLRSCR;
   FOR Row := 1 TO 2 DO                  { Display the prices }
      FOR Col := 1 TO 4 DO
         WRITELN( Disks[Row, Col]:1:2 );
END.  {Disks2}
```

In the typed constant, Disks, notice how parentheses organize the information. As a rule of thumb, the number of dimensions determines the number of parentheses at the start and end of the typed constant.

4. The preceding disk inventory would be displayed better if the output had descriptive titles. Before you add titles, it is helpful for you to see how to display a table in its native row and column format.

Typically, a nested FOR loop such as the one in the preceding example is used. If you use the WRITE statement rather than the WRITELN statement, however, the values do not display one number per line; rather, they display next to each other on one line.

You do not want to see every disk price on one line, but you want each row of the table displayed on a separate line. Because a blank WRITELN statement sends the cursor to the next line, insert a WRITELN statement before the row number changes (immediately before the END; {for} statement). Doing so displays the table in its row and column format, as shown here.

```
{ Filename: C18DISK3.PAS

{ Assigns disk prices to a table. }
PROGRAM Disks3;
{
  Display disk prices in table format and
  display the prices with a few spaces before
  them to separate them from each other when displayed
}
```

```
USES Crt;
CONST Spc = ' ';
        Disks: ARRAY[1..2,1..4] OF REAL =
                (( 2.30, 2.75, 3.20, 3.50 ),
                 ( 1.75, 2.10, 2.60, 2.95 ));

VAR Row: INTEGER;
    Col: INTEGER;

BEGIN
   CLRSCR;
   FOR Row := 1 TO 2 DO
      BEGIN
         FOR Col := 1 TO 4 DO
            WRITE( Disks[Row, Col]:1:2,Spc:4 );
            WRITELN;                        { Forces cursor to next row }
      END;  {for}
END.  {Disks3}
```

The following code shows the result of a run of this program in table format. The only things missing are the titles.

```
2.30    2.75    3.20    3.50
1.75    2.10    2.60    2.95
```

5. To add the titles, simply display a row of titles before the first row of values, and then display a new column title before each column, as shown in the following program.

```
{ Filename: C18DISK4.PAS }

{ Assigns disk prices to a table. }

PROGRAM Disks4;
{
  Display disk prices in table format.
  Display the prices with a few spaces before
  them to separate them from each other when displayed.
  Add spaces to center numbers under titles.
}
```

```
USES Crt;
CONST Spc = ' ';
      W1  = 14;
      W2  = 10;
      Disks: ARRAY[1..2,1..4] OF REAL =
              (( 2.30, 2.75, 3.20, 3.50 ),
               ( 1.75, 2.10, 2.60, 2.95 ));

VAR Row: INTEGER;
    Col: INTEGER;

BEGIN
   CLRSCR;
   WRITELN( Spc:17,'SS = Single Sided     DS = Double Sided' );
   WRITELN( Spc:17,'DS = Double Density   HD = High Density' );
   WRITELN;
   WRITELN( Spc:14, 'SS','DS':W1,'SS':W1,'DS':W1 );
   WRITELN( Spc:14, 'DD','DD':W1,'HD':W1,'HD':W1 );
   FOR Row := 1 TO 2 DO
      BEGIN
         IF Row = 1                    { Display row title }
            THEN WRITE( '3-1/2 inch    ' )
            ELSE WRITE( '5-1/4 inch    ' );
         FOR Col := 1 TO 4 DO
            WRITE( Disks[Row, Col]:1:2, Spc:W2 );
         WRITELN;                      { Force cursor to }
                                       { next row }
      END; {for}
END. {Disks4}
```

The following displays the output from this program in table format.

| | SS = Single Sided | DS = Double Sided |
| | DD = Double Density | HD = High Density |

| | SS | DS | SS | DS |
	DD	DD	HD	HD
3-1/2 inch	2.30	2.75	3.20	3.50
5-1/4 inch	1.75	2.10	2.60	2.95

6. The following program is a comprehensive program that reads in the softball team's hits table shown earlier in this chapter. The values are read from typed constants.

This example shows the usefulness of such tables. Rather than simply display the complete table, it processes the table's raw data into meaningful information by supplying the following information:

A list showing each player's total hits for the season

The name of the player with the most hits

The name of the player with the fewest hits

The game with the most hits

The game with the fewest hits

The player names cannot be stored in the table with the hit data because the names are string data and the hits are stored as integers. Therefore, a separate array (single-dimensional) that holds the player names is read. When the numbers of the rows with the most and fewest hits are known, those two players' names are displayed from the player name array using the row number.

```
{ Filename: C18HITS.PAS }
{
  Program to display stats from the team's softball league.
  Reserve storage for hits and player names.
}
PROGRAM Hits1;
USES Crt;
CONST Width     = 15;
      MaxPlayers = 15;
      MaxGames  = 10;
```

BEGIN

Analyze rows to
get players with
highest and lowest hits

Analyze columns to
get games with
highest and lowest hits

END

```
Hits:    ARRAY[1..MaxPlayers, 1..MaxGames] OF INTEGER =
             (( 2, 1, 0, 0, 2, 3, 3, 1, 1, 2 ),
              ( 1, 0, 3, 2, 5, 1, 2, 2, 1, 0 ),
              ( 1, 0, 2, 1, 0, 0, 0, 0, 2, 0 ),
              ( 0, 3, 6, 4, 6, 4, 5, 3, 6, 3 ),
              ( 2, 2, 3, 2, 1, 0, 2, 3, 1, 0 ),
              ( 1, 3, 2, 0, 1, 5, 2, 1, 2, 1 ),
              ( 3, 1, 1, 1, 2, 0, 1, 0, 4, 3 ),
              ( 2, 2, 1, 2, 4, 1, 0, 7, 1, 0 ),
              ( 5, 4, 5, 1, 1, 0, 2, 4, 1, 5 ),
              ( 2, 2, 3, 1, 0, 2, 1, 3, 1, 2 ),
              ( 1, 1, 2, 1, 3, 4, 1, 0, 3, 2 ),
              ( 1, 0, 1, 2, 1, 0, 3, 4, 1, 2 ),
              ( 0, 0, 0, 0, 0, 0, 1, 0, 0, 0 ),
              ( 2, 2, 2, 2, 2, 1, 1, 3, 1, 3 ),
              ( 2, 3, 1, 0, 1, 2, 1, 2, 0, 3 ));

   Player: ARRAY[1..MaxPlayers] OF STRING[20] =
   ('Adams', 'Berryhill', 'Downing',  'Edwards', 'Franks',
    'Grady', 'Howard',    'Jones',     'Martin', 'Powers',
    'Smith', 'Smithtown', 'Townsend', 'Ulmer',    'Williams' );

VAR Highest:  INTEGER;        { highest hits }
    Lowest:   INTEGER;        { lowest hits }
    Row:      INTEGER;        { FOR loop index }
    Col:      INTEGER;        { FOR loop index }
    Total:    INTEGER;        { total hits }
    HighRow:  INTEGER;        { row of player with most hits }
    LowRow:   INTEGER;        { row of player with least hits }
    HighGame: INTEGER;        { col of game with most hits }
    LowGame:  INTEGER;        { col of game with least hits }
BEGIN
   CLRSCR;
        {
         Find and display each player's total hits, and
         find highest and lowest
        }
```

```
Highest := 0;                    { Ensure first player's }
                                 { hits > highest }
Lowest  := 999;                  { and < lowest to start }
                                 { the ball rolling }
WRITELN( 'Name':Width, 'Total Hits':Width );
FOR Row := 1 TO MaxPlayers DO
   BEGIN
      Total := 0;                { Init before each }
                                 { player's hit total }
                                 { begins }

      FOR Col := 1 TO MaxGames DO
         Total := Total + Hits[Row, Col];
      WRITELN( Player[row]:Width, Total:Width );
      IF (Total > Highest)
         THEN BEGIN
                 HighRow := Row;
                 Highest := Total;
              END;
      IF (Total < Lowest)
         THEN BEGIN
                 LowRow := Row;
                 Lowest := Total;
              END;
   END;  {for}
WRITELN;

WRITELN( Player[HighRow],
         ' had the highest number of hits at ', Highest );
WRITELN( Player[LowRow],
         ' had the lowest number of hits at ', Lowest );

Highest := 0;                    { Ensure that first game's }
                                 { hits > highest }
Lowest  := 999;                  { and < lowest to start }
                                 { the ball rolling. }
FOR Col := 1 TO MaxGames DO       { This time step through }
                                 { columns first to add }
                                 { game totals }

   BEGIN
      Total := 0;                { Init before each }
                                 { game's hit totals }
                                 { begin }
```

```
              FOR Row := 1 TO MaxPlayers DO
                 Total := Total + Hits[Row, Col];
              IF (Total > Highest)
                 THEN BEGIN
                         HighGame := Col;
                         Highest  := Total;
                      END;
              IF (Total < Lowest)
                 THEN BEGIN
                         LowGame := Col;
                         Lowest  := Total;
                      END;
         END;  {for}
      WRITELN;
      WRITELN( 'Game number ', HighGame,
               ' had the highest number of hits at ', Highest );
      WRITELN( 'Game number ', LowGame,
               ' had the lowest number of hits at ', Lowest );
   END.  {Hits1}
```

Figure 18.2 shows the result of this program's table computations.

```
            Name       Total Hits
            Adams          15
         Berryhill        17
          Downing           6
          Edwards          40
           Franks          16
            Grady          18
           Howard          16
            Jones          20
           Martin          28
           Powers          17
            Smith          18
         Smithtown        15
          Townsend          1
            Ulner          19
          Williams         15

Edwards had the highest number of hits at 40
Townsend had the lowest number of hits at 1

Game number 8 had the highest number of hits at 33
Game number 4 had the lowest number of hits at 19
```

Figure 18.2. Displaying table data and computations.

Summary

You know how to create, initialize, and process multidimensional arrays. Although not all data fits in the compact format of tables, much does. Using nested FOR loops makes stepping through a multidimensional array straightforward.

One of the limitations of a multidimensional array is that each element must be the same data type. This limitation keeps you from being able to store several kinds of data in tables. The next chapter looks at the record data type. With arrays of records, you can store several kinds of data in tables.

Review Questions

Answers to the Review Questions appear in Appendix B.

1. What statement reserves a two-dimensional table of integers called Scores with five rows and six columns?

2. What statement reserves a three-dimensional table of string variables called Names with two sets of 10 rows and 20 columns?

3. Given the following ARRAY statement

   ```
   Names: ARRAY[1..5, 1..10] OF STRING[30];
   ```

   which subrange (first or second) represents rows and which represents columns?

4. How many elements are reserved with the following statements:

   ```
   Ara: ARRAY[1..5, 1..6] OF INTEGER;
   ```

5. Given the following table of integers in the matrix called Ara

4	1	3	5	9
10	2	12	1	6
25	43	2	91	8

what values do the following elements contain?

    A. `Ara[2, 2]`

    B. `Ara[1, 2]`

    C. `Ara[3, 4]`

    D. `Ara[3, 5]`

6. Given the typed constant

```
CONST Grades: ARRAY[1..3, 1..5] OF INTEGER =
        (( 80, 90, 96, 73, 65 ),
         ( 67, 90, 68, 92, 84 ),
         ( 70, 55, 95, 78, 100 ));
```

what are the values of

    A. `Grades[2, 3]`

    B. `Grades[3, 5]`

    C. `Grades[1, 1]`

7. What control statement usually is best used for "stepping" through multidimensional arrays?

8. How many elements do the following statements reserve?

    `Accounts: ARRAY[-10..12, 30..35, -1..2] OF INTEGER;`

Review Exercises

1. Write a program that reserves storage for three years of sales data for five salespeople. Use assignment statements to fill the matrix with data and display it one value per line. (*Hint:* Use columns for the years, and rows for the salespeople.)

2. Rather than assignment statements, use a typed constant to fill the salespeople data from the preceding exercise.

3. Write a program that tracks the grades for five classes that have 10 students each. Read the data from a typed constant, and display the table in its native row and column format.

4. Add appropriate titles to the table you displayed in the preceding exercise.

5. Read the softball team hits into a table. Compute and display the average number of hits per game and the average number of hits per player. (*Hint:* This exercise requires that you step through the rows and columns twice, similar to the C18HITS.PAS example that displayed the maximum and minimum values.)

6. Given the following table of distances between cities

	Tulsa	Okla. City	Joplin	Dallas
Tulsa	0	101	89	400
Okla. City	101	0	178	420
Joplin	89	178	0	532
Dallas	400	420	532	0

write a program to read this data into a table of mileage and display the following:

The city closest to Tulsa (not including Tulsa)

The city farthest from Dallas

The average mileage of surrounding towns (not including itself) to Joplin

The two cities closest together

Although it is easy to look at the table and see the answers, your program should search the table to find this data. If you add many more cities to the table, your program does not change except for a few subscripts and typed constant values.

An Introduction to Records

This chapter introduces a new approach to the concept of storing data in variables. Whereas arrays can store data with the same type, records can store mixed types. This chapter introduces

- ◆ Storing data in records
- ◆ The RECORD statement
- ◆ The WITH statement
- ◆ Arrays of records
- ◆ Nested records

The main advantage of records is that you can model real-world problems more closely. As in Chapter 17, in the neighborhood association example, separate arrays were needed for the family names and the dues. What if you wanted to keep track of how long each family has lived in the neighborhood? With arrays you would need to declare another array. You learn how to solve this problem with records later in this chapter.

What Is a Record?

A *record* is a way of packaging information of different types into one box. All the types you have studied so far (including arrays) may be used in a record definition. The format for declaring a record variable is

```
VAR RecordName: RECORD
                FieldVar1: Type1;
                FieldVar2: Type2;
                   ⋮
            END;
```

If you need to use more than one record variable of the same type, you can define the record type in the TYPE section:

```
TYPE RecordType = RECORD
                    FieldVar1: Type1;
                    FieldVar2: Type2;
                       ⋮
                END;
VAR   RecordName1: RecordType;
      RecordName2: RecordType;
```

FieldVar1, *FieldVar2*, ... make up a field list of variables (or identifiers), as you have seen before. Now, however, they are inside a RECORD definition. Programmers often refer to *FieldVar1*, *FieldVar2*, ... as the *fields* of the record.

Good Record Candidates

Whenever you have information that is somehow related, you probably can use RECORDS to organize it. Here are some examples:

```
TYPE   OrientationType = (PortraitOT, LandscapeOT);
       MenuString      = STRING[15];
       FamilyString    = STRING[30];
       FamilyRecord    = RECORD
```

```
                        Name: FamilyString;
                        Dues: REAL;
                     END;
        PageRecord      = RECORD
                        TopMargin:    REAL;
                        LeftMargin:   REAL;
                        RightMargin:  REAL;
                        BottomMargin: REAL;
                        Orientation:  OrientationType;
                        PageLines:    BYTE;
                     END;
        MenuRecord      = RECORD
                        Name:   MenuString;
                        X:      BYTE;
                        Y:      BYTE;
                        HiLite: BYTE;
                        Help:   INTEGER;
                     END;

VAR  Family: FamilyRecord;
     Page:   PageRecord;
     Menu:   MenuRecord;
```

> **TIP:** Although it is not necessary to use the phrase "record" as part of the name of a record type, it improves the readability of your program.

FamilyRecord shows you how to package Name and Dues inside a record. After RECORD, the two identifiers and their types are listed. An END; statement closes the package.

The PageRecord record could be part of a package of information your program needs when it is printing to a laser printer. Inside the PageRecord, four REAL fields define the boundaries for printing. An Orientation field specifies whether printing should be in Landscape or Portrait mode. The last field, PageLines, determines how many lines should print before doing a form feed.

The MenuRecord could be used in designing a menu system. When you display a menu option, you need to know the screen coordinates (X,Y), the letter in the menu option to highlight, and maybe a reference to online help for your program.

An important requirement for using a type is that the type must be defined before it can be used. In the preceding examples, OrientationString, MenuString, and FamilyString all are defined before they are included in the record definition.

Assigning Data to a Record Variable

Let's use the FamilyRecord example to show how you assign data to a field inside a RECORD definition. If a family's name is Smith and the dues are $15.00, you would write:

```
Family.Name := 'Smith';
Family.Dues := 15.00;
```

Family is a variable of type FamilyRecord. Name and Dues are fields in FamilyRecord. Just separate the record variable from a field list variable with a period.

The WITH Statement

If you have several field identifiers in a record, you must type the record variable repeatedly. As a shortcut, you can use the WITH statement. Here is its format:

```
WITH RecordVar DO
   BEGIN
     FieldVar1 statement;
     FieldVar2 statement;
     ⋮
   END;  {with}
```

For example,

```
WITH Family DO
   BEGIN
     Name := 'Smith';
     Dues := 15.00;
   END;  {with}
```

When you use the WITH statement, the period no longer is needed (or allowed). The WITH statement not only saves you some typing, but also makes the code less cluttered and therefore easier to read. Use the BEGIN-END pair when you have more than one field variable to use. If there is only one field variable to use, the BEGIN-END pair is optional; in fact, you may not even want to use the WITH statement in this case.

Arrays of Records

A particularly powerful structure is an array of records. Because each element of the array is a record, you satisfy the array's requirement that each element have the same type. You commonly find this structure when you have several packages of information that must be tied together.

Examples

1. The FamilyRecord can be used to illustrate an array of records. The following program is a rewrite of C17FAM1.PAS:

```
{ Filename: C19FAM3.PAS }

{ Program to gather and display 35 names and dues. }
PROGRAM Family3;
USES Crt;

CONST MaxFamily = 35;
      FamilyLen = 30;

TYPE  FamilyString = STRING[FamilyLen];
      FamilyRecord = RECORD
                        Name: FamilyString;
                        Dues: REAL;
                     END;

VAR   Family: ARRAY[1..MaxFamily] OF FamilyRecord;
      i:      INTEGER;                 { subscript }
BEGIN
```

```
                    { Initialize array }
          FOR i := 1 TO MaxFamily DO
             WITH Family[i] DO
                BEGIN
                   Name := '';
                   Dues := 0.0;
                END;  {with}
          CLRSCR;
          FOR i := 1 TO MaxFamily DO
             WITH Family[i] DO
                BEGIN
                   WRITE( 'What is the name of family ',i,'? ' );
                   READLN( Name );
                   WRITE( 'What are their dues? ' );
                   READLN( Dues );
                END;  {with}
          FOR i := 1 TO MaxFamily DO
             WITH Family[i] DO
                BEGIN
                   WRITELN( 'Family ', i, ' is ', Name );
                   WRITELN( 'Their dues are ', Dues:1:2 );
                END;  {with}
      END.  {Family3}
```

C17FAM1.PAS used parallel arrays to keep track of family names and dues. By using a record, you can package family name and dues together. This not only is less awkward, but also illustrates Turbo Pascal's capability to be self-documenting. With parallel arrays, you need to add comments to document that two (or more) arrays are related. When you look at a record definition, such as FamilyRecord, it is clear that the fields of the record are related.

2. Now we can answer the question posed at the beginning of this chapter: What if you want to keep track of how long each family has lived in the neighborhood? You just add a new field to the record definition for FamilyRecord.

```
{ Filename: C19FAM4.PAS }

{ Program to gather and display 35 names and dues. }
PROGRAM Family4;
```

```
USES Crt;

CONST MaxFamily = 35;
      FamilyLen = 30;

TYPE   FamilyString = STRING[FamilyLen];
       FamilyRecord = RECORD
                           Name:  FamilyString;
                           Dues:  REAL;
                           Years: INTEGER;
                       END;

VAR    Family: ARRAY[1..MaxFamily] OF FamilyRecord;
       i:      INTEGER;                   { subscript }
BEGIN
          { Initialize array }
    FOR i := 1 TO MaxFamily DO
       WITH Family[i] DO
          BEGIN
             Name  := '';
             Dues  := 0.0;
             Years := 0;
          END;  {with}


    CLRSCR;
    FOR i := 1 TO MaxFamily DO
       WITH Family[i] DO
          BEGIN
             WRITE( 'What is the name of family ',i,'? ' );
             READLN( Name );
             WRITE( 'What are their dues? ' );
             READLN( Dues );
             WRITE( 'How long has family ',i,' lived here? ');
             READLN( Years );
          END;  {with}
    FOR i := 1 TO MaxFamily DO
       WITH Family[i] DO
          BEGIN
             WRITELN( 'Family ', i, ' is ', Name );
             WRITELN( 'Their dues are ', Dues:1:2 );
             IF Years = 1
                 THEN WRITELN( 'They have lived here 1 year')
```

```
                        ELSE WRITELN( 'They have lived here ',
                                      Years,' years');
                END;  {with}
        END.  {Family4}
```

Using Record Typed Constants

A record typed constant is a convenient way to initialize the fields of a record. When you use a record typed constant, you must follow these steps:

1. List each field name in order.

2. Follow each field name with a colon and valid data.

3. Separate fields with a semicolon.

4. Enclose the definition inside parentheses.

The `PageInfoRecord` illustrates how to do this:

```
CONST OrigPage: PageInfoRecord =
          (TopMargin:   1.0; LeftMargin:   0.5;
           RightMargin: 0.5; BottomMargin: 1.0;
           Orientation: LandscapeOT; PageLines: 45);
```

As you gain experience in programming, you probably will find that you use a special array typed constant more often than others. In this array typed constant, the array element is a record. The preceding definition of `MenuRecord` illustrates how to define such a typed constant. When you define an array typed constant with records, you combine the techniques for defining an array typed constant and a record typed constant:

1. Include each field name in order.

2. Follow each name with a colon and valid data.

3. Separate fields with a semicolon.

4. Enclose each array element in parentheses.

5. Separate array elements with a comma.

6. Enclose the definition in parentheses.

Examples

1. Suppose that you have a program with the following menu options: Backup, NewSale, OldSale, ToolBox, eXit. These menu options are to be displayed horizontally across the top of the screen. (eXit has an uppercase *X* to inform the user to press X to exit your program.)

The following short program illustrates this idea:

```
{ Filename: C19REC1.PAS }

{ Illustrating an array typed constant with records. }

PROGRAM Record1;
USES Crt;
CONST MaxMenuOpt  = 7;
TYPE  MenuString  = STRING[15];
      MenuRecord  = RECORD
                      Name:   MenuString;
                      X:      BYTE;
                      Y:      BYTE;
                      HiLite: BYTE;
                      Help:   INTEGER;
                    END;
      MenuArray   = ARRAY[1..MaxMenuOpt] OF MenuRecord;
CONST MenuOption: MenuArray =
      ((Name: 'Backup';  X:  2; Y: 1; HiLite: 1; Help: 100),
       (Name: 'NewSale'; X: 11; Y: 1; HiLite: 1; Help: 101),
       (Name: 'OldSale'; X: 21; Y: 1; HiLite: 1; Help: 102),
       (Name: 'ToolBox'; X: 31; Y: 1; HiLite: 1; Help: 103),
       (Name: 'eXit';    X: 41; Y: 1; HiLite: 2; Help: 104),
       (Name: '';        X:  1; Y: 1; HiLite: 1; Help:   0),
       (Name: '';        X:  1; Y: 1; HiLite: 1; Help:   0));
```

```
VAR i: INTEGER;
BEGIN
   CLRSCR;
   i := 1;
   WHILE ((i <= MaxMenuOpt) AND (MenuOption[i].Name <> '')) DO
      WITH MenuOption[i] DO
         BEGIN
            GOTOXY(X,Y);
            TEXTCOLOR( LIGHTGRAY );
            WRITE( Name );                    { write full menu name }
            GOTOXY(X+HiLite-1,Y);
            TEXTCOLOR( LIGHTRED );
            WRITE( Name[HiLite] );         { highlight hot key }
            INC(i);
         END;   {with}
END.   {Record1}
```

Let's take a closer look at the typed constant, MenuOption. MenuOption has a type of MenuArray. When you look at the definition for MenuArray, you see an array of seven MenuRecord records. The seven rows of data in MenuOption correspond to the seven elements of the array. Parentheses enclose each element, and a comma separates the elements.

Notice that the last two elements have a Name of '' (the null string). Turbo Pascal is very strict. If you define an array to have seven elements, then you must have seven elements in MenuOption. Because your menu has only five options, you must fill MenuOption with dummy data. The last two elements are not used by your program, but they still must contain valid data.

Inside each element, you see the field list of variables: Name, X, Y, HiLite, and Help. These variables are from the definition of MenuRecord. A colon and valid data follow each field name. A semicolon separates the fields.

Finally, another set of parentheses enclose the record. When you run the preceding program, you see the following horizontal menu:

Backup NewSale OldSale ToolBox eXit

You will be using arrays of records more in Chapter 28, "Random-Access Disk Processing."

2. The following program illustrates another array typed constant with records.

```pascal
{ Filename: C19OCEAN.PAS }

{ Illustrating an array typed constant with records }

PROGRAM Oceans2;
USES Crt;
TYPE  OceanTypes    = (Atlantic,Indian,Pacific );
      OceanString   = STRING[9];
      OceanRecord   = RECORD
                          Name:    OceanString;
                          Depth:   WORD;
                          Surface: WORD;
                      END;
      OceanNameArray = ARRAY[OceanTypes] OF OceanRecord;
CONST Oceans: OceanNameArray =
              ((Name: 'Atlantic'; Depth: 30246;
                Surface: 31830),
               (Name: 'Indian';   Depth: 24442;
                Surface: 28360),
               (Name: 'Pacific';  Depth: 36200;
                Surface: 63800));
VAR   Ocean: OceanTypes;
BEGIN
   CLRSCR;
   WRITELN( '*** Major Oceans ***' );
   WRITELN;
   FOR Ocean := Atlantic TO Pacific DO
      WITH Oceans[Ocean] DO
         BEGIN
            WRITELN( 'The ',Name,' Ocean: ',
                     'Depth = ',Depth,
                     ' feet    and Surface Area = ',
                     Surface,' square miles.' );
            WRITELN;
         END;   {with}
END.   {Oceans2}
```

Nested Records

Records are similar to arrays in another respect. Records also can be nested, which means that, inside a record definition, at least one of the field variables has its own record definition.

Example

You might have to write a program that generates form letters. To structure the letter, you decide to break it into three parts: the heading address, the inside address, and the body of the letter. This arrangement could describe the overall structure of the letter. Each of these parts also can be broken down as follows:

```
{ Filename: C19LTR1.PAS }

CONST MaxBody        = 45;
      AddressLen     = 40;
      CityLen        = 30;
      StateLen       = 20;
      ZipLen         = 10;
      BusNameLen     = 30;
      BusCompanyLen  = 40;
      SalutationLen  = 30;
      BodyLineLen    = 50;
      ClosingLen     = 30;
      SignatureLen   = 30;

TYPE  AddressString     = STRING[AddressLen];
      CityString        = STRING[CityLen];
      StateString       = STRING[StateLen];
      ZipString         = STRING[ZipLen];
      BusNameString     = STRING[BusNameLen];
      BusCompanyString  = STRING[BusCompanyLen];
      SalutationString  = STRING[SalutationLen];
      ClosingString     = STRING[ClosingLen];
      SignatureString   = STRING[SignatureLen];
      BodyLineString    = STRING[BodyLineLen];
      HeadingRecord     = RECORD
                            Address1:  AddressString;
                            Address2:  AddressString;
```

```
                  Address3:   AddressString;
                  City:       CityString;
                  State:      StateString;
                  Zip:        ZipString;
                END;
  InsideRecord    = RECORD
                  BusName:    BusNameString;
                  BusCompany: BusCompanyString;
                  Address1:   AddressString;
                  Address2:   AddressString;
                  City:       CityString;
                  State:      StateString;
                  Zip:        ZipString;
                END;
  BodyLineArray   = ARRAY[1..MaxBody] OF BodyLineString;
  BodyRecord      = RECORD
                  Salutation:   SalutationString;
                  Lines:        BodyLineArray;
                  Closing:      ClosingString;
                  Signature:    SignatureString;
                END;
  LetterRecord    = RECORD
                  Heading: HeadingRecord;
                  Inside:  InsideRecord;
                  Body:    BodyRecord;
                END;
```

LetterRecord is the overall definition of the structure. Within LetterRecord, you see the three parts of a letter: Heading, Inside, and Body. These parts are nested inside LetterRecord. Both HeadingRecord and InsideRecord consist of various strings. Body also has an array of strings, however, called Lines. This discussion gives you a taste of how to set up more complicated structures.

Summary

With an array, all elements must have the same type, and you can use an index to access individual elements. With a record, you can package almost any combination of types, and you must specify each field and its associated type.

You can use a WITH statement to more conveniently access the fields of a record.

Arrays of records are a common application structure. This structure combines the ease of use of arrays with the power of records.

As your applications become more complicated, you probably will notice that your records become more complicated as well. Nested records are one example of more complicated records.

Review Questions

Answers to the Review Questions appear in Appendix B.

1. True or False: Records must have more than one variable.

2. True or False: Records must have field identifiers with different types.

3. What is always the last Turbo Pascal reserved word that marks the end of a record definition?

4. True or False: Records always are defined in the TYPE section.

5. How do you assign a value to a record field identifier?

6. True or False: A record's fields must be a simple data type: integer, real, BOOLEAN, CHAR, or string.

7. Is the following definition correct?

```
TYPE ModelRecord = RECORD
                   Kind:       ModelType;
                   Date:       WORD;
                   OnDisplay:  BOOLEAN;
                   ID:         IDString;
                   Company:    CompanyString;
                 END;
    ModelType = (Aircraft, Auto, Helicopter, Ship, Truck,
                 Van);
    IDString   = STRING[40];
    CompanyString = STRING[20];
```

8. Given the following definition, replace the code between the BEGIN-END pair using a WITH statement.

```
TYPE TreeType    = (DeciduousTT, EvergreenTT);
     BranchType  = (AlternateBT, OppositeBT);
     LeafType    = (SimpleLT, CompoundLT, NeedleLT);
     TreeRecord  = RECORD
                       Kind:   TreeType;
                       Branch: BranchType;
                       Leaf:   LeafType;
                   END;
VAR  Tree: TreeRecord;
BEGIN
   Tree.Kind   := DeciduousTT;
   Tree.Branch := AlternateBT;
   Tree.Leaf   := SimpleLT;
   :
END.
```

Review Exercises

1. Write a TYPE definition to store a friend's name, sex, eye color, and hair color.

2. Write a TYPE definition to store the name of a favorite song, artist, label, and year purchased.

3. Write a program that uses a typed constant to display the following information:

```
*** World Tea Production ***
India: 690000 metric tons for 27.6% of the world total.
China: 566000 metric tons for 22.6% of the world total.
Sri Lanka: 225000 metric tons for 9.0% of the world total.
```

4. Write a program that uses a typed constant to store the following 1990 information and then sort it by Franchise Fee:

Franchise	Franchise Fee	Number of Franchises
McDonald's	22500	7919
KFC	20000	7009
Burger King	40000	5101
Subway Sandwiches	10000	4760
Wendy's	25000	2451
Hardee's	15000	2359

Part VI

Subroutines

Numeric Functions

You already have seen several methods of writing routines that make your computer work for you. This chapter is the first of a series of chapters designed to show you ways to increase Turbo Pascal's productivity on your computer. This chapter shows you ways to use many built-in routines, called *numeric functions*, that work with numbers. By learning the Turbo Pascal numeric functions, you can let Turbo Pascal manipulate your mathematical data. This chapter introduces you to

♦ Ordinal functions

♦ Number functions

♦ Arithmetic functions

♦ Trigonometric functions

♦ Math functions

♦ The SIZEOF function

♦ Random-number processing

Although some of these functions are highly technical, many of them are used daily by Turbo Pascal programmers who do not use much math in their programs. Most of these functions are useful for reducing your programming time. Instead of having to "reinvent the wheel" every time you need Turbo Pascal to perform a numeric operation, you might be able to use one of the many built-in functions to do the job for you.

An Overview of Functions

Turbo Pascal has several built-in routines that you can call to get results. When you call a routine that returns a value, that routine is called a *function*. Possible return values include all the simple data types you have seen in earlier chapters: INTEGER, REAL, BOOLEAN, CHAR, and STRING.

You already have seen the CHR function. By specifying a number, you can display the character that corresponds to that number on the ASCII table. The statement

```
WRITELN( CHR(65), CHR(66), CHR(67), CHR(7) );
```

displays the letters A, B, and C, and then rings the bell (ASCII value 7 is the bell character).

CHR illustrates what many functions have in common: the function name followed by parentheses. The value in the parentheses, called an *argument* or *parameter*, is the input to the function. The format of a *function call* (using a function anywhere in your program) is

```
ReturnValue := FunctionName [( Arg1 [, Arg2 ] [, ..., ArgN ] )];
```

Notice that a function can have no parameters, one parameter, or more than one parameter, depending on how it is defined. You usually combine functions with other statements (assignment statements, output statements, and so on).

A function always *returns* a value as well. The numeric functions return a number based on the parameter you send it. Similarly, string functions return a string based on the parameter you send it. When a numeric function returns a value, you must do something with that value: Either display it, assign it to a variable, or use it in an expression. Because the purpose of a function is to return a value, you cannot put a function on the left side of a colon-equal sign in an assignment statement.

A function always returns a value.

> **NOTE:** A function name always has parentheses following it if it requires a parameter, as most of them do.

Ordinal Functions

Ordinal means related to a sequence or enumeration. For example, the CHR function has been mentioned already. The CHR function is an ordinal function in the sense that it returns a character based on a sequence of numbers defined to be the ASCII table.

The ordinal functions are

♦ CHR

♦ ORD

♦ SUCC

♦ PRED

The ORD function is the inverse of the CHR function.

> **NOTE:** ORD returns the relative position of an item in a sequence.

The set of ASCII characters form such a sequence. For example, if you want to know the ASCII number of the uppercase character *A*, write

```
X := ORD('A');
```

where X is an integer variable. With A as the parameter, ORD's return value is 65. After this statement, X has a value of 65.

You can use ORD also on an enumerated type to determine its relative position in the type definition; for example, with

```
TYPE Colors = (Red, White, Blue);
VAR  X: BYTE;
     c: Colors;
```

```
BEGIN
   X := ORD(Red);
END.
```

Because the first item in an enumerated type has position 0, the preceding assignment statement gives x a value of 0.

> **NOTE:** The succ (for successor) function returns the next item in a sequence.

succ can be used with any type of ordinal list, such as the counting numbers or your own enumerated type. For example, to find the successor of 4, write:

```
X := SUCC(4);
```

This statement assigns a value of 5 to x.

You often see succ used with enumerated types. For example, to find the next color after Red in your Colors definition, write:

```
c := SUCC(Red);
```

After this statement, c has a value of White. What do you get when you write the following?

```
c := SUCC(Blue);
```

> **NOTE:** Turbo Pascal does not have a convenient way of checking whether you are at the end of an enumerated list.

The preceding assignment statement results in c being undefined. You must be very careful to check for the end of such a list. For example, if you want to wrap around, write:

```
IF c = Blue
   THEN c := Red
   ELSE c := SUCC(c);
```

The PRED (for predecessor) function is the opposite of succ.

> **NOTE:** PRED returns the preceding item in a sequence.

For example, to find the color before Blue, write:

```
c := PRED(Blue);
```

After this statement, c has a value of White. Just as you must be very careful with SUCC and the last item in a sequence, you must be very careful with PRED also and the first item of a sequence. If you use PRED on the first item of a sequence, the result is undefined. If you want to wrap around as before, write:

```
IF c = Red
   THEN c := Blue
   ELSE c := PRED(c);
```

Number Functions

Several functions are related to integers and reals:

♦ INT

♦ TRUNC

♦ FRAC

♦ ROUND

One of the most common integer functions is the INT function. It returns the integer value of the number you send it. If you send it a real number, INT converts it to the integer part of the real. For example:

```
WRITELN( INT(8.93):1:2 );
```

displays an 8.00 (the return value of INT) on the screen. Note that even though 8.93 is closer to 9 than 8, INT rounds down to 8.

> **NOTE:** INT returns a whole number (as a real) that is rounded toward 0.

You can use a variable or expression as the numeric function parameter, as shown here:

```
Num := 8.93;
WRITELN( INT(Num):1:2 );
```

The preceding lines and the lines

```
Num := 8;
WRITELN( INT(Num + 0.93):1:2 );
```

as well as the lines

```
Num1 := 8.93;
Num2 := INT(Num1);
WRITELN( Num2:1:2 );
```

All produce the same output: 8.00.

INT works for negative parameters as well. The following section of code

```
WRITELN( INT(-7.6) );
```

displays -7.00. –7.6 is between –7 and –8. Because –7 is closer to 0, INT returns –7.

> **NOTE:** TRUNC returns (as a LONGINT) the *truncated* whole number value of the parameter.

Truncation means that the fractional part of the parameter (the part of the number to the right of the decimal point) is taken off the number. TRUNC always returns a LONGINT value. The line

```
WRITELN( TRUNC(8.93) );
```

displays the value of 8. INT and TRUNC return the same value for both positive and negative numbers.

INT and TRUNC both use real parameters. INT returns a real whole number. TRUNC returns a LONGINT.

NOTE: FRAC returns the fractional value of the parameter.

The parameter to FRAC must be real, and the result is real as well. Therefore, the statement

```
WRITELN( FRAC(8.1):5:2, FRAC(8.5):5:2, FRAC(8.5001):8:4 );
```

produces the following output:

```
0.10    0.50    0.5001
```

NOTE: ROUND rounds a real number to a whole number.

The parameter to ROUND must be real, and the result is a LONGINT. The statement

```
WRITELN( ROUND(1.1),' ', ROUND(1.5), ' ',ROUND(1.8) );
```

produces the following:

```
1  2  2
```

Example

The following program summarizes the four integer functions. The program displays the return values of each integer function using several different parameters. Pay attention to how each function differs for both positive and negative numbers.

```
{ Filename: C20INTRF.PAS }

{ Illustrates the way the four integer functions compare. }
PROGRAM IntRealFunctions1;
USES Crt;

CONST W = 15;                          { width }
      D = 4;                           { decimal places }
VAR   Num: REAL;
BEGIN
```

```
        CLRSCR;
        WRITELN( 'Parameter':W, 'INT':W, 'TRUNC':W, 'FRAC':W,
                'ROUND':W );
        WRITELN( '---------':W, '---':W, '-----':W, '----':W,
                '-----':W );
        Num := 10;                              { integer parameter }
        WRITELN( Num:W:D, INT(Num):W:D, TRUNC(Num):W, FRAC(Num):W:D,
                ROUND(Num):W );
        Num := 10.5;
        WRITELN( Num:W:D, INT(Num):W:D, TRUNC(Num):W, FRAC(Num):W:D,
                ROUND(Num):W );
        Num := 10.51;
        WRITELN( Num:W:D, INT(Num):W:D, TRUNC(Num):W, FRAC(Num):W:D,
                ROUND(Num):W );
        Num := 0.1;
        WRITELN( Num:W:D, INT(Num):W:D, TRUNC(Num):W, FRAC(Num):W:D,
                ROUND(Num):W );
        Num := 0.5;
        WRITELN( Num:W:D, INT(Num):W:D, TRUNC(Num):W, FRAC(Num):W:D,
                ROUND(Num):W );
        Num := 0.51;
        WRITELN( Num:W:D, INT(Num):W:D, TRUNC(Num):W, FRAC(Num):W:D,
                ROUND(Num):W );
        Num := -0.1;
        WRITELN( Num:W:D, INT(Num):W:D, TRUNC(Num):W, FRAC(Num):W:D,
                ROUND(Num):W );
        Num := -0.5;
        WRITELN( Num:W:D, INT(Num):W:D, TRUNC(Num):W, FRAC(Num):W:D,
                ROUND(Num):W );
        Num := -0.51;
        WRITELN( Num:W:D, INT(Num):W:D, TRUNC(Num):W, FRAC(Num):W:D,
                ROUND(Num):W );
        Num := -10;
        WRITELN( Num:W:D, INT(Num):W:D, TRUNC(Num):W, FRAC(Num):W:D,
                ROUND(Num):W );
        Num := -10.5;
        WRITELN( Num:W:D, INT(Num):W:D, TRUNC(Num):W, FRAC(Num):W:D,
                ROUND(Num):W );
        Num := -10.51;
        WRITELN( Num:W:D, INT(Num):W:D, TRUNC(Num):W, FRAC(Num):W:D,
                ROUND(Num):W );
END.  {IntRealFunctions}
```

Figure 20.1 shows the output of this program.

Parameter	INT	TRUNC	FRAC	ROUND
10.0000	10.0000	10	0.0000	10
10.5000	10.0000	10	0.5000	10
10.5100	10.0000	10	0.5100	11
0.1000	0.0000	0	0.1000	0
0.5000	0.0000	0	0.5000	0
0.5100	0.0000	0	0.5100	1
-0.1000	-0.0000	0	-0.1000	0
-0.5000	-0.0000	0	-0.5000	0
-0.5100	-0.0000	0	-0.5100	-1
-10.0000	-10.0000	-10	0.0000	-10
-10.5000	-10.0000	-10	-0.5000	-10
-10.5100	-10.0000	-10	-0.5100	-11

Figure 20.1. Comparing the four integer functions.

Arithmetic Functions

You don't have to be an expert in math to use many of the Turbo Pascal mathematical functions. Often, even in business applications, the following functions come in handy:

♦ SQR

♦ SQRT

♦ ABS

Each function takes a numeric parameter (integer or real) and returns a value.

NOTE: SQR returns the square of its parameter.

The SQR function is "smart" in the sense that it returns the same type you sent as the parameter. If you use an integer parameter, the function returns an integer result. If you use a real parameter, the function returns a real result. This line:

```
WRITELN( SQR(5),'  ', SQR(1.1):1:2 );
```

produces the following output:

```
25  1.21
```

NOTE: SQRT returns the square root of its parameter.

The parameter can be any positive integer or real. The square root is not defined for negative numbers. If you use a negative value as a parameter to SQRT, you see the message `Error 207: Invalid floating point operation`. The section of code

```
WRITELN( SQRT(4):6:1, SQRT(64):6:1, SQRT(4096):6:1 );
```

produces the following output:

```
2.0     8.0     64.0
```

The *n*th Root

There are no functions to return the *n*th root of a number; there are only functions to return the square root. In other words, there is no Turbo Pascal function that you can call to give you the fourth root of 65,536.

(By the way, 16 is the fourth root of 65,536 because 16 times 16 times 16 times 16 is 65,536.)

The ABS function also can be used in many programs. Whatever parameter you pass to ABS, its positive value is returned. For example, the section of code

```
WRITELN( ABS(-5):7,ABS(-5.76):7:2,ABS(0):7,ABS(5):7,
         ABS(5.76):7:2 );
```

produces the following output:

```
5     5.76     0     5     5.76
```

Absolute value is used for distances (which are always positive), accuracy measurements, age differences, and other calculations that require a positive result.

Examples

1. This program uses the ABS function to tell the difference between two ages.

```
{ Filename: C20ABS.PAS }

{ Displays the differences between two ages. }
PROGRAM Abs1;
USES Crt;
VAR Age1: BYTE;
    Age2: BYTE;
BEGIN
   CLRSCR;
   WRITE( 'What is the first child''s age? ' );
   READLN( Age1 );
   WRITE( 'What is the second child''s age? ' );
   READLN( Age2 );
   WRITELN( 'They are ', ABS(Age1 - Age2), ' years apart.' );
END.   {Abs1}
```

2. The following program asks for a number and displays the square root of it. Notice that it tests whether the number is greater than or equal to 0 to ensure that the square root function works properly.

```
{ Filename: C20SQRT.PAS }

{ Program to compute square roots. }
PROGRAM SquareRoot1;
USES Crt;
VAR Num: REAL;
BEGIN
```

```
CLRSCR;
REPEAT
   WRITELN( 'What number do you want to see the' );
   WRITE( 'square root of (it cannot be negative)? ');
   READLN( Num );
UNTIL (Num >= 0);

WRITELN;
WRITELN( 'The square root of ',Num:1:2,' is ',SQRT(Num):1:2 );
END.  {SquareRoot1}
```

You should always be aware of the limits of function parameters and make sure the program does not exceed those limits by performing input validation checking, as this example program does.

Trigonometric Functions

The following four functions are available for trigonometric applications:

♦ PI

♦ ARCTAN

♦ COS

♦ SIN

These functions are probably the least-used functions in Turbo Pascal. This is not to belittle the work of scientific and mathematical programmers who need them. Thank goodness Turbo Pascal supplies these functions; otherwise, programmers would have to write their own routines to perform these four basic trigonometric functions.

NOTE: PI returns the value of pi, approximately 3.14159265358979.

> **NOTE:** The ARCTAN function returns the arctangent of the parameter in radians. The parameter is assumed to be an expression representing an angle of a right triangle.
>
> The result of ARCTAN always falls between –*pi/2* and +*pi/2*.

For example, the following statement displays the arctangent of the angle stored in the variable ang:

```
WRITELN( ARCTAN(ang):1:4 );
```

> **TIP:** If you need to pass an angle expressed in degrees to these functions, convert the angle to radians by multiplying it by (pi/180).

> **NOTE:** The COS function returns the cosine of the angle, expressed in radians, of the parameter.

For example, the following statement displays the cosine of an angle with the approximate value of pi:

```
WRITELN( COS(PI):1:4 );
```

The output is -1.0000.

> **NOTE:** The SIN function returns the sine of the angle, expressed in radians, of the parameter.

For example, the following statement displays the sine of an angle with the approximate value of pi divided by two:

```
WRITELN( SIN(PI / 2):1:4 );
```

The output is 1.0000.

If you want to compute the tangent, you can use the trigono-metric identity:

```
Tan := SIN(x)/COS(x);
```

The following statement displays the tangent of an angle with the approximate value of pi divided by 4:

```
WRITELN( SIN(PI/4)/ COS(PI/4):1:7 );
```

The output is 1.0000.

Math Functions

Two highly mathematical functions sometimes are used in business and mathematics:

◆ EXP

◆ LN

If you understand the trigonometric functions, you should have no trouble with these. You use them the same way. (If you do not understand these mathematical functions, that's OK. Some people program in Turbo Pascal for years and never need them.)

> **NOTE:** EXP returns the base of natural logarithm (*e*) raised to a specified power.

The parameter to EXP can be any constant, variable, or expression. *e* is the mathematical expression for the value 2.718282.

The following program shows the EXP function in use:

```
FOR Num := 1 TO 5 DO
    WRITELN( EXP(Num):1:6 );
```

This produces the following output:

```
  2.718282
  7.389056
 20.085537
 54.598150
148.413159
```

Notice the first number. *e* raised to the first power does indeed equal itself.

> **NOTE:** LN returns the natural logarithm of the parameter.

The parameter to LN can be any positive constant, variable, or expression. The following program shows the LN function in use:

```
FOR Num := 1 TO 5 DO
   WRITELN( LN(num):1:6 );
```

This produces the following output:

```
0.000000
0.693147
1.098612
1.386294
1.609438
```

The natural logarithm of *e* is 1. If you type

```
WRITELN( LN(2.718282):1:6 );
```

`1.000000` is the result.

The SIZEOF Function

The SIZEOF function is one of the few functions that can take a variable or a type as a parameter.

> **NOTE:** SIZEOF returns the number of bytes needed to hold a variable or type.

The variable can have any data type. You can use this function later when you work with data files. Most programmers do not care what internal size each variable takes. If you are preparing to allocate a real array of 200 elements and you want to see how much internal memory the array will take, however, you can code this program:

```
Test := 0.0;                  { A sample REAL variable }
WRITELN( 'The 200-element real array will take' );
WRITELN( SIZEOF(Test) * 200, ' bytes of storage.' );
```

This program displays the following:

```
1200
```

Each REAL number takes six bytes of internal storage.

You can use SIZEOF also to determine the size of a type. For example, you can determine the size of your MenuRecord from Chapter 19:

```
WRITELN( 'MenuRecord has ',SIZEOF(MenuRecord),' bytes.' );
```

The preceding statement displays 21 bytes.

Random-Number Processing

Random events happen every day of your life. It might be rainy or sunny when you wake up. You might have a good day or a bad day. You might get a phone call or you might not. Your stock portfolio might go up in value or down in value. Random events are especially important in games. Part of the fun of games is the luck involved with the roll of a die or the draw of a card when it is combined with your playing skills.

Simulating random events is important for a computer to do also. Computers, however, are *finite* machines; that is, given the same input, they always produce the same output. This consistency makes for boring game programs.

The designers of Turbo Pascal knew this and found a way to overcome it. They wrote a function that generates random numbers. With it, you can get a random number to compute a die roll or a draw of a card. The format of the RANDOM function is

```
RANDOM [(n)]
```

Using RANDOM

RANDOM is the first function you have seen that might or might not require a parameter. RANDOM without any parameters returns a random real number greater than or equal to 0 and less than 1. For instance, the section of code

```
WRITELN( RANDOM:10:6, RANDOM:10:6, RANDOM:10:6, RANDOM:10:6 );
```

might produce the following output:

```
0.000000   0.533424   0.579518   0.289562
```

For some strange reason, Turbo Pascal returns a 0.0 the first time you use RANDOM. The following section introduces the RANDOMIZE statement. RANDOMIZE makes sure that you do not start with the same random number. Without using RANDOMIZE, you can work around this problem by first assigning RANDOM to some dummy variable.

Depending on your computer, you might get different results. Try the preceding WRITELN statement on your machine to see the results. Each of these numbers is between 0 and 1, which is the definition of the RANDOM function's output.

If you write a program with this one WRITELN statement and run it repeatedly, you get the same four random numbers. You will see how to change this in the next section.

Using a parameter with the RANDOM function results in a WORD value being returned. The parameter determines the maximum number that can be returned. Only 0 and positive numbers can be used as parameters.

For example, if you use 0 as the RANDOM parameter, RANDOM returns 0. Writing RANDOM(10) generates random numbers from 0 to 9.

The RANDOMIZE Statement

The RANDOMIZE statement *reseeds* the random-number generator. This means that you get a different set of random numbers every time you run your program. In almost every program that uses the RANDOM function, you see the RANDOMIZE statement toward the beginning of the code. The format of RANDOMIZE is

```
RANDOMIZE;
```

Using the Random-Number Generator for Applications

So far, the random-number generation of Turbo Pascal might seem like a mixed blessing. The ability to generate random numbers is nice, but the numbers don't seem truly random.

Your computer's internal clock keeps ticking away every second. Because there are 86,400 seconds in a day, the odds of running the same program at exactly the same second twice in a row are slim.

Therefore, why not put the following RANDOMIZE statement at the beginning of any program that uses the RANDOM function?

Including this statement ensures you that you will get different random results every time you run the program (there is only a 1 in 86,400 chance that you will get the same value in any given day).

When would you not want to include the RANDOMIZE statement? Many applications no longer would work if the random-number generator were randomized for you. Computer simulations are used all the time in business, engineering, and research to simulate the pattern of real-world events. Researchers have to be able to duplicate these simulations repeatedly. Although the events inside the simulations might be random from each other, the running of the simulations cannot be random if researchers are to study several different effects.

Mathematicians and statisticians also need to repeat random-number patterns for their analysis, especially when they are working with risk, probability, and gaming theory.

Because so many computer users need to repeat their random-number patterns, the designers of Turbo Pascal wisely have chosen to give you, the programmer, the option of keeping the same random patterns or changing them.

If you want to generate a set of random numbers for a specific range, such as 1 to 6 for a die, write:

```
X := RANDOM(6) + 1;
```

The RANDOM function returns numbers 0 through 5. By adding 1 to the result, the range becomes 1 through 6.

What if you need a range from 5 to 10? Write:

```
X := RANDOM(6) + 5;
```

The basic idea for defining a range is to send the RANDOM function the maximum – minimum + 1 (10 – 5 + 1) and then add the minimum (5) to the result.

If you write a program to simulate the drawing of a card from a deck of 52 cards, you can use the following statement:

```
NextCard := RANDOM(52) + 1;
```

Assuming that you stored the 52 cards in a string array, this statement would choose the subscript of the next card.

Examples

1. The following program displays 10 random numbers from 0 to 1 on the screen. Run this program on your computer to look at the results. Run it several times. The output is always the same because the random-number seed never changes.

```
{ Filename: C20RAN1.PAS }

{ Demonstrates unseeded random numbers. }
PROGRAM Random1;
USES Crt;
VAR i: INTEGER;
BEGIN
   CLRSCR;
   FOR i := 1 TO 10 DO
      WRITELN( RANDOM:10:6 );
END.  {Random1}
```

Because RANDOM has no parameter, a real is returned. Some formatting has been added to make the results easier to read.

2. The next example improves on the preceding one by including the RANDOMIZE statement. Every time the program is run, you get a different set of random numbers.

```
{ Filename: C20RAN2.PAS }

{ Seeds a new random-number generator. }
PROGRAM Random2;
USES Crt;
```

```
VAR i: INTEGER;
BEGIN
   CLRSCR;
   RANDOMIZE;
   FOR i := 1 TO 10 DO
      WRITELN( RANDOM:10:6 );
END.   {Random2}
```

3. The following program displays random numbers based on the user's READLN value. It displays them in the range of 1 to the number the user enters.

```
{ Filename: C20RAN3.PAS }

{
  Program to display several random-numbers in a
  range from 1 to whatever value is typed by the user.
}
PROGRAM Random3;
USES Crt;
VAR i:   INTEGER;
    Num: INTEGER;
BEGIN
   CLRSCR;
   REPEAT
      WRITE( 'Please enter a positive number: ' );
      READLN( Num );
   UNTIL (Num >= 1);                    { Ensure # is good }
   WRITELN( '20 Random numbers from 1 to ',Num );
   FOR i := 1 TO 20 DO
      WRITELN( RANDOM(Num) + 1 );       { Put # in range }
END.   {Random3}
```

Summary

This chapter showed you Turbo Pascal's many built-in numeric functions. Functions save you programming time because they perform some of the computing tasks for you, leaving you time to concentrate on your program. There are functions that convert numbers from one data type to another, round numbers, perform advanced mathematical operations, and generate random numbers.

Along with the numeric functions, there are several string functions that work on character string data. With the string functions, you can write better input routines and manipulate string data in ways you were not able to before. The next chapter discusses string functions.

Review Questions

Answers to the Review Questions appear in Appendix B.

1. What advantage does using built-in functions have over writing your own routines?

2. What is a function parameter?

3. What is the difference between SQRT and SQR?

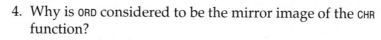

4. Why is ORD considered to be the mirror image of the CHR function?

5. Describe the expected ranges of each RANDOM statement in the following WRITELN.

```
RANDOMIZE;
WRITELN( RANDOM:5:2, RANDOM(2):5, RANDOM(7):5, RANDOM(11)+2 );
```

6. Name the function that can return the size of a variable or type.

7. What is the output of the following program?

```
Num := -5.6;
WRITELN( INT(Num):10:2, TRUNC(Num):10, FRAC(Num):10:2 );
```

8. Assume that you have a game with the following:

```
TYPE Direction = (North, East, South, West);
VAR  Dir: Direction;
```

How do you assign a random direction for Dir?

9. True or False: The following two statements are equivalent:

```
WRITELN( 64 * (1/2) );
WRITELN( SQRT(64) );
```

10. What does the following statement produce?

```
WRITELN( ORD(CHR(72)) );
```

Review Exercises

1. Write a program that returns one number higher than input by the user.

2. Write a program to compute the square root and square of the numbers from 10 to 25.

3. Write a program that displays the 26 letters of the alphabet down the screen so that the *A*s fill one 80-column line, the *B*s fill the next 80-column line, and so on until all 26 letters are displayed across the screen.

4. Write a program that builds a table of sines and cosines for angles 0 degrees through 90 degrees in 10-degree increments. (Remember to convert degrees to radians.)

5. Write a program to ask for two children's ages. Display the positive difference between the ages without using an IF statement.

6. Write a game to test the user's knowledge of squares from 1 to 25.

7. Write a program that simulates the rolling of two dice. Display the random dice values, from 1 to 6 for each die, for five separate rolls.

8. Modify the card-drawing routine so that it uses two decks of cards. This is an easy modification requiring only a few extra FOR loops, but it tests your grasp of the routine and random numbers.

String and CHAR Functions

This chapter shows you Turbo Pascal's string and CHAR functions. These functions work in a manner similar to numeric functions: when you pass them a parameter, they return a value—in this case a string or CHAR value. These functions enable you to display strings and CHAR variables in ways you never could before, as well as look at individual characters from a string.

This chapter introduces you to the following functions and statements:

- ♦ CHAR conversion function
- ♦ String functions
- ♦ The READKEY input function

After completing this chapter, you will know the more common built-in functions of Turbo Pascal, and you will be ready in the next chapter to write your own functions.

CHAR **Conversion Function**

The CHAR conversion function is UPCASE. This function converts a letter to uppercase.

> **NOTE:** UPCASE converts its CHAR parameter to an uppercase letter. If the parameter is already an uppercase letter, no conversion is done.

This function is straightforward. It can convert a CHAR variable, constant, or expression to uppercase.

The following section of code explains this function:

```
WRITELN( UPCASE('a'),'  ', UPCASE('A') );
```

The preceding statement would display:

```
A  A
```

This function has many uses. In asking your user a question, such as a yes-or-no question, you can ensure that the answer is in uppercase and perform an IF statement. For example:

```
IF (UPCASE(AnsCh) = 'Y') THEN ...
```

where AnsCh is a CHAR variable. Without the UPCASE function, you would have to test for both an uppercase Y and a lowercase y. A later example builds on this discussion.

String Functions

There are several string functions that manipulate strings. They let you find the length of a string, find the position of a string within another string, break strings apart, and put strings together. The string functions explained in this section are

- ◆ LENGTH
- ◆ POS
- ◆ COPY
- ◆ CONCAT

The LENGTH function is good to use when you want to know the length of a string.

> **NOTE:** LENGTH returns the length (the number of characters) of the string variable, constant, or expression inside its parentheses.

Recall that strings have the length byte in index 0 of the string. Because the length byte is in CHAR format, LENGTH converts the CHAR value into an integer. The WRITELN statement:

```
WRITELN( LENGTH('abcdef') );
```

produces 6 as its output. LENGTH usually is combined with other string functions when a string length is required. If the string inside the parentheses is a null string (if it does not contain any data), LENGTH returns a 0. You can test to see whether a string variable has data (to see whether the user typed anything before pressing Enter) with the following section of code:

```
WRITE( 'Please type an answer ');
READLN(Ans);
IF LENGTH(Ans) = 0
   THEN WRITELN( 'You did not type anything...' );
```

> **NOTE:** The POS function searches for a CHAR or substring within another string. It returns the index of the string where the substring was found.

If the CHAR or substring is not found, POS returns 0. POS requires two parameters. The first is the CHAR or substring you want to find. The second parameter is the string you want to search. For example,

```
tStr := 'This is a test string';
WRITELN( 'The position of "test" is ',POS('test',tStr) );
WRITELN( 'The position of "is" is ',POS('is',tStr) );
WRITELN( 'The position of "xyz" is ',POS('xyz',tStr) );
```

The preceding statements would display

```
The position of "test" is 11
The position of "is" is 3
The position of "xyz" is 0
```

Notice that the second example returns 3 and not 6. POS finds the first match and stops. Because "xyz" is not in the search string, POS returns 0 for the last WRITELN.

With the COPY function, you can specify which part of a string to return.

> **NOTE:** COPY requires three parameters: a string variable, a constant, or an expression followed by two integer constants or variables. The first integer determines the starting point of the string. The second number determines how many characters are returned.

COPY can pull any number of characters from anywhere in the string. The following example shows how the COPY function works:

```
tStr := 'Turbo Pascal FORTRAN COBOL C BASIC';
WRITELN( COPY(tStr, 1, 12) );
WRITELN( COPY(tStr, 14, 7) );
WRITELN( COPY(tStr, 22, 5) ):
WRITELN( COPY(tStr, 28, 1) );
WRITELN( COPY(tStr, 30, 5) );
```

This example produces a listing of these five programming languages, one per line, as shown in the following output:

```
Turbo Pascal
FORTRAN
COBOL
C
BASIC
```

CONCAT concatenates two or more strings. The resulting string can have as many as 255 characters, the maximum string size. For example,

```
tStr1 := 'This is only a test. If this ';
tStr2 := 'had been an actual emergency, you ';
tStr3 := 'would have been instructed ...';
WRITELN( CONCAT(tStr1, tStr2, tStr3) );
```

The preceding WRITELN would display This is only a test. If this had been an actual emergency, you would have been instructed ....

Turbo Pascal has an alternative form that is much easier to use. When you want to concatenate two or more strings, use plus signs. For example, the above WRITELN could be replaced with

```
WRITELN( tStr1 + tStr2 + tStr3 );
```

Many times, string functions are used together to search for and test for strings. One string function's return value can be a parameter to another function.

Examples

1. The following program uses POS to see whether a name is included in the typed constant.

```
{ Filename: C21DATNM.PAS }

{ Check to see if user's name is in the data. }
PROGRAM DataName1;
USES Crt;

CONST MaxNames = 15;

TYPE  NameString = STRING[10];
      NameArray  = ARRAY[1..MaxNames] OF NameString;

CONST DataName: NameArray =
          ('George', 'Sam',   'Mary',   'Abby',  'Carol',
           'Lou',    'Sally', 'Martha', 'James', 'Kerry',
           'Luke',   'Judy',  'Bill',   'Mark',  'John');
```

```
VAR i:     INTEGER;           { index to move thru array }
    Found: BOOLEAN;           { check for a match }
    First: NameString;        { name typed by user }
BEGIN
  CLRSCR;
  WRITE( 'What is your first name? ' );
  READLN( First );
  First[1] := UPCASE(First[1]); { make sure 1st letter }
                                { capitalized }
  Found := FALSE;             { init BOOLEAN flag }
  i     := 1;                 { init loop var }
  REPEAT
     IF (POS(First, DataName[i])) <> 0
        THEN BEGIN             { Name in data so stop }
               WRITELN( 'Your name is already on record.' );
               Found := TRUE;
             END
        ELSE INC(i);
  UNTIL ((i > MaxNames) OR Found);
  IF NOT Found
     THEN WRITELN( 'Your name is not on record' );
END.   {DataName1}
```

After you get the user's name, First, you force the first letter to be uppercase. Although this increases the chances of finding the name in the list, it does not find the name if the user typed all letters as uppercase.

Notice that the REPEAT loops check two conditions. The BOOLEAN variable, Found, is initialized false. If a match is found, then Found is set true and the loop stops. If the user types a name that is not in the list, there must be a safety check to stop when all names have been checked. The variable i is initialized to 1 and then incremented if there is no match. For example, if you type Kathy, i will be incremented to 16 and the program will display a message that Your name is not on record.

> **TIP:** When testing your code, always be careful to test first and last cases. For example, in the above program, type George and John to verify that the first and last names can be found. Also try a name from the middle of the list. After you are convinced that all nominal cases work, type examples that should fail.

2. The book database program in Appendix E uses string functions for some of the book titles. If a book's title begins with *The...*, the book database program deletes *The* from the front of the title and appends it to the end. Therefore, the title

```
The Rain in Spain
```

becomes

```
Rain in Spain, The
```

The following program asks for a book's title, saves all characters except for the leading *The,* and concatenates

```
", The"
```

to the end of the title. If the title does not begin with *The,* the program does not change the title.

```
{ Filename: C21BOOKT.PAS }

{ Moves leading THE from the front of a book's title. }
PROGRAM BookTitle1;
USES Crt;
VAR AnsCh:  CHAR;         { user's response to do another }
                          { title }
    Title:  STRING[30];   { book title typed by user }
    RTitle: STRING[30];   { right side of title w/o "THE" }
BEGIN
   CLRSCR;
   REPEAT
      WRITE( 'What is the title of the book? ');
```

```
        READLN( Title );
        IF (COPY(Title,1,4) = 'The ')
           THEN BEGIN
                   RTitle := COPY(Title,5,LENGTH(Title));
                   Title  := RTitle + ', The';
                END;
        WRITELN;
        WRITELN( 'Please file the book under:' );
        WRITELN( Title );
        WRITELN;
        WRITE( 'Do you want to enter another book title? (Y/N) ');
        READLN( AnsCh );
        WRITELN;
     UNTIL (UPCASE(AnsCh) = 'N');
END.  {BookTitle1}
```

The program uses COPY twice. First, COPY checks the first four letters of the user's string. The fourth character is compared to a space to make sure that titles such as *Theoretical Physics* are not affected. Second, COPY is used to strip *The* by storing only the remaining characters. When the third parameter of COPY specifies a number that is greater than the remaining characters in the string, COPY is smart enough to return only the remainder of the string.

Notice how the program also uses an embedded UPCASE function in the UNTIL part of the REPEAT loop. The user can enter Y or y, and the program knows that the user wants to loop again.

The READKEY Input Function

One function, the READKEY function, seems to be a distant relative of the READLN statement. As with READLN, READKEY gets input from the keyboard. Unlike READLN, however, READKEY can get only one character at a time from the keyboard, not an entire string of characters, as READLN can.

The format of the READKEY function is

READKEY

Because you never pass a parameter to READKEY, it requires no parentheses. The return value of READKEY is the character typed at the keyboard.

Any character you type at the keyboard is returned from READKEY, except the following keystrokes:

Shift, Ctrl, Alt, Ctrl–Break, Ctrl–Alt–Del, Ctrl–NumLock,

DisplayScreen (or PrintScrn), Shift–DisplayScreen

The return value of READKEY usually is assigned to a CHAR variable.

You might wonder why anyone would want to use READKEY, because it can accept only one character at a time. It has one advantage over READLN, however: when you press a key, you can store the key in a CHAR variable without having to press Enter. READLN *requires* that you press Enter, whereas READKEY gets its character input and passes control to the next statement without waiting for an Enter keypress. Users often appreciate not having to press Enter after a menu choice or a yes-or-no question.

READKEY is often used with KEYPRESSED, which was introduced in Chapter 15, "The IF-THEN-ELSE Statement." KEYPRESSED is a BOOLEAN function that returns true if a key has been pressed on the keyboard; it returns false if no key has been pressed. There is a special area in memory where all keystrokes are stored as bytes. This area is called the *keyboard buffer*. When you press most keys (such as an alphabet character) only one character is stored. If a user types the letter *k*, you can use KEYPRESSED to detect that there is a keystroke in the keyboard buffer.

When you press certain other keys (such as the function keys) or combinations of keys (such as Alt–D or Ctrl–F5), the keyboard stores two characters instead of one. If two characters are stored, the first one is always the null character (#0). The second character can then be used to identify what key was pressed.

The following examples illustrate READKEY.

Examples

1. This program beeps at users when they press B on the keyboard. If the user presses Q, the program quits. The program is simply a loop that gets the character with READKEY. The program ignores characters other than B or Q. It shows you the quick response of READKEY. Without READKEY, the user would have to press Enter after the B or Q.

   Because the program converts the READKEY value to upper-case, it does not matter whether the CapsLock or Shift key is pressed.

```
{ Filename: C21BEEP }

{ Beeps if user presses B; otherwise, quits when user presses Q. }
PROGRAM Beep1;
USES Crt;
VAR AnsCh: CHAR;
BEGIN
   CLRSCR;
   WRITELN( 'I will beep if you press B' );
   WRITELN( 'and I will quit if you press Q.' );
   REPEAT
      AnsCh := READKEY;   { Get a character if one is waiting }
      IF (UPCASE(AnsCh) = 'B')
         THEN WRITE( #7 );
   UNTIL (UPCASE(AnsCh) = 'Q');
END.  {Beep1}
```

2. You can use the following section of code to check for a user's answer to a yes-or-no question without the user having to press Enter.

```
{ Filename: C21YN1.PAS }

{ Routine to loop until the user enters Y or y or N or n. }
PROGRAM YesNo1;
USES Crt;
VAR AnsCh: CHAR;
BEGIN
   CLRSCR;
   WRITE( 'Do you want to continue (Y/N)? ' );
```

```
    REPEAT
        AnsCh := READKEY;
    UNTIL ((UPCASE(AnsCh) = 'Y') OR (UPCASE(AnsCh) = 'N'));
END.  {YesNo1}
```

An alternative to the preceding UNTIL line would be to use a set:

```
UNTIL (UPCASE(AnsCh) IN ['Y','N']);
```

As discussed in Chapter 13, "The WHILE Loop," sets are convenient when used with CHAR types and enumerated types.

3. The following is a menu routine that uses READKEY. It is only a portion of a larger program, but it is the basis of the menus used in the book management application in Appendix E. As soon as the user presses one of the menu options, control leaves the menu routine.

```
{ Filename: C21MENU.PAS }

{ Beginning of a menu routine. }
PROGRAM Menu1;
USES Crt;
VAR ChoiceCh: CHAR;                  { character typed by user }
BEGIN
    CLRSCR;
    WRITELN( 'What do you want to do? ' );
    WRITELN;
    WRITELN( '1. Display a report' );
    WRITELN( '2. Enter more data' );
    WRITELN( '3. Quit the program' );
    WRITELN;
    WRITE( 'Please press the number of your choice... ' );
    REPEAT
        ChoiceCh := READKEY;             { Wait until get 1-3 }
    UNTIL (ChoiceCh IN ['1','2','3']);
    WRITELN( ChoiceCh );                 { Echo response to }
                                         { user }
            { rest of program would go here }
END.  {Menu1}
```

Notice that the test in the UNTIL part of the REPEAT loop uses a set of CHARS because ChoiceCh is a CHAR. Because READKEY does not echo to the screen (as READLN does), you must display ChoiceCh if you want to echo the user's input to the screen.

4. This example shows how you can use KEYPRESSED and READKEY together to clear the keyboard buffer. You can use this at the beginning of a program to prevent your program from responding to keystrokes that may have been typed beforehand. Or, in some game situations, you may need to clear the keyboard buffer when you switch to a new part of the game.

```
{Filename C21Kbd1.PAS}

{ Illustrate how you can clear the keyboard buffer. }
PROGRAM ClearKbd;
USES Crt;
VAR Ch: CHAR;
BEGIN
   CLRSCR;
   WHILE KEYPRESSED DO Ch := READKEY;
   WHILE KEYPRESSED DO Ch := READKEY;
          { rest of program would go here }
END.   {ClearKbd}
```

Using a WHILE loop with KEYPRESSED ensures that all regular keystrokes are removed from the keyboard buffer. For example, if someone pressed *k*, the first WHILE loop would remove the *k* from the keyboard buffer. The second WHILE loop would not execute because KEYPRESSED would return false.

However, if someone pressed a function key, the first WHILE loop would only remove the null character (#0). Including a second WHILE loop ensures that all keystrokes are removed from the keyboard buffer.

5. This example shows you how you can read any character that READKEY can return. You can read characters of the alphabet, function keys, and special combinations that use Alt and Ctrl. The program loops until you press Esc.

```
{Filename C21Kbd2.PAS}

{ Illustrate how you can read any key that READKEY can return.}
PROGRAM ReadKbd;
USES Crt;
VAR Ch: CHAR;                        { character typed by user }
BEGIN
   CLRSCR;
         { Clear keyboard buffer }
   WHILE KEYPRESSED DO Ch := READKEY;
   WHILE KEYPRESSED DO Ch := READKEY;
   WRITELN( 'This program responds to Enter, 0, A, z, and Esc' );
   WRITELN( ' as well as Alt-Q, F1, F2, Up arrow, and Ctrl PgDn' );
   REPEAT
      Ch := READKEY;
      IF KEYPRESSED                  { test if #0 in keyboard buffer }
         THEN BEGIN
                 Ch := READKEY;
                 CASE Ch OF
                    #16: WRITELN( 'You pressed Alt Q');
                    #59: WRITELN( 'You pressed F1' );
                    #60: WRITELN( 'You pressed F2' );
                    #72: WRITELN( 'You pressed the up arrow key' );
                   #118: WRITELN( 'You pressed Ctrl PgDn' );
                 END;  {case}
              END
         ELSE CASE Ch OF
                 #13: WRITELN( 'You pressed Enter' );
                 #27: WRITELN( 'You pressed Esc' );
                 #48: WRITELN( 'You pressed 0' );
                 #65: WRITELN( 'You pressed A' );
                #122: WRITELN( 'You pressed z' );
              END;  {case}
   UNTIL Ch = #27;
END.  {ReadKbd}
```

The program starts by using the idea from Example 3 to
clear the keyboard buffer. After READKEY returns a CHAR from
the user, KEYPRESSED is called to test if a function key or
combination of keys was pressed. If so, then READKEY is called
again to replace the null character currently in Ch with

another character. A CASE statement then determines which key was pressed. You can expand the constants in this CASE statement with values from Table B.2 in the *Turbo Pascal Programmer's Guide* that accompanies Turbo Pascal. If #0 is not in the keyboard buffer, another CASE statement determines which character was typed. You can use the ASCII table in Appendix A of this book to expand the constants in the second CASE statement. Notice that no BEGIN–END pair is needed with ELSE to block this second CASE statement.

Summary

You have seen the Turbo Pascal string functions and the UPCASE function. Many string functions often are used in programs.

You have seen many built-in Turbo Pascal functions. Although Turbo Pascal has many functions, there is not a function for everything you will ever need. That is why you need to learn how to program computers.

Not every routine must be a complete program, however. The next chapter shows you how to create your own functions. When you create a function, your program can call it and pass it parameters as though it were built-in.

Review Questions

Answers to the Review Questions appear in Appendix B.

1. True or False: If you send an uppercase character to UPCASE, you get a lowercase character as a result.

2. True or False: The LENGTH function returns the maximum number of characters that a string can store.

3. Write a WRITELN statement that displays only the first seven characters of a string variable, tStr, where tStr is declared as:

```
VAR tStr: STRING[10];
```

4. What value does the following POS statement return?

```
X := POS('C','cCcC');
```

5. When do you use the READKEY function rather than the READLN statement?

6. What does the following WRITELN statement display?

```
A := 'Turbo Pascal is fun!';
b := COPY(A, 1, 12);
WRITELN( b );
```

7. What string is returned by COPY in the following code fragment?

```
a := 'Turbo Pascal';
b := COPY(a,1,25);
```

8. Use WRITELN with LENGTH to display the following title centered at the top of an 80-column screen (use only one statement):

```
Turbo Pascal by Example
```

Review Exercises

1. Write a program to ask users for their first and last names. Then display only their initials.

2. Write a program that asks users for their first, middle, and last names. Display the names as last name, first name, and middle initial.

3. Study the fancy name-displaying program toward the end of Chapter 3, "What Is a Program?" that lets you practice using the Turbo Pascal editor. It is full of string and number functions. Add a few more of your own routines to display the name in unique ways, such as across the screen diagonally.

User-Defined Functions

Now that you have seen Turbo Pascal's built-in functions, it's time to learn how to define your own. Although there are many built-in functions in Turbo Pascal, there is not a built-in function for everything you could possibly want to do.

Consequently, Turbo Pascal enables you to define your own functions, called *user-defined functions*. You can pass parameters to a user-defined function just as you did with the built-in functions. You can write user-defined functions to return simple data types. As with some of Turbo Pascal's built-in functions, your user-defined functions do not have to require parameters.

This chapter introduces you to

♦ What user-defined functions are

♦ How to use user-defined functions

♦ How to write user-defined functions

This chapter contains several examples of user-defined functions that you might want to include in your own programs. The more routines you write that are user-defined functions, the less work you have to do in the future. You can reuse your user-defined functions instead of typing the same routine in every program you write.

Overview of User-Defined Functions

When you write a user-defined function, you are writing a miniprogram that will be called from your main program. In other words, a user-defined function is simply one or more Turbo Pascal statements that you write and assign a name to. After you write a user-defined function, you only have to type the function name, just as you did with INT and CHR, plus any required parameters.

Over time, you likely will write a large number of user-defined functions. When you write a useful function, you cannot add it to the Turbo Pascal language. In Chapter 25, "Units," you learn how to save a function to a file, called a *unit*. A unit is nothing more than a file containing many of your functions. Storing functions in units saves you typing time and errors—you can write functions and use them again at a later time.

How to Use a Function

The format of a function is

```
FUNCTION FunctionName [ ( Var1: Type1
                       [ ;Var2: Type2]
                       [ ; ... )] ] : FunctionType;
   BEGIN
     ⋮
     FunctionName := ...;
   END;   {FunctionName}
```

A function requires a *FunctionName* that you devise and use to call the function later. The name must conform to the same naming rules as do variable names. The function has a data type, just as variables do, which is the last part of a function header and is separated from the rest of the header by a colon. For instance, if the first part of a function looks like

```
FUNCTION Cut( ...): STRING;
```

the `FunctionName` is `Cut`. You call that function (execute it) by referring to that name in the program. This function returns a `STRING`.

The list of parameters (`Var1: Type1`; `Var2: Type2`; ...) is a list of one or more variable names and the corresponding data type. The parameter list defines the number and data type of each parameter you pass to your function. If your function does not need any parameters, there is no parameter list.

> **NOTE:** A user-defined function can have more than one parameter passed to it, but it can have only one return value. This return value will be either a `BOOLEAN`, `CHAR`, integer, real, `STRING`, or one of your own defined enumerated types. An additional return type is the `POINTER`, which is beyond the scope of this book.

Inside the `BEGIN-END` pair is the block of code where your function does all the work. After the body of the function, you must assign the function name to a final expression (which can be a variable, a constant, or a mixture of both). This is the function's *return value.* To return a value (and every function in Turbo Pascal must return a value), you are required to define a type for the function.

> **NOTE:** Turbo Pascal does not check that you assigned the `FunctionName` to a result inside the `BEGIN-END` pair. If you forget to do this, your function's result will be undefined.

To get you started with the feel of functions, the first set of examples shows functions that require no parameters.

Examples

1. User-defined functions that have no parameters are fairly limited; however, you can perform some simple, timesaving operations with them. If you have a long name, you can define a function with the sole purpose of displaying your name. Look at the following program.

```
{ Filename: C22FNAME.PAS }

{ Defines a function that returns a long, full name. }
PROGRAM FullName1;
USES Crt;

FUNCTION MyFullName: STRING;
   BEGIN
     MyFullName := 'Stephen Alonzo Jackson';
   END;   {MyFullName}

BEGIN
   CLRSCR;
   WRITELN( MyFullName );              { Show function's }
                                       { return value }
   WRITELN( MyFullName );              { Show it a second time }
   WRITELN( COPY(MyFullName, 1, 7 ) ); { A function's return }
                                       { value is like any }
                                       { other type }
END.   {FullName1}
```

In the following output from this program, notice that the
return value is a string. You know that the return value is a
string by looking at the data type of the function.

```
Stephen Alonzo Jackson
Stephen Alonzo Jackson
Stephen
```

2. One good use of a user-defined function without parameters
   might be a multiple-character displaying routine. For example, the following user-defined function saves typing:

```
{ Defines a multiple-character displaying function. }
FUNCTION Dash80:  STRING;
   VAR tStr: STRING;
       i:    INTEGER;
   BEGIN
     tStr := '';
```

```
    FOR i := 1 TO 80 DO tStr := tStr + '-';
    Dash80 := tStr;          { define return value }
 END;   {Dash80}

{ A program only has to call Dash80 }
{ in order to display a string of 80 dashes }
```

Notice how the function has its own variables, which only this function may use. The main program does not even know they exist. This topic is called *variable scope* and is discussed in Chapter 24.

When you use a FOR loop in a function, the index variable must be declared in the function. In the above example, i is the index variable. This topic is also discussed more fully in Chapter 24.

3. Functions can use variables declared by the main program. For example, the following program uses a user-defined function that calculates the area of a room. It assumes that the variables RoomLength and RoomWidth are already defined with a value before they are used.

```
{ Filename: C22AREA1.PAS }

PROGRAM Area1;
USES Crt;
VAR RoomWidth:  INTEGER;
    RoomLength: INTEGER;

    { User-defined function to calculate area. }

FUNCTION Area: LONGINT;
   BEGIN
      Area := RoomLength * RoomWidth;
   END;   {Area}

BEGIN
   CLRSCR;
   RoomWidth := 25;                    { Use a fixed width }
```

```
    FOR RoomLength := 10 TO 20 DO   { Loop through several }
                                    { length values }
       WRITELN( 'Width: ',    RoomWidth,
                ' Length: ', RoomLength,
                ' Area: ',    Area );
END.  {Area1}
```

The following output shows the calculations of different areas.

```
Width: 25  Length: 10  Area: 250
Width: 25  Length: 11  Area: 275
Width: 25  Length: 12  Area: 300
Width: 25  Length: 13  Area: 325
Width: 25  Length: 14  Area: 350
Width: 25  Length: 15  Area: 375
Width: 25  Length: 16  Area: 400
Width: 25  Length: 17  Area: 425
Width: 25  Length: 18  Area: 450
Width: 25  Length: 19  Area: 475
Width: 25  Length: 20  Area: 500
```

Using Parameters with Functions

As shown in the previous examples, using functions without parameters is not always better than simply writing the code without the functions. When you use parameters, however, this changes dramatically. Parameters enable the expressions to take on useful jobs by working on data passed to them. This means that the functions do not always perform the same function every time they are called; they are data-driven and return different values based on the parameters passed to them.

Variables in a parameter list do not have to be variables that are used in the rest of the program. They can simply be referred to in the function's parameter list. For example, the following user-defined function has a single REAL parameter called N:

```
FUNCTION Half(N: REAL): REAL;
   BEGIN
      Half := N / 2;
   END;  {Half}
```

The function name is Half. The parameter is N. The function takes whatever number is sent to it, divides that number by 2, and returns the result as a REAL value.

The program that uses this function does not have to have a variable called N. Actually, it is best that it does not. N is just a placeholder for the parameter. N's primary job is to give the function the following message:

"Whatever value my programmer passes me, use that value in place of N."

You could call the function with the following line:

```
HalfLife := Half(84);
```

When this line of code executes, the function assumes that the 84 passed to it will replace N. The expression N / 2 becomes 84 / 2 when 84 is passed to it.

Although it would have been easier to type the statement

```
HalfLife := 84 / 2;
```

without a function, parameters give your functions much more flexibility, as the following examples show.

Examples

1. You can have more than one parameter in the parameter list. The following program uses the RANDOM function. Instead of RANDOM returning a random number from 0 to 1, this user-defined function called RandomInterval returns a random number between the two numbers the programmer passes to it. This keeps programmers from having to remember and retype the complete integer random-number formula every time they want a whole-number random number.

```
{ Filename: C22RND.PAS }

{ Show 20 random numbers ranging from 1 to 6.}
PROGRAM RandomInterval1;
USES Crt;
VAR i: INTEGER;                               { FOR loop index }

           { Whole-number random-number generator. }

FUNCTION RandomInterval(Left:  INTEGER;
                        Right: INTEGER): INTEGER;
   BEGIN
      RandomInterval := RANDOM(Right - Left + 1) + Left;
   END;  {RandomInterval}

BEGIN
   CLRSCR;
   FOR i := 1 TO 20 DO
      WRITELN( RandomInterval(1,6) ); { Return # from 1 to 6 }
END.  {RandomInterval1}
```

As you can see from the following output, only random numbers from 1 to 6 are generated when the program executes, because the values 1 and 6 were passed to the function. The function assumes that Left will be less than Right.

```
1
5
6
5
1
2
6
2
6
3
5
1
5
3
```

```
3
4
2
4
3
5
```

2. The following example shows two handy functions: *minimum* and *maximum functions*. These functions accept two values each. The maximum function returns the greater of the two values, and the minimum function returns the lesser of the two values. This saves you from having to write an IF statement every time you want to know which of two numbers is bigger or smaller than the other.

```
{ Filename: C22MINMX.PAS }


{ Show how to find the minimum and maximum of two numbers. }
PROGRAM MinMax1;
USES Crt;
VAR N1: INTEGER;                    { 1st number typed by user }
    N2: INTEGER;                    { 2nd number typed by user }


            { A minimum and maximum function for integers. }


FUNCTION MinInt(N1: INTEGER;
                N2: INTEGER): INTEGER;
   BEGIN
      IF N1 < N2
         THEN MinInt := N1
         ELSE MinInt := N2;
   END;  {MinInt}


FUNCTION MaxInt(N1: INTEGER;
                N2: INTEGER): INTEGER;
   BEGIN
      IF N1 > N2
         THEN MaxInt := N1
         ELSE MaxInt := N2;
   END;  {MaxInt}
```

```
BEGIN
   CLRSCR;
   WRITE( 'Please enter two values, separated by spaces ' );
   READLN( N1, N2 );
   WRITELN;
   WRITELN( 'The highest value is: ', MaxInt(N1, N2) );
   WRITELN( 'The lowest value is: ',  MinInt(N1, N2) );
END.  {MinMax1}
```

The parameters passed to MaxInt and MinInt in the WRITELN statements did not have to be named N1 and N2. This program still would have worked if they were named x and y because the N1 and N2 in the user-defined functions are just placeholders for the expression.

Notice that each function name is given a return value in two places depending on which part of the IF statement is true. Although the function can return only one value, you can have more than one function assignment statement. The output for this program is as follows:

```
Please enter two values, separated by spaces 33 54

The highest value is: 54
The lowest valuie is: 33
```

3. Earlier you saw how to compute the square of a number using the Turbo Pascal function SQR. What if you wanted the cube of a number? Turbo Pascal lacks an exponential function. However, you can use some math inside a function to create your own. The following function takes two parameters. The first one is the number you want to raise to some power. The second number is the power or exponent.

```
{ Filename: C22POWER.PAS }


{ Compute the first 15 cubes. }

PROGRAM Power1;
USES Crt;
```

```
VAR i: INTEGER;                         { FOR loop index }


        { Compute the powers of numbers. }

FUNCTION Power(Base:     REAL;
              Exponent: REAL): REAL;
    BEGIN
        Power := EXP(LN(Base)*Exponent);
    END;  {Power}


BEGIN
    CLRSCR;
    FOR i := 1 TO 15 DO
        WRITELN( i, '  ',Power(i, 3):1:2 );  { Compute cubes }
END.  {Power1}
```

You can also use Power to compute roots by using the appropriate fraction for the exponent. For example, to compute the cube root of the numbers above, change the exponent parameter from 3 to 1/3.

4. Here is a function that reverses the characters in a string:

```
FUNCTION ReverseStr(s: STRING): STRING;
    VAR tStr: STRING;              { temp str }
        i:     INTEGER;            { FOR loop index }
    BEGIN
        tStr := '';                { Init as null string }
        FOR i := LENGTH(s) DOWNTO 1 DO
            tStr := tStr + s[i];   { Build new string }
        ReverseStr := tStr;        { Define return value! }
    END; {ReverseStr}
```

The parameter is s. The function's return value is tStr because it is assigned to the function's name. Remember that all functions must return a value. The return value is the value you assign to the function name.

To call this function (to execute it), you simply have to pass it a string value. As long as you have defined the function before you use it, you can call it from anywhere in the program. The following line sends the function a string constant:

```
BackStr := ReverseStr('Larry');
```

Because ReverseStr's return value is a string, this line of code puts the reversed Larry in the variable called BackStr. If you then display BackStr, you see the following result:

```
yrraL
```

Advantages of Functions

Defining a rather complicated function just to reverse the letters in *Larry* might seem like a lot of work. You might be asking why you can't type the reverse string routine in the program when you need it without bothering with all the function definition code at the top of the program. The power of user-defined functions comes in when you need the same routine several times in one program (or in several programs).

For instance, to reverse only one string in a program, it probably would be easier to type the code that reverses it at the point in the program where it's required. If you have to reverse several strings in the same program, however, your coding time is shortened if you define a function to reverse the strings. After you define the function, you can call it from several places in your program and pass it several different values without retyping the routine. Your program might have the following statements:

```
:
WRITELN( ReverseStr('Larry') );
BackName := ReverseStr(First) + ReverseStr(Last);

Mir     := ReverseStr('This string gets reversed');
WRITELN( Mir );     { display the reversed string }
:
```

Although this example might be slightly exaggerated, if you have to reverse more than one string (as this example code does four times), you must write four sets of string-reversal routines in your program. Because you defined the function at the top of the program, however, you only have to call it from then on. Whatever string variable, constant, or string expression you pass to it will be received in the function's parameter list and reversed.

Another advantage to using your own functions is to improve your code's readability. It is much easier to see ReverseStr and have a good idea what the code does than to interpret a detailed FOR loop.

If a function defines the return value in an IF statement, you must be careful that the function is always defined. In the previous examples with MinInt and MaxInt, these functions were defined no matter which part of the IF statement was true.

EXIT is not the same as HALT.

Turbo Pascal also has an option to quickly exit a function. When you know that there is no need to continue executing statements in a function, you can include the EXIT statement. This is really a GOTO in disguise. When Turbo Pascal finds an EXIT statement, it jumps to the end of the function without executing the rest of the function's code. The EXIT statement can be placed in the main program block. A brief example makes this clear.

The following user-defined function is an expanded version of the string-reversal function you saw earlier. It simply returns the reversed parameter *unless* it is passed 'Don't reverse' as a parameter. If it receives the 'Don't reverse' string, it simply returns the string untouched.

```
    { Reverse the characters in a string }

FUNCTION ReverseStr(s: STRING): STRING;
    VAR tStr: STRING;
        i:    INTEGER;
    BEGIN
        IF (s = 'Don''t reverse')
            THEN BEGIN
                    ReverseStr := s;      { Don't change string }
                    EXIT;
                END;
        tStr := '';                       { Init as null string }
        FOR i := LENGTH(s) DOWNTO 1 DO
            tStr := tStr + s[i];          { Build a new string }
        ReverseStr := tStr;                { The return value }
    END;  {ReverseStr}
```

Notice that the string is returned to the calling program untouched if the string contains `Don't reverse`. Otherwise, the string is reversed. Although there are two `ReverseStr := ...` statements, only one of them executes because the `IF` statement conditionally controls them. The `EXIT` is necessary to keep the string reversal from happening if the parameter equals `Don't reverse`.

> **TIP:** When you use `EXIT` to quit a function, be sure the function name is used in an assignment statement before you call `EXIT`.

You can put statements other than calculations inside a function. For instance, in the function just shown, you could have included `WRITELN` and `READLN` statements. These types of statements, however, cloud the function. You should keep your functions as tight as possible and not include many input or output statements in them. Functions are a great way to perform routine calculations, `BOOLEAN` checks, and string manipulations on parameters you pass to them.

Examples

1. The following user-defined function requires an integer parameter. When you pass it an integer, the function adds the numbers from 1 to that integer. In other words, if you pass the function a 6, it returns the result of the following calculation:

$$1 + 2 + 3 + 4 + 5 + 6$$

This is known as the *sum of the digits* calculation and is sometimes used in accounting to calculate depreciation.

```
{ Filename: C22SUMD.PAS }

PROGRAM Sum1;
USES Crt;
VAR N1: INTEGER;
    N2: INTEGER;
    N3: INTEGER;
```

```
                    { Function that computes sum of digits for its }
                    { parameter. }

        FUNCTION SumDep(n: INTEGER): INTEGER;
            VAR Sum: INTEGER;                   { running total }
                i:   INTEGER;                   { FOR loop index }
            BEGIN
                IF (n <= 0)
                    THEN BEGIN
                            SumDep := n;        { Return parameter }
                                EXIT;           { if too small }
                        END
                    Sum := 0;                   { Init total variable }
                    FOR i := 1 TO n DO
                        INC(Sum,i);
                    SumDep := Sum;              { Return the result }
            END;  {SumDep}

        BEGIN
            CLRSCR;
                    { Pass the function several values }
            N1 := SumDep(6);
            WRITELN( 'The sum of the digits for 6 is ', N1 );

            WRITELN( 'The sum of the digits for 0 is ', SumDep(0) );
            WRITE( 'The sum of the digits for 18 is ' );
            WRITELN( SumDep(18) );

            N2 := 25;
            N3 := SumDep(N2);
            WRITELN( 'The sum of the digits for ', N2, ' is ', N3 );
        END.   {Sum1}
```

The function is called four times. The second time, the
parameter is 0, so the function simply returns it unchanged.
The output from this program follows.

```
The sum of the digits for 6 is 21
The sum of the digits for 0 is 0
The sum of the digits for 18 is 171
The sum of the digits for 25 is 325
```

2. The program that follows includes two user-defined string functions. This example illustrates how you can call a function from inside another function. The function, FirstWordUC, returns the first word of a string in uppercase by calling the two functions, FirstWord and Caps. They perform these actions

◆ FirstWord returns the first word of the string.

◆ Caps returns a string in uppercase letters.

```
{ Filename: C22STR2F.PAS }


{
  Illustrates a single program with multiple user
  string functions.
}
PROGRAM String1;
USES Crt;
VAR tStr: STRING;

            { Find the first word of a string by locating the
              position of the first space. Then copy from
              the first character of the string to one place
              before the space. }

FUNCTION FirstWord(s1: STRING): STRING;
   BEGIN
      FirstWord := COPY(s1, 1, POS(' ', s1) - 1 );
   END;  {FirstWord}

FUNCTION Caps(s: STRING): STRING;
   VAR i: INTEGER;                  { FOR loop index }
   BEGIN
      FOR i := 1 TO LENGTH(s) DO s[i] := UPCASE(s[i]);
      Caps := s;                    { define return value! }
   END;  {Caps}

FUNCTION FirstWordUC(s: STRING): STRING;
   BEGIN
      FirstWordUC := Caps(FirstWord(s));
   END;  {FirstWordUC}
```

```
BEGIN
        CLRSCR;
        tStr := 'The rain in Spain';
        WRITELN( 'String                  = ', tStr );
        WRITELN( 'First Word              = ', FirstWord(tStr) );
        WRITELN( 'First word capitalized = FirstWordUC(tStr) );
END.   {String1}
```

3. The following program includes a user-defined function that centers within 80 spaces any string passed to it and builds an output line on-screen. This example also illustrates how a function (Blanks) can be called from another function (Center). When you need to center a string, simply pass it to this function. The function returns the string so that you can display it centered on-screen.

```
{ Filename: C22CENT.PAS }

{ Routine that returns a centered string. }
PROGRAM Center1;
USES Crt;
TYPE MaxString = STRING[80];
VAR  InStr: MaxString;


          { Build a string of n spaces. }

FUNCTION Blanks(n: INTEGER): MaxString;
    VAR i:    INTEGER;              { FOR loop index }
       tStr: MaxString;            { temp string }
    BEGIN
       tStr := '';                 { init to null string }
       FOR i := 1 TO n DO tStr := tStr + ' ';
       Blanks := tStr;             { define return value! }
    END; {Blanks}

FUNCTION Center(s: STRING): MaxString;
    VAR Indent: INTEGER;           { # of spaces before string }
    BEGIN
       IF (LENGTH(s) > 80)
          THEN BEGIN
```

```
                          Center := s;      { Return string if too long }
                          EXIT;
                       END;
                 Indent := (80 - LENGTH(s)) DIV 2;
                 Center := Blanks(Indent) + s + Blanks(Indent);
            END;   {Center}


            { Show user how it works }
        BEGIN
            CLRSCR;
            WRITELN( 'Please type a string, and I will display it' );
            WRITELN( 'centered on the next line...' );
            READLN( InStr );
            WRITELN( Center(InStr) );      { Display it centered }
        END.   {Center1}
```

You can add this routine to your own library to use when you need to center a title on-screen. The following is the output of a sample run.

```
Please type a string, and I will display it
centered on the next line...
Turbo Pascal By Example
                                Turbo Pascal By Example
```

4. Many programs have BOOLEAN functions to verify input. Here are two such functions:

```
FUNCTION Yes(AnsCh: CHAR): BOOLEAN;
    BEGIN
        Yes := UPCASE(AnsCh) = 'Y';
    END;   {Yes}


FUNCTION ValidDigit(Digit: CHAR): BOOLEAN;
    BEGIN
        ValidDigit := Digit IN ['0'..'9'];
    END;   {ValidDigit}
```

For example, to check if a user responded with 'Y', 'y', 'N', or 'n', use an IF statement like this:

```
IF Yes(UserCh)
   THEN ...     { do something with the Yes answer }
   ELSE ...;    { do something with the No answer }
```

You can use the second function to verify that a user has typed all digits in an input string:

```
TYPE UserCh: CHAR;
BEGIN
   ⋮
   WRITE( 'Please type a number from 0 to 9: ' );
   READLN(UserCh);
   IF ValidDigit(UserCh)
      THEN ...   {do something with the valid digit }
      ELSE ...;  {do something with an invalid digit }
   ⋮
END.
```

Summary

This chapter has shown you how to build your own collection of user-defined functions. When you write a user-defined function, you save programming time later. Instead of writing the routine a second or third time, you only have to call the function by its name. Over time, you will develop a good library of your own functions to accent Turbo Pascal's built-in functions. In Chapter 25, "Units," you learn how to organize your library into files called units.

Review Questions

Answers to the Review Questions appear in Appendix B.

1. Why do you sometimes need to define your own functions?

2. True or False: A user-defined function without any parameter list can return more than one value.

3. Given the user-defined function:

```
FUNCTION Fun(i: INTEGER): STRING;
    BEGIN
        Fun := CHR(i) + CHR(i) + CHR(i);
    END;   {Fun}
```

A. What is the return data type?

B. How many parameters are passed to it?

C. What is the data type of the parameter(s)?

4. True or False: If a function includes several function name assignment statements, it returns more than one value when it is called.

5. Which built-in numeric function does the following user-defined function simulate?

```
FUNCTION A(x: INTEGER): INTEGER;
    BEGIN
        A := x * x;
    END;   {A}
```

Review Exercises

1. Write a function to reverse a string of characters and convert them to uppercase.

2. For the function, RandomInterval, presented earlier in this chapter, add error checking to verify that parameter Left is less than parameter Right.

3. Write a function that computes the real area of a circle, given its real radius. The formula to calculate the radius of a circle is

```
Area := PI * SQR(radius);
```

4. Write a function to verify that a character is a valid alphabetical character.

5. Modify the Power function to make sure that the function does not try to calculate the power if the Base parameter is 0.

6. Use the RandomInterval function presented earlier to test how random the results are for "throwing" a die. After 100 throws, display the totals for each number 1-6.

7. Write a function to return the value of a polynomial (the answer), given this formula:

$$9x^4 + 15x^2 + x^1$$

User-Defined Procedures

The preceding three chapters taught you how to use Turbo Pascal's built-in functions and how to design your own. This chapter builds on that knowledge by extending the power of routines you write yourself.

Computers never get bored. They loop and perform the same input, output, and computations that your programs require as long as you want them to. You can take advantage of their repetitive nature by looking at your programs in a new way: as a series of small routines that execute when and as many times as you need them to execute.

Most of the material in this chapter and the next chapter improves on the subroutine concept. This chapter covers

♦ An overview of procedures

♦ Building your own subroutine library

This chapter stresses the use of *modular programming*. Turbo Pascal was designed to make it easy for you to write your programs in several modules rather than as one long program. By breaking programs into several smaller routines, you can isolate problems better, write correct programs faster, and produce programs that are much easier to maintain than if you wrote them as one long program.

An Overview of Procedures

When you approach an application that needs to be programmed, it is best not to sit down at the keyboard and start typing. Rather, you should think about the program and what it is to do. One of the best ways to attack a program is to start with the program's overall goal and break it into several smaller modules. You should never lose sight of the overall goal of the program, but you should try to think of how the individual pieces fit together to accomplish that goal.

When finally you sit down to start coding the problem, continue to think in terms of those individual pieces that fit together. Do not approach a program as if it were one giant entity; rather, continue to write the small pieces individually.

This does not mean you should write separate programs to do everything. You can keep individual pieces of the overall program together by writing *procedures*. Procedures are sections of programs you can execute repeatedly. Many good programmers write programs that consist solely of procedures, even if they are to execute one or more of the procedures only once.

Look at the following code to get a feel for the way procedures work. It is not a Turbo Pascal program, but a preliminary outline for one—an outline of a problem that needs to be programmed. The program is to receive a list of numbers from the keyboard, sort the numbers, and display them on the screen. You have seen examples of such programs in previous chapters.

```
{ Program to receive a list of numbers, sort them, and display }
{ them. }

BEGIN
   ⋮
   Turbo Pascal statements to get list of numbers into an array.
   ⋮
```

```
    ⋮
    Turbo Pascal statements to sort those numbers
    ⋮
    Turbo Pascal statements to display those numbers to screen

END.
```

It turns out that this is not a good way to approach this program. Until now, you were too busy concentrating on the individual Turbo Pascal language elements to worry about procedures, but now it is time for you to improve the way you think of programs. The problem with the approach shown in the preceding outline is that it is one long program with one Turbo Pascal statement after another, yet there are three distinct sections (or better yet, *sub*sections) in the program.

Because the overall program is obviously a collection of smaller routines, you can group these routines by making them procedures. The following shows an outline of the same program, but it has broken the routines into distinct procedures and added a new block at the bottom of the program that controls the other procedures.

```
{
   Program with three routines.
   The main (bottom) block controls the execution of the others.
   The first routine gets a list of numbers.
   The second one sorts those numbers.
   The third one displays them to the screen.
}
PROGRAM Sort1;

PROCEDURE GetNumbers;                      { First Routine }
   BEGIN
      Turbo Pascal statements to get list of numbers
      ⋮
   END;   {GetNumbers}

PROCEDURE SortNumbers;                      { Second Routine }
   BEGIN
```

```
        Turbo Pascal statements to sort numbers
        ⋮
    END;   {SortNumbers}


PROCEDURE DisplayNumbers;                   { Third Routine }
    BEGIN
      Turbo Pascal statements to display numbers on screen

        ⋮
    END;   {DisplayNumbers}


BEGIN
    GetNumbers;
    SortNumbers;
    DisplayNumbers;
END.   {Sort1}
```

This program outline is a much better way of writing the program. It is longer to type, but it's organization is better. The main (bottom) block simply controls, or *calls*, the other procedures to do their work in the proper order. After all, it would be silly to sort the numbers before the user types them. Therefore, the main block ensures that the other routines execute in the proper sequence.

The main block is not actually a procedure. It is the main program block. (The main program block is often called the *main module, main body,* or *main block.*) This is where you previously would have typed the full program. Now, however, the program only consists of a group of procedure calls. The main program block in all but the shortest of programs should be simply a series of procedure-controlling statements.

Using the above code outlines makes it easier to write the full program. Before going to the keyboard, you know there are four distinct sections of this program: a procedure-calling main module, a keyboard data-entry procedure, a sorting procedure, and a displaying procedure.

Remember, you should never lose sight of the original programming problem. With the approach just described, you never do. Look at the main program block in the last code outline again. Notice that you can glance at this block and get a feel for the overall program without the entire program's statements getting in the way. This is a good example of modular programming. A large programming problem has been broken into distinct modules called procedures. Each procedure performs a primary job in a few Turbo Pascal statements.

The length of each procedure varies depending on what the procedure is to do. A good rule of thumb is that a procedure's length should not be more than one screen long. If it is, it becomes more difficult to edit and maintain with the Turbo Pascal editor. Not only that, if a procedure is more than one screen long, it probably does too much and should be broken into two or more procedures. This is not a requirement; you must make the final judgment on whether a procedure is too long.

Notice that a procedure is like a detour on a highway. You are traveling along in the primary program and then you run into a procedure-calling statement. You must temporarily leave the main block and go execute the procedure's code. When that procedure's code is finished, control of the program is passed back to the main program block at the exact point where it left. (When you finish a detour, you end up back on your main route to continue your trip.) Control continues as the primary block continues to call each procedure one at a time and in the proper order.

You used this calling pattern with the built-in and user-defined functions in the previous chapters. Control of your main program was temporarily suspended while the function executed. Control then returned to your program. As with functions, you can execute a procedure call repeatedly in a loop without having to write the code more than once.

The Procedure

A procedure is a completely separate section of code you call from your main program block. You also can call user-defined and built-in procedures and functions from another procedure or function.

By using procedures, you see only what you want to see. You are forced (thankfully) to think more in terms of modules.

To designate a subroutine as a procedure, you must use the PROCEDURE statement.

The format of a PROCEDURE is

```
PROCEDURE ProcedureName [Var1: Type1][; Var2: Type2] [;...];
   BEGIN
     A block of one or more Turbo Pascal statements
   END;   {ProcedureName}
```

You must give the procedure a unique *ProcedureName*. The name must follow the same rules governing variable names. The *block of one or more Turbo Pascal statements* is one or more statements making up the body of the procedure. Unlike functions, a procedure never has a data type or return value associated with it. The name simply informs Turbo Pascal where to look when the main program calls it. As with functions, a procedure can have its own CONST, TYPE, and VAR sections. Only the statements in this procedure can use these locally defined declarations.

The following section of a program shows a block of statements that constitute a procedure:

```
   .
   .
   .
{
      CalcInt calculates an interest rate. The procedure
      uses a function, Power, from the previous chapter.
}
PROCEDURE CalcInt;
   BEGIN
      WRITE( 'What is the interest rate? (e.g., 0.13) ' );
      READLN( IntRate );
      WRITE( 'How many years is the loan? ' );
      READLN( Term );
      WRITE( 'What is the original loan principal? ' );
      READLN( Prin );
      TotalInt := Prin * Power((1 + Rate),Term);
   END;   {CalcInt}
   .
   .
   .
```

The procedure's name is CalcInt. It is common to indent the body of a procedure. Turbo Pascal knows that it should always return from a procedure to the statement that called it.

If you must exit a procedure before its natural end, use an EXIT statement. This is the same statement you used in the previous chapter when you needed to exit a function. When Turbo Pascal finds an EXIT statement it immediately jumps to the end of the procedure.

> **CAUTION:** You must be very careful when using the EXIT statement in a subroutine (function or procedure), especially when you edit an existing subroutine by adding an EXIT statement. Make sure that no statements following the EXIT statement are required for proper execution of the subroutine.

To call the interest-calculation procedure shown earlier, you must put the procedure name on a separate line as:

```
CalcInt;
```

This statement is located in the main program or in another procedure or function that needs to call CalcInt.

A Procedure Example

This section is different from many of those you have seen earlier in this book. It is a complete walk-through example that takes you from the beginning of a programming problem to its conclusion. It is the application described when this chapter opened: Sort a list of numbers typed by the user and then display them.

The layout of this program is fairly obvious. As shown earlier, there is a main program that calls four procedures. The first procedure simply shows a title for the program. The second procedure gets the list of numbers from the user. The third procedure sorts those numbers. The fourth procedure displays the numbers on the screen. Therefore, the following code is a good outline for the main block:

```
{ Filename: C23SRT1.PAS }

{
  Get a list of numbers, sort them, and
  then display them on the screen.
}

PROGRAM SortNum1;
USES Crt;
CONST MaxNum = 100;
TYPE  NumArray = ARRAY[1..MaxNum] OF INTEGER;

VAR Nums:      NumArray;                  { array for user's # }
    TotalNums: INTEGER;                   { total # typed by user }
BEGIN
   TEXTCOLOR(WHITE);
   TEXTBACKGROUND(BLUE);
   CLRSCR;
   ShowTitle;
   GetNums;                               { Get the input }
   SortNums;                              { Sort them }
   DisplayNums;                           { Display them }
END.   {SortNum1}
```

For now, type this program (but don't run it). Turbo Pascal requires a procedure to be defined before it is called. Type the following (shown in **bold**) after the TotalNums declaration and before the BEGIN of the main program block. Your program should now look like this:

```
{ Filename: C23SRT1.PAS }

{
  Get a list of numbers, sort them, and
  then display them on the screen.
}

PROGRAM SortNum1;
USES Crt;
CONST MaxNum = 100;
```

```
TYPE  NumArray = ARRAY[1..MaxNum] OF INTEGER;

VAR Nums:     NumArray;                { array for user's # }
    TotalNums: INTEGER;                { total # typed by user }

PROCEDURE ShowTitle;
  BEGIN
  END;  {ShowTitle}

PROCEDURE GetNums;
  BEGIN
  END;  {GetNums}

PROCEDURE SortNums;
  BEGIN
  END;  {SortNums}

PROCEDURE DisplayNums;
  BEGIN
  END;  {DisplayNums}

BEGIN
  TEXTCOLOR(WHITE);
  TEXTBACKGROUND(BLUE);
  CLRSCR;
  ShowTitle;
  GetNums;                             { Get the input }
  SortNums;                            { Sort them }
  DisplayNums;                         { Display them }
END.  {SortNum1}
```

These skeleton procedures satisfy Turbo Pascal's requirement that all procedures be defined before being called. By pressing Alt–C, you can even compile this outline. In fact, writing skeleton procedures like this is a common programming technique.

Typically, the next step would be to complete the first procedure and test it. After you convince yourself it works correctly, you would start the process over again with the next procedure.

GetNums introduces the built-in Turbo Pascal procedure VAL. VAL uses three parameters to convert a string value to a number. The first parameter is the string you want to convert. The second parameter is the converted number. If the string was successfully converted to a number, the third parameter returns 0. If the string was not successfully converted, the third parameter returns the index of the first character that could not be converted. For instance, if you send VAL the string '123', VAL would successfully convert it to the number 123 and the third parameter would be 0. However, if you send VAL the string, '12a', the number would not be converted and the third parameter would return a 3.

Complete the ShowTitle procedure with the following:

```
PROCEDURE ShowTitle;
   BEGIN
      WRITELN( '*** Number Sorting Program ***' );
      WRITELN;
   END;  {ShowTitle}
```

Complete the GetNums procedure with the following:

```
          { GetNums gets a list of user numbers }

PROCEDURE GetNums;
    VAR i:       INTEGER;    { counter to stay within array }
        Done:    BOOLEAN;    { true if user presses only Enter }
        tNum:    INTEGER;    { user's string converted to number }
        NumStr:  STRING[6];  { string typed by user }
        ErrCode: INTEGER;    { chk to verify good conversion }
    BEGIN
        i    := 1;
        Done := FALSE;
        WHILE ((i <= MaxNum) AND (NOT Done)) DO
          BEGIN
            WRITELN;
            WRITELN( 'To quit, press Enter without typing '+
                     'anything' );
            WRITE( 'Please type the next number in the list ' );
            READLN( NumStr );
            IF NumStr = ''
               THEN Done := TRUE
               ELSE BEGIN
                     VAL(NumStr,tNum,ErrCode);
                     IF ErrCode = 0
                        THEN BEGIN
```

```
                        Nums[i] := tNum;
                        INC(i);
                    END
                 ELSE WRITELN( 'Please check number' );
            END;
      END;  {while}
   TotalNums := PRED(i);
END;  {GetNums}
```

You now are ready to type the sorting and displaying procedures. Complete the SortNums and DisplayNums procedures with the following:

```
      { SortNums uses a bubble sort }

PROCEDURE SortNums;
   VAR i:    INTEGER;              { FOR loop index }
       j:    INTEGER;              { FOR loop index }
      tNum: INTEGER;               { temp num for swapping order }
   BEGIN
      FOR i := 1 TO TotalNums DO
         FOR j := i TO TotalNums DO
            IF (Nums[i] > Nums[j])
               THEN BEGIN                { swap array elements }
                     tNum    := Nums[j];
                     Nums[j] := Nums[i];
                     Nums[i] := tNum;
                  END;
   END;  {SortNums}


      { DisplayNum displays the sorted list of numbers }

PROCEDURE DisplayNums;
   VAR i: INTEGER;                  { FOR loop index }
   BEGIN
      WRITELN;
      WRITELN( 'Here are the ',TotalNums,' sorted numbers' );
      WRITELN;
      FOR i := 1 TO TotalNums DO
         WRITELN( Nums[i] );                { Display each sorted # }
   END;  {DisplayNums}
```

When you use a FOR loop in a procedure (or function), the index variable must be declared in the procedure. In procedure SortNums, i and j are the index variables. In procedure DisplayNums, i is the index variable. This topic is discussed more fully in Chapter 24, "Identifier Scope."

You have now typed the complete program, including procedures. Notice that each procedure is preceded with a comment to briefly explain the procedure. This is good habit to develop.

To run this program, you only have to select **Run Run** from the menu (or press Ctrl–F9) as you have done with previous Turbo Pascal programs. If you typed the program correctly, you should be able to run it, type several numbers, and see them displayed. Figure 23.1 shows a sample run.

Save the program to disk under the filename in the comments: C23SRT1.PAS (with the **File Save** menu option).

```
*** Number Sorting Program ***

To quit, press Enter without typing anything
Please type the next number in the list 87
Please type the next number in the list 66
Please type the next number in the list 43
Please type the next number in the list 48
Please type the next number in the list 19
Please type the next number in the list 8
Please type the next number in the list 24
Please type the next number in the list

Here are the 7 sorted numbers

8
19
24
43
48
66
87
```

Figure 23.1. Showing a list of sorted numbers.

Wrapping Up Procedures

The body of the main program reads almost as though it were English. It looks like:

Get the numbers, sort the numbers, and then display the numbers.

Although this might be stretching things a bit, by making up meaningful procedure labels, you can make your programs more self-documenting.

The following program makes you feel good about your age *and* your weight! It contains a menu that controls the three things you might want to do. Typing the main program block first is a common technique. This provides an overall view for your program. For now, type the main module of the program, which is listed here:

```
{ Filename: C23AGEWT.PAS }


{
  Program to compute age in dog years and weight on the moon
  to illustrate function and procedure calls.
}

PROGRAM AgeWeight1;
USES Crt;
VAR Choice: INTEGER;              { menu option selected by user }
    Quit:   BOOLEAN;              { flag to quit program }

BEGIN
   TEXTCOLOR(WHITE);
   TEXTBACKGROUND(BLUE);
   CLRSCR;
   Quit := FALSE;
   REPEAT
      DisplayMenu;                     { Call menu procedure }
      CASE Choice OF
         1: ShowDogAge;                { Call dog age procedure }
         2: ShowMoonWeight;            { Call moon wt procedure }
         3: Quit := TRUE;
         ELSE WRITELN( 'Please type 1 - 3 for a menu option' );
```

```
      END;  {case}
   UNTIL Quit;
END.  {AgeWeight1}
```

Now that you have typed the main module, you are ready to begin with the procedures. Type the following procedure, shown in **bold** (DisplayMenu), after the Quit declaration and before the BEGIN of the main program block:

```
{ Filename: C23AGEWT.PAS }


{
  Program to compute age in dog years and weight on the moon
  to illustrate function and procedure calls.
}

PROGRAM AgeWeight1;
USES Crt;
VAR Choice: INTEGER;             { menu option selected by user }
    Quit:   BOOLEAN;             { flag to quit program }

PROCEDURE DisplayMenu;
   BEGIN
      WRITELN;
      WRITELN( 'Do you want to?' );
      WRITELN;
      WRITELN( '1. Compute your age in dog years' );
      WRITELN( '2. Compute your weight on the moon' );
      WRITELN( '3. Quit this program' );
      WRITELN;
      WRITE( 'What is your choice? ' );
      READLN( Choice );
   END;  {DisplayMenu}

BEGIN
   TEXTCOLOR(WHITE);
   TEXTBACKGROUND(BLUE);
   CLRSCR;
   Quit := FALSE;
   REPEAT
```

```
        DisplayMenu;                        { Call menu procedure }
        CASE Choice OF
           1: ShowDogAge;                    { Call dog age procedure }
           2: ShowMoonWeight;               { Call moon wt procedure }
           3: Quit := TRUE;
           ELSE WRITELN( 'Please type 1 - 3 for a menu option' );
        END;  {case}
     UNTIL Quit;
END.   {AgeWeight1}
```

Type the following lines after the DisplayMenu procedure. Because the procedure ShowDogAge calls the function DogAgeCalc, you must define DogAgeCalc before ShowDogAge.

```
{ Filename: C23AGEWT.PAS }


{
  Program to compute age in dog years and weight on the moon
  to illustrate function and procedure calls.
}

PROGRAM AgeWeight1;
USES Crt;
VAR Choice: INTEGER;               { menu option selected by user }
    Quit:   BOOLEAN;               { flag to quit program }


PROCEDURE DisplayMenu;
   BEGIN
      WRITELN;
      WRITELN( 'Do you want to?' );
      WRITELN;
      WRITELN( '1. Compute your age in dog years' );
      WRITELN( '2. Compute your weight on the moon' );
      WRITELN( '3. Quit this program' );
      WRITELN;
      WRITE( 'What is your choice? ' );
      READLN( Choice );
   END;  {DisplayMenu}


FUNCTION DogAgeCalc(Age: INTEGER): INTEGER;
   BEGIN
```

```
            DogAgeCalc := Age DIV 7;
        END;  {DogAgeCalc}

    PROCEDURE ShowDogAge;
        VAR Ch:     CHAR;              { removes char from kbd buffer }
            Age:    INTEGER;           { age typed by user }
            DogAge: INTEGER;           { age converted to dog years }
        BEGIN
          WRITELN;
          WRITE( 'How old are you ' );
          READLN( Age );
          DogAge := DogAgeCalc(Age);        { Call dog age function }
          WRITELN;
          WRITELN( 'Your age in dog years is only ', DogAge, '!' );
          WRITELN( 'You''re younger than you thought...' );
          WRITELN;
          WRITELN( 'Press any key to return to the main menu...' );
          REPEAT UNTIL KEYPRESSED;
          Ch := READKEY;
        END;  {ShowDogAge}

BEGIN
    TEXTCOLOR(WHITE);
    TEXTBACKGROUND(BLUE);
    CLRSCR;
    Quit := FALSE;
    REPEAT
        DisplayMenu;                        { Call menu procedure }
        CASE Choice OF
            1: ShowDogAge;                  { Call dog age procedure }
            2: ShowMoonWeight;              { Call moon wt procedure }
            3: Quit := TRUE;
            ELSE WRITELN( 'Please type 1 - 3 for a menu option' );
        END; {case}
    UNTIL Quit;
END.  {AgeWeight1}
```

Because the procedure ShowMoonWeight also calls a function (MoonWeightCalc), you must define that function before the procedure (ShowMoonWeight). Type the following after the ShowDogAge procedure.

```
{ Filename: C23AGEWT.PAS }


{
  Program to compute age in dog years and weight on the moon
  to illustrate function and procedure calls.
}

PROGRAM AgeWeight1;
USES Crt;
VAR Choice: INTEGER;                 { menu option selected by user }
    Quit:   BOOLEAN;                 { flag to quit program }

PROCEDURE DisplayMenu;
   BEGIN
      WRITELN;
      WRITELN( 'Do you want to?' );
      WRITELN;
      WRITELN( '1. Compute your age in dog years' );
      WRITELN( '2. Compute your weight on the moon' );
      WRITELN( '3. Quit this program' );
      WRITELN;
      WRITE( 'What is your choice? ' );
      READLN( Choice );
   END;  {DisplayMenu}

FUNCTION DogAgeCalc(Age: INTEGER): INTEGER;
   BEGIN
      DogAgeCalc := Age DIV 7;
   END;  {DogAgeCalc}

PROCEDURE ShowDogAge;
   VAR Ch:    CHAR;               { removes char from kbd buffer }
       Age:    INTEGER;           { age typed by user }
       DogAge: INTEGER;           { age converted to dog years }
   BEGIN
      WRITELN;
      WRITE( 'How old are you ' );
      READLN( Age );
```

```
        DogAge := DogAgeCalc(Age);          { Call dog age function }
        WRITELN;
        WRITELN( 'Your age in dog years is only ', DogAge, '!' );
        WRITELN( 'You''re younger than you thought...' );
        WRITELN;
        WRITELN( 'Press any key to return to the main menu...' );
        REPEAT UNTIL KEYPRESSED;
        Ch := READKEY;
    END;   {ShowDogAge}


FUNCTION MoonWeightCalc(Weight: INTEGER): INTEGER;
    BEGIN
        MoonWeightCalc := Weight DIV 6;
    END;   {MoonWeightCalc}


PROCEDURE ShowMoonWeight;
    VAR Ch:         CHAR;        { removes char from kbd buffer }
        Weight:     INTEGER;     { weight typed by user }
        MoonWeight: INTEGER;     { weight converted to moon weight }
    BEGIN
        WRITELN;
        WRITE( 'How much do you weigh? ' );
        READLN( Weight );
        MoonWeight := MoonWeightCalc(Weight);
        WRITELN;
        WRITELN( 'Your weight on the moon is only ', MoonWeight,
                 ' pounds!' );
        WRITELN( 'You are light enough to fly! (on the moon...)' );
        WRITELN;
        WRITELN( 'Press any key to return to the main menu...' );
        REPEAT UNTIL KEYPRESSED;
        Ch := READKEY;
    END;   {ShowMoonWeight}


BEGIN
    TEXTCOLOR(WHITE);
    TEXTBACKGROUND(BLUE);
    CLRSCR;
    Quit := FALSE;
    REPEAT
```

```
    DisplayMenu;                         { Call menu procedure }
    CASE Choice OF
        1: ShowDogAge;                   { Call dog age procedure }
        2: ShowMoonWeight;               { Call moon wt procedure }
        3: Quit := TRUE;
        ELSE WRITELN( 'Please type 1 - 3 for a menu option' );
    END;  {case}
  UNTIL Quit;
END.  {AgeWeight1}
```

Figure 23.2 shows a sample run.

```
Do you want to?

1. Compute your age in dog years
2. Compute your weight on the moon
3. Quit this program

What is your choice? 2

How much do you weigh? 198

Your weight on the moon is only 33 pounds!
You are light enough to fly! (on the moon...)

Press any key to return to the main menu...
```

Figure 23.2. **Showing a sample weight run.**

Do you see any other way this program can be improved? There is one section of code repeated in both procedures. It is the final four statements in the procedure that simply display a message and wait for the user to press a key. Because this code is duplicated, it is a good candidate for a procedure. If you put it in its own procedure (aptly named something meaningful such as WaitForKey), these two procedures need only to call it by name.

Building Your Own Library

Over time, you will develop several useful procedures and functions that you might want to reuse in the future. Each time you write a new procedure, that's one routine you will never have to write again. For now, keep these routines in a file as your personal library of functions and procedures. Chapter 25, "Units," shows how to organize these files into units.

By creating a library file, you invest in your programming future. These routines help you in future programs, and they help promote a structured, modular approach to Turbo Pascal programming.

Summary

You now have been exposed to truly structured programs. Rather than typing long programs, you are able to break them into separate routines. This isolates your routines from each other so that surrounding code does not confuse things when you are concentrating on a section of your program.

The examples in this chapter were longer than previous examples. Even so, they showed that long programs are easy to manage and maintain when you break them into modules. Chapter 24, "Identifier Scope," wraps up procedures and functions by introducing the concepts of variable scope. Now that you have learned to isolate code, you must learn how to isolate variables as well, to protect their values and write even better programs.

Review Questions

Answers to the Review Questions appear in Appendix B.

1. When your main program block calls a procedure, the procedure must be defined

   A. Before the calling statement

   B. After the calling statement

   C. Before or after the calling statement

2. True or False: A procedure always has a BEGIN-END pair.

3. True or False: A procedure can have its own CONST, TYPE, and VAR sections.

4. What is wrong with the following procedure?

```pascal
PROCEDURE Weight;
   VAR Weight: INTEGER;
   BEGIN
      WRITE( 'Please type your weight ' );
      READLN( Weight );
   END;   {Weight}
```

5. True or False: A procedure must have at least two statements.

6. True or False: A procedure can have only one parameter in its parameter list.

7. True or False: The main program block could consist of only calls to procedures.

Review Exercises

1. Write a program with two procedures. The first procedure is to ask for a name, and the second is to display it randomly on the screen 10 times.

2. Rewrite the example program, AgeWeight1, shown earlier in this chapter, to use a new procedure, WaitForKey. See the comments after the program for help.

3. Write a procedure called Beep that beeps the computer's speaker.

4. Write a procedure that clears the keyboard. Refer to Example 4 in Chapter 21.

5. Write a procedure so that a user can type a string on one line. Allow the user to press F1 at any time to simulate getting help. When the user presses F1, display some message in line 25. Refer to Example 5 in Chapter 21.

Identifier Scope

The concept of *identifier scope* is most important when you write functions and procedures. Identifier scope specifies where your constants, types, and variables may be legally used. It especially protects variables in one routine from other routines. If a function or procedure does not need access to a variable located in another routine, that variable's scope keeps it protected.

Most of this chapter discusses the concept of identifier scope. To understand identifier scope fully, you must learn the difference between local and global identifiers and the two ways to pass parameters. This chapter introduces

- ♦ The CONST statement
- ♦ Global identifiers
- ♦ Local identifiers
- ♦ Passing parameters by value
- ♦ Passing parameters by address

When you understand the concept of identifier scope, the programs you write should run more reliably and should be easier to debug. Identifier scope requires only a little more overhead and forethought in programming but rewards you with much more accurate code.

The CONST **Statement**

Although you have been using constants in previous programs, they need to be discussed in more detail at this time. Up to this point, a constant was a BOOLEAN, CHAR, integer, real, or STRING, such as the following examples:

43   'A string'   32234   545.6544432   6.323E+102

The format of CONST is

```
CONST ConstantName1 = expression1;
      ConstantName2 = expression2;
      ⋮
```

The name for a constant (ConstantName1 and ConstantName2 in preceding code) follows the normal rules for identifier names. The expression can be any BOOLEAN, CHAR, integer, real, or string expression. The expression can also involve a previously defined enumerated type. A numerical expression can contain math operators.

Turbo Pascal interprets the expression to determine the data type. If the expression is a string expression, Turbo Pascal assumes the constant is a string constant. If the expression is a numeric expression or constant, Turbo Pascal tries to find the numeric data type (BYTE, SHORTINT, INTEGER, LONGINT, or WORD for integer types) with the smallest range that can hold the entire expression.

You must define a constant with CONST before using it in a program. There are usually two places where you declare the CONST section: At the top of your program and just before the BEGIN statement of the main body. If your program has no functions or procedures, these two locations are the same.

If you declare the CONST section at the top of your program, all functions and procedures before the declaration may use these constants. If you declare the CONST section after all subroutines and before the main body, only the main body may use these constants. TYPE and VAR sections can be declared similarly.

There is nothing to prevent you from declaring a CONST, TYPE, or VAR section between subroutines. However, using such a location makes these declarations more difficult to find and is not recommended.

Examples

1. Many programmers prefer to use defined constants for extremes of data such as age limits or the maximum number of customers. If those extremes change, it is easy to change the CONST statement without having to change the constant value everywhere it appears in a program. The following program shows a maximum and minimum employee age limit defined as a constant.

```
{ Filename: C24CON1.PAS }


{ Illustrate minimum and maximum constants. }
PROGRAM Constant1;
USES Crt;
CONST MinAge = 18;
      MaxAge = 67;
VAR   Age: BYTE;                        { age typed by user }
BEGIN
   CLRSCR;
   WRITE( 'How old are you? ' );
   READLN( Age );
   IF (Age < MinAge)
      THEN WRITELN( 'You are too young' )
      ELSE IF (Age > MaxAge)
              THEN WRITELN( 'You are too old' )
              ELSE WRITELN( 'Your age is with company limits' );
END.  {Constant1}
```

Turbo Pascal assumes MinAge and MaxAge are BYTE because the BYTE data type is the data type with the smallest range that can hold 18 and 67.

This is a simple example, but it illustrates the advantage of using defined constants. If the company changes its age limits, it has to change only the CONST declarations. If the constant is used several places in the program, it changes in all those places as well.

2. By defining unchanging data as constants, you can ensure that you do not inadvertently change the constant. For example, the following program produces an error:

```
{ Filename: C24BAD.PAS }

{ Shows incorrect use of a defined constant. }

PROGRAM BadConstUse;
CONST MaxCircles = 100;
      Height     =  10;
VAR   Radius: INTEGER;
      Area:   REAL;
      Volume: REAL;
BEGIN
   FOR Radius := 1 TO MaxCircles DO
      BEGIN
         Area   := PI * SQR(Radius);   { area of a circle }
         Volume := Area * Height;      { volume of cylinder }
         INC(Height);                  { *** ERROR *** }
      END; {for}
END.  {BadConstUse}
```

Because the value of Height should not be changed, this programming bug will be found quickly, whereas if Height were a variable, Turbo Pascal would let you add 1 to it each time through the loop.

Turbo Pascal tells you that you cannot change a constant by issuing Error 20: Variable identifier expected.

3. The following program illustrates how the location of a CONST declaration affects how the constants may be used.

```
{Filename: C24CON2.PAS}

{ Declare CONST sections in 2 locations.}
PROGRAM Constant2;
USES Crt;
CONST Max1 = 100;

PROCEDURE Sub;
```

```
    BEGIN
        WRITELN( 'At Sub, Max1 = ',Max1);
    END;   {Sub}

CONST Max2 = 200;

BEGIN
    CLRSCR;
    WRITELN( 'In main body, Max1 = ',Max1);
    WRITELN( 'In main body, Max2 = ',Max2);
    Sub;
END.   {Constant2}
```

If you replace Max1 in procedure Sub with Max2, Turbo Pascal returns this compile error: Error 3: Unknown identifier and positions the cursor at Max2. Although this example shows how the location of the CONST declaration can affect where constants are used, the same applies to where TYPE and VAR sections are declared.

4. Turbo Pascal also supports expressions in a CONST declaration. The expression may include some of the built-in functions, such as ABS, CHR, LENGTH, ODD, ORD, PRED, ROUND, SIZEOF, SUCC, and TRUNC. The expression may also contain previously defined constants. Here are some sample declarations:

```
CONST MinNum    = 0;
      MaxNum    = 99;
      MaxRange  = MaxNum - MinNum;
      BadNumMsg = 'Please check your number';
      BadNumLen = LENGTH(BadNumMsg);
      NoteChar  = CHR(13);
```

Global and Local Variables

You now are ready for a new concept that will improve your functions and procedures. It deals with how subroutines share variables.

The scope of a variable (sometimes called the *visibility of variables*) describes how variables are "seen" by your program. Some variables have *global* scope. A global variable can be seen from (and used by) every statement in the program, including functions and procedures. The programs you wrote before learning about functions and procedures had variables with global scope; a variable defined in the first statement could be used by (and is visible from) the last statement in the program.

Local scope is a new concept. A local variable can be seen from (and used by) only the code in which it is defined.

If you use no functions or procedures, the concept of local and global variables is a moot point. You should, however, use functions and procedures because it is best to write modular programs. When you include a function or procedure, you must understand how local and global variables work so that each routine can "see" the variables it requires.

A variable is global if it is defined in the VAR section at the top of the *main* program block. At the top of the main program block, constants defined in the CONST section and types defined in the TYPE section are global as well.

Inside a function or procedure, constants defined in the CONST section, types defined in the TYPE section, and variables defined in the VAR section are local to that function or procedure. A variable also can be local if it is defined in a parameter list of a function or procedure. Using a variable with a parameter list will be discussed later in this chapter.

Global and Local Variable Example

In the VAR section of the following main program block, Loc1, Loc2, Glob1, and Glob2 are declared as globals (all program statements can "see" them). Procedure Sub also has a VAR section with Loc1 and Loc2. These are local to the procedure. Even though they have the same name as those declared as globals, they are completely separate and distinct variables.

```
{ Filename: C24LCGL1.PAS }

{ Shows local and global variables. }
```

```
PROGRAM LocalGlobal;
VAR Loc1:  INTEGER;                    { global }
    Loc2:  INTEGER;                    { global }
    Glob1: INTEGER;                    { global }
    Glob2: STRING;                     { global }

PROCEDURE Sub;
   VAR Loc1: INTEGER;                  { local }
       Loc2: INTEGER;                  { local }
   BEGIN
      WRITELN( Loc1:4, Loc2:4, Glob1:4, Glob2:20 );
      { This displays: ?   ?   100   A global string }
      { Notice that loc1 and loc2 ARE NOT KNOWN HERE!!! }
   END;  {Sub}

BEGIN
   Loc1  := 25;
   Loc2  := 50;
   Glob1 := 100;
   Glob2 := 'A global string';

   WRITELN( Loc1:4, Loc2:4, Glob1:4, Glob2:20 );
   { This displays: 25   50   100   A global string }

   Sub;                               { Call the procedure }
END.  {LocalGlobal}
```

The preceding program begins by initializing all the global variables. A WRITELN statement then displays values for all these global variables. As you would expect, the values output by this WRITELN statement match the initialized values. The last statement of the main body calls the Sub procedure. Sub's only statement is a WRITELN that is a copy of the WRITELN in the main body. Because Loc1 and Loc2 are declared locally and have not been initialized, the results of displaying Loc1 and Loc2 are unpredictable. The displayed values are whatever happens to be in memory. However, the two global variables, Glob1 and Glob2, display the same values as in the WRITELN in the main body.

> **TIP:** If your program behaves unpredictably, double-check that all variables have been initialized.

In your own programs, you should avoid declaring local variables with the same name as a global variable. From this simple example, you can see how duplicate names can be confusing.

> **TIP:** Douglas Hergert, author of *Turbo Pascal 6 Programming for the PC*, has an excellent suggestion to help keep global variables distinct. He suggests prefacing all global variables with a lowercase *g*. Using this suggestion, the four global variables, Loc1, Loc2, Glob1, and Glob2 become gLoc1, gLoc2, gGlob1, and gGlob2.

Try to avoid using global variables.

You might be wondering what to do with this new-found information. Here is the bottom line: Global variables can be dangerous because code can inadvertently overwrite a variable that was initialized in another place in the program. It is better to assign most variables in your program *local* to the subroutine that needs to access them.

Read the previous sentence once more. It means that although you know how to make variables global, you should not do so. Try to stay away from using global variables. It is easier to program using global variables at first. If you make every variable in your program global, including those in every function and procedure, you never have to worry about whether a variable is known. If you do this, however, even those routines that have no need for certain variables can change them.

The Advantages of Passing Variables

You saw the difference between local and global variables. You saw that by making your variables local, you protect their values because only the procedure or function that owns the local variable (the scope is visible from that subroutine only) can modify it.

What do you do, however, if you have a local variable that you want to use in two or more subroutines? In other words, you might have a need for a variable's value to be input from the keyboard in one subroutine, and that same variable is to be displayed in another subroutine. If the variable is local to the first subroutine, the second one can't display it because only the first sees it and knows its value.

The two subroutines are either in the main program body or they are in another subroutine. If the subroutines are in the main program body, there are two solutions. First, you could make the variable global by declaring it in a VAR section at the top of your program. This is not a good idea because you want only those two subroutines to see the variable. All subroutines could see it if it were global. The second, and more acceptable, solution is to declare a VAR section just before the main program body. The variable would not be visible to any subroutine declared before the main program body. By including the variable in such a VAR section, you can *pass* the variable from the first subroutine to the other subroutine. The variable would be known only to the main program body and the two subroutines.

If the subroutines are in another subroutine, there are also two possible solutions. First, you could again make the variable global by declaring it at the top of your program. As before, you want to avoid global variables. The second, and better, solution is to pass the variable from the first routine to the other routine. This has a big advantage: The variable is known only to those two routines.

When you pass a variable from one routine to another, you are *passing a parameter* from the first routine to the next. You can pass more than one parameter (variable) at a time if you want several variables sent from one routine to another. The receiving routine *receives parameters* (variables) from the routine that sent them.

You have already passed parameters to routines when you passed values to a user-defined function (which received those parameters in its parameter list). For example, when you used the UPCASE function, you passed it a lowercase letter as a parameter.

When a routine passes parameters, it is called the *calling routine*. The calling routine can be in the main body, a function, or procedure.

The routine that receives those parameters is called the *receiving routine*. The receiving routine can be either a function or procedure. Figure 24.1 is a pictorial representation of what is going on.

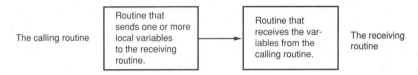

Figure 24.1. Overview of calling and receiving routines.

To pass a local variable from one routine to another, you place the local variable in parentheses in the calling routine. The following program shows how to declare a VAR section just before the main program body. Use this technique when you want to pass variables from the main program body. The following program is slightly changed from that one. The two variables are passed to the procedure. Because of this, the procedure "knows" the values and can display them correctly.

TIP: When passing parameters, the calling routine's variable names do not have to match the receiving routine's variable names. They must, however, match in number and type.

```
{ Filename: C24LCGL2.PAS }

{ Shows passing of local variables. }

PROGRAM LocalGlobal2;
VAR Glob1: INTEGER;                    { global }
    Glob2: STRING;                     { global }


PROCEDURE Sub(Loc1: INTEGER;
             Loc2: INTEGER);
   BEGIN
     WRITELN( Loc1:4, Loc2:4, Glob1:4, Glob2:20 );
     { This displays: 25   50   100   A global string }
     { Notice that loc1 and loc2 display correctly now }
   END;  {Sub}
```

```
VAR Loc1: INTEGER;
    Loc2: INTEGER;

BEGIN
   Loc1 := 25;
   Loc2 := 50;

   Glob1 := 100;
   Glob2 := 'A global string';

   WRITELN( Loc1:4, Loc2:4, Glob1:4, Glob2:20 );
   { This displays: 25   50   100   A global string }

   Sub(Loc1, Loc2);
END.   {LocalGlobal2}
```

If two subroutines are not in the main program body, the following program shows how to pass variables from one subroutine to another.

```
{ Filename: C24LOC1.PAS }

{ Shows passing of local variables. }

PROGRAM Local1;

PROCEDURE ShowVars(Loc1: INTEGER;
                   Loc2: INTEGER);
   BEGIN
      WRITELN( 'Inside ShowVars, Loc1 = ',Loc1:4,' Loc2 = ',
               Loc2:4;
      Loc1 := 25;
      Loc2 := 35;
      WRITELN( 'Inside ShowVars, Loc1 = ',Loc1:4,' Loc2 = ',
               Loc2:4);
   END;   {ShowVars}

PROCEDURE Sub;
   VAR Loc1: INTEGER;            { local vars }
       Loc2: INTEGER;
   BEGIN
      Loc1 := 5;
      Loc2 := 10;
```

```
        ShowVars(Loc1, Loc2);    { pass 5 and 10 to ShowProc1 }
        WRITELN( 'Inside Sub, Loc1 = ',Loc1:4, ' Loc2 = ',
                Loc2:4);
    END;   {Sub}

BEGIN
    Sub;
END.   {Local1}
```

In the preceding example, Loc1 and Loc2 are local variables. Only the Sub procedure and the ShowVars procedure can see these local variables. Sub can see the variables because they are declared there. ShowVars can see them because they were passed to it from Sub. After ShowVars shows the initial values of 5 and 10, these values are changed to 25 and 35. The last statement of ShowVars displays values of 25 and 35. However, when control returns to Sub, the last line of Sub executes a WRITELN statement. This WRITELN displays values of 5 and 10. This proves that Loc1 and Loc2 were not permanently changed in ShowVars. The next section shows how to permanently change parameters.

Passing by Address

The previous example shows how you pass a parameter by value. Once you are inside the routine, you can change the parameters, however, the change is local. When control returns to the main program block, the parameters are not changed.

If you want the parameters to be changed by the routine, you must *pass by address*. Sometimes this is called being passed *by reference*. When a parameter is passed by address, the variable's *address in memory* is sent to, and is assigned to, the receiving routine's parameter list. (If more than one variable is passed by address, each of their addresses is sent to and assigned to the receiving function's parameters.)

All variables in memory are stored at separate addresses of memory. Figure 24.2 shows addresses of memory.

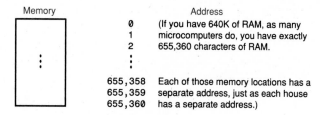

Figure 24.2. **Memory and its addresses.**

When you instruct Turbo Pascal to declare a variable, you are telling it to find a blank place in memory and assign that memory's address to the variable name. When your program displays or uses the variable, Turbo Pascal knows to go to that variable's address and display what is there.

If you were to declare three variables as shown here,

```
VAR   Ara: ARRAY[0..2] OF CHAR;
      j:   BYTE;
      k:   BYTE;
BEGIN
   Ara[0] := 'A';
   Ara[1] := 'B';
   Ara[2] := 'C';
   j       := 8;
   k       := 3;
   .
   .
   .
```

Turbo Pascal might arbitrarily set them up in memory at the addresses shown in Figure 24.3.

Actually, the integer and real variables take more than one memory location each, but this figure illustrates the idea of how variables are stored at their addresses.

When a variable is passed by address, the address of the variable is copied to the receiving routine. Any time a variable is passed by address, if you change that variable in the receiving routine, the variable also is changed in the calling routine.

To tell Turbo Pascal you want to pass a parameter by reference, you precede the parameter with VAR in the function or procedure definition.

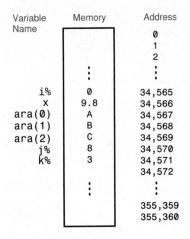

Figure 24.3. **The variables in memory.**

Passing by Address Example

The following example is a sorting procedure. You have seen several bubble sorting examples in this book. This one is a procedure, however, rather than a stand-alone program.

Before this sort procedure is discussed further, take a look at it:

```
{
  This procedure assumes it will be passed a string
  array (SArr), and an integer count (ct) that includes the
  number of strings in that array.

  This routine sorts the array using a bubble sort.
  Once sorted, control is passed back to the calling routine.

  Because the array is preceded by a VAR, the array will be
  passed by address. Therefore, when this routine sorts the
  array, it will remain sorted when the calling routine
  gets control again.
}
```

```
PROCEDURE SortIt(VAR SArr: StrArray;
                     ct:   INTEGER);
   VAR i:    INTEGER;
       j:    INTEGER;
       tNum: CHAR;
   BEGIN
      FOR i := 1 TO (ct - 2) DO
         FOR j := (i + 1) TO (ct - 1) DO
            IF (SArr[i] > SArr[j])
               THEN BEGIN
                       tNum    := SArr[j];
                       SArr[j] := SArr[i];
                       SArr[i] := tNum;
                    END;
   END;  {SortIt}
```

The first things to notice are the extensive remarks at the top. It is a good idea to tell what the routine does, what kind of values it expects (in this case, a string array passed by address and the integer count of the elements in that array, not passed by address), and what it expects to happen when it finishes (the array is sorted when it gets back to the calling routine because it was passed by address).

This routine does not care what kind of program, procedure, or function calls it. It is almost a stand-alone procedure, although it has to be passed some data. This is where the power of this routine comes into play. It can be used in any program that needs a string array sorted of type strArray. All you have to do is copy this routine to that program. If the main program or any other procedure or function wants a string array sorted of type strArray, it only has to pass the string array to this routine, along with the number of elements in that array, as in

```
TYPE StrArray = ARRAY[1..2000] OF STRING[30];
VAR  NameArr:   StrArray;
     Employees: StrArray;

SortIt( NameArr, 1200 );
```

or

```
SortIt( Employees, NumEmp );
```

495

This makes the sorting routine extremely flexible. SortIt does not care what the data is called that is passed to it. SortIt only knows it is getting a string array of type StrArray and an integer count from some other routine.

This routine also has three local variables called i, j, and tNum. Because the i and j variables are required only for subscripting and because tNum is just used for swapping array elements, they are defined locally and do not have to be passed back to the calling routine.

NOTE: Whenever you have a FOR loop, the index variable must be declared for the block that has the FOR loop. If the FOR loop is in a function or procedure, Turbo Pascal requires that the index variable be declared locally. If the FOR loop is in the main program body, the index variable must be declared before the main program body. Including a VAR section just before the main program body satisfies this requirement.

The SortIt routine assumes the array elements start at 1. To be more flexible, the SortIt routine should be rewritten as

```
{
  This procedure assumes it will be passed a string
  array, the starting array index, and the ending array
  index.

  This routine sorts the array using a bubble sort.
  Once sorted, control is passed back to the calling routine.

  Because the array is preceded by a VAR, the array will be
  passed by address. Therefore, when this routine sorts the
  array, it also will be sorted when the calling routine
  gets control again.
}

PROCEDURE SortIt(VAR SArr:  StrArray;
                     First: INTEGER;
                     Last:  INTEGER);
```

```
VAR i:    INTEGER;
    j:    INTEGER;
   tNum: STRING;
BEGIN
   FOR i := Start TO (Last - 2) DO
      FOR j := (i + 1) TO (Last - 1) DO
         IF (SArr[i] > SArr[j])
            THEN BEGIN
                    tNum    := SArr[j];
                    SArr[j] := SArr[i];
                    SArr[i] := tNum;
                 END;
END;  {SortIt}
```

This version is much improved. You should ensure that every function or procedure where you are passing an array has some way to determine the correct array index. Otherwise, the routines will not be truly portable from one routine to another; they will assume a starting or ending subscript that might be incorrect.

Passing by Value

Sometimes you hear passing by value called *passing by copy*. When you pass a parameter by value, the receiving routine or function can change it. If it does, however, the variable is *not* changed in the calling routine.

For instance, if you pass an array to the SortIt routine by value, SortIt sorts the array. When control is returned to the calling routine, however, that procedure's array is not sorted.

Any time you must pass parameters to a *function* and return the function result, you should consider passing the parameters by value. If the function has to return a changed parameter in addition to its function result, you must pass by address.

If a function needs to return a changed parameter, many programmers use a procedure rather than a function. Typically, you use a function to return one value—the function result.

To pass a variable by value, do not simply precede the parameter with VAR. In this procedure header, all parameters are passed by value:

```
PROCEDURE SCALAWAGS(Hours: INTEGER;
                    Rate:  REAL;
                    TAXER: REAL);
```

All built-in functions such as INT and CHR assume that their values are passed by value. For example, in the section of code

```
i    := 5.2;
NewI := INT(i);
```

the variable i is passed by value. It is not changed in the INT function (remember that no built-in functions change their parameters, but instead they return a value based on their parameters).

Passing by Value Example

The following procedures are similar to two routines you saw in earlier programs. The first procedure, MoonWeight, calculates and displays the moon-equivalent of any weight passed to it. The second procedure, DogYears, calculates and displays any age in dog years based on its passed value.

```
{
  This routine calculates and displays the moon weight of
  any weight passed to it. Because it does not have to
  change any data passed to it, it is best called by value.
  Because the gravity of the moon is one-sixth of the earth's
  gravity, Weight is divided by 6.
}
PROCEDURE MoonWeight(Weight: INTEGER);
   BEGIN
     MoonWt := Weight DIV 6;
     WRITELN( 'Your weight on the moon is: ',MoonWt );
   END;  {MoonWeight}

PROCEDURE DogYears(Years: INTEGER);
   {
     This routine calculates and displays the dog years of
     any years passed to it. Because it does not have to
     change any data passed to it, it is best called by value.
```

No built-in functions change their parameters; instead, they return a value based on their parameters.

```
   Because dog years are seven times standard years, Years is
   divided by 7.
 }
 BEGIN
   DogYrs := Years DIV 7;
   WRITELN( 'You age in dog years is: ', DogYrs );
 END;   {DogYears}
```

No data passed to these procedures is changed. To use these procedures, type:

```
 .
 .
 .
WRITE( 'What is your weight? ' );
READLN( UserWeight );
MoonWeight( UserWeight );                { Passed by value }

WRITE( 'How old are you? ' );
READLN( Age );
DogYears ( Age );                        { Passed by value }
 .
 .
 .
```

The choice between passing by value and passing by address might not seem as critical as it can be. If you are writing routines that should never change the passed variables, pass them by value. Later, if you (or someone else) change the routine and accidentally change one of the passed variables, at least the changed variable is not harmed in both routines (and hopefully the error becomes easier to find).

The following is a nonsense program that doesn't do much. Yet if you look at it, you might sense there is something wrong with it. The program passes numbers from 1 to 20 to the procedure called TripleIt, which triples the number and displays it.

```
{ Filename: C24STAT1.PAS }

PROGRAM Triple1;
USES Crt;
```

```
      {
        Triples whatever value is passed to it
        and adds up the total
      }

PROCEDURE TripleIt(Num: INTEGER);
   VAR Total:  INTEGER;
       NumBy3: INTEGER;
   BEGIN
      Total  := 0;
      NumBy3 := 3 * Num;                  { Triple number passed }
      Total  := Total + NumBy3;           { Add up triple numbers }
      WRITELN( 'The number, ', Num:2, ' multiplied by 3 is: ',
                 NumBy3:2 );
      IF (Total > 300)
         THEN WRITELN( 'The total of the triple numbers '+
                        'is over 300' );
   END;  {TripleIt}

VAR i: INTEGER;

BEGIN
   CLRSCR;
   FOR i := 1 TO 20 DO
      TripleIt(i);
END.  {Triple1}
```

The variable called Total is automatically set to 0. Its purpose is to add the triple numbers and display a message when the total of the triples goes over 300. However, this WRITELN statement never executes. Each of the 20 times this procedure is called, Total is set back to 0 again.

If, however, you want Total to retain its value even after the procedure ends, you can declare it just before the main program body.

The following program corrects the intent of the previous one.

```
{ Filename: C24STAT2.PAS }

PROGRAM Triple2;
USES Crt;
```

```
{
   Triples whatever value is passed to it
   and adds up the total
}

PROCEDURE TripleIt(    Num:   INTEGER;  {number to add}
                   VAR Total: INTEGER);  {running total}
VAR NumBy3: INTEGER;
BEGIN
   NumBy3 := Num * 3;                   { Triple number passed }
   Total  := Total + NumBy3;            { Add up triple numbers }
   WRITELN( 'The number, ', Num:2, ' multiplied by 3 is: ',
            NumBy3:2 );
   IF (Total > 300)
      THEN WRITELN( 'The total of the triple numbers '+
                    'is over 300' );
   END;  {TripleIt}

VAR i:     INTEGER;
   Total: INTEGER;

BEGIN
   CLRSCR;
   Total := 0;
   FOR i := 1 TO 20 DO
      TripleIt(i,Total);
END.   {Triple2}
```

Figure 24.4 shows the first part of this program's output.
Because Total is a global variable, its value is not erased when the
procedure finishes. When the procedure is called again, Total's
previous value (its value when you left the routine) is still there.

Rather than declaring Total just before the main program body,
you also could declare a typed constant local to the TripleIt procedure. Turbo Pascal stores typed constants in the Data Segment. This
means that typed constants retain their values each time the routine
is called. In the following example, Total is 0 when procedure
TripleIt is called the first time. When the procedure completes, Total
is 3. When the procedure is called the second time, Total is still 3.
When the procedure completes the second time, Total is 9. And
so on.

```
The number,  1 multiplied by 3 is:  3
The number,  2 multiplied by 3 is:  6
The number,  3 multiplied by 3 is:  9
The number,  4 multiplied by 3 is: 12
The number,  5 multiplied by 3 is: 15
The number,  6 multiplied by 3 is: 18
The number,  7 multiplied by 3 is: 21
The number,  8 multiplied by 3 is: 24
The number,  9 multiplied by 3 is: 27
The number, 10 multiplied by 3 is: 30
The number, 11 multiplied by 3 is: 33
The number, 12 multiplied by 3 is: 36
The number, 13 multiplied by 3 is: 39
The number, 14 multiplied by 3 is: 42
The number, 15 multiplied by 3 is: 45
The number, 16 multiplied by 3 is: 48
The number, 17 multiplied by 3 is: 51
The number, 18 multiplied by 3 is: 54
The number, 19 multiplied by 3 is: 57
The number, 20 multiplied by 3 is: 60
```

Figure 24.4. **Displaying tripled numbers and a running total.**

```pascal
{ Filename: C24STAT3.PAS }

PROGRAM Triple3;
USES Crt;

PROCEDURE TripleIt(Num: INTEGER);
   {
     Triples whatever value is passed to it
     and adds up the total
   }
   CONST Total: INTEGER = 0;              { typed constant }
   VAR   NumBy3: INTEGER;
   BEGIN
      NumBy3 := 3 * Num;                  { Triple number passed }
      Total  := Total + NumBy3;           { Add up triple numbers }
      WRITELN( 'The number, ', Num:2, ' multiplied by 3 is: ',
               NumBy3:2 );
      IF (Total > 300)
         THEN WRITELN( 'The total of the triple numbers '+
                       'is over 300' );
   END; {TripleIt}

VAR i: INTEGER;
```

```
BEGIN
   CLRSCR;
   FOR i := 1 TO 20 DO
      TripleIt(i);
END.   {Triple3}
```

The preceding program produces exactly the same results as Figure 24.4.

Summary

This chapter has been unlike most in this book. It is much more theoretical in nature because there is so much to learn about passing parameters. The entire concept of parameter passing is required because local variables are better than global; they are protected in their own routines but must be shared between other routines. Turbo Pascal lets you pass by address or by value. If the receiving routine is to change the parameters in both places, you should pass by address.

Most of the information in this chapter will become more obvious as you use functions and procedures in your own programs. Start using them right away; the longer your programs are the happier you'll be that you wrote several small functions and procedures rather than one long program. You can test and modify individual modules easier.

Review Questions

Answers to the Review Questions appear in Appendix B.

1. Why would you want to use the CONST statement to give a name to a constant, such as SalesMinimum, rather than using the actual value, such as 20,000, throughout your program?

2. True or False: A local variable is local only to the function or procedure in which it is declared, and the routines that call it.

3. How can you specify that a parameter is passed by address?

4. What is the output of the following section of code?

```
PROCEDURE Add(    Num1: INTEGER;
                  Num2: INTEGER;
              VAR Sum: INTEGER);
   BEGIN
      Sum := Num1 + Num2;
   END.  {Add}

PROCEDURE AddMenu;
   VAR Sum: INTEGER;
   BEGIN
      Add(5,7,Sum);
      WRITELN( 'The sum is ',Sum );
   END;  {AddMenu}
```

5. When would you pass a global variable from one routine to another? (*Hint: Be careful, this is tricky!*)

6. How would you set up a procedure to keep track of how many times the procedure is called?

7. If you want parameters to be changed in both the calling routine and the receiving routine, would you pass by address or pass by value?

Review Exercises

1. Write a function that returns the total amount of money you have spent on diskettes in the past year. Assume it is passed two parameters: the number of diskettes bought and the average price per diskette. Do not display the price in the function; just compute and return it. Use only local variables.

2. Write a procedure that simply counts the number of times it is called. Name the procedure CountIt. Assume it never is passed anything, but that it simply keeps track of every time you call it. Display the following message inside the procedure:

```
The number of times this procedure has been called is: xx
```

in which *xx* is the actual number.

3. Write a procedure that draws a box on the screen using ASCII characters. Write the procedure so it receives two parameters: the number of columns wide and the number of rows high that the box should be. (This would be a great procedure for drawing boxes around titles.)

4. Write a string-blanking routine that blanks whatever string is passed to it. Assume the string is passed by address (or else the blank string could not be used in the calling procedure).

5. Write a complete application program that keeps track of a holiday and birthday mailing list. The main program should consist of variable, function, and procedure declarations, and procedure calls. One of the procedures should let the user enter the data, and another should display the data. Before displaying it, the display procedure should call another procedure to sort the list alphabetically (this sort routine is never called or declared in the main program). Include a function that returns the number of out-of-state names (be sure you use CONST for your home state name).

Units

As you add more functions and procedures to your programming library, you eventually need some way to organize them. Turbo Pascal provides the answer: store functions and procedures into files called *units*. To access a function or procedure in a unit, you include a USES statement, followed by the name of the unit. This chapter covers

- ♦ Using a unit
- ♦ The structure of a unit
- ♦ Expanding a unit
- ♦ Including CONST, TYPE, and VAR sections in a unit

Turbo Pascal Units

You have seen several examples of a program using the Turbo Pascal unit Crt. In programs where you needed to use procedure CLRSCR, you had a USES Crt; statement at the top of the program. This is because the CLRSCR procedure is in the Crt unit. When you needed to print to the printer with WRITELN(LST,...); you included a USES Printer; statement for a similar reason.

If you use a Turbo Pascal procedure or function, and you receive `Error 3: Unknown identifier`, you probably have to include the appropriate Turbo Pascal unit. With on-line help you can quickly determine the required unit. Position the cursor on the "unknown identifier" and press Ctrl–F1 for topic help. The editor provides a help window on the procedure or function. The help window identifies the required unit.

Using a Unit

The format of the USES statement is

```
USES UnitName1 [, UnitName2] [, UnitName3] [,...,UnitNameN];
```

If your program needs more than one unit, you can list them on one USES statement. For example, you have seen

```
USES Crt, Printer;
```

For most programs, when there is more than one unit to include on a USES statement, you can list them in any order.

The Structure of a Unit

Now that you know how to call a unit from a program, it's time to create a unit to illustrate the process. As an example, create a unit that includes functions and procedures related to writing text to a screen. Units do not have to include related routines, however, when naming a unit, it is most efficient to have related routines together.

Deciding on a good name for a unit is probably the hardest thing to do when creating one. There are some restrictions. The extension must be .PAS. That leaves one to eight characters for a meaningful name. Because your unit is a file, the name must conform to DOS rules for naming files. Use SCRTOOL.PAS as the name. "Scr" suggests that the screen is involved, whereas "Tool" suggests that the unit includes general utility functions and procedures.

The next step is to open a file called SCRTOOL.PAS. Before you type anything, here is an overview of the general format of a unit. Introducing just what you need for now.

```
UNIT UnitName;

INTERFACE

IMPLEMENTATION

END.   {UnitName}
```

The `UnitName` must match the name of the file without the .PAS extension. In this case, `UnitName` is `ScrTool`.

The INTERFACE section is where you include all function and procedure headers that your program needs to use. The header consists of the word PROCEDURE or FUNCTION, the name of the subroutine, and any parameter list.

The IMPLEMENTATION section is where you define all the function and procedure bodies declared in the INTERFACE section. The IMPLEMENTATION section also can include other functions and procedures that act as support routines. Any function or procedure not included in the INTERFACE section cannot be accessed outside of the unit.

Creating a Unit

Begin your `ScrTool` unit by including a procedure to paint the screen in any background color. Call it `PaintScreen`.

```
{Filename: SCRTOOL.PAS}

UNIT ScrTool;

INTERFACE

   PROCEDURE PaintScreen(BG: BYTE);    { header }

IMPLEMENTATION
```

```
USES Crt;

   PROCEDURE PaintScreen(BG: BYTE);
      BEGIN
         TEXTCOLOR(LIGHTGRAY);          { so cursor doesn't disappear }
         TEXTBACKGROUND(BG);
         CLRSCR;                        { CLRSCR in Crt unit }
      END;  {PaintScreen}

END.   {ScrTool}
```

This routine takes advantage of the fact that CLRSCR erases the screen using the current background color. Earlier, it was indicated that CLRSCR is in the Turbo Pascal unit Crt. Because the ScrTool unit is separate from any program, you must tell it how to find the Crt unit. This can be done with a USES statement inside the ScrTool unit. Because the CLRSCR procedure is in the IMPLEMENTATION section, the USES statement immediately follows the IMPLEMENTATION keyword.

The unit name (ScrTool) matches the name of the unit file (without the .PAS extension). The INTERFACE houses the procedure header (PROCEDURE PaintScreen(BG: BYTE);). The IMPLEMENTATION keyword is followed by the USES statement that tells your unit that it needs to use the Crt unit. After the USES statement, you include the complete procedure.

NOTE: Although you can have just one procedure (or function) in a unit, you usually have a collection of related routines.

Press F2 to save the unit to disk. Before compiling the unit, make sure that option Destination under menu option Compile is set to Disk. If it is set to Memory, press D to toggle the option to Disk. To verify that your typing is correct, press Alt–F9 to compile the unit. When you compile a unit to disk, Turbo Pascal creates a TPU (Turbo Pascal Unit) file. Turbo Pascal uses the first part of the unit's filename (the part without the extension) and adds TPU as the extension. For unit ScrTool, the TPU file is called SCRTOOL.TPU. If you need to compile unit ScrTool in the future and SCRTOOL.TPU exists, Turbo Pascal is "smart" in the sense that it can determine if the unit has been changed. If the unit has not been changed, Turbo Pascal uses the existing TPU file. If the unit has been changed, Turbo Pascal creates a new TPU file. When Turbo Pascal can use an existing TPU file, it dramatically reduces the time it takes to compile your program.

> **TIP:** You probably have been saving all your files in the same directory. You might consider creating a special subdirectory to store your units. In order for Turbo Pascal to find the subdirectory, press Alt–O to select the **O**ptions menu. Now select **D**irectories. Tab to the line labeled Unit directories and type the name of the subdirectory in which your unit is stored. Press Alt–K to exit the dialog box. Turbo Pascal returns to the editor. Press Alt–O again. Select **S**ave Options.... When the Save Options dialog box appears, you should see Turbo.TP. Press Alt–K to exit the dialog box. Now Turbo Pascal can find your unit subdirectory.

Example

This example shows you how to use the ScrTool unit.

```
{ Filename: C25UNIT1.PAS }

PROGRAM DemoUnit1;
USES Crt, ScrTool;
VAR i: BYTE;

BEGIN
    FOR i := 7 DOWNTO 0 DO
        BEGIN
            PaintScreen(i);
            DELAY(500);
        END;
END.  {DemoUnit1}
```

Because the DELAY procedure is in the Crt unit, you must include Crt in the program USES statement. With ScrTool included in this USES statement, Turbo Pascal can find the PaintScreen procedure. This means you do not have to paste a copy of the procedure into every program that uses PaintScreen. As you develop your own general procedures and functions, include them in units.

Expanding a Unit

Another screen-related routine that can be included in your ScrTool unit is a procedure that places a string at any designated screen location, in any designated color.

```
PROCEDURE ScrWrite(X,Y:  INTEGER;
                   FG:   BYTE;
                   BG:   BYTE;
                   S:    STRING);
   BEGIN
      GOTOXY(X,Y);
      TEXTCOLOR(FG);
      TEXTBACKGROUND(BG);
      WRITE(S);
   END;   {ScrWrite}
```

This routine conveniently packages the Turbo Pascal routines for positioning the cursor, defining colors, and writing a string. Because the user specifies exactly where to place the string, the routine uses WRITE rather than WRITELN. To include this procedure in your ScrTool unit, you must place the procedure header in the INTERFACE section and the complete procedure in the IMPLEMENTATION section. You also must recompile the unit by pressing Alt–F9. Here is the updated ScrTool unit:

```
{Filename: SCRTOOL.PAS}

UNIT ScrTool;

INTERFACE

   PROCEDURE PaintScreen(BG: BYTE);
```

```
PROCEDURE ScrWrite(X,Y: INTEGER;
                   FG:   BYTE;
                   BG:   BYTE;
                   S:    STRING);


IMPLEMENTATION

USES Crt;

    PROCEDURE PaintScreen(BG: BYTE);
        BEGIN
            TEXTCOLOR(LIGHTGRAY);
            TEXTBACKGROUND(BG);
            CLRSCR;
        END;   {PaintScreen}


    PROCEDURE ScrWrite(X,Y: INTEGER;
                       FG:   BYTE;
                       BG:   BYTE;
                       S:    STRING);
        BEGIN
            GOTOXY(X,Y);
            TEXTCOLOR(FG);
            TEXTBACKGROUND(BG);
            WRITE(S);
        END;   {ScrWrite}
END.   {ScrTool}
```

Units can call other units.

GOTOXY, TEXTCOLOR, and TEXTBACKGROUND are all in the Crt unit. The USES Crt; statement after the IMPLEMENTATION section tells Turbo Pascal where to find these additional procedures. You also can include your own units in a USES statement. In other words, units can call other units.

If a declaration (CONST, TYPE, or VAR) or subroutine header in the INTERFACE section needs to refer to another unit, include the USES statement just after the word INTERFACE. If a declaration or a statement in the body of a subroutine needs to refer to another unit, include the USES statement just after the word IMPLEMENTATION.

Example

The following program illustrates both ScrTool procedures by clearing the screen in black and then displaying all the possible color combinations for displaying a string.

```
{ Filename: C25UNIT2.PAS }

{ Demo ScrTool procedures PaintScreen and ScrWrite }

PROGRAM DemoUnit2;

USES Crt, ScrTool;

VAR BG: BYTE;                          { background color }
    FG: BYTE;                          { foreground color }

BEGIN
   PaintScreen(BLACK);                 { color constants in Crt }
   FOR BG := 0 TO 7 DO
     FOR FG := 0 TO 15 DO
        ScrWrite(10*BG+1,FG+1,FG,BG,' Test ');
   ScrWrite(28,25,WHITE,BLACK,'Press Enter to continue');
   READLN;
   PaintScreen(BLACK);                 { clean up screen }
END.   {DemoUnit2}
```

Because the color constants BLACK and WHITE are in the Crt unit, you must include Crt along with ScrTool in the USES statement.

Including CONST, TYPE, and VAR Statements in a Unit

In addition to including procedures and functions in a unit, you also can include a CONST, TYPE, and VAR section. Add one final procedure to your ScrTool unit. This routine draws a box inside a window.

```
PROCEDURE Frame(W1,W2,W3,W4: BYTE;
                FG:          BYTE;
                BG:          BYTE;
```

```
                InsideColor: BYTE;
                Title:       FrameString;
                Msg:         MsgString);
    VAR i: INTEGER;
    BEGIN
       WINDOW(W1,W2,W3,W4);
       PaintScreen(InsideColor);
       WINDOW(W1,W2,W3,W4+1);
       FOR i := 2 TO W3-W1 DO ScrWrite(i,1,FG,BG,#196);
       FOR i := 2 TO W4-W2 DO ScrWrite(1,i,FG,BG,#179);
       FOR i := 2 TO W4-W2 DO ScrWrite(W3-W1+1,i,FG,BG,#179);
       FOR i := 2 TO W3-W1 DO ScrWrite(i,W4-W2+1,FG,BG,#196);
       ScrWrite(1,1,FG,BG,#218);
       ScrWrite(1,W4-W2+1,FG,BG,#192);
       ScrWrite(W3-W1+1,1,FG,BG,#191);
       ScrWrite(W3-W1+1,W4-W2+1,FG,BG,#217);
       ScrWrite((W3-W1+1-LENGTH(Title)) DIV 2,1,FG,BG,Title);
       ScrWrite(3,W4-W2+1,FG,BG,Msg);
    END;  {Frame}
```

This routine introduces the Turbo Pascal procedure WINDOW. With WINDOW, you can create windows on your screen. A window acts like the full screen in that you can write messages and scroll; it is just smaller. Windows often help organize a screen for your users. Many programs use windows, and as you probably know, there is also a software package by Microsoft called Windows. Turbo Pascal's IDE uses windows extensively. For example, when you are using the editor, you are in the editor window. If you press F1 while in the editor window, a help window appears. When you use procedure Frame above, you can create windows in your own programs.

One disadvantage of a window involves its lower right corner. Just like the full screen, a window scrolls when you write a character in the lower right corner. Because you want to draw a frame for your window, the window scrolls when you write a frame character in the lower-right corner, which is why the procedure calls WINDOW twice. The second time, it makes the window a line deeper. This, however, is transparent to all the ScrWrite statements in the procedure.

Even though ScrWrite will be placed before PaintScreen and ScrWrite in the IMPLEMENTATION section, these previous two procedures were declared in the INTERFACE section. This satisfies Turbo Pascal's requirement that a procedure (or function) be declared before it can be used.

ScrWrite also makes extensive use of some extended ASCII characters. Refer to Appendix A to see the character associated with the numbers used in the previous ScrWrite statements.

> **TIP:** With the Turbo Pascal editor, you can use the Alt key and number pad to include extended ASCII characters directly. This only works for extended ASCII characters. For example, rather than typing #196 in the previous ScrWrite statement, hold down the Alt key and type 196 on the number pad (NumLock can be either on or off). When you release the Alt key, the editor displays the extended ASCII character.

After the frame is drawn, the Title is centered in the top frame of the window. When you pass a string as the Title, many people think it looks better if you include a leading and trailing space. This avoids having the frame bump into your title. You can also display a message in the lower-left frame of the window. If you do not want to display a Title or Msg, pass a null string (' ') to the procedure.

When you include the procedure header for Frame in the INTER-FACE section, you are going to have a slight problem. Turbo Pascal will not know the types FrameString and MsgString referenced in the parameter list. To solve this problem, you can define a TYPE section in the INTERFACE.

```
TYPE FrameString = STRING[30];
     MsgString   = STRING[30];
```

You could not include this TYPE definition in the IMPLEMENTATION section because you would be defining it after using it. Turbo Pascal requires the opposite. By including these two types in the INTERFACE, any program that uses ScrTool can use FrameString and MsgString. After adding the type definitions and the Frame procedure, here is the latest version of the ScrTool unit:

```
{Filename: SCRTOOL.PAS}

UNIT ScrTool;

INTERFACE

    TYPE FrameString = STRING[30];
         MsgString   = STRING[30];

    PROCEDURE Frame(W1,W2,W3,W4: BYTE;
                    FG:          BYTE;
                    BG:          BYTE;
                    InsideColor: BYTE;
                    Title:       FrameString;
                    Msg:         MsgString);

    PROCEDURE PaintScreen(BG: BYTE);

    PROCEDURE ScrWrite(X,Y: INTEGER;
                       FG:  BYTE;
                       BG:  BYTE;
                       S:   STRING);

IMPLEMENTATION

USES Crt;

    PROCEDURE Frame(W1,W2,W3,W4: BYTE;
                    FG:          BYTE;
                    BG:          BYTE;
                    InsideColor: BYTE;
                    Title:       FrameString;
                    Msg:         MsgString);
      VAR i: INTEGER;
      BEGIN
        WINDOW(W1,W2,W3,W4);
        PaintScreen(InsideColor);
        WINDOW(W1,W2,W3,W4+1);
        FOR i := 2 TO W3-W1 DO ScrWrite(i,1,FG,BG,#196);
        FOR i := 2 TO W4-W2 DO ScrWrite(1,i,FG,BG,#179);
        FOR i := 2 TO W4-W2 DO ScrWrite(W3-W1+1,i,FG,BG,#179);
```

```
                    FOR i := 2 TO W3-W1 DO ScrWrite(i,W4-W2+1,FG,BG,#196);
                    ScrWrite(1,1,FG,BG,#218);
                    ScrWrite(1,W4-W2+1,FG,BG,#192);
                    ScrWrite(W3-W1+1,1,FG,BG,#191);
                    ScrWrite(W3-W1+1,W4-W2+1,FG,BG,#217);
                    ScrWrite((W3-W1+1-LENGTH(Title)) DIV 2,1,FG,BG,Title);
                    ScrWrite(3,W4-W2+1,FG,BG,Msg);
                 END;  {Frame}

         PROCEDURE PaintScreen(BG: BYTE);
            BEGIN
               TEXTCOLOR(LIGHTGRAY);
               TEXTBACKGROUND(BG);
               CLRSCR;
            END;  {PaintScreen}

         PROCEDURE ScrWrite(X,Y: INTEGER;
                            FG:  BYTE;
                            BG:  BYTE;
                            S:   STRING);
            BEGIN
               GOTOXY(X,Y);
               TEXTCOLOR(FG);
               TEXTBACKGROUND(BG);
               WRITE(S);
            END;  {ScrWrite}

      END.  {ScrTool}
```

Examples

1. This example draws windows randomly all over the screen.

```
{ Filename: C25UNIT3.PAS }

{ Demo ScrTool procedure Frame }

PROGRAM DemoUnit3;
```

```
USES Crt, ScrTool;

CONST MaxWindows = 20;

VAR   X1:    BYTE;                    { X1 and Y1 define the }
      Y1:    BYTE;                    { top left corner }
      X2:    BYTE;                    { X2 and Y2 define the }
      Y2:    BYTE;                    { lower right corner }
      i:     INTEGER;
      Title: FrameString;
      Msg:   MsgString;
      iStr:  STRING[2];               { identify frame & msg }

BEGIN
   RANDOMIZE;
   PaintScreen(BLACK);
   FOR i := 1 TO MaxWindows DO
     BEGIN
        STR(i,iStr);
        Title := ' Frame ' + iStr + ' ';
        Msg   := ' Message ' + iStr + ' ';
        X1 := RANDOM(40) + 1;     { start window in scr left }
                                  { half }
        X2 := X1 + RANDOM(68-X1) + 12;
        Y1 := RANDOM(LENGTH(Msg)) + 1;
        Y2 := Y1 + RANDOM(22-Y1) + 3;
        Frame(X1,Y1,X2,Y2,RANDOM(16),RANDOM(8),RANDOM(8),
              Title,Msg);
        DELAY(500);
     END;
   WINDOW(1,1,80,25);                  { restore full screen }
   ScrWrite(28,25,WHITE,BLACK,'Press Enter to continue');
   READLN;
   PaintScreen(BLACK);                 { clean up screen }
END.   {DemoUnit3}
```

To make sure the windows fit on the screen, the program carefully calculates X1, Y1, X2, and Y2. With X2, you must be sure the window will be wide enough for your text strings to fit. Add LENGTH(Msg) to the X2 calculation so that the Msg string will fit in the window. When the foreground and background colors are the same, you will not see any frame title or message. Figure 25.1 shows a sample run of DemoUnit3.

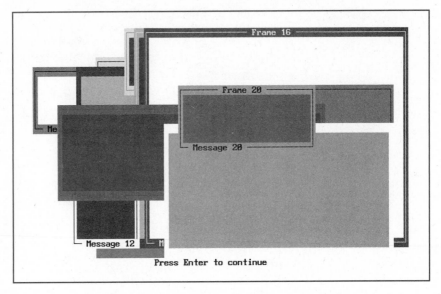

Figure 25.1. A sample run of DemoUnit3 to show random frames.

2. Instead of declaring the types, FrameString and MsgString, in the INTERFACE of ScrTool, you can include them instead in another unit, called ScrGlob (for screen globals). First, open a file called SCRGLOB.PAS. Second, write the code for the unit. Third, update ScrTool. Here is the code for the ScrGlob unit:

```
{Filename: SCRGLOB.PAS}

{ Declare all globals used by the ScrTool unit. }

UNIT ScrGlob;

INTERFACE
```

```
TYPE FrameString = STRING[30];
     MsgString   = STRING[30];

IMPLEMENTATION

END.  {ScrGlob}
```

Notice that there is nothing in the IMPLEMENTATION section. The purpose of this unit is to declare all globals associated with the ScrTool unit. Although this unit has only a TYPE section, you could also include CONST and VAR sections.

To update the ScrTool unit, delete FrameString and MsgString. After the INTERFACE section, add:

USES ScrGlob;

The INTERFACE section of the ScrTool unit should be:

```
{Filename: SCRTOOL.PAS}

UNIT ScrTool;

INTERFACE

USES ScrGlob;

    PROCEDURE Frame(W1,W2,W3,W4: BYTE;
                    FG:          BYTE;
                    BG:          BYTE;
                    InsideColor: BYTE;
                    Title:       FrameString;
                    Msg:         MsgString);

    PROCEDURE PaintScreen(BG: BYTE);

    PROCEDURE ScrWrite(X,Y: INTEGER;
                       FG:  BYTE;
                       BG:  BYTE;
                       S:   STRING);
```

If another unit needs to use FrameString or MsgString and not any of the procedures in unit ScrTool, that unit needs to include:

```
USES ScrGlob;
```

If another unit needs to use FrameString or MsgString and one or more procedure in unit ScrTool, that unit needs to include:

```
USES ScrGlob, ScrTool;
```

Include all program global constants, types, or variables in the INTERFACE section of a unit (for example, you could call the unit, ProgGlob). When another unit needs to access a global, include:

```
USES ProgGlob;
```

Summary

Units provide a convenient way to organize your Turbo Pascal files. As you develop your units you should carefully assign their names. For example, you used the word *Tool* to indicate a utility unit. The disadvantage of using *Tool* is that it leaves you only four characters for your unit name. Another idea would be to preface all unit files with a *U*; rather than ScrTool, you could have used UScr. Or, perhaps, you would rather end all unit names in a *U*.

As you build your library of units, you will probably develop some routines that do not seem to fit well into any of your existing units. It would probably be best to include these routines in a new unit.

The examples in this chapter emphasized having procedures in a unit. Sometimes, you need only the CONST, TYPE, or VAR section in the INTERFACE and no functions or procedures. This occurs when a unit must refer only to a specific constant, type definition, or variable declaration.

If something in the INTERFACE section of a unit needs to refer to a unit, include the USES statement just after the word, INTERFACE. If something in the IMPLEMENTATION section of a unit needs to refer to a unit, include the USES statement just after the word, IMPLEMENTATION.

Review Questions

Answers to the Review Questions appear in Appendix B.

1. What is a unit?

2. What is the purpose of the INTERFACE section?

3. What is always the last statement of a unit?

4. What is the relationship between the name of a unit and the name of the file containing the unit?

5. How does a program or unit call another unit?

6. How do you decide if a USES statement needs to go in the INTERFACE or IMPLEMENTATION section of a unit?

Review Exercises

1. Add error checking to the procedures in the ScrTool unit. Make sure the PaintScreen procedure uses only valid background colors, the ScrWrite procedure uses only valid numbers for GOTOXY, and the Frame procedures uses only valid numbers for the WINDOW procedure.

2. Create a string unit that has at least one procedure or function. For example, include a function that returns a string of repeating characters (see Chapter 22, "User-Defined Functions").

3. Create a unit that has only constants and type definitions in the INTERFACE.

Part VII

Disk File Processing

Reading and Writing to Disk

So far, every example in this book has processed data that resides inside the program listing or comes from the keyboard. You learned about typed constants that store data, you assigned constants and variables to other variables, and you created new data values from existing ones. The programs also received input with READLN and READKEY and processed the user's keystrokes.

The data created by the user with typed constants is sufficient for some applications. With the large volumes of data most real-world applications must process, however, you need a better way of storing that data. For all but the smallest computer programs, the hard disk offers the solution.

By storing data on the disk, the computer helps you enter the data, find it, change it, and delete it. The computer and Turbo Pascal are simply tools to help you manage and process data.

This chapter focuses on disk and file theory before you get to numerous disk examples in the next chapter. Because disk processing takes some preliminary work to understand, it helps to cover some introductory explanations about disk files and their uses before looking at Turbo Pascal's specific disk file commands in Chapter 27, "Sequential Disk Processing."

This chapter introduces:

◆ An overview of disks

◆ Types of files

◆ Processing data on the disk

◆ Filenames

◆ Types of disk file access

After this chapter, you will be ready to tackle the Turbo Pascal examples and specific disk file processing commands in Chapter 27. If you are new to disk file processing, study this chapter before delving into Turbo Pascal's file-related commands. The overview presented here rewards you with a deeper and better understanding of how Turbo Pascal and your disk work together.

Why Use a Disk?

The typical computer system has 640K of RAM and a 30- to 40-megabyte hard disk drive. (Chapter 1, "Welcome to Turbo Pascal," explained your computer's internal hardware and devices.) Figure 26.1 shows your RAM layout. The first part of conventional memory in most PCs is taken up by DOS, DOS information, and memory-resident programs. DOS always resides in your computer's RAM. When you start Turbo Pascal, it shares memory with DOS. Whatever is left of the 640K is the room you have for your programs and data. There is not too much room left.

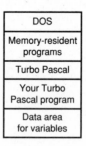

| DOS |
| Memory-resident programs |
| Turbo Pascal |
| Your Turbo Pascal program |
| Data area for variables |

Figure 26.1. **Your RAM storage.**

Your disk drive holds much more data than can fit in your computer's RAM. This is the primary reason for using the disk for your data. The disk memory, because it is nonvolatile, lasts longer. When you power-off your computer, the disk memory is not erased, whereas RAM is erased. Also, when your data changes, you (or more important, your users) do not have to edit the program and look for a set of typed constants. Instead, users run previously written programs that make changes to the disk data. This makes programming more difficult at first because programs have to be written to change the data on the disk. However, nonprogrammers can then use the programs and modify the data without knowing how to program.

The capacity of your disk makes it a perfect place to store your data as well as your programs. Think about what would happen if all data had to be stored in a program's typed constants. What if the Social Security office in Washington, D.C., asked you to write a Turbo Pascal program to compute, average, filter, sort, and display each person's name and address in their files? Would you want your program to include millions of typed constants? Not only would you not want the program to hold that much data, but it could not do so because only relatively small amounts of data fit in a program before you run out of RAM.

You have more storage by storing data on your disk, so you are much less limited. Your disk can hold as much data as you have disk capacity. Also, if your disk requirements grow, you can usually increase your disk space, whereas you cannot always add more RAM to your computer. Although Turbo Pascal can access *expanded* memory with overlays (beyond the scope of this book), it cannot access the special *extended* memory some computers have. Expanded memory is memory you add to an original PC or XT. Extended memory is memory you add to an AT (286 and above).

Your program does not have to access much RAM at once, however, because it can read data from your disk drive and process it. Not all your disk data has to reside in RAM for your program to process it. Your program reads some data, processes it, and then reads some more. If your program requires disk data a second time, it rereads that place on the disk.

Data Files and Filenames

A DATA FILE is a collection of related information stored on your disk.

You can store two types of files on your computer's disk drive: *program files* and *data files*. You are used to program files, which are the programs you write and store on the disk with the **File Save...** command. Data files do not contain programs, but rather, they contain the data the programs process. For the rest of this book, *files* refers to data files unless *program file* is specifically mentioned.

To understand the computer's data files, you can think of files in a filing cabinet. Files on your computer are treated just as files are in a filing cabinet. You probably have a cabinet or box at home containing several filing folders. You might have a file of your insurance papers, a file of your automobile papers, a file of your home and mortgage information, and several other files. Do you see that these files fit the definition of computer data files? These files are sets of *related* information.

You would not (intentionally) mix your insurance and mortgage files. If you did, your file integrity would be lost. The files would no longer contain related information, so they would not be useful files.

Computer File Example

It helps to take the analogy of computer files and regular paper files one step further. Think about colleges 25 years ago, before they computerized. How did they store their information about students, professors, and classes? They probably had three filing cabinets, and one of the cabinets probably held the student files.

As each student enrolled, the enrollment clerk completed a form similar to that in Figure 26.2, which includes the student's Social Security number, name, address, city, state, ZIP code, age, and so forth. The clerk would then file that piece of paper in the cabinet.

Later, if that student moved and needed his or her address changed, the student would tell the clerk. The clerk would have to go to the filing cabinet, find the student's form, change the address, and then put the form back in the student filing cabinet. The professor file and the class file would be handled similarly.

```
┌─────────────────────────────────────┐
│           ┌──────────────────┐       │
│           │ School Application│       │
│           └──────────────────┘       │
│                                       │
│   Social Security #:_____     │
│                                       │
│   Name:_____      │
│                                       │
│   Address:_____      │
│                                       │
│   City:_____  State:_____  Zip:_____ │
│                                       │
│   Grade:_____    Sex:_____      │
│                                       │
│   GPA:_____      Age:_____      │
│                                       │
│                                       │
│                                       │
│                                       │
└─────────────────────────────────────┘
```

Figure 26.2. A college student's enrollment form to be filled out and filed in a manual data file.

Look forward in time about 25 years to today and think of how that same college handles students, professors, and classes with the help of computerized data files. Rather than three filing cabinets, the college would have a huge disk drive with three files on it: the student file, the professor file, and the class file.

As students enroll, the clerk does not fill out a form. Instead, the clerk sits in front of a computer and answers questions on the screen. These questions, or *prompts*, might look like those in Figure 26.3. Do you notice anything familiar? The clerk is filling out the same information on the screen that might have been filled out on a piece of paper 25 years ago. When the information is complete, the clerk presses a key and the computer stores that information in the student file on the disk. If that student's information changes, the clerk displays the student's information on the screen again, changes it, and saves it back to the disk file.

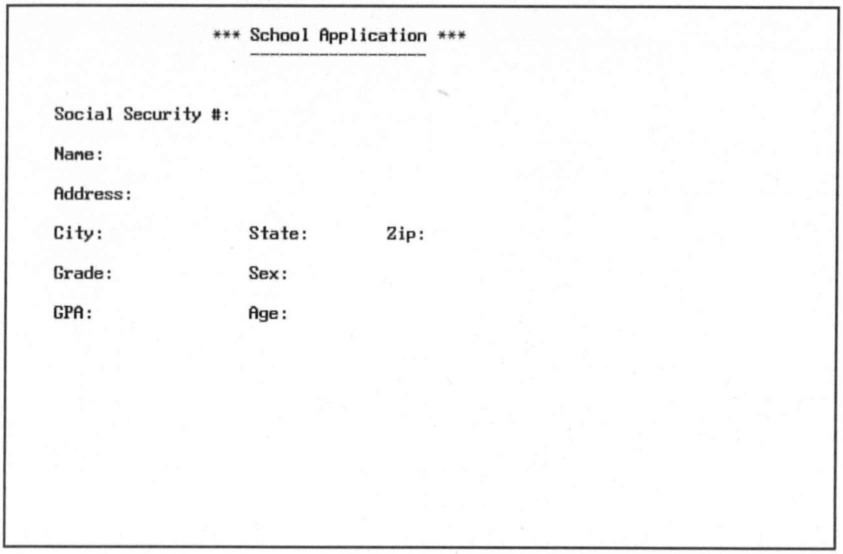

```
                    *** School Application ***
                    ---------------------------


    Social Security #:

    Name:

    Address:

    City:              State:        Zip:

    Grade:             Sex:

    GPA:               Age:
```

Figure 26.3. The school's computerized data-entry screen.

The operations are the same in both the manual and the computerized filing systems, except the computer takes over much of the work required to retrieve a blank form and manually file it in the proper location. The sooner you realize that computer files and files in cabinets are handled in the same way, the easier it is to learn to use Turbo Pascal to write programs that create, modify, and delete disk information.

Records and Fields

Before writing a program that creates a data file on disk, you must think through the data to be stored in the file. The programmer decides exactly what information is stored and how it is stored. To make proper file decisions, you should understand exactly how data is stored on the disk.

The student data file described in the preceding section might look like the file in Table 26.1. The table shows data for four students. There is no specified order of the file; files are generally kept in the same physical order in which their data was entered (in this case, the order in which the students enrolled in the school). This does not mean file access can be made only in that order. Turbo Pascal programs can read this file and display a file listing in any order, including numerical order by Social Security number and alphabetical order.

Table 26.1. Sample student data.

Social Security #	Name	Age	Address	City	State ZIP
434-54-3223	Jones, Michael	21	9 W. Elm	Miami	FL 22332
231-34-5767	Brown, Larry	19	505 Baker	Tampa Bay	FL 23227
945-65-2344	Smith, Kim	20	14 Oak Rd.	Miami	FL 22331
294-78-9434	Lawton, Jerry	21	6 Main St.	Miami	FL 22356
.	.		.	.	
.	.		.	.	
.	.		.	.	.

Your computer files are broken into *records* and *fields*. A record is an individual occurrence in the file. In this case, the file is a collection of students, so each student's information is called a complete student record. If there are 12,000 students in the file, there must be 12,000 records in the file.

In Table 26.1, you can view a record as a row from the file. This is not a technically accurate description because a record can span more than one row in a data file; however, for small data files (with relatively few columns of data), a record can be viewed as a row in the file.

The fields are the columns in the file. The student data file has seven columns: Social Security number, name, age, address, city, state, and ZIP. Even if 5,000 student records are added to the file, there will still be only seven fields because there will still be seven columns of data.

You can create files with *fixed-length records* or *variable-length records*. If the records are fixed-length, each field takes the same amount of disk space, even if that field's data value does not fill the field. Fixed strings are typically used for fixed-length records. For instance, most programmers create a data file table for their files such as the one shown in Table 26.2. This table lists each field name, the type of data in each field, and the length of each field.

Table 26.2. Student description table for a fixed-length data file.

Field Name	Length	Data Type
SocSec	9	STRING
StName	25	STRING
StAge	2	INTEGER
StAddr	30	STRING
StCity	10	STRING
StState	2	STRING
StZip	5	STRING

83 total characters per record

The total record length is 83 characters. Every record in this file takes exactly 83 characters of disk space. Just because a city takes only 5 characters of the 10-character field does not mean 5 characters are all that are stored. Each field is padded with spaces to the right, if needed, to fill the complete 10 characters for each student's city. This has a major drawback: It wastes much disk space. But each field is large enough to hold the largest possible data value.

Files with variable-length records, on the other hand, do not waste space like files with fixed-length records. When a field's data value is saved to the file, the next field's data value is stored immediately after it. There is usually a special separating character between the fields so that your programs know where the fields begin and end.

Files with variable-length records save disk space, but it is not always as easy to write programs that process them as it is to write programs that process files with fixed-length records. If limited disk space is a consideration, there is more of a need for the space-saving variable-length records, even if the programs to process them are more difficult to write. The next two chapters discuss each of these file types.

Filenames

Each file in your filing cabinet has a label on it. Without those labels, finding a certain file would be difficult, and the files would tend to get mixed up. You want your data to be as easy to find as possible, so you label the files as accurately as possible.

Files on a computer also have names. Each file on your disk has a unique filename. You cannot have two files on the same disk that have the same name (unless they are in different directories). If that were possible, your computer would not know which file you wanted when you asked it to use one of them.

Some files are named for you. Others you must name. Just as Turbo Pascal variables have naming rules, so do filenames on the disk. Filenames can be from one to eight characters long with an optional one-to-three-character *extension*. The filename and extension must be separated from each other with a period. For example, here are some valid filenames:

Sales89.Dat	Checks.Apr	a.3	TestData
Turbo.exe	emp_name.ap	Students	employee.q

Notice that some filenames have an extension and some do not. No filename extension is longer than three characters. A filename can consist of letters, numbers, and the underscore (_) character. Because spaces are not allowed in filenames, the underscore character is good to use when you want to separate parts of a filename, as in emp_name.ap in the preceding list.

Although a few other special characters are allowed in filenames, such as the pound sign and the exclamation point, many are not allowed, such as the asterisk and the question mark. To be safe, use just letters, numbers, and the underscore.

> **TIP:** Make your filenames meaningful. Although you could call your December 1991 checkbook data file `x_5.q`, calling it `checkdec.91` would make much more sense.

When you write a program to create a data file, you have to create a name for that file, and it must conform to the file-naming rules listed previously. The file is created on the DOS default disk drive (the active drive at the DOS prompt when you started Turbo Pascal).

If you want to override the default and save the file some other place, you must precede the filename with the appropriate information. This information consists of two parts: the disk drive letter and the file path. Assume that the file, SALES89.DAT, is on drive C: and in subdirectory, OldData. To completely specify this file location, use C:\OldData\SALES89.DAT. Notice that a backslash (\) separates the disk drive name (C:), path (OldData), and filename (SALES89.DAT). In general, specify a filename with

dd:\FilePath\FileName

where `dd` represents the disk drive letter. If you wish to save a file on the same disk drive, the disk drive letter is optional. `FilePath` can contain other subdirectories, to a maximum of 63 characters. Separate subdirectories in `FilePath` with backslashes. Table 26.3 lists some examples:

Table 26.3. Some file naming examples.

File Specification	Location
`a:\SALES89.DAT`	drive A:
`d:\Sales\SALES89.DAT`	drive D:, subdirectory Sales
`d:\Business\Sales\SALES89.DAT`	drive D:, subdirectory Sales under the directory Business
`\OldData\SALES89.DAT`	current drive, subdirectory OldData

Types of Disk File Access

Your programs can access files two ways: through *sequential access* or through *random access.* Your application determines the method you should choose. The access mode of a file determines how you read, write, change, and delete data from the file. Some of your files can be accessed both sequentially and randomly.

A sequential file has to be accessed one record at a time in the same order the records were written. This is analogous to cassette tapes: You play music in the same order it was recorded. You can quickly fast forward or rewind over songs that you do not want to listen to, but the order of the songs dictates what you must do to play the song you want.

It is difficult, and sometimes impossible, to insert file records in the middle of a sequential file. How easy is it to insert a new song in the middle of two other songs on a tape? The only way to add or delete records from the middle of a sequential file is to create a completely new file that combines both old and new records. For example, to insert a new record #10 into an existing 20-record sequential file, you must create a new file, copy the first nine records from the old file into the new file, write the new record, and then continue copying the remaining records from the old file.

It might seem that sequential files are limiting, but it turns out that many applications lend themselves to sequential file processing. In Chapter 27, you will see several ways to best use sequential files.

You can access a random-access file in any order you want. Think of records in a random-access file as you would songs on a compact disc or record; you can go directly to any song you want without having to play or fast-forward over the other songs. If you want to play the first song, the sixth song, and then the fourth song, you can do so. The order of play has nothing to do with the order in which the songs were originally recorded.

Random file access takes more programming, but rewards that effort with a more flexible file access method. Chapter 28 discusses how to program for random-access files.

Summary

This chapter introduced Turbo Pascal file processing. You now have the tools you need to understand the statements that are covered by the next two chapters. You understand the difference between records and fields, and between sequential file access and random file access modes.

When you learn how to write disk file programs, you rarely use typed constants except to initialize program control variables such as age limits, month names, day of the week names, and other small groups of data required to control the incoming data on the disk and produce output.

Review Questions

Answers to the Review Questions appear in Appendix B.

1. What are the two modes that access disk files?

2. The following table shows some inventory records from a disk file:

Part No.	Description	Quantity	Price
43223	Bolt #45	12	0.45
52912	Long Widget	42	3.43
20328	Stress Clip	39	2.00
94552	Turn Mold	2	12.32
45357	#1 Roller	30	7.87

   A. How many records are in this file?

   B. How many fields are there?

   C. What are the field names?

3. Why is it important to be able to save data on a hard disk?

4. Name two drawbacks of keeping all your data in typed constants.

5. Which are usually more flexible and easier to program, fixed-length records or variable-length records?

6. The following three filenames contain three months of video rental data for a video store. What, if anything, is wrong with the filenames?

   ```
   0_0.0       bbbwws4.12a      hatdata.apr
   ```

7. Of the following list of filenames, which ones are not valid?

sales.89.may	employees.dec	userfile
pipe.dat	sales.txt	PROG1.PAS

Sequential Disk Processing

Turbo Pascal supports three different types of files: text, typed, and untyped. Text files are discussed in this chapter. Typed files are discussed in the next chapter. Untyped files are beyond the scope of this book.

Text files typically consist of ASCII characters. For example, when you use the IDE to edit one of your Pascal files, you are using a text file. Text files are usually associated with sequential file processing.

This chapter introduces Turbo Pascal sequential file processing commands. You will learn how to create, modify, and manage sequential files on the disk. Using the disk for your data storage dramatically increases the power of your programs. You can process large amounts of data and store it for later use.

This chapter introduces

♦ How to open and close a file

♦ Testing for file existence

♦ Creating sequential files

♦ The WRITE and WRITELN statements

◆ Reading sequential files

◆ The READ and READLN statements

◆ The EOF function

◆ Appending to sequential files

The concepts and commands you learn here are helpful for almost every Turbo Pascal application you write. Separating the data from the programs that process it makes your programs much more useful for long-term use and for real-world data processing.

How to Open a File

Chapter 26, "Reading and Writing to Disk," described the analogy between files in cabinets and files on a disk. Before you use a file from your filing cabinet, you must open the filing cabinet. Before creating, modifying, or displaying a disk data file in Turbo Pascal, you also must open the file.

There are several steps you must take when opening a text file. First, you must declare a file variable of type TEXT. Second, you must use the ASSIGN statement to associate the file variable with the name of the file to be opened. The format of the ASSIGN statement is

```
ASSIGN( FileVar, FileName );
```

The FileName must be a string, a string variable, or a constant specifying a valid filename. You can open more than one file in one program. Rather than referring to the filename every time you access a file, you refer to the FileVar. FileVar also is known as the *file handle*.

After the ASSIGN statement, the next statement depends on how you want to use the file. There are two possibilities. You can open a text file either to read from or to write to, but not both at the same time.

If you want to read data from an existing text file, the next statement after the previous ASSIGN statement is

```
RESET( FileVar );
```

After using ASSIGN and RESET, the file is now open. Turbo Pascal uses a *file pointer* to keep track of the current location inside an open file. RESET moves the file pointer to the beginning of the file. If you use RESET on a non-existent file, Turbo Pascal returns an error. A later section in this chapter shows you how to deal with such errors.

If you wish to write data to an existing text file, you can *append* data to the text file or add to the end of the text file. The next statement after the previous ASSIGN statement is

```
APPEND( FileVar );
```

After using ASSIGN and APPEND, the file is now open. APPEND moves the file pointer to the beginning of the file. If you use APPEND on a non-existent file, Turbo Pascal returns an error.

If you wish to create a new text file, the next statement after the previous ASSIGN statement is

```
REWRITE( FileVar );
```

After using ASSIGN and REWRITE, the file is now open. If the file associated with *FileVar* already exists, REWRITE deletes the old file and creates a new file. REWRITE moves the file pointer to the beginning of the empty file. If you use REWRITE on a non-existent file, a new file is created and Turbo Pascal returns no error.

Examples

1. Suppose you must create a sequential file containing an inventory of your household items. Assuming the following file declaration, these statements do just that:

   ```
   VAR HouseFile: TEXT;

   ASSIGN( HouseFile, 'House.inv' );
   REWRITE( HouseFile );
   ```

   The file is ready to accept data from the program.

2. If you previously created the household inventory file and must read values from it, you have to write a program containing the following statements:

```
ASSIGN( HouseFile, 'House.inv' );
RESET( HouseFile );
```

3. After buying several items, you want to add to the household inventory file. To add to the end of the file, you would open it in the following way:

```
ASSIGN( HouseFile, 'House.inv' );
APPEND( HouseFile );
```

4. Suppose you want to create a backup copy of the household inventory file. You have to create a new file from the old one. This involves reading the old file and writing data to another file. The backup file can even reside on another disk drive, as shown in the following statements:

```
VAR OldHouse: TEXT;
    NewHouse: TEXT;
BEGIN
   ⋮
   ASSIGN( OldHouse, 'c:House.inv' );  { Old file }
   RESET( OldHouse );                  { open for reading }
   ASSIGN( NewHouse, 'a:House.inv' );  { New file }
   REWRITE( NewHouse );                { open for writing }
   ⋮
END.
```

If the file resides on the DOS default drive, you do not have to put a disk drive name before the filename. When you open more than one file in a program, the files must have different file handles.

DOS Determines the Total Number of Open Files

The FILES= command resides in your DOS CONFIG.SYS file. It determines the number of open files you can have at any one time in Turbo Pascal. Turbo Pascal requires one of the files for its own use, and you can open additional files until the total equals the number set in the FILES= statement.

If you find your programs must open several files at the same time and you receive the following error messages

```
Too many files open
```

you will have to increase the number following the FILES= statement in your CONFIG.SYS file.

You can use the IDE to edit your CONFIG.SYS file. Press F3 to open a file and type

```
C:\CONFIG.SYS
```

If you see a FILES statement, edit the number to be greater. If you do not see a FILES statement, insert the following line at the top of the file:

```
FILES=20
```

The CLOSE Statement

After using a file, just as with a filing cabinet, you must close the file with the CLOSE statement. You should close all files that are open in your program when you are through with them. By closing the files, Turbo Pascal frees the file handle for use by other files that are opened later. DOS also does some bookkeeping on the file when you close it.

TIP: If you need a file open for only part of a program, close it immediately after you finish with it rather than at the end of the program as some programmers do. In the event of a power failure, some of the data in open files might be lost.

The format of the CLOSE statement is

```
CLOSE( FileVar );
```

CLOSE works for all Pascal output files, whether opened with APPEND, RESET, or REWRITE.

For example, to close an output file associated with file handle HouseFile, you would type

```
CLOSE( HouseFile );
```

Testing for File Existence

If you try to open a file for reading data and the file does not yet exist, your program will crash with runtime error 002 File not found. Turbo Pascal has a function, IORESULT, that returns I/O (Input/Output) status. If IORESULT returns 0, then all is well. To avoid crashing, you must temporarily disable Turbo Pascal's I/O checking. You can do this with a special compiler directive. Here is one way to check whether a file exists:

```
    ASSIGN( FileVar,'Some.dat' );
{$I-}                                    { turn off I/O checking }
    RESET( FileVar );
{$I+}                                    { turn on I/O checking }
    IF IORESULT <> 0
      THEN BEGIN
              WRITELN( 'File does not exist');
              EXIT;
           END;
```

If IORESULT <> 0 there are several possible things that could have gone wrong. When checking for a file, however, the most likely problem is that the file was not found. Table 27.1 shows some possible values and what they indicate.

Table 27.1. Possible IORESULT values.

IORESULT	Meaning
2	File not found
3	Path not found
4	Too many open files
5	File access denied
6	Invalid file handle

IORESULT	Meaning
8	Not enough memory
10	Invalid environment
11	Invalid format
12	Invalid file access code
15	Invalid drive number
16	Cannot remove current directory
17	Cannot rename across drives
18	No more files
100	Disk read error
101	Disk write error
102	File not assigned
103	File not open
104	File not open for input
105	File not open for output
106	Invalid numeric format
150	Disk is write-protected
151	Unknown unit
152	Drive not ready
153	Unknown command
154	CRC error in data
155	Bad drive request
156	Disk seek error
157	Unknown media type
158	Sector not found
159	Printer out of paper
160	Device write fault
161	Device read fault
162	Hardware failure

After you call IORESULT, it immediately resets itself to 0. To store the return value, you must save the value in a variable. You can use this variable with a CASE statement to display a problem message. By defining a BOOLEAN function, you can determine whether a text file exists.

```
FUNCTION FileExists(FName: STRING): BOOLEAN;
   VAR TFile:    TEXT;
       IOStatus: INTEGER;
   BEGIN
      FileExists := FALSE;
      ASSIGN( TFile,FName );
{$I-}                                     { turn off I/O checking }
      RESET( TFile );
{$I+}                                     { turn off I/O checking }
      IOStatus := IORESULT;               { save IORESULT }
      IF IOStatus = 0
         THEN BEGIN
                 FileExists := TRUE;
                 CLOSE( TFile );
              END
         ELSE CASE IOStatus OF
                 4: WRITELN( 'Too many open files' );
                 5: WRITELN( 'File access denied' );
               104: WRITELN( 'File not open for input' );
               105: WRITELN( 'File not open for output' );
               152: WRITELN( 'Drive not ready' );
              END;  {case}
   END;  {FileExists}
```

Although the preceding function uses RESET, you can use it to test for file existence whether or not you are opening the file for reading or writing. If your program is accessing a floppy drive and the drive door is not closed, IORESULT returns 152. This kind of error checking helps prevent DOS from disrupting your screen with Abort, Retry, Ignore?.

An alternative technique uses a function from Turbo Pascal's Dos unit. FSEARCH does not display the Abort, Retry, Ignore? message if a floppy drive is not ready. You do not even have to turn off I/O error checking. If FSEARCH cannot find a desired file, it returns a null string. If FSEARCH finds the file, it returns the filename (including the path) where the file is located. To use this function, include a USES Dos; statement.

```
FUNCTION FileExists(FName: STRING): BOOLEAN;
   VAR TFile: TEXT;
       S:      STRING;
   BEGIN
     S := FSEARCH(FName,'');
     FileExists := S <> '';
   END;  {FileExists}
```

The second parameter to FSEARCH specifies a list of directories to search. Use '' to search the current subdirectory. You could easily modify the function to include another parameter to search alternative directories.

Creating Sequential Files

If you want to create a file (or overwrite one that already exists), open it with REWRITE:

```
ASSIGN( FileVar, FileName );
REWRITE( FileVar );
```

After you have opened the file, you need a way to write data to it. Most data going to a file comes from user input, calculations, or a combination of these. If you save your data in a disk file, it will be there the next time you need it, and you will not have to re-create it each time you run your program.

Although you can use both WRITE and WRITELN to send output data to a sequential file, you usually use WRITELN. When you use WRITE, it becomes difficult to read the file because the data is not organized in any way. When you use WRITELN, you are actually writing lines of text to a file. These lines do not have to be the same length. Turbo Pascal automatically terminates a line of text with a carriage return–line feed combination.

The format of WRITELN is

```
WRITELN( FileVar, ExpressionList );
```

The *FileVar* must be the file handle of the opened file to which you want to write. The *ExpressionList* is one or more variables, constants, expressions, or a combination of each separated by commas. The only difference between WRITELN and WRITELN(*FileVar*,...) is *FileVar*, which redirects the output to a file rather than to the screen. Recall that the full format of using WRITELN to write to the screen is

WRITELN(OUTPUT, *ExpressionList*);

Similarly, writing data to the printer uses

WRITELN(LST, *ExpressionList*);

It is important to remember that WRITELN(*FileVar*,   ) displays data to a file *exactly* as that data would appear on the screen with the regular WRITELN statement.

The following program writes three lines of customer data to a file:

```
{ Filename: C27CUST1.PAS }

{ Write three lines of customer data to a file. }

PROGRAM Cust1;
USES Crt;
VAR CustFile: TEXT;

BEGIN
   CLRSCR;
   ASSIGN( CustFile, 'Cust.dat' );
   REWRITE( CustFile );                    { create file on }
                                           { default drive }
   WRITELN( CustFile, 'Johnson, Mike', 34, '5th and Denver',
           'Houston', 'TX', '74334' );
   WRITELN( CustFile, 'Abel, Lea', 28, '85 W. 123th', 'Miami',
           'FL', '39443' );
   WRITELN( CustFile, 'Madison, Larry', 32, '4 North Elm',
           'Lakewood', 'IL', '93844' );
   CLOSE( CustFile );                      { Always close open }
                                           { files when you are }
                                           { through with them }
END.   {Cust1}
```

This program produces a file called CUST.DAT that looks like this:

```
Johnson, Mike345th and DenverHoustonTX74334
Abel, Lea2885 W. 123thMiamiFL39443
Madison, Larry324 North ElmLakewoodIL93844
```

As with the WRITELN statement, you can also add formatting when writing data to a disk file. This lets you format numbers and strings when you send them to disk files, just as when you send them to the screen and printer.

Because there was not any formatting with the previous example, there is no easy method of reading the data back into memory. Notice in the preceding file that the data runs together in some places and is separated in other places. When you are ready to read this file, Turbo Pascal will have a difficult time reading the data.

Because the following program includes formatting with the WRITELN statement, it is an improved version of the program described earlier:

```
{ Filename: C27CUST2.PAS }

{ Write three lines of customer data to a file. }

PROGRAM Cust2;
USES Crt;
VAR CustFile: TEXT;

BEGIN
   CLRSCR;
   ASSIGN( CustFile, 'Cust.Dat' );
   REWRITE( CustFile );                  { Open file on default
                                         { drive }
   WRITELN( CustFile, 'Johnson, Mike':20, 34:3,
            '5th and Denver':20, 'Houston':10,
            'TX':3, '74334':10 );
   WRITELN( CustFile, 'Abel, Lea':20, 28:3,
            '85 W. 123th':20, 'Miami':10,
            'FL':3, '39443':10 );
   WRITELN( CustFile, 'Madison, Larry':20, 32:3,
            '4 North Elm':20, 'Lakewood':10,
            'IL':3, '93844':10 );
```

```
        CLOSE( CustFile );                  { Always close open }
                                            { files when you are }
                                            { through with them }
END.   {Cust2}
```

Because the program uses formatting with WRITELN, the output file's fields are separated much better. Here is the output file, called Cust.Dat, created from this program:

```
Johnson, Mike 34      5th and Denver    Houston  TX      74334
      Abel, Lea 28      85 W. 123th       Miami  FL      39443
Madison, Larry 32       4 North Elm    Lakewood  IL      93844
```

This file can later be read by sequential input programs like those described in the next section. To read the file, the exact same formatting must be used.

Turbo Pascal inserts a carriage return and a line feed character at the end of each line of data you write with WRITELN.

> **TIP:** When outside of the Turbo Pascal program, you can use the DOS command TYPE to view the contents of a text file. For example, to view the previous file from DOS, use:
>
> TYPE Cust.dat

As mentioned earlier, Turbo Pascal keeps track of where you are in a text file with a file pointer. When you open a file for reading or when you create a new file, the file pointer points to the beginning of the file. When you open a file to append data, the file pointer points to the end of the file. When you use READLN or WRITELN, the file pointer advances to the next line of data.

Examples

1. The following program creates a data file of books from a collection. This is similar to the way the book database program in Appendix E gets its data. It loops through prompts that ask the user for book information and writes that information to a file.

```
{ Filename: C27BOOK1.PAS }

{ Get book data and create a file. }

PROGRAM Book1;
USES Crt;
CONST TitleLen   = 30;
      AuthorLen  = 20;
      EditionLen = 8;
      CopiesLen  = 8;
      YearLen    = 6;

TYPE  TitleString   = STRING[TitleLen];
      AuthorString  = STRING[AuthorLen];
      EditionString = STRING[EditionLen];
      YearString    = STRING[YearLen];

VAR   BookFile:  TEXT;
      BookTitle: TitleString;
      Author:    AuthorString;
      Copies:    INTEGER;
      Edition:   EditionString;
      CopyDate:  YearString;
      AnsCh:     CHAR;
BEGIN
   CLRSCR;
   ASSIGN( BookFile, 'Book.Dat' );
   REWRITE( BookFile );               { create file }
   REPEAT                             { Loop asking for data }
      WRITELN;
      WRITE( 'What is the next book title? ');
      READLN( BookTitle );
      WRITE( 'Who is the author? ');
      READLN( Author );
      WRITE( 'How many copies do you have? ');
      READLN( Copies );
      WRITE( 'What edition (1st, 2nd, etc.) is the book? ');
      READLN( Edition );
      WRITE( 'What is the copyright date? ');
      READLN( CopyDate );
          { Now write the data to the file }
```

```
     WRITELN( BookFile, BookTitle:TitleLen,
                 Author:AuthorLen,
                 Copies:CopiesLen, Edition:EditionLen,
                 CopyDate:YearLen );
     WRITELN;
     WRITE( 'Do you have another book to enter? (y/n) ');
     READLN( AnsCh );
   UNTIL (UPCASE(AnsCh) = 'N');     { Loop until user wants }
                                    { to quit }

   CLOSE( BookFile );
 END.   {Book1}
```

2. Many programmers remember that new computer users are accustomed to filling out forms by hand when they are filing information. Therefore, they design their input screens to look similar to a form. The GOTOXY command is useful for this. The following program enters the same information in the book file that the previous one did. As you can see from the input screen shown in Figure 27.1, however, the user probably feels more at home with this screen than with a group of individual questions.

```
                   ***************************
                   * Book Data-Entry Screen *
                   ***************************


 Book's Title The Rain in Spain

 Book's Author Welby, Kerry

 --------------------------------------------------------------------

 No. of Copies 2     Edition (1st, 2nd, etc.) 3rd    Copyright Date 1989
```

Figure 27.1. A formlike data-entry screen.

The program displays the entire data-entry screen, then uses GOTOXY to position the cursor after each prompt. Because of the modular nature of this program (and of most programs), procedures are called from the main program to perform their individual tasks, such as displaying titles and prompts and getting the input data. Only the input routine and data-saving routine require the values of the book data, so the data is local to those routines and is passed between them. Users are asked whether they want to enter another book in a function that returns their answer.

Due to space limitations, not all data-entry routines in this book are in a complete formlike program. You should, nevertheless, consider this for your applications that users will see.

```
{ Filename: C27BOOK2.PAS }

{
 Get book data from a formlike data-entry screen
  and create a file.
}

PROGRAM Book2;
USES Crt;

CONST Spc = ' ';
      TitleLen   = 30;
      AuthorLen  = 20;
      EditionLen = 8;
      CopiesLen  = 8;
      YearLen    = 6;

TYPE  TitleString   = STRING[TitleLen];
      AuthorString  = STRING[AuthorLen];
      EditionString = STRING[EditionLen];
      YearString    = STRING[YearLen];

VAR   BookFile: TEXT;
      BookTitle: TitleString;
      Author:   AuthorString;
```

```
      Copies:    INTEGER;
      Edition:   EditionString;
      CopyDate:  YearString;


  {
    BooksDone: Ask if the user wants to enter another book,
    and return the uppercase answer
  }

FUNCTION BooksDone: BOOLEAN;
VAR AnsCh: CHAR;
   BEGIN
      GOTOXY(10,16);
      WRITE( 'Do you want to enter another book? (y/n) ');
      READLN(AnsCh);
      BooksDone := UPCASE(AnsCh) = 'N';
   END;   {AskAgain}


   { MakeLineCh: build string of repeating chars }

FUNCTION MakeLineCh(Len: INTEGER;
                    Ch:  CHAR): STRING;
   VAR tStr: STRING;
   BEGIN
      FILLCHAR(tStr[1],Len,Ch);
      tStr[0]    := CHR(Len);
      MakeLineCh := tStr;
   END;   {MakeLineCh}


   {
     DisplayScreen: This subroutine places each data-entry
     prompt on various locations around the screen so the
     user gets a feel of a data-entry form.
   }

PROCEDURE DisplayScreen;
   BEGIN
      GOTOXY(1,7);
      WRITELN( 'Book''s Title' );

      GOTOXY(1,9);
      WRITELN( 'Book''s Author' );
```

```
      GOTOXY(1,11);
      WRITELN( MakeLineCh(80,'-') );

      GOTOXY(1,13);
      WRITELN( 'No. of Copies' );

      GOTOXY(21,13);
      WRITELN( 'Edition (1st, 2nd, etc.)' );

      GOTOXY(53,13);
      WRITELN( 'Copyright Date' );
END;  {DisplayScreen}


  {
    DisplayTitle: This subroutine simply displays the
    program's title on the screen
  }

PROCEDURE DisplayTitle;
   BEGIN
      TEXTCOLOR( 7);
      TEXTBACKGROUND( 1);            { white on blue }
      CLRSCR;

      WRITELN( Spc:25, MakeLineCh(26, '*') );
      WRITELN( Spc:25, '* Book Data-Entry Screen *' );
      WRITELN( Spc:25, MakeLineCh(26, '*' ) );
   END;  {DisplayTitle}


  {
    SaveBookData: This subroutine saves
    the entered data to the disk
  }

PROCEDURE SaveBookData(BookTitle: TitleString;
                       Author:    AuthorString;
                       Copies:    INTEGER;
                       Edition:   EditionString;
                       CopyDate:  YearString);
```

```
        BEGIN
          WRITELN( BookFile,BookTitle:TitleLen,
                    Author:AuthorLen, Copies:CopiesLen,
                    Edition:EditionLen, CopyDate:YearLen );
        END;  {SaveBookData}


   {
     GetBookData: After each input, display the value left
     two places to get rid of question marks from the input
     prompt.
   }

   PROCEDURE GetBookData;
     BEGIN
        TEXTCOLOR( 14);
        TEXTBACKGROUND( 1);        { Change color of user's }
                                   { input values }
        GOTOXY(14,7);              { Place data-input value }
                                   { after prompt }

        WRITE( '? ');
        READLN( BookTitle );

        GOTOXY(14,7);
        WRITELN( BookTitle, '  ' );

        GOTOXY(15,9);
        WRITE( '? ');
        READLN( Author );
        GOTOXY(15,9);
        WRITELN( Author, '  ' );

        GOTOXY(15,13);
        READLN( Copies );
        GOTOXY(15,13);
        WRITELN( Copies, '  ' );

        GOTOXY(46,13);
        READLN( Edition );
        GOTOXY(46,13);
        WRITELN( Edition, '  ' );
```

```
                GOTOXY(68,13);
                READLN( CopyDate );
                GOTOXY(68,13);
                WRITELN( CopyDate, '  ' );

                { Write the input data to disk }
                SaveBookData(BookTitle, Author, Copies,
                             Edition, CopyDate);
           END;   {GetBookData}

  BEGIN
     CLRSCR;
     ASSIGN( BookFile, 'Book.Dat' );
     REWRITE( BookFile );                   { create the file }
     REPEAT                                 { Loop asking for data }
        DisplayTitle;                       { Show title at top }
        DisplayScreen;                      { Show data-entry scr }
        GetBookData;                        { Get user's input data }
     UNTIL BooksDone;
     CLOSE( BookFile );
  END.   {Book2}
```

NOTE: Because the program formats the data, each line of data has the same length. Without formatting, the length of each line would probably be different.

Reading Sequential Files

To read data files created with WRITELN, you must use the READLN(*FileVar*,...) statement. READLN (*FileVar*,...) works with data files as READLN works with the keyboard. As your program executes each READLN (*FileVar*,...) in a text file, another line of data is input from the disk file. The format of the READLN statement is

READLN(*FileVar*, *VariableList*);

get input
from disk file

The *VariableList* might consist of one or more variables separated by commas. You must have already opened the file referred to by the *FileVar* with RESET.

READLN reads any data sent to the file with WRITELN.

The following statement reads four variables from the input file opened as text file CityFile. Two are numeric, and two are string.

```
READLN( CityFile, Group, Total, City, Amount );
```

The data types of the variables must match the data file's data types.

> **NOTE:** You also can use the READ(*FileVar*, ...) statement to read values from a file. However, you usually use READLN (*FileVar*, ...) with exactly the same formatting used to WRITELN (*FileVar*, ...) the data to the file.

When you read data from an input file, one of two things always happens:

♦ The input values are read

♦ The end of the input file is reached

Most of the time, READLN returns whatever values were input from the file. When all the values are input, however, there will be no more data. If you try to READLN past the end of the file, you get only empty strings and no error message.

With file input, Turbo Pascal supplies a built-in *end of file function*, EOF, that tells you whether you have just read the last line of data from the file. The format of EOF is

```
ReturnValue := EOF( FileVar );
```

EOF returns TRUE if you just input the last line from the file. EOF returns FALSE if there are more lines of data to be input. *ReturnValue* tells you whether you should continue looping to input more values.

Call the EOF function after each READLN to see whether there are more values to input or whether you have just input the last one.

Examples

1. The following program reads the first three lines of data from an inventory file. The program that created the file probably used a WRITELN statement that looked similar (in the number of variables and data types) to the READLN used here. Notice that the file must be opened with RESET. The next example shows you how to use EOF.

```
{ Filename: C27INV.PAS }

{
  Reads and displays first three lines of data
  from an input file.
}

PROGRAM Inventory1;
USES Crt, Dos;
CONST PartLen  =  6;
      DescLen  = 20;
      QuanLen  =  5;
      PriceLen =  7;
TYPE  PartNoString      = STRING[PartLen];
      DescriptionString = STRING[DescLen];

VAR   InvFile:     TEXT;
      PartNo:      PartNoString;
      Description: DescriptionString;
      Quantity:    INTEGER;
      Price:       REAL;

FUNCTION FileExists(FName: STRING): BOOLEAN;
   VAR TFile: TEXT;
       S:      STRING;
   BEGIN
      S := FSEARCH(FName,'');
      FileExists := S <> '';
   END;  {FileExists}
```

```
BEGIN
   CLRSCR;
   IF NOT FileExists('Inv.Dat')
      THEN BEGIN
              WRITELN( 'Inv.Dat file not found' );
              EXIT;
           END;
   ASSIGN( InvFile, 'Inv.Dat' );
   RESET( InvFile );
   WRITELN( 'First three lines of data from the file:' );
   WRITELN;
   WRITELN( 'Part #', 'Description', 'Quantity', 'Price' );
      { Get the first line }
   READLN( InvFile, PartNo, Description, Quantity, Price );
   WRITELN( PartNo:PartLen, Description:DescLen,
            Quantity:QuanLen, Price:PriceLen:2 );
      { Get the second line }
   READLN( InvFile, PartNo, Description, Quantity, Price );
   WRITELN( PartNo:PartLen, Description:DescLen,
            Quantity:QuanLen, Price:PriceLen:2 );
      { Get the third line }
   READLN( InvFile, PartNo, Description, Quantity, Price );
   WRITELN( PartNo:PartLen, Description:DescLen,
            Quantity:QuanLen, Price:PriceLen:2 );
   CLOSE( InvFile );
END.   {Inventory1}
```

2. The following program reads and displays the book data.
   The input is performed in a loop so that the end of the file
   can be tested for with EOF. You want to keep reading lines of
   data until you reach the end of the file.

```
{ Filename: C27BOOK3.PAS }

{ Input book data from a file and display it. }

PROGRAM Book3;
USES Crt, Dos;

CONST TitleLen   = 30;
      AuthorLen  = 20;
      EditionLen = 8;
```

```
          CopiesLen  = 8;
          YearLen    = 6;


TYPE  TitleString   = STRING[TitleLen];
      AuthorString  = STRING[AuthorLen];
      EditionString = STRING[EditionLen];
      YearString    = STRING[YearLen];


VAR   BookFile:  TEXT;
      BookTitle: TitleString;
      Author:    AuthorString;
      Copies:    INTEGER;
      Edition:   EditionString;
      CopyDate:  YearString;


FUNCTION FileExists(FName: STRING): BOOLEAN;
   VAR TFile: TEXT;
       S:     STRING;
   BEGIN
     S := FSEARCH(FName,'');
     FileExists := S <> '';
   END;  {FileExists}


PROCEDURE ShowHeadings;
   BEGIN
      WRITELN( 'Title':TitleLen, 'Author':AuthorLen,
               'Copies':CopiesLen, 'Edition':EditionLen,
               'Date':YearLen );
   END;  {ShowHeadings}


BEGIN
   CLRSCR;
   IF NOT FileExists('Book.Dat')
      THEN BEGIN
             WRITELN( 'Book.Dat file not found' );
             EXIT;
           END;
   ASSIGN( BookFile, 'Book.Dat' );
   RESET( BookFile );
   ShowHeadings;
   WRITELN;
```

```
        WHILE NOT EOF( BookFile ) DO          { Read lines of data }
           BEGIN                              { until none left }
              READLN( BookFile, BookTitle, Author, Copies,
                       Edition, CopyDate );
              WRITELN( BookTitle:TitleLen, Author:AuthorLen,
                       Copies:CopiesLen, Edition:EditionLen,
                       CopyDate:YearLen );
           END;  {while}

        CLOSE( BookFile );
     END.  {Book3}
```

3. The following program counts the number of lines of data in
   the file that the user enters. This program enables the user to
   find out how many students are in a student file, how many
   customers are in a customer file, or how many books are in a
   book data file.

```
{ Filename: C27CNT1.PAS }

{ Counts the number of lines in a file. }

PROGRAM Count1;
USES Crt, Dos;
VAR X:      TEXT;                  { generic file var }
    dfName: STRING[12];           { data file name }
    Count:  INTEGER;              { number of lines }
    Line:   STRING;               { line of text read }
    FileOK: BOOLEAN;              { if file exists or not }

FUNCTION FileExists(FName: STRING): BOOLEAN;
   VAR TFile: TEXT;
       S:      STRING;
   BEGIN
      S := FSEARCH(FName,'');
      FileExists := S <> '';
   END;  {FileExists}

BEGIN
   CLRSCR;
   FileOK := FALSE;
   WRITELN( 'A Line Counting Program' );
   REPEAT
```

```
        WRITELN;
        WRITE( 'What is the name of the datafile you want to use '
               + 'for the count? ' );
        READLN( dfName );
        FileOK := FileExists(dfName);
     UNTIL (FileOK OR (dfName = ''));
     IF dfName = '' THEN HALT;
     Count := 0;                              { Initialize count }
     ASSIGN( X, dfName );
     RESET( X );
     WHILE NOT EOF(X) DO
        BEGIN
           READLN(X, Line);
           INC( Count );
        END;   {while}

     WRITELN;
     WRITELN( 'The number of lines of data in the file is: ',
              Count );
     CLOSE( X );
  END.   {Count1}
```

The following output is the result of running this program. The user must know the name of the data file and type the complete filename and extension.

```
A Line Counting Program
What is the name of the datafile you want to use for the count? Cust.dat
The number of lines of data in the file is: 4
```

Appending Data to Sequential Files

After creating and reading files, you might want to add data to the end of a sequential file. This is easy when you open the file with APPEND. All subsequent writes to that file are added to the end of it. This lets users add data to a file over time.

Examples

1. The following program adds to the book file you created in a previous program (C27BOOK1.PAS). It simply opens the file with APPEND and prompts the user through each input, while writing the values to the disk.

```
{ Filename: C27BOOK4.PAS }

{ Append to end of book data file. }

PROGRAM Book4;
USES Crt, Dos;
CONST TitleLen   = 30;
      AuthorLen  = 20;
      EditionLen = 8;
      CopiesLen  = 8;
      YearLen    = 6;

TYPE  TitleString   = STRING[TitleLen];
      AuthorString  = STRING[AuthorLen];
      EditionString = STRING[EditionLen];
      YearString    = STRING[YearLen];

VAR   BookFile:  TEXT;
      BookTitle: TitleString;
      Author:    AuthorString;
      Copies:    INTEGER;
      Edition:   EditionString;
      CopyDate:  YearString;

FUNCTION FileExists(FName: STRING): BOOLEAN;
   VAR TFile: TEXT;
       S:     STRING;
   BEGIN
      S := FSEARCH(FName,'');
      FileExists := S <> '';
   END;  {FileExists}

PROCEDURE GetBookData;
   BEGIN
      WRITELN;
```

```
            WRITE( 'What is the next book title? ' );
            READLN( BookTitle );
            WRITE( 'Who is the author? ' );
            READLN( Author );
            WRITE( 'How many copies do you have? ' );
            READLN( Copies );
            WRITE( 'What edition (1st, 2nd, etc.) is the book? ' );
            READLN( Edition );
            WRITE( 'What is the copyright date? ' );
            READLN( CopyDate );
        END;   {GetBookData}


    PROCEDURE SaveBookData;
        BEGIN
            { Now write the data to the file }
            WRITE( BookFile, BookTitle:TitleLen, Author:Authorlen,
                    Copies:CopiesLen, Edition:EditionLen,
                    CopyDate:YearLen );
        END;   {SaveBookData}


    FUNCTION BooksDone: BOOLEAN;
        VAR AnsCh: CHAR;
        BEGIN
          WRITE( 'Do you have another book to enter? (y/n) ' );
            READLN( AnsCh );
            BooksDone := (UPCASE(AnsCh) = 'N' );
        END;   {BooksDone}


    BEGIN
        CLRSCR;
        WRITELN( 'This program adds to end of book data file.' );
        WRITELN;
        IF NOT FileExists('Book.Dat')
            THEN BEGIN
                    WRITELN( 'Book.Dat file not found' );
                    HALT;
                END;
        ASSIGN( BookFile, 'Book.Dat' );
        APPEND( BookFile );                  { Open for appending }
        REPEAT                               { Loop asking for data }
            WRITELN;
            GetBookData;
```

```
        SaveBookData;
    UNTIL BooksDone;
    CLOSE( BookFile );
END.  {Book4}
```

2. The following program appends two data files together. It asks the user for the names of two files. It then adds the second file to the end of the first one. READLN is used to read an entire line. Users must make sure that the two data files have the same type and number of fields if they later want to sequentially read the newly appended file.

```
{ Filename: C27APND.PAS }

{ Appends one file to the end of the other. }

PROGRAM Append1;
USES Crt, Dos;
TYPE FileNameString = STRING[12];
VAR  File1:     TEXT;
     File2:     TEXT;
     FileName1: FileNameString;
     FileName2: FileNameString;

     Line:      STRING;
     FileOK:    BOOLEAN;

FUNCTION FileExists(FName: STRING): BOOLEAN;
   VAR TFile: TEXT;
       S:      STRING;
   BEGIN
      S := FSEARCH(FName,'');
      FileExists := S <> '';
   END;  {FileExists}

BEGIN
   CLRSCR;
   FileOK := FALSE;
   REPEAT
      WRITE( 'What is the name of the first file? ' );
      READLN( FileName1 );
```

```
            IF FileName1 = ''
               THEN HALT
               ELSE IF FileExists(FileName1)
                       THEN FileOK := TRUE
                       ELSE WRITELN(FileName1 + ' not found');
        UNTIL FileOK;
        FileOK := FALSE;
        REPEAT
           WRITE( 'What file do you want to append to ',
                  FileName1,' ' ); READLN( FileName2 );
           IF FileName2 = ''
               THEN HALT
               ELSE IF FileExists(FileName2)
                       THEN FileOK := TRUE
                       ELSE WRITELN(FileName2 + ' not found');
        UNTIL FileOK;
        ASSIGN( File1, FileName1 );
        APPEND( File1 );
        WRITELN( File1 );
        ASSIGN( File2, FileName2 );
        RESET( File2 );
        REPEAT
           READLN( File2, Line );
           WRITELN( File1, Line );
        UNTIL ( EOF(File2) );
        CLOSE( File2 );
        CLOSE( File1 );
     END.   {Append1}
```

Summary

Now that you have been exposed to sequential data file processing, you will be able to keep permanent data on your disk and
add to it or look at it when you need to without using typed
constants. Sequential file processing is fairly easy to do, but it is
limited; you read the data in the same order it was stored on the disk.

Much data lends itself to sequential file processing. You can
search sequential data files one line of data at a time looking for the

line of data you desire (using the same concept as the parallel array key fields). But there is an even faster and more flexible way to search files for data. Using random-access files makes your data-processing programs true data-retrieval programs that can quickly find any data you have to find. Chapter 28, "Random-Access Disk Processing," introduces you to the concept of random file processing.

Review Questions

Answers to the Review Questions appear in Appendix B.

1. What statement must you always use to associate a file variable to a filename?

2. What are the three ways of accessing a TEXT file?

3. What command reads data from a sequential data file?

4. When you open a file where is the file pointer?

5. What happens if you open a file with RESET and the file does not exist?

6. What happens if you open a file with APPEND when the file does not exist?

7. What is wrong with the following:

```
{ DelTrailCh deletes trailing characters


FUNCTION DelTrailCh(Ch: CHAR;
                    s: STRING): STRING;
   BEGIN
      WHILE Ch = s[LENGTH(S)] DO DELETE(s,1,LENGTH(S));
   END;   {DelTrailCh}
```

8. What is the difference between the WRITELN statement and the WRITE statement?

9. What does the EOF function do?

10. Which DOS command determines how many files Turbo Pascal can open at once?

11. What statement reads an entire line of a text file at once into a string variable?

Review Exercises

1. Write a program that stores your holiday mailing list in a data file.

2. Write a program that reads and prints the mailing list from the preceding example to the printer.

3. Add a menu to the holiday mailing list program to let the user add more data or see the data that already exists in the file.

4. Write a program to count the number of characters in a file.

5. Write a program that creates a backup copy of a TEXT file. The users are to enter the name of the file they want backed up. Your program is then to open that file with the extension BAK and create a copy of it by reading and writing (using WRITELN) one line at a time.

6. Add data-checking routines to the book data-entry program (C27BOOK2.PAS) to ensure that the user enters a proper date and edition. Check to ensure the data is within valid ranges.

7. Expand on the book database presented throughout this chapter to put the routines together in procedures and call them based on the user's menu choice. The program does not have to be as complete as the one in Appendix E, but make sure it combines the concepts of creating the file, reading the file, and adding to it.

Random-Access Disk Processing

This chapter introduces the concept of random file access. Random file access lets you read or write any record in your data file without having to read or write every record before it. You can quickly search for, add, retrieve, change, and delete information in a random-access file. Although you need a few new commands to access files randomly, you will find that the extra effort pays off in flexibility, power, and speed of disk access.

This chapter introduces

♦ How to open a random-access file

♦ The SEEK statement

♦ The FILESIZE statement

♦ Random file access records

♦ Testing for file existence

This chapter concludes Part VII, "Disk File Processing." With Turbo Pascal's sequential and random-access files, you can do most everything you would ever want to do with data files.

Random File Records

Random-access files exemplify the power of data processing with Turbo Pascal. Sequential file processing is slow unless you read the entire file into arrays and process them in memory. As explained in Chapter 26, "Reading and Writing to Disk," you have much more disk space than RAM. Most disk data files do not even fit in your RAM at one time. Therefore, you need a way to quickly read individual records from a file in any order needed and process them one at a time.

Think about the data files of a large credit card organization. When you make a purchase, the store calls the credit card company to receive an authorization. There are millions of people in the credit card company's files. Without fast computers, there would be no way the credit card company could read every record from the disk that comes before yours in a timely manner. Sequential files do not lend themselves to quick access. It is not feasible in many situations to look up individual data file records using sequential access.

The credit card companies must use random file access so that their computers can go directly to your record, just as you go directly to a song on a compact disk or record album. The file must be set up differently for random file access, but the power that results from the preparation is worth the effort.

All random file records must be fixed-length records. Chapter 26 explained the difference between fixed-length and variable-length records. The sequential files you read and wrote in the previous chapter used variable-length records. When you are reading or writing sequentially, there is no need for fixed-length records because you input each field one record at a time, looking for the data you want. With fixed-length records, your computer can better calculate exactly where a desired record is located on the disk.

Although you waste some disk space with fixed-length records (because of the spaces that pad some of the fields), the advantages of random file access make up for the "wasted" disk space.

> **TIP:** With random-access files, you can read or write records in any order. Therefore, even if you want to perform sequential reading or writing of the file, you can use random-access processing and "randomly" read or write the file in sequential record number order.

How to Open a Random-Access File

Turbo Pascal supports fixed-length records with *typed files*. Typed files are basically files of records. After creating a record definition to include all the different kinds of data your application needs, you must declare a file variable. The following lines illustrate this process:

```
TYPE NameString    = STRING[30];
     AddressString = STRING[40];
     CityString    = STRING[20];
     StateString   = STRING[15];
     ZipString     = STRING[10];

     FileRecord    = RECORD
                        Name:    NameString;
                        Address: AddressString;
                        City:    CityString;
                        State:   StateString;
                        Zip:     ZipString;
                     END;

VAR  AddrFile: FILE OF FileRecord;    { typed file }
```

When declaring a text file in Turbo Pascal, you declare the file variable to be of type TEXT. With typed files, you must specify the structure of the file by using FILE OF along with the file's record definition, as AddrFile is declared above.

FileRecord defines the structure of the file. AddrFile refers to a file consisting of FileRecords.

Just as with sequential files, you must open random-access files before reading or writing to them. However, after a random-access file is open, you can read from *and* write to the file.

As with TEXT files, random-access files require two statements to open them. First, you must associate a file handle with the file:

```
ASSIGN( FileVar, FileName );
```

prepare file
for random access

Second, you must either create a new file or open an old one. To create a new file (or overwrite an old one), use

```
REWRITE( FileVar );
```

To open an existing file, use

```
RESET( FileVar );
```

FileVar is the file handle used in the rest of the program to refer to this open file.

The following statements open an existing file called ADDRESS.89 on disk drive D:.

```
ASSIGN( AddrFile, 'D:Address.89' );
RESET( AddrFile );
```

As with other filenames, you can type the name in uppercase or lowercase letters.

> **NOTE:** You cannot use APPEND on a typed file. APPEND can be used only with text files.

Examples

The following examples prepare you for reading and writing random-access files. They illustrate the first part of the process: defining the record and its fields.

1. Suppose you want to save a list of friends' names to a random-access file. You must first decide how much storage per name your program requires. All random-access records must be fixed-length. Even if the records contain only one

field, the friend's name, that field must be a fixed-length field.

You might quickly scan through your friends' names and try to determine who has the longest name. You can make the length of that name the length for all the names. Of course, you might meet someone with a longer name later and not have room for it, but you would waste too much space if you gave the field a length of 1,000 characters! Therefore, think of a good trade-off length, such as 20.

Here are the first few lines of a program that sets up this simple random-access file:

```
TYPE NameRecord = RECORD
                      FirstName: STRING[10];
                      LastName:  STRING[10];
                  END;
VAR  Names:    ARRAY[1..100] OF NameRecord;
     NameFile: FILE OF NameRecord;      { typed file }
BEGIN
   ASSIGN( NameFile, 'Friend.Lst' );
   RESET( NameFile );
```

This code fragment allows up to 100 names to be stored in an array of records. Each record is 22 bytes in length (don't forget to add the length byte for each string in the record definition). You could input values in this array with a FOR loop such as

```
FOR i := 1 TO 100 DO
   WITH Names[i] DO
      BEGIN
         WRITE( 'What is the first name? ' );
         READLN( FirstName );
         WRITE( 'What is the last name? ' );
         READLN( LastName );
      END;   {with}
```

Of course, if you do not have exactly 100 names, you need a way to exit this loop early. When the array is filled, you could then write it to a random-access file with the random-access statements explained in the next section.

This illustrates one point you might want to think about while planning your data file programs. There really is no good reason to store every name in the array of records before writing them to the disk file. When the user enters a name, the program can write that name to disk before asking for the next name. This procedure eliminates the need for an array of records. You have to define only one record variable, such as this one:

```
VAR FriendName: NameRecord;
```

2. The following section of code prepares an inventory record for random-access processing:

```
TYPE InvRecord = RECORD
                     PartNo:       STRING[5];
                     Description: STRING[10];
                     Quantity:    INTEGER;
                     Price:        REAL;
                 END;
VAR  Item:    InvRecord;
     InvFile: FILE OF InvRecord;        { typed file }
BEGIN
   ASSIGN( InvFile, 'd:Inven.Dat' );
   RESET( InvFile );
```

Reading and Writing to Random-Access Files

After defining a record, you are ready to have your program read or write data to a file. Use the WRITE statement to write a record to a file. Use the READ statement to read a record from a file.

The location of a record in the file becomes important when working with random-access files. A record number is the key to finding whatever record you want to write or read. Turbo Pascal keeps track of where you are in the file with a *file pointer*. When you first open a file with RESET or REWRITE, the file pointer points to the first record. When you read a record from a typed file, you use READ(*FileVar*, ...). Each time you use READ(*FileVar*, ...), Turbo Pascal advances the file pointer one record. When you write a record to a typed file, you use WRITE(*FileVar*, ...). Each time you use WRITE(*FileVar*, ...), Turbo Pascal advances the file pointer one record.

> **CAUTION:** READLN(*FileVar*, ...) and WRITELN(*FileVar*, ...) can only be used with text files.

> **NOTE:** Turbo Pascal starts counting records from 0. In other words, the first record is always record 0.

Creating Random-Access File Data

After you define the record you want to write, and initialize the fields in that record with data, WRITE that record to the disk. The format of WRITE is

```
WRITE( FileVar, RecordData );
```

FileVar is the file handle that refers to the random-access file opened earlier. *RecordData* is a record of data as defined in a TYPE statement.

Examples

1. Here is the complete random-access friends' name program. This program places the names in a random-access file using WRITE.

```
{ Filename: C28FRND1.PAS }

{ Stores friends' names in a random-access file. }
```

```
PROGRAM Friend1;
USES Crt;

TYPE NameRecord = RECORD
                      FirstName: STRING[10];
                      LastName:  STRING[10];
                 END;

VAR NameRec:  NameRecord;                  { A record variable }
    NameFile: FILE OF NameRecord;
    Done:     BOOLEAN;

BEGIN
    CLRSCR;
    ASSIGN( NameFile, 'Friend.Lst' );
    REWRITE( NameFile );              { File pointer at rec 0 }
    Done := FALSE;
    REPEAT
       WRITELN;
       WRITELN( 'What is the first name? ' );
       WRITE( '(Press ENTER if no more) ' );
       WITH NameRec DO
          BEGIN
             READLN( FirstName );
             IF (FirstName = '')
                THEN Done := TRUE
                ELSE BEGIN
                        WRITE( 'What is the last name? ' );
                        READLN( LastName);
                        WRITE( NameFile, NameRec );
                     END;
          END;  {with}
    UNTIL Done;
    CLOSE( NameFile );
END.  {Friend1}
```

Notice how the WITH statement is used to avoid extra typing.
This program also uses a BOOLEAN flag, Done, to end the loop. The
file pointer automatically advances to the next record position
after the program writes the data (WRITE(NameFile, NameRec);).

2. Here is the inventory program that creates the inventory file:

```
{ Filename: C28INV1.PAS }

{ Creates an inventory random-access file. }

PROGRAM Inventory1;
USES Crt;
TYPE InvRecord = RECORD
                    PartNo:   STRING[5];
                    Descrip:  STRING[10];
                    Quantity: INTEGER;
                    Price:    REAL;
                 END;
VAR ItemRec: InvRecord;
    InvFile: FILE OF InvRecord;

PROCEDURE GetInteger(    Prompt: STRING;
                     VAR IntVal: INTEGER);

   VAR IntStr:     STRING[6];
       GoodNumber: BOOLEAN;
       ErrCode:    INTEGER;
       I:          INTEGER;

   BEGIN
     REPEAT
        GoodNumber := FALSE;
        WRITE( Prompt );
        READLN( IntStr );
        VAL(IntStr,I,ErrCode);
        IF ErrCode = 0
           THEN BEGIN
                   IntVal    := I;
                   GoodNumber := TRUE;
                END
           ELSE WRITELN( 'Please check your number');
     UNTIL GoodNumber;
   END;  {GetString}

PROCEDURE GetReal(    Prompt:  STRING;
                  VAR RealVal: REAL);
```

```
VAR RealStr:    STRING[6];
    GoodNumber: BOOLEAN;
    ErrCode:    INTEGER;
    R:          REAL;

BEGIN
   REPEAT
      GoodNumber := FALSE;
      WRITE( Prompt );
      READLN( RealStr );
      VAL(RealStr,R,ErrCode);
      IF ErrCode = 0
         THEN BEGIN
                 RealVal    := R;
                 GoodNumber := TRUE;
              END
         ELSE WRITELN( 'Please check your number');
   UNTIL GoodNumber;
END;   {GetString}


FUNCTION PartsDone: BOOLEAN;
   VAR AnsCh: CHAR;
   BEGIN
      WRITE( 'Is there another part? (Y/N) ' );
      READLN( AnsCh );
      PartsDone := UPCASE(AnsCh) = 'N';
   END;   {PartsDone}

BEGIN
   CLRSCR;
   ASSIGN( InvFile, 'Inven.Dat' );
   REWRITE( InvFile );                { File pointer at rec 0 }
   REPEAT
      WRITELN;
      WITH ItemRec DO                 { Get data from user }
         BEGIN
            WRITE( 'What is the part number? ' );
            READLN( PartNo );
            WRITE( 'What is the description? ' );
            READLN( Descrip );
            GetInteger( 'What is the quantity? ', Quantity);
```

EXAMPLE

```
        GetReal( 'What is the price? ', Price);
      END;   {with}
    WRITE( InvFile, ItemRec );
  UNTIL PartsDone;
  CLOSE( InvFile );
END.   {Inventory1}
```

> **NOTE:** Keep in mind that although you created it in a sequential manner, this is a random-access file. The first record is followed by the second, and so on. Later, you can read this file randomly or sequentially using random-access commands.

Notice that special input routines are used to get the integer and real values. If READLN had been used with an integer or real variable and the user typed a character rather than a valid number, the program would crash. By using a string variable and VAL, the program has control over invalid input data.

Reading Random-Access Files

You must use the READ statement to read from random-access files. READ reads records from the disk file to the record you define. The format of READ is

```
READ( FileVar, RecordData );
```

FileVar is the file handle that refers to the random-access file opened earlier. *RecordData* is a declared record that holds the data read from the disk file.

Examples

1. The following program reads the inventory file created earlier. It reads the file with READ, but it reads from the first record to the last as if it were a sequential file.

```
{ Filename: C28INV2.PAS }

{ Reads an inventory random-access file created earlier. }

PROGRAM Inventory2;
USES Crt;
TYPE InvRecord = RECORD
                    PartNo:   STRING[5];
                    Descrip:  STRING[10];
                    Quantity: INTEGER;
                    Price:    REAL;
                 END;
VAR  ItemRec: InvRecord;
     InvFile: FILE OF InvRecord;
BEGIN
   CLRSCR;
   ASSIGN( InvFile, 'Inven.Dat' );
   RESET( InvFile );
   WHILE NOT EOF(InvFile) DO              { Loop through file }
      BEGIN
         READ( InvFile, ItemRec );     { Get record }
         WRITELN;
         WITH ItemRec DO
            BEGIN
               WRITELN( 'The part number: ', PartNo );
               WRITELN( 'The description: ', Descrip );
               WRITELN( 'The quantity: ', Quantity );
               WRITELN( 'The price: ', Price:1:2 );
            END;  {with}
      END;  {while}
   CLOSE( InvFile );
END.  {Inventory2}
```

Notice you can use EOF with typed files just as you can with TEXT files.

Figure 28.1 shows this program displaying an inventory listing. It displays the records in exactly the same order they were entered in the file.

```
What is the part number? 321
What is the description? Widgets
What is the quantity? 23
What is the price? 4.95
Is there another part? (Y/N) y

What is the part number? 190
What is the description? A-bolts
What is the quantity? 434
What is the price? 2
Is there another part? (Y/N) y

What is the part number? 662
What is the description? Crane top
What is the quantity? 4
What is the price? 544.54
Is there another part? (Y/N) y

What is the part number? 541
What is the description? Seal
What is the quantity? 32
What is the price? 5.66
```

Figure 28.1. Reading and displaying the inventory data.

2. Here is the same program, except it reads and displays the inventory file in reverse order. You could not do this with sequential files.

The FILESIZE statement determines how many records are in a typed file. You can use FILESIZE only after a file is open. Because record numbers start counting from 0, you must subtract 1 (by using PRED) from FILESIZE to get the actual number of the last record. See Figure 28.2.

```
LastRecNum := PRED(FILESIZE( InvFile ));
```

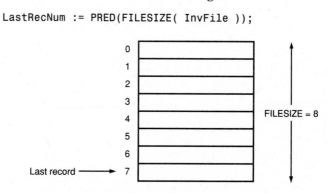

Figure 28.2. Determining the number of the last record.

The SEEK statement positions the file pointer to the desired record. SEEK also must be used only on an open file. First use FILESIZE to find the number of the last record in the file, and then use SEEK to position the file pointer to this last record. In this program, RecNum starts at this last record in the file and counts down. This should begin to give you an idea of what you can do with random-access files.

```pascal
{ Filename: C28INV3.PAS }


{
  Reads an random-access inventory file created earlier
  and displays it backward.
}
PROGRAM Inventory3;
USES Crt;
TYPE InvRecord = RECORD
                    PartNo:   STRING[5];
                    Descrip:  STRING[10];
                    Quantity: INTEGER;
                    Price:    REAL;
                 END;
VAR  ItemRec:    InvRecord;
     InvFile:    FILE OF InvRecord;
     LastRecNum: INTEGER;
     RecNum:     INTEGER;
BEGIN
   CLRSCR;
   ASSIGN( InvFile, 'Inven.Dat' );
   RESET( InvFile );              { set file ptr to rec 0 }
       { next line calculates position of last record }
   LastRecNum := PRED(FILESIZE( InvFile ));
   FOR RecNum := LastRecNum DOWNTO 0 DO
      BEGIN
         SEEK( InvFile, RecNum );
         READ( InvFile, ItemRec );    { Get record }
         WRITELN;
         WITH ItemRec DO
            BEGIN
               WRITELN( 'The part number: ', PartNo );
```

```
                     WRITELN( 'The description: ', Descrip );
                     WRITELN( 'The quantity: ', Quantity );
                     WRITELN( 'The price: ', Price:1:2 );
              END;   {with}
        END;   {for}
     CLOSE( InvFile );
END.   {Inventory3}
```

3. The following program asks users for the record number they want to see. The program then reads and displays only that record from the inventory file. This is a true random-access file. With a sequential file, you have to read every record until you get to the one the users want to see.

```
{ Filename: C28INV4.PAS }

{
  Asks the user for a record number, and
  displays that record from the inventory file.
}

PROGRAM Inventory4;
USES Crt;
TYPE InvRecord = RECORD
                     PartNo:   STRING[5];
                     Descrip:  STRING[10];
                     Quantity: INTEGER;
                     Price:    REAL;
                 END;
VAR   ItemRec:    InvRecord;
      InvFile:    FILE OF InvRecord;
      LastRecNum: INTEGER;
      RecNum:     INTEGER;

PROCEDURE ShowGoodRange;
   BEGIN
      WRITELN;
      WRITELN( 'You must enter a record number from 0 to ',
              LastRecNum);
   END;   {ShowGoodRange}
```

```
FUNCTION TimeToQuit: BOOLEAN;
    VAR AnsCh: CHAR;
    BEGIN
        WRITE( 'Do you want to enter another record? (Y/N) ' );
        READLN( AnsCh );
        TimeToQuit := UPCASE(AnsCh) = 'N';
    END;  {TimeToQuit}

BEGIN
    CLRSCR;
    ASSIGN( InvFile, 'Inven.Dat' );
    RESET( InvFile );
    LastRecNum := PRED(FILESIZE( InvFile ));
    REPEAT
        WRITELN( 'First record number is 0' );
        WRITE( 'What inventory record number do you want? ' );
        READLN( RecNum );
        IF ((RecNum <= LastRecNum) AND (RecNum >= 0))
            THEN BEGIN
                    SEEK( InvFile, RecNum );
                    READ( InvFile, ItemRec );    { Get record }
                    WRITELN;
                    WITH ItemRec DO
                        BEGIN
                            WRITELN( 'The part number: ',
                                        PartNo );
                            WRITELN( 'The description: ',
                                        Descrip );
                            WRITELN( 'The quantity: ', Quantity );
                            WRITELN( 'The price: ', Price:1:2 );
                        END;  {with}
                END
            ELSE ShowGoodRange;
    UNTIL TimeToQuit;
    CLOSE( InvFile );
END.  {Inventory4}
```

4. Your users certainly might not know the record number of each customer. Therefore, you can search random-access files, just as you had to do with sequential files. The following program asks the user for an inventory part number.

It then reads the random-access file sequentially (using READ). When it finds a matching part number, it displays that part's record information.

```
{ Filename: C28INV5.PAS }

{
  Asks the user for an inventory part number, and
  displays that record from the inventory file.
}
PROGRAM Inventory5;
USES Crt;
TYPE InvRecord = RECORD
                   PartNo:   STRING[5];
                   Descrip:  STRING[10];
                   Quantity: INTEGER;
                   Price:    REAL;
                 END;


VAR  ItemRec:    InvRecord;
     InvFile:    FILE OF InvRecord;
     SearchPart: INTEGER;
     ErrCode:    INTEGER;
     Found:      BOOLEAN;
     Part:       INTEGER;
     LastRecNum: INTEGER;


FUNCTION GetPartNo: INTEGER;

   VAR GoodNumber: BOOLEAN;
       PartStr:    STRING[5];
       PartNum:    INTEGER;
       ErrCode:    INTEGER;

  BEGIN
     WRITELN;
     REPEAT
       GoodNumber := FALSE;
       WRITELN( 'What part number do you want to see?' );
       WRITE( '(Type 0 to quit) ' );
       READLN( PartStr );
```

```
                    VAL(PartStr,PartNum,ErrCode);
                    GoodNumber := (ErrCode = 0);
                UNTIL GoodNumber;
                GetPartNo := PartNum;
        END;  {GetPartNo}


PROCEDURE ShowMatch;
    BEGIN
        WITH ItemRec DO
            BEGIN
                WRITELN;
                WRITELN( 'The part number: ', PartNo );
                WRITELN( 'The description: ', Descrip );
                WRITELN( 'The quantity: ', Quantity );
                WRITELN( 'The price: ', Price:1:2 );
            END;  {with}
    END;  {ShowMatch}


PROCEDURE ShowNoMatch;
    BEGIN
        WRITELN;
        WRITELN( 'That part is not in the inventory file' );
        WRITELN;
     END;  {ShowNoMatch}


BEGIN
    CLRSCR;
    ASSIGN( InvFile, 'Inven.Dat' );
    RESET( InvFile );
    LastRecNum := PRED(FILESIZE( InvFile ));
    SearchPart := GetPartNo;
    WHILE (SearchPart <> 0) DO
        BEGIN
            Found := FALSE;
            WHILE NOT EOF( InvFile ) DO
                BEGIN
                    READ( InvFile, ItemRec );      { Get record }
                    WITH ItemRec DO
                        BEGIN
                            VAL(PartNo,Part,ErrCode);
                            IF (Part = SearchPart)
                                THEN BEGIN
```

```
                           ShowMatch;
                           Found := TRUE;
                        END;
                  END;  {with}
            END;  {while}
         IF NOT Found THEN ShowNoMatch;
         SearchPart := GetPartNo;
         RESET( InvFile );                    { reset file pointer }
       END;  {while}
    CLOSE( InvFile );
END.  {Inventory5}
```

Figure 28.3 shows the screen as a user looks for an inventory item.

```
What part number do you want to see?
(Type 0 to quit) 812

That part is not in the inventory file

What part number do you want to see?
(Type 0 to quit) 321

The part number: 321
The description: Widgets
The quantity: 23
The price: 4.95

What part number do you want to see?
(Type 0 to quit)
```

Figure 28.3. The user requests an inventory record by entering the part number.

The next section shows you how to change record data in random-access files. One of the first steps needed to change a record is for this search routine to find it, given a *key field* or a field value to look for. A key field usually contains unique data. Because no two inventory part numbers should have the same value, the inventory part number is a good field to search with (the unique key field).

Changing a Random-Access File

When you find the desired random-access record, you can change it and write it back to the file. The advantage of random-access files over sequential files is that the entire file does not have to be rewritten; only the record you want to change must be rewritten.

When you determine the record to change, point to the record (using SEEK) and READ the record into a variable. After changing the record's field data (you can change any or all field data by assigning them other values), issue another SEEK to the same record location and WRITE the record back in its place.

Example

Suppose a company decides to add a letter *C* to each customer number stored in a customer file, and a *V* to each vendor number in a vendor file. (The company left enough room in these fields to add the prefix letter.) The following program opens the customer file and reads each customer record. It inserts a *C* before the customer number and writes each record back to the file. No other customer data is changed. Then the program does the same for the vendors.

```
{ Filename: C28CV1.PAS }

{
  This program reads each record in a customer and vendor
  file and inserts a C or V in each file's customer and
  vendor number. No other fields in the files are changed.
}

PROGRAM CustVendor1;
USES Crt;
```

```
TYPE CustRecord = RECORD
                        Num:  STRING[8];
                        Name: STRING[15];
                        Addr: STRING[20];
                        City: STRING[10];
                        St:   STRING[2];
                        Zip:  STRING[5];
                        Bal:  REAL;
                  END;

TYPE VendRecord = RECORD
                        Num:  STRING[10];
                        Name: STRING[20];
                        Addr: STRING[20];
                        City: STRING[10];
                        St:   STRING[2];
                        Zip:  STRING[5];
                   END;

VAR CustRec:     CustRecord;
    VendRec:     VendRecord;
    CFile:       FILE OF CustRecord;
    VFile:       FILE OF VendRecord;
    LastFileRec: INTEGER;
    Rec:         INTEGER;

BEGIN
   CLRSCR;
   ASSIGN( CFile, 'CustData.Dat' );
   RESET( CFile );
   LastFileRec := PRED(FILESIZE( CFile ));

        { Add the C to the Customer number field }
   FOR Rec := 0 TO LastFileRec DO
      BEGIN
         READ( CFile, CustRec );
         INSERT('C', CustRec.Num, 1);  { Insert C }
         SEEK( CFile, Rec );
         WRITE( CFile, CustRec );       { No other data}
                                        { changed }

      END;  {for}
   CLOSE( CFile );
```

```
                    { Add the V to the Vendor number field }
          ASSIGN( VFile, 'c:Vendor.dat' );
          RESET( VFile );
          LastFileRec := PRED(FILESIZE(VFile));
          FOR Rec := 0 TO LastFileRec DO
             BEGIN
                 READ(VFile, VendRec );
                 INSERT('V',VendRec.Num,1);      { Insert the V }
                 SEEK(VFile,Rec);
                 WRITE( VFile, VendRec );         { No other data}
                                                  { changed }

             END;  {for}
          CLOSE( VFile );
      END.  {CustVendor1}
```

Testing for File Existence

If you try running the previous program without first creating some data for the files, the program crashes. You can use exactly the same technique to check for file existence as you did in the previous chapter with TEXT files.

```
   ASSIGN( FileVar,'Some.dat');
{$I-}                                    {turn off I/O checking}
   RESET( FileVar );
{$I+}                                    {turn on I/O checking}
   IF IORESULT <> 0
      THEN BEGIN
           WRITELN( 'File does not exist');
           EXIT;
         END;
```

To create a procedure to test for file existence, you need to borrow an idea used with untyped files. Untyped files are declared with a type of FILE. Because you just want to know whether a file exists, you are not interested in the file structure. If you did not use a type of FILE, you would have to define a separate file existence function for each record type, such as FILE OF NameRecord or FILE OF

InvRecord. You can use the following function to test whether a text file exists.

```
FUNCTION FileExists(FName: STRING): BOOLEAN;
   VAR X: FILE;
       IOStatus: INTEGER;
   BEGIN
      FileExists := FALSE;
      ASSIGN( X, FName );
   {$I-}
      RESET( X );
   {$I+}
      IOStatus := IORESULT;
      IF IOStatus = 0
         THEN BEGIN
                 FileExists := TRUE;
                 CLOSE( X );
              END
         ELSE CASE IOStatus OF
                 4: WRITELN( 'Too many open files' );
                 5: WRITELN( 'File access denied' );
               152: WRITELN( 'Drive not ready' );
              END;  {case}
   END;  {FileExists}
```

You also could use the function FileExists2 from the last chapter. The advantage to using the preceding function is that you have control over all errors returned by IORESULT. To expand the above CASE statement to include more error conditions, refer to Table 27.1 in the preceding chapter.

Summary

Now, you can work with random-access files in Turbo Pascal. You saw that random-access files still can be read sequentially, but you also can read and write them in any order. You also can change a record in the middle of the file without affecting any surrounding records in the file. By ensuring that your random-access files have a unique field key, you can search the files for a record using this key field; the first occurrence of that key field match will be the record the user wants.

This concludes the section on Turbo Pascal data files. Your program now has the capability to store a large amount of data without relying on typed constants to hold data. By using random-access files for your changing data, you ensure that you can easily update that data later.

Review Questions

Answers to the Review Questions appear in Appendix B.

1. What is the advantage of random-access files over sequential files?

2. What is the basic unit of a random-access file?

3. How does Turbo Pascal number records in a typed file?

4. After you have opened a file, what Turbo Pascal statement can you use to move the file pointer anywhere in the file?

5. True or False: Random-access records are fixed-length records.

6. What Turbo Pascal statement helps save you some typing when working with fields of a record?

7. Why should a key field be unique?

8. What statement returns the number of records in a typed file?

9. What is wrong with the following code to update a record?

```
SEEK(X,RecNum);
READ(X,Rec);
    { code to update Rec }
WRITE(X, Rec);
```

10. How can a procedure receive a passed record variable as a parameter?

Review Exercises

1. Create a record a hospital could use to track a patient's name, address, patient number, doctor's name, and current account balance.

2. Write a simple data-entry program that fills the hospital's file with the patient data from the previous exercise.

3. Write a program to read all the records from Exercises 1 and 2 in sequential order.

4. Combine Exercises 1 and 2 to produce a program that the hospital's accounting department can use to display the name and number of every patient who owes more than $1,000.

5. Add a routine to the preceding exercise's program that lets the accounting department change the current balance of a patient, given the patient number.

6. Add to the inventory program presented earlier so the user can see a displayed listing of every inventory part. Send the listing to the printer with appropriate titles.

7. Modify the student database program C27CNT1.PAS in Chapter 27 so that the students' names are stored in a random-access file rather than in a sequential file. Improve the add-student routine so no two students can have the same student number. Also, let the user change a student's address and telephone number information if necessary.

Part VIII

Appendixes

ASCII Table
(Including IBM Extended Character Codes)

Dec X_{10}	Hex X_{16}	Binary X_2	ASCII Character
000	00	0000 0000	null
001	01	0000 0001	☺
002	02	0000 0010	●
003	03	0000 0011	♥
004	04	0000 0100	◆
005	05	0000 0101	♣
006	06	0000 0110	♠
007	07	0000 0111	●
008	08	0000 1000	■
009	09	0000 1001	○
010	0A	0000 1010	■
011	0B	0000 1011	♂
012	0C	0000 1100	♀
013	0D	0000 1101	♪
014	0E	0000 1110	♪♪
015	0F	0000 1111	☼
016	10	0001 0000	►

Dec X_{10}	Hex X_{16}	Binary X_2	ASCII Character
017	11	0001 0001	◄
018	12	0001 0010	↕
019	13	0001 0011	!!
020	14	0001 0100	¶
021	15	0001 0101	§
022	16	0001 0110	−
023	17	0001 0111	↨
024	18	0001 1000	↑
025	19	0001 1001	↓
026	1A	0001 1010	→
027	1B	0001 1011	←
028	1C	0001 1100	FS
029	1D	0001 1101	GS
030	1E	0001 1110	RS
031	1F	0001 1111	US
032	20	0010 0000	SP
033	21	0010 0001	!
034	22	0010 0010	"
035	23	0010 0011	#
036	24	0010 0100	$
037	25	0010 0101	%
038	26	0010 0110	&
039	27	0010 0111	'
040	28	0010 1000	(
041	29	0010 1001	)
042	2A	0010 1010	*
043	2B	0010 1011	+
044	2C	0010 1100	,
045	2D	0010 1101	-
046	2E	0010 1110	.
047	2F	0010 1111	/

Dec X_{10}	Hex X_{16}	Binary X_2	ASCII Character
048	30	0011 0000	0
049	31	0011 0001	1
050	32	0011 0010	2
051	33	0011 0011	3
052	34	0011 0100	4
053	35	0011 0101	5
054	36	0011 0110	6
055	37	0011 0111	7
056	38	0011 1000	8
057	39	0011 1001	9
058	3A	0011 1010	:
059	3B	0011 1011	;
060	3C	0011 1100	<
061	3D	0011 1101	=
062	3E	0011 1110	>
063	3F	0011 1111	?
064	40	0100 0000	@
065	41	0100 0001	A
066	42	0100 0010	B
067	43	0100 0011	C
068	44	0100 0100	D
069	45	0100 0101	E
070	46	0100 0110	F
071	47	0100 0111	G
072	48	0100 1000	H
073	49	0100 1001	I
074	4A	0100 1010	J
075	4B	0100 1011	K
076	4C	0100 1100	L
077	4D	0100 1101	M
078	4E	0100 1110	N

Dec X_{10}	Hex X_{16}	Binary X_2	ASCII Character
079	4F	0100 1111	O
080	50	0101 0000	P
081	51	0101 0001	Q
082	52	0101 0010	R
083	53	0101 0011	S
084	54	0101 0100	T
085	55	0101 0101	U
086	56	0101 0110	V
087	57	0101 0111	W
088	58	0101 1000	X
089	59	0101 1001	Y
090	5A	0101 1010	Z
091	5B	0101 1011	[
092	5C	0101 1100	\
093	5D	0101 1101	]
094	5E	0101 1110	^
095	5F	0101 1111	–
096	60	0110 0000	`
097	61	0110 0001	a
098	62	0110 0010	b
099	63	0110 0011	c
100	64	0110 0100	d
101	65	0110 0101	e
102	66	0110 0110	f
103	67	0110 0111	g
104	68	0110 1000	h
105	69	0110 1001	i
106	6A	0110 1010	j
107	6B	0110 1011	k
108	6C	0110 1100	l
109	6D	0110 1101	m

Dec X_{10}	Hex X_{16}	Binary X_2	ASCII Character
110	6E	0110 1110	n
111	6F	0110 1111	o
112	70	0111 0000	p
113	71	0111 0001	q
114	72	0111 0010	r
115	73	0111 0011	s
116	74	0111 0100	t
117	75	0111 0101	u
118	76	0111 0110	v
119	77	0111 0111	w
120	78	0111 1000	x
121	79	0111 1001	y
122	7A	0111 1010	z
123	7B	0111 1011	{
124	7C	0111 1100	¦
125	7D	0111 1101	}
126	7E	0111 1110	~
127	7F	0111 1111	DEL
128	80	1000 0000	Ç
129	81	1000 0001	ü
130	82	1000 0010	é
131	83	1000 0011	â
132	84	1000 0100	ä
133	85	1000 0101	à
134	86	1000 0110	å
135	87	1000 0111	ç
136	88	1000 1000	ê
137	89	1000 1001	ë
138	8A	1000 1010	è
139	8B	1000 1011	ï
140	8C	1000 1100	î

Dec X_{10}	Hex X_{16}	Binary X_2	ASCII Character
141	8D	1000 1101	ì
142	8E	1000 1110	Ä
143	8F	1000 1111	Å
144	90	1001 0000	É
145	91	1001 0001	æ
146	92	1001 0010	Æ
147	93	1001 0011	ô
148	94	1001 0100	ö
149	95	1001 0101	ò
150	96	1001 0110	û
151	97	1001 0111	ù
152	98	1001 1000	ÿ
153	99	1001 1001	Ö
154	9A	1001 1010	Ü
155	9B	1001 1011	¢
156	9C	1001 1100	£
157	9D	1001 1101	¥
158	9E	1001 1110	P_t
159	9F	1001 1111	ƒ
160	A0	1010 0000	á
161	A1	1010 0001	í
162	A2	1010 0010	ó
163	A3	1010 0011	ú
164	A4	1010 0100	ñ
165	A5	1010 0101	Ñ
166	A6	1010 0110	ª
167	A7	1010 0111	º
168	A8	1010 1000	¿
169	A9	1010 1001	⌐
170	AA	1010 1010	¬
171	AB	1010 1011	½

Dec X_{10}	Hex X_{16}	Binary X_2	ASCII Character
172	AC	1010 1100	¼
173	AD	1010 1101	¡
174	AE	1010 1110	«
175	AF	1010 1111	»
176	B0	1011 0000	▒
177	B1	1011 0001	▓
178	B2	1011 0010	█
179	B3	1011 0011	│
180	B4	1011 0100	┤
181	B5	1011 0101	╡
182	B6	1011 0110	╢
183	B7	1011 0111	╖
184	B8	1011 1000	╕
185	B9	1011 1001	╣
186	BA	1011 1010	║
187	BB	1011 1011	╗
188	BC	1011 1100	╝
189	BD	1011 1101	╜
190	BE	1011 1110	╛
191	BF	1011 1111	┐
192	C0	1100 0000	└
193	C1	1100 0001	┴
194	C2	1100 0010	┬
195	C3	1100 0011	├
196	C4	1100 0100	─
197	C5	1100 0101	┼
198	C6	1100 0110	╞
199	C7	1100 0111	╟
200	C8	1100 1000	╚
201	C9	1100 1001	╔
202	CA	1100 1010	╩

Dec X_{10}	Hex X_{16}	Binary X_2	ASCII Character
203	CB	1100 1011	⊤⊤
204	CC	1100 1100	⊩
205	CD	1100 1101	=
206	CE	1100 1110	╬
207	CF	1100 1111	⊥
208	D0	1101 0000	⊥⊥
209	D1	1101 0001	⊤
210	D2	1101 0010	π
211	D3	1101 0011	⊔
212	D4	1101 0100	⊢
213	D5	1101 0101	F
214	D6	1101 0110	π
215	D7	1101 0111	╫
216	D8	1101 1000	╪
217	D9	1101 1001	⌐
218	DA	1101 1010	⌐
219	DB	1101 1011	■
220	DC	1101 1100	▬
221	DD	1101 1101	▌
222	DE	1101 1110	▐
223	DF	1101 1111	▀
224	E0	1110 0000	α
225	E1	1110 0001	β
226	E2	1110 0010	Γ
227	E3	1110 0011	π
228	E4	1110 0100	Σ
229	E5	1110 0101	σ
230	E6	1110 0110	μ
231	E7	1110 0111	τ
232	E8	1110 1000	Φ
233	E9	1110 1001	θ

Dec X_{10}	Hex X_{16}	Binary X_2	ASCII Character
234	EA	1110 1010	Ω
235	EB	1110 1011	δ
236	EC	1110 1100	∞
237	ED	1110 1101	ø
238	EE	1110 1110	∈
239	EF	1110 1111	∩
240	F0	1111 0000	≡
241	F1	1111 0001	±
242	F2	1111 0010	≥
243	F3	1111 0011	≤
244	F4	1111 0100	⌠
245	F5	1111 0101	⌡
246	F6	1111 0110	÷
247	F7	1111 0111	≈
248	F8	1111 1000	°
249	F9	1111 1001	•
250	FA	1111 1010	·
251	FB	1111 1011	
252	FC	1111 1100	η
253	FD	1111 1101	2
254	FE	1111 1110	■
255	FF	1111 1111	

Answers to Review Questions

Chapter 1

1. RAM stands for *r*andom-*a*ccess *m*emory. This is the computer's internal memory.

2. RAM usually is measured in kilobytes, where a kilobyte is 1,024 bytes of data. Recall that a byte is the amount of memory needed to store one character.

3. Data in RAM is lost when you turn off your computer. Data on a hard disk is not lost when you turn off your computer.

4. The disk usually holds many times more bytes than RAM.

5. A modem.

6. B. The mouse acts like an input device. Remember that it can be used in place of the keyboard's arrow keys to move the cursor on the screen.

7. NumLock. Pressing it again turns off the numbers.

8. Pascal is a very structured language. This makes it easier to develop new programs and to read existing programs.

9. Turbo Pascal integrated an editor and compiler. The current version of Turbo Pascal integrates a debugger as well.

10. DOS.

11. Because it is erased every time the power is turned off.

12. True. The greater resolution means that there are more dots that make up a graphics image.

13. 524,288 (512 times 1,024).

14. *M*odulate-*dem*odulate.

Chapter 2

1. Type Turbo Arty.

2. The program editing window.

3. Clicking means pressing and releasing the left mouse button; double-clicking means pressing and releasing the button twice in succession; dragging means pressing a button and moving the mouse while still holding down the button.

4. The menus display every command you can request so that you do not have to remember commands.

5. F10.

6. When you press F1, the Turbo Pascal Help shortcut key, Turbo Pascal displays a help message about what you are doing; it looks at the *context* of the help request.

7. It is important that you save your work and return to DOS before turning off your computer. Turbo Pascal properly ensures that you do not lose any work.

8. You can get help from the **Help** menu option, you can press F1 for context-sensitive help, you can press Shift–F1 for the

Help Index, and you can position the cursor on a word and press Ctrl–F1 to get help on that word (topic help).

9. C. (The left-arrow key does not erase, although it does move the cursor backward over the text.)

10. Command-line options change the Turbo Pascal environment so that the program starts the way you prefer.

11. You can execute many menu commands without displaying the menus by typing their keyboard-shortcut equivalents.

Chapter 3

1. A set of instructions that makes the computer do something.

2. Either buy it or write it yourself. Using Turbo Pascal can make the latter easy!

3. False. They can do only exactly what *you* (the programmer) tell them to do.

4. The program is the instructions (like a recipe). The output is the result of executing those instructions (like the cake you make by following a recipe).

5. The Turbo Pascal program editor.

6. PAS.

7. You must thoroughly plan the program before typing it. By thinking it out ahead of time, defining the problem to be solved, and breaking it into logical pieces, you can write the program faster than if you type it as you plan it.

8. False. Backspace erases as the cursor moves to the left. The left-arrow key does not erase.

9. The clipboard.

10. You can have as many as ten bookmarks in a Turbo Pascal program.

Chapter 4

1. **File Open...**

2. Because a program in memory is erased if you power-off your computer.

3. You can use as many as eight letters in a filename.

4. A. False. You can have no spaces in a filename.

   B. False. If a filename has more than the maximum eight characters, Turbo Pascal truncates the filename and uses only the first eight.

   C. True.

5. You can have as many source files in memory as will fit in your system's memory.

6. False. You must use the DOS DEL command to erase files from the disk.

7. Free-form means that you can add a lot of white space and blank lines to make your programs more readable.

8. Save your programs often as you type them, in case of power failure or computer problems. Your work will be safe as of the last save to disk.

Chapter 5

1. Commands and data.

2. A storage location in your computer that holds values.

3. DataFile. Variable names cannot start with a number and cannot include spaces or dashes in their names.

4. False. There is no such type as Single Integer or Double Integer.

5. True. Only REAL, however, does not need the special compiler directive, {$N+}, to be valid.

6. One.

7. WRITELN (or WRITE).

8. CLRSCR.

9. −300.0

   4,541,000,000,000

   0.0019

10. 1.5E+1   −4.3E-05   −5.4543E+4   5.312349E+5

Chapter 6

1. Enclose a comment inside braces, {}, or (* *).

2. The computer ignores the statement and goes to the next line in the program.

3. False. The computer ignores the third line because it is a comment.

4. True.

5. The semicolon.

6. A. Include a USES Printer statement at the top of your program.

   B. Use WRITELN(LST,...) to print to the printer.

7. False. To nest comments, use alternative forms of comment delimiters. For example,

   ```
   (* WRITELN('This is a test');  {this is a nested comment} *)
   ```

8. If the printer is ready, the line prints 20 spaces and then the word Computer.

9. If the printer is ready, the line prints three spaces, Month, a space, Day, a space, and Year.

10. Here are two ways:

```
WRITELN( ' ':27, 'Hello' );

WRITELN('                        Hello');
```

11. Remember to use `''` to indicate an apostrophe inside a string.

```
WRITELN('Bob''s Sales');
```

12. `86 and 99 are secret agents.`

Chapter 7

1. A. 5

   B. 6

   C. 5

2. A. 5

   B. 7

3. `a:5, b:5`
   `    6   10`

   (Don't be fooled. In the first WRITELN statement, because the letters are inside quotation marks, the variable values cannot be printed.)

4. A. `a := (3 + 3) / (4 + 4);`

   B. `x := (a - b) * (a - c) * (a - c);`

   C. `f := SQRT(a) / b;`

   D. `d := ((8 - x*x) / (x - 9)) - ((4 * 2 - 1) / x*x*x);`

5. `WRITELN( 'A circle with a radius of 4 has an area of ',`
   `        (PI * 4 * 4):1:2);`

   (In a later chapter, you will learn that PI is a Turbo Pascal function that returns the value for pi.

6. `WRITELN( 'The remainder is: ', (100 MOD 4) );`

Chapter 8

1. If the string variable is declared as STRING, then it can hold 255 characters of data.

2. The plus sign, +.

3. Use CONCAT.

4. The length byte is the number of bytes of data in the string. This value is stored in character format in position 0 of the string.

5. B, C, and D. In D, FirstName and LastName are longer strings than EmpName. EmpName stores only the first 20 characters.

6. False. '40' is a string. To do this calculation, remove the single quotation marks.

7. Assuming that City and State are declared as string variables, write:

```
WRITELN( City, ', ', State );
```

8. `FileName := 'C:\' + FileName + '.DAT';`

Chapter 9

1. READ and READLN.

2. Without a prompt message, the user does not know what to type at the keyboard.

3. True.

4. WRITE.

5. Use an assignment statement:

```
x := 5;
```

Or, use a READLN statement:

```
READLN( x );
```

6. A space.

7. You must use a comma to separate two variables in a READLN statement.

8.
```
WRITELN( '*** Miles Per Gallon ***' );
WRITELN;
WRITE( ' Type the mileage driven ');
READLN( Miles);
WRITE( ' Type the gallons of fuel used' +
       ' since your last fill up? ');
READLN( Gallons );
```

9. Runtime error 106.

Chapter 10

1. Use WRITELN(x:20); where x previously was declared as an integer.

2. True.

3. 77, 36, 156, 122.

4. C.

5. Turbo Pascal rounds the number to an integer.

6. Turbo Pascal automatically expands the field width.

7. By overriding the sequential order of the program, control passes to the statement after the GOTO's label.

8. False. The first statement beeps the computer's speaker. The second statement beeps the printer's speaker.

9. Blinking light magenta text on a magenta background. (This may not be the prettiest combination you can create!)

10. No output is produced. The next WRITE, however, occurs in the middle of the screen at row 12, column 40.

11. There are three ways to beep the system speaker:

```
WRITE( CHR(7) );
WRITE( #7 );
WRITE( ^G );
```

Chapter 11

1. A. False.

   B. True.

   C. True.

   D. True.

2. False. Because 54 is not less than or equal to 50, the WRITELN never happens.

3. A. False. Uppercase characters have lower ASCII numbers.

   B. True. The null string has an ASCII value of 0. The character 0 (zero) has an ASCII value of 48.

   C. False.

   D. False.

4. C.

5. A. False.

   B. False.

   C. True.

   D. True.

Chapter 12

1. A repetition of statements in a Turbo Pascal program.

2. A nested loop occurs when you put one loop inside another.

3. The inside loop acts as though it moves faster because it must complete all its iterations before the outer loop can finish its next one.

4. ```
   10
    9
    8
    7
    6
    5
    4
    3
    2
    1
   ```

5. True.

6. The loop stops execution, and the program resumes at the statement following the end of the FOR loop.

7. True.

8. ```
   1
   2
   3
   4
   5
   ```

Remember that the FOR statement looks at the StartVal and EndVal only once: when the FOR statement first begins. Changing those values inside the FOR loop does not affect the control of the FOR loop. Changing the counter variable, however, affects it because the control variable is changed and compared to the ending value each time through the loop.

Chapter 13

1. True.

2. False. If the condition initially is false, the WHILE loop is skipped.

3. INC and DEC.

4. A WHILE loop performs a relational test. It is an indeterminate loop. A FOR loop, on the other hand, executes the body of the FOR loop a certain number of times controlled by the FOR's control values.

5. Forever. Because A is not changed, the WHILE loops endlessly.

6. Here's the loop:

   Because the condition, A < 10, is false, the last WRITELN statement never executes.

Chapter 14

1. True.

2. A. Bottom.

   B. Top.

3. True.

4. A WHILE loop performs a relational test at the beginning of the loop and executes as long as the relational test is true. A REPEAT loop performs a relational test at the end of the loop and executes as long as the relational test is false.

5. The loop keeps repeating until A becomes greater than 5. Because A is fixed at 0, the loop repeats forever.

6. The program displays the following:

```
Here's the loop:
Turbo Pascal
```

Chapter 15

1. True.

2. False. If the IF statement does not have an ELSE, a semicolon separates the IF-THEN from the next statement.

3. The compact BOOLEAN expression is equivalent to

```
IF Num = 0
    THEN Done := TRUE
    ELSE Done := FALSE;
```

4. True. If a decision requires one branch, then an IF-THEN is all that is required. If a decision requires two branches, then an IF-THEN-ELSE statement is required.

5. Henry.

6. If Num = 100, the code fragment displays Num should be less than 100.

Chapter 16

1. The CASE statement.

2. If an ELSE is part of the CASE statement, then the statement or statements associated with ELSE executes. If there is no ELSE, then the CASE does nothing.

3. False. EXIT causes the program to jump to the end of the procedure, function, or program. If EXIT is in the main program block, then EXIT is the same as HALT. HALT stops the execution at any point within the program.

4. False. Turbo Pascal is very strict in requiring the same type.

5. False. Putting the most often executed CASE option first speeds up your programs. (You do not always know in advance which this will be, however, but sometimes you do.)

6.
```
CASE Num OF
    1:    WRITELN( 'Alpha' );
    2:    WRITELN( 'Beta' );
    3:    WRITELN( 'Gamma' );
    ELSE WRITELN( 'Other' );
END;  {case}
```

```
7. CASE Grade OF
     100:    WRITELN('You got an A+');
     95..99: WRITELN('You got an A');
     88..94: WRITELN('You got a B');
     77..87: WRITELN('You got a C');
     70..76: WRITELN('Yellow Alert: You got a D');
     ELSE    WRITELN('Red Alert: You got an F');
   END;  {case}
```

```
8. CASE Sales OF
     0..2500:    Bonus :=  0;
     2501..5000: Bonus := 25;
     ELSE        Bonus := 50;
   END;
```

Chapter 17

1. True.

2. By the subscript.

3. No. Every element in an array must be the same type.

4. False. Arrays can start with any integer.

5. 79.

6. Range checking. You can select this option under Options | Compiler or by including the {$R+} compiler directive at the top of your program.

7. By using a swap routine. The swap routine needs to use a temporary variable to store intermediate results. For example, to swap two integers, x and y, you use:

```
VAR x,y,t: INTEGER;
BEGIN
    t := x;
    x := y;
    y := t;
END.
```

8. You often use FOR loops to increment through an array.

9. 23. (4 – (–18) + 1 = 23.)

Chapter 18

1. Scores: ARRAY[1..5,1..6] OF INTEGER;

2. Names: ARRAY[1..10, 1..20, 1..2] OF STRING;

3. The first subrange, 1..5, is the row subrange; the second subrange, 1..10, is the column subrange.

4. 30 (5 times 6).

5. A. 2

   B. 1

   C. 91

   D. 8

6. A. 68

   B. 100

   C. 80

7. The nested FOR loop is best because its control variables simulate the row and column (and depths, and so on for more than two dimensions) numbers of a matrix.

8. 552 (23 times 6 times 4).

Chapter 19

1. False. Records must have at least one field identifier.

2. False. Although records may have field identifiers with the same type, it is more common for them to have field identifiers with different types.

3. END.

4. False. Records usually are defined in the TYPE section. If there is only one variable to declare, you can define the record variable in the VAR section.

5. Use the name of the record, a period, and the name of the field identifier. If you want to assign values to several field identifiers, you can use a WITH statement.

6. False. Records can include other records.

7. No. The definitions for ModelType, IDString, and CompanyString must come before the definition for ModelRecord.

8.
```
BEGIN
    WITH Tree DO
        BEGIN
            Kind   := DeciduousTT;
            Branch := AlternateBT;
            Leaf   := SimpleLT;
        END;  {with}
    ⋮
END.
```

Chapter 20

1. They are already written for you.

2. It is a constant, a variable, or an expression inside the function's parentheses that the function works on.

3. SQRT computes the square root, and SQR computes the square.

4. ORD returns the ASCII number of whatever character is passed to it. CHR returns the ASCII character of whatever number is passed to it.

5. RANDOM:5:2 returns real values from 0.00 to 0.99.
RANDOM(2):5 returns values from 0 to 1.
RANDOM(7):5 returns values from 0 to 6.
RANDOM(11)+2 returns values from 2 to 12.

6. SIZEOF.

7. The WRITELN statement displays:

```
    -5.00          -5      -0.60
```

8.
```
CASE RANDOM(4) OF
   0: Dir := North;
   1: Dir := East;
   2: Dir := South;
   3: Dir := West;
END;  {case}
```

9. False. The first statement displays 32; the second statement displays 8.

10. 72. This illustrates how ORD and CHR are inverse functions.

Chapter 21

1. False.

2. False. LENGTH returns the current number of characters in the string.

3. WRITELN(COPY(tStr,1,7));.

4. POS assigns a value of 2 to X.

5. When you want to get one character from the keyboard without the user having to press Enter.

6. Turbo Pascal.

7. Turbo Pascal. Although the COPY parameter specifies 25 characters to be copied, the string has only 12. Only 12 characters therefore are returned.

8. You use the following statement:

```
WRITELN( ' ':((80 - LENGTH('Turbo Pascal By Example')) DIV 2),
         'Turbo Pascal By Example' );
```

Chapter 22

1. Turbo Pascal does not have a built-in function to do everything.

2. False.

3. A. STRING.

   B. 1.

   C. INTEGER.

4. False. A function never can return more than one value. If the function has more than one function name assignment statement, the data conditionally controls which of the assignment statements is executed.

5. The square function, SQR.

Chapter 23

1. A.

2. True. (Turbo Pascal has an advanced feature called in-line directives in which procedures and functions do not use a BEGIN-END pair.)

3. True.

4. Weight is used as the name of the procedure as well as the name of a variable. Turbo Pascal accepts the Weight used as a variable inside the procedure. This is a good example, however, of how not to name identifiers.

5. False. Although it does not do anything, a procedure can have no statements. Sometimes it improves your code's readability to put a single complicated statement inside a well-named procedure.

6. False.

7. True.

Chapter 24

1. You can change it easily if the value for SalesMinimum changes. Rather than change the value everywhere it appears, you have to change only the CONST statement.

2. False. A local variable is local only to the module in which it is defined.

3. Preface the parameter with VAR in the function's or procedure's parameter list.

4. The sum is 12.

5. A global variable does not have to be passed, because it is known throughout every procedure in the program anyway. However, there is no harm in doing so.

6. Use a locally defined typed constant because it retains its value. Or, declare a global variable and initialize it to 0 at the start of your program.

7. Pass by address. Passing by value ensures that arguments are changed only in the procedure to which they are sent (copied).

Chapter 25

1. A unit is a self-contained module that enables you to build your own library of code.

2. The INTERFACE section determines what other modules can see inside a unit.

3. END.

4. They are the same.

5. The calling program or unit simply includes the name of the unit in a USES statement.

6. Put the unit in the INTERFACE section if a declaration (CONST, TYPE, or VAR) or parameter type in a function or procedure needs to refer to the unit. Otherwise, put the unit in the IMPLEMENTATION section.

Chapter 26

1. Sequential access and random access.

2. A. 5.

   B. 4.

   C. Part No., Description, Quantity, Price.

3. By saving data on a hard disk, you can permanently store data. Otherwise, you have to retype data every time you run a program.

4. A. There is not enough RAM to hold large amounts of data.

   B. Nonprogrammers cannot always be expected to change the program when the data changes. You want anyone to be able to use your programs without having to know Turbo Pascal.

5. Fixed-length records typically require less programming.

6. The filenames are technically valid filenames. They are not meaningful, however, and do not help describe the data contained in them.

7. The file `sales.89.may` has one too many periods in the name (a filename cannot have more than one file extension). The file called `employees.dec` contains too many letters in the first part of the filename. The rest of the filenames are valid.

Chapter 27

1. The `ASSIGN` statement.

2. After using `ASSIGN` to associate a file variable to a filename, use `APPEND`, `RESET`, or `REWRITE` to open the file. If you use `APPEND` or `REWRITE`, you can only write to the file. If you use `RESET`, you may only read from the file.

3. The `READ` statement.

4. When you open a text file with RESET or REWRITE, the file pointer points to the first record, which Turbo Pascal counts as record #0. When you open a text file with APPEND, the file pointer points to the end of the file.

5. Unless I/O checking was disabled temporarily, the program crashes.

6. Unless I/O checking was disabled temporarily, the program crashes.

7. The comment before the FUNCTION header does not have a closing comment brace. Turbo Pascal ignores this function because the next right brace is after the END; statement marking the end of the function.

8. With respect to text files, WRITE adds data to a file. WRITELN adds data and an end-of-line marker.

9. It tells whether the record just read was the last one.

10. The FILES = statement in the CONFIG.SYS file.

11. WRITELN.

Chapter 28

1. You can read and write random-access files in any record order without having to read every record up to the one you want.

2. A record.

3. Turbo starts counting records from 0.

4. SEEK.

5. True.

6. The WITH statement.

7. So that a search on that field will always find the record for which you are looking. If more than one record key were the same, you would not know whether you found the record wanted by the user when you found a match of a key value.

8. `FILESIZE`.

9. After the record to be updated is read and updated, another `SEEK` is needed to move the file pointer back to the correct record. As it stands, the code will overwrite the record following the one updated. Before the `WRITE` statement, insert `SEEK(X,RecNum);`.

10. In the procedure's parameter list, include the name of the record and the record type.

Keyword and Subroutine Reference

Turbo Pascal Keywords

ABSOLUTE	FAR	NOT
AND	FILE	OBJECT
ARRAY	FOR	OF
ASM	FORWARD	OR
ASSEMBLER	FUNCTION	PACKED
BEGIN	GOTO	PRIVATE
CASE	IF	PROCEDURE
CONST	IMPLEMENTATION	PROGRAM
CONSTRUCTOR	IN	RECORD
DESTRUCTOR	INLINE	REPEAT
DIV	INTERFACE	SET
DO	INTERRUPT	SHL
DOWNTO	LABEL	SHR
ELSE	MOD	STRING
END	NEAR	THEN
EXTERNAL	NIL	TO

```
TYPE              USES              WHILE
UNIT              VAR               WITH
UNTIL             VIRTUAL           XOR
```

Selected Built-in Turbo Pascal Subroutines

Function	Unit	Description
ABS(X)	System	Returns the absolute value of X
CHR(I)	System	Returns characters with ASCII value of I
CONCAT(S1,S2,...)	System	Concatenate strings S1, S2, ...
COPY(S,I,N)	System	Returns N characters of string S starting at I
EOF(F)	System	Returns end-of-file status
EOLN(F)	System	Returns end-of-line status
EXP(R)	System	Returns exponential of R
FILESIZE(F)	System	Returns current size of file
FRAC(R)	System	Returns fractional part of R
FSEARCH(F,S)	Dos	Returns path of file F in directory S
INT(R)	System	Returns integer part of R
IORESULT	System	Returns status of last I/O
KEYPRESSED	Crt	Returns True if keyboard buffer is not empty
LENGTH(S)	System	Returns current length of string S
LN(R)	System	Returns natural logarithm of R
ODD(I)	System	Returns true if I is odd number

Function	Unit	Description
ORD(X)	System	Returns ordinal number of ordinal-type value
PI	System	Returns value of pi
POS(S1,S)	System	Returns position of string S1 inside string S
PRED(X)	System	Returns predecessor of X
RANDOM	System	Returns random number between 0 and 1
RANDOM(W)	System	Returns random number between 0 and W
READKEY	Crt	Returns character in keyboard buffer
ROUND(R)	System	Returns R rounded to integer
SIN(R)	System	Returns sine of R
SIZEOF(X)	System	Returns number of bytes used by X
SQR(X)	System	Returns square of X
SQRT(R)	System	Returns square root of R
SUCC(X)	System	Returns successor of X
TRUNC(R)	System	Returns X truncated to integer
UPCASE(C)	System	Returns character C converted to uppercase
WHEREX	Crt	Returns cursor's current X-coordinate
WHEREY	Crt	Returns cursor's current Y-coordinate

Procedure	*Unit*	*Description*
APPEND(T)	System	Opens a text file; file pointer at end of file
ASSIGN(F)	System	Associates a file variable to a file
CLOSE(F)	System	Closes an opened file
CLREOL	Crt	Clears all characters on current line starting from cursor position
CLRSCR	Crt	Clears active window
DEC(X)	System	Decrements X
DEC(X,I)	System	Decrements X by I
DELAY(W)	Crt	Delays system by W milliseconds
ERASE(F)	System	Erases closed file F
EXIT	System	Jumps to end of current block
FILLCHAR(X,C,V)	System	Fills X with C bytes of V
FLUSH(T)	System	Flushes buffer of open text file
GETDATE(Y,M,D,N)	Dos	Returns current system date
GETDIR(D,S)	System	Returns current directory S of drive D
GETTIME(H,M,S,S100)	Dos	Returns current system time
GOTOXY(x,y)	Crt	Positions cursor at (x,y)
HALT(W)	System	Stops your program
INC(X)	System	Increments X
INC(X,I)	System	Increments X by I
INSERT(S,S1,I)	System	Inserts S into S1 at I
MKDIR(S)	System	Creates subdirectory S
NOSOUND	Crt	Turns off sound
RANDOMIZE	System	Initializes random number generator

Procedure	Unit	Description
READ(F,V1,...)	System	Reads from file F into variable V1, ...
READLN(F,V1,...)	System	Reads from file F into variable V1, ... and then goes to next line
RENAME(F)	System	Renames a closed file
RESET(F)	System	Opens an existing file
REWRITE(F)	System	Creates and opens a new file
RMDIR(S)	System	Removes empty subdirectory S
SEEK(F,I)	System	Positions file pointer at record I
SETDATE(Y,M,D)	Dos	Sets current system date
SETTEXTBUF(F,B,W)	System	Resets I/O buffer for text file
SETTIME(H,M,S,S100)	Dos	Sets current system time
SOUND	Crt	Turns on sound
STR(X,S)	System	Converts number X into string S
TEXTBACKGROUND(B)	Crt	Resets background color to B
TEXTCOLOR(B)	Crt	Resets foreground color to B
VAL(S,X,C)	System	Converts string S into number X and returns conversion status in C
WINDOW(X1,Y1,X2,Y2)	Crt	(X1,Y1) specifies the upper left corner of a window. (X2,Y2) specifies the lower right corner of the window.
WRITE(F,V1,...)	System	Write variables V1, ... to file F
WRITELN(F,V1,...)	System	Write variables V1, ... to file F and then an end-of-line marker

Memory Addressing, Binary, and Hexadecimal Review

You do not have to understand the concepts in this appendix to become well-versed in Turbo Pascal. You can master Turbo Pascal, however, only if you spend some time learning about the "behind-the-scenes" roles played by binary numbers. The material presented here is not difficult, but many programmers do not take the time to study it. Hence, a handful of Turbo Pascal masters learn this material and understand how Turbo Pascal works "under the hood," whereas others never will be as expert in the language as they could be.

You should take the time to learn about addressing, binary numbers, and hexadecimal numbers. These fundamental principles are presented here for you to learn, and although a working knowledge of Turbo Pascal is possible without knowing them, they will greatly enhance your Turbo Pascal skills (and your skills in every other programming language).

After reading this appendix, you will better understand why different Turbo Pascal data types hold different ranges of numbers. You also will see the importance of being able to represent hexadecimal numbers in Turbo Pascal, and you will better understand Turbo Pascal pointer addressing.

Computer Memory

Each memory location inside your computer holds a single character called a *byte*. A byte is any character, whether it is a letter of the alphabet, a numeric digit, or a special character such as a period, question mark, or even a space (a blank character). If your computer contains 640K of memory, it can hold a total of approximately 640,000 bytes of memory. This means that as soon as you fill your computer's memory with 640K, there is no room for an additional character unless you overwrite something else.

Before describing the physical layout of your computer's memory, it might be best to take a detour and explain exactly what 640K means.

Memory and Disk Measurements

K means approximately 1000 and exactly 1024.

By appending the *K* (from the metric word *kilo*) to memory measurements, the manufacturers of computers do not have to attach as many zeros to the end of numbers for disk and memory storage. The K stands for approximately 1000 bytes. As you will see, almost everything inside your computer is based on a power of 2. Therefore, the K of computer memory measurements actually equals the power of 2 closest to 1000, which is 2 to the 10th power, or 1024. Because 1024 is very close to 1000, computerists often think of K as meaning 1000, even though they know it only approximately equals 1000.

M means approximately 1,000,000 and exactly 1,048,576.

Think for a moment about what 640K exactly equals. Practically speaking, 640K is about 640,000 bytes. To be exact, however, 640K equals 640 times 1024, or 655,360. This explains why the PC DOS command CHKDSK returns 655,360 as your total memory (assuming that you have 640K of RAM) rather than 640,000.

Because extended memory and many disk drives can hold such a large amount of data, typically several million characters, there is an additional memory measurement shortcut called *M*, which stands for *meg*, or *megabytes*. The M is a shortcut for approximately one million bytes. Therefore, 20M is approximately 20,000,000 characters, or bytes, of storage. As with K, the M literally stands for 1,048,576 because that is the closest power of 2 (2 to the 20th power) to one million.

How many bytes of storage is 60 megabytes? It is approximately 60 million characters, or 62,914,560 characters to be exact.

Memory Addresses

Each memory location in your computer, just as with each house in your town, has a unique *address.* A memory address is simply a sequential number, starting at 0, which labels each memory location. Figure D.1 shows how your computer memory addresses are numbered if you have 640K of RAM.

By using unique addresses, your computer can keep track of memory. When the computer stores a result of a calculation in memory, it finds an empty address, or one matching the data area where the result is to go, and stores the result at that address.

Your Turbo Pascal programs and data share computer memory with DOS. DOS must always reside in memory while you operate your computer. Otherwise, your programs would have no way to access disks, printers, the screen, or the keyboard. Figure D.2 shows computer memory being shared by DOS and a Turbo Pascal program. The exact amount of memory taken by DOS and a Turbo Pascal program is determined by the version of DOS you use, how many DOS extras (such as device drivers and buffers) your computer uses, and the size and needs of your Turbo Pascal programs and data.

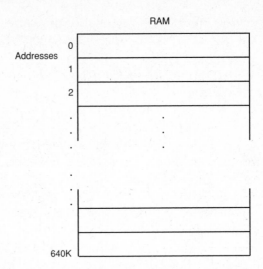

Figure D.1. Memory addresses for a 640K computer.

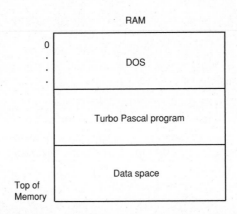

Figure D.2. DOS, your Turbo Pascal program, and your program's data share the same memory.

Bits and Bytes

You now know that a single address of memory might contain any character, called a byte. You know that your computer holds many bytes of information, but it does not store those characters in the same way that humans think of characters. For example, if you type a letter *W* on your keyboard while working in your Turbo Pascal editor, you see the *W* on the screen, and you also know that the *W* is stored in a memory location at some unique address. Actually, your computer does not store the letter *W*; it stores electrical impulses that stand for the letter *W*.

Electricity, which is what runs through the components of your computer, making it understand and execute your programs, can exist in only two states—on or off. As with a lightbulb, electricity is either flowing (it is on) or it is not flowing (it is off). Even though you can dim some lights, the electricity is still either on or off.

Today's modern digital computers employ this on-or-off concept. Your computer is nothing more than millions of on and off switches. You might have heard about integrated circuits, transistors, and even vacuum tubes that computers have contained over the years. These electrical components are nothing more than switches that rapidly turn electrical impulses on and off.

This two-state on and off mode of electricity is called a *binary* state of electricity. Computer people use a 1 to represent an on state (a switch in the computer that is on) and a 0 to represent an off state (a switch that is off). These numbers, 1 and 0, are called *binary digits.* The term binary digits is usually shortened to *bits.* A bit is either a 1 or a 0 representing an on or an off state of electricity. Different combinations of bits represent different characters.

Several years ago, someone listed every single character that might be represented on a computer, including all uppercase letters, all lowercase letters, the digits 0 through 9, the many other characters (such as %, *, {, and +), and some special control characters. When you add the total number of characters that a PC can represent, you get 256 of them. These 256 characters are listed in the ASCII (pronounced *as-kee*) table in Appendix A.

The order of the ASCII table's 256 characters is basically arbitrary, just as the telegraph's Morse code table is arbitrary. With Morse code, a different set of long and short beeps represent

> The binary digits 1 and 0 (called bits) represent on and off states of electricity.

different letters of the alphabet. In the ASCII table, a different combination of bits (1s and 0s strung together) represent each of the 256 ASCII characters. The ASCII table is a standard table used by almost every PC in the world. ASCII stands for American Standard Code for Information Interchange. (Some minicomputers and mainframes use a similar table called the EBCDIC table.)

It turns out that if you take every different combination of eight 0s strung together, to eight 1s strung together (that is, from 00000000, 00000001, 00000010, and so on until you get to 11111110, and finally, 11111111), you will have a total of 256 of them. (256 is 2 to the 8th power.) Each memory location in your computer holds eight bits each. These bits can be any combination of eight 1s and 0s. This brings us to the following fundamental rule of computers.

> **NOTE:** Because it takes a combination of eight 1s and 0s to represent a character, and because each byte of computer memory can hold exactly one character, eight bits equals one byte.

To bring this into better perspective, consider that the bit pattern needed for the uppercase letter *A* is 01000001. No other character in the ASCII table "looks" like this to the computer because each of the 256 characters is assigned a unique bit pattern.

Suppose that you press the *A* key on your keyboard. Your keyboard does *not* send a letter *A* to the computer; rather, it looks in its ASCII table for the on and off states of electricity that represent the letter *A*. As Figure D.3 shows, when you press the *A* key, the keyboard actually sends 01000001 (as on and off impulses) to the computer. Your computer simply stores this bit pattern for *A* in a memory location. Even though you can think of the memory location as holding an *A*, it really holds the byte 01000001.

If you were to print that *A*, your computer would not send an *A* to the printer; it would send the 01000001 bit pattern for an *A* to the printer. The printer receives that bit pattern, looks up the correct letter in the ASCII table, and prints an *A*.

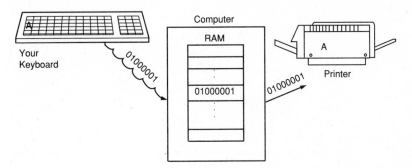

Figure D.3. **Your computer keeps track of characters by their bit patterns.**

From the time you press the *A* until the time you see it on the printer, it is *not* a letter *A!* It is the ASCII pattern of bits that the computer uses to represent an *A*. Because a computer is electrical, and because electricity is easily turned on and off, this is a nice way for the computer to manipulate and move characters, and it can do so very quickly. Actually, if it were up to the computer, you would enter everything by its bit pattern, and look at all results in their bit patterns. This would not be good, so devices such as the keyboard, screen, and printer know that they have to work part of the time with letters as we know them. That is why the ASCII table is such an integral part of a computer.

There are times when your computer treats two bytes as a single value. Even though memory locations are typically eight bits wide, many CPUs access memory two bytes at a time. If this is the case, the two bytes are called a *word* of memory. On other computers (commonly mainframes), the word size might be four bytes (32 bits) or even eight bytes (64 bits).

Summarizing Bits and Bytes

A bit is a 1 or a 0 representing an on or an off state of electricity.

Eight bits represents a byte.

A byte, or eight bits, represents one character.

---

continues

Each memory location of your computer is eight bits (a single byte) wide. Therefore, each memory location can hold one character of data. Appendix A is an ASCII table listing all possible characters.

If the CPU accesses memory two bytes at a time, those two bytes are called a word of memory.

The Order of Bits

To further understand memory, you should understand how programmers refer to individual bits. Figure D.4 shows a byte and a two-byte word. Notice that the bit on the far right is called bit 0. From bit 0, keep counting by ones as you move left. For a byte, the bits are numbered 0 to 7, from right to left. For a double-byte (a 16-bit word), the bits are numbered from 0 to 15, from right to left.

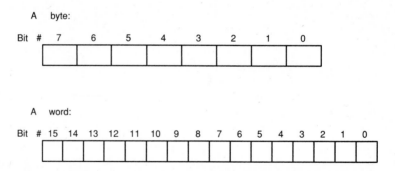

Figure D.4. The order of bits in a byte and a two-byte word.

Bit 0 is called the *least-significant bit,* or sometimes the *low-order bit.* Bit 7 (or bit 15 for a two-byte word) is called the *most-significant bit,* or sometimes the *high-order bit.*

Binary Numbers

Because a computer works best with 1s and 0s, its internal numbering method is limited to a *base-2* (binary) numbering system. People work in a *base-10* numbering system in the real world. The base-10 numbering system is sometimes called the decimal numbering system. There are always as many different digits as the base in a numbering system. For example, in the base-10 system, there are ten digits, 0 through 9. As soon as you count to 9 and run out of digits, you have to combine some that you already used. The number 10 is a representation of ten values, but it combines the digits 1 and 0.

The same is true of base 2. There are only two digits, 0 and 1. As soon as you run out of digits, after the second one, you have to re-use digits. The first seven binary numbers are 0, 1, 10, 11, 100, 101, and 110.

It is okay if you do not understand how these numbers were derived; you will see how in a moment. For the time being, you should realize that no more than two digits, 0 and 1, can be used to represent any base-2 number, just as no more than ten digits, 0 through 9, can be used to represent any base-10 number in the regular "real-world" numbering system.

You should know that a base-10 number, such as 2981, does not really mean anything by itself. You must assume what base it is. You get very used to working with base-10 numbers because that is what the world uses. However, the number 2981 actually represents a quantity based on powers of 10. For example, Figure D.5 shows what the number 2981 actually represents. Notice that each digit in the number represents a certain number of a power of 10.

This same concept applies when you work in a base-2 numbering system. Your computer does this, because the power of 2 is just as common to your computer as the power of 10 is to you. The only difference is that the digits in a base-2 number represent powers of 2 and not powers of 10. Figure D.6 shows you what the binary numbers 10101 and 10011110 are in base-10. This is how you convert any binary number to its base-10 equivalent.

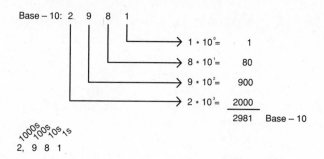

Figure D.5. The base-10 breakdown of the number 2981.

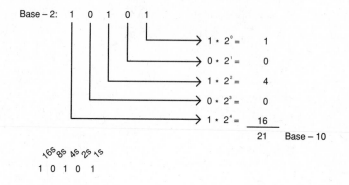

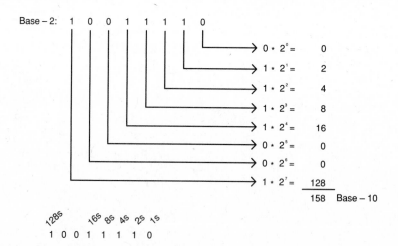

Figure D.6. The base-2 breakdown of the numbers 10101 and 10011110.

A binary number can contain only the digits 1 and 0.

A base-2 number contains only 1s and 0s. To convert any base-2 number to base-10, add each power of 2 everywhere a 1 appears in the number. The base-2 number 101 represents the base-10 number 5. (There are two 1s in the number, one in the 2 to the 0 power, which equals 1, and one in the 2 to the second power, which equals 4.) Table D.1 shows the first 18 base-10 numbers and their matching base-2 numbers.

Table D.1. The first 18 base-10 and base-2 (binary) numbers.

Base-10	Base-2
0	0
1	1
2	10
3	11
4	100
5	101
6	110
7	111
8	1000
9	1001
10	1010
11	1011
12	1100
13	1101
14	1110
15	1111
16	10000
17	10001

You do not have to memorize this table; you should be able to figure the base-10 numbers from their matching binary numbers by adding the powers of two for each 1 (on) bit. Many programmers do memorize the first several binary numbers, however, because it comes in handy in advanced programming techniques.

What is the largest binary number a byte can hold? The answer is all 1s, or 11111111. If you add the first eight powers of 2, you get 255.

A byte holds either a number or an ASCII character, depending on how it is accessed. For example, if you were to convert the base-2 number 01000001 to a base-10 number, you would get 65. However, this also happens to be the ASCII bit pattern for the uppercase letter *A*. If you check the ASCII table, you will see that the *A* is ASCII code 65. Because the ASCII table is so closely linked with the bit patterns, the computer knows whether to work with a number 65 or a letter *A*—by the context of how the patterns are used.

A binary number is not limited to a byte, as an ASCII character is. Sixteen or 32 bits at a time can represent a binary number (and usually do). There are more powers of 2 to add when converting that number to a base-10 number, but the process is the same. By now you should be able to figure out that 1010101010101010 is 43,690 in base-10 decimal numbering system (although it might take a little time to calculate).

To convert from decimal to binary takes a little more effort. Luckily, you rarely need to convert in that direction. Converting from base-10 to base-2 is not covered in this appendix.

Binary Arithmetic

At their lowest level, computers can only add and convert binary numbers to their negative equivalents. Computers cannot truly subtract, multiply, or divide, although they simulate these operations through judicious use of the addition and negative-conversion techniques.

If a computer were to add the numbers 7 and 6, it could do so (at the binary level). The result is 13. If, however, the computer were instructed to subtract 7 from 13, it could not do so. It can, however, take the negative value of 7 and add that to 13. Because –7 plus 13 equals 6, the result is a simulated subtraction.

To multiply, computers perform repeated addition. To multiply 6 by 7, the computer adds seven 6s together and gets 42 as the answer. To divide 42 by 7, a computer keeps subtracting 7 from 42 repeatedly until it gets to a 0 answer (or less than 0 if there is a remainder), then counts the number of times it took to reach 0.

Because all math is done at the binary level, the following additions are possible in binary arithmetic:

$0 + 0 = 0$

$0 + 1 = 1$

$1 + 0 = 1$

$1 + 1 = 10$

Because these are binary numbers, the last result is not the number 10, but the binary number 2. (Just as the binary 10 means "no ones, and carry an additional power of 2," the decimal number 10 means "no ones, and carry a power of 10.") No binary digit represents a 2, so you have to combine the 1 and the 0 to form the new number.

Because binary addition is the foundation of all other math, you should learn how to add binary numbers. You will then understand how computers do the rest of their arithmetic.

Using the binary addition rules shown previously, look at the following binary calculations:

```
 01000001    (65 decimal)
+00101100    (44 decimal)
 _____

 01101101    (109 decimal)
```

The first number, 01000001, is 65 decimal. This also happens to be the bit pattern for the ASCII A, but if you add with it, the computer knows to interpret it as the number 65 rather than the character A.

The following binary addition requires a carry into bit 4 and bit 6:

```
  00101011   (43 decimal)
+ 00100111   (39 decimal)
  --------
  01010010   (82 decimal)
```

Typically, you have to ignore bits that carry past bit 7, or bit 15 for double-byte arithmetic. For example, both of the following binary additions produce incorrect positive results:

```
  10000000   (128 decimal)        1000000000000000   (65536 decimal)
+ 10000000   (128 decimal)      + 1000000000000000   (65536 decimal)
  --------                        ----------------
  00000000   (0 decimal)          0000000000000000   (0 decimal!)
```

There is no 9th or 17th bit for the carry, so both of these seem to produce incorrect results. Because the byte and 16-bit word cannot hold the answers, the magnitude of both these additions is not possible. The computer must be programmed, at the bit level, to perform *multiword arithmetic*, which is beyond the scope of this book.

Binary Negative Numbers

Negative binary numbers are stored in their 2's complement format.

Because subtracting requires understanding binary negative numbers, you need to learn how computers represent them. The computer uses *2's complement* to represent negative numbers in binary form. To convert a binary number to its 2's complement (to its negative) you must

1. Reverse the bits (the 1s to 0s and the 0s to 1s).

2. Add 1.

This might seem a little strange at first, but it works very well for binary numbers. To represent a binary –65, you need to take the binary 65 and convert it to its 2's complement, such as

```
01000001   (65 decimal)
10111110   (Reverse the bits)
      +1   (Add 1)
--------
10111111   (-65 binary)
```

By converting the 65 to its 2's complement, you produce –65 in binary. You might wonder what makes 10111111 mean –65, but by the 2's complement definition it means –65.

If you were told that 10111111 is a negative number, how would you know which binary number it is? You perform the 2's complement on it. Whatever number you produce is the positive of that negative number. For example:

```
10111111   (-65 decimal)
01000000   (Reverse the bits)
     +1    (Add 1)
_____

01000001   (65 decimal)
```

Something might seem wrong at this point. You just saw that 10111111 is the binary –65, but isn't 10111111 *also* 191 decimal (adding the powers of 2 marked by the 1s in the number, as explained earlier)? It depends whether the number is a *signed* or an *unsigned* number. If a number is signed, the computer looks at the most-significant bit (the bit on the far left), called the *sign bit*. If the most-significant bit is a 1, the number is negative. If it is 0, the number is positive.

Most numbers are 16 bits long. That is, two-byte words are used to store most integers. This is not always the case for all computers, but it is true for most PCs.

In the Turbo Pascal programming language, you can designate numbers as either signed integers (SHORTINT, INTEGER, or LONGINT) or unsigned integers (BYTE or WORD). If you designate a variable as a signed integer, the computer interprets the high-order bit as a sign bit. If the high-order bit is on (1), the number is negative. If the high-order bit is off (0), the number is positive. If, however, you designate a variable as an unsigned integer, the computer uses the high-order bit as just another power of 2. That is why the magnitude of unsigned integer variables goes higher (a WORD uses two bytes and ranges from 0 to 65535) than for signed integer variables (an INTEGER uses two bytes and ranges from –32768 to +32768).

After so much description, a little review is in order. Assume that the following 16-bit binary numbers are unsigned:

0011010110100101

1001100110101010

1000000000000000

These numbers are unsigned, so the bit 15 is not the sign bit, but just another power of 2. You should practice converting these large 16-bit numbers to decimal. The decimal equivalents are

13733

39338

32768

If, on the other hand, these numbers are signed numbers, the high-order bit (bit 15) indicates the sign. If the sign bit is 0, the numbers are positive and you convert them to decimal in the usual manner. If the sign bit is 1, you must convert the numbers to their 2's complement to find what they equal. Their decimal equivalents are

+13733

−26197

−32768

To compute the last two binary numbers to their decimal equivalents, take their 2's complement and convert it to decimal. Put a minus sign in front of the result and you find what the original number represents.

TIP: To make sure that you convert a number to its 2's complement correctly, you can add the 2's complement to its original positive value. If the answer is 0 (ignoring the extra carry to the left), you know that the 2's complement number is correct. This is like saying that decimal opposites, such as −72 + 72, add up to zero.

Hexadecimal Numbers

All those 1s and 0s get confusing. If it were up to your computer, however, you would enter *everything* as 1s and 0s! This is unacceptable to people because we do not like to keep track of all those 1s and 0s. Therefore, a *hexadecimal* numbering system (sometimes called *hex*) was devised. The hexadecimal numbering system is based on base-16 numbers. As with other bases, there are 16 unique digits in the base-16 numbering system. Here are the first 19 hexadecimal numbers:

0 1 2 3 4 5 6 7 8 9 A B C D E F 10 11 12

Hexadecimal numbers use 16 unique digits, 0 through F.

Because there are only 10 unique digits (0 through 9), the letters A through F represent the remaining six digits. (Anything could have been used, but the designers of the hexadecimal numbering system decided to use the first six letters of the alphabet.)

To understand base-16 numbers, you should know how to convert them to base-10 so that they represent numbers people are familiar with. Perform the conversion to base-10 from base-16 the same way you did with base-2, but instead of using powers of 2, represent each hexadecimal digit with powers of 16. Figure D.7 shows how to convert the number 3C5 to decimal.

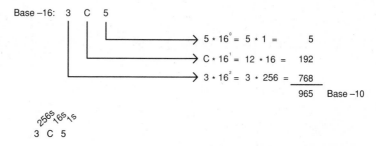

Figure D.7. Converting hexadecimal 3C5 to its decimal equivalent.

TIP: There are calculators available that convert numbers between base-16, base-10, and base-2, and also perform 2's complement arithmetic.

You should be able to convert 2B to its decimal 43 equivalent, and E1 to decimal 225 in the same manner. Table D.2 shows the first 20 decimal, binary, and hexadecimal numbers.

Table D.2. The first 20 base-10, base-2 (binary), and base-16 (hexadecimal) numbers.

Base-10	Base-2	Base-16
1	1	1
2	10	2
3	11	3
4	100	4
5	101	5
6	110	6
7	111	7
8	1000	8
9	1001	9
10	1010	A
11	1011	B
12	1100	C
13	1101	D
14	1110	E
15	1111	F
16	10000	10
17	10001	11
18	10010	12
19	10011	13
20	10100	14

Why Learn Hexadecimal?

Because of its close association to the binary numbers your computer uses, hexadecimal notation is extremely efficient for describing memory locations and values. It is much easier for you (and more importantly at this level, for your computer) to convert from base-16 to base-2 than from base-10 to base-2. Therefore, you sometimes want to represent data at the bit level, but using hexadecimal notation is easier (and requires less typing) than using binary numbers.

To convert from hexadecimal to binary, convert each hex digit to its four-bit binary number. You can use Table D.2 as a guide for this. For example, the following hexadecimal number

5B75

can be converted to binary by taking each digit and converting it to four binary numbers. If you need leading zeroes to "pad" the four digits, use them. The number becomes

0101 1011 0111 0101

It turns out that the binary number 0101101101110101 is exactly equal to the hexadecimal number 5B75. This is much easier than converting them both to decimal first.

To convert from binary to hexadecimal, reverse this process. If you were given the following binary number

1101000011110111111010

you could convert it to hexadecimal by grouping the bits into groups of four, starting with the bit on the far right. Because there is not an even number of groups of four, pad the one on the far left with zeroes. You then have the following:

0011 0100 0011 1101 1111 1010

Now you only have to convert each group of four binary digits into their hexadecimal number equivalent. You can use Table D.2 to help. You then get the following base-16 number:

343DFA

How Binary and Addressing Relate to Turbo Pascal

The material presented here may seem foreign to many programmers. The binary and 2's complement arithmetic reside deep in your computer, shielded from most programmers (except assembly language programmers). Understanding this level of your computer, however, explains everything else you learn.

Many Turbo Pascal programmers learn Turbo Pascal before delving into binary and hexadecimal representation. For them, much about the Turbo Pascal language seems strange; it could be explained very easily, however, if they understood the basic concepts.

For example, a signed integer holds a different range of numbers than an unsigned integer. You now know that this is due to the sign bit's being used in two different ways, depending on whether the number is designated as signed or unsigned.

The ASCII table also should make more sense to you after this discussion. The ASCII table is an integral part of your computer. Characters are not actually stored in memory and variables; rather, their ASCII bit patterns are stored.

The hexadecimal notation taught to many Turbo Pascal programmers also makes much more sense if they truly understand base-16 numbers. For example, if you see the following line in a Turbo Pascal program

```
i := $41;
```

you could convert the hex 41 to decimal (65 decimal) if you want to know what is being assigned. Programmers also find that they can better interface with assembly language programs when they understand the concepts presented in this appendix.

If you gain only a cursory knowledge of this material at this point, you will be very much ahead of the game when you program in Turbo Pascal.

The Complete Application

```
{ Filename: BOOK.PAS }

{
  Book Management Database Program
  ---- ---------- -------- -------

  This program illustrates using Turbo Pascal to create a
  book-tracking database program. You can keep track of your
  book inventory, the authors in your library, the condition of
  the book, and more.

  The program's easy-to-use data-entry screens and reports
  make keeping track of your personal collection of books easy.
}

PROGRAM BookFileSystem;
USES Crt, Printer, ScrTool;

CONST Spc          = ' ';
      MaxNumBooks = 300;                  { Maximum number of books }
      TitleLen    = 30;
      AuthorLen   = 25;
```

```
                    CondLen     = 10;
                    DateLen     =  8;
                    EditionLen  =  3;
                    NoteLen     = 80;
                    BookNameLen = 40;
                    YBot        = 25;
                    FNameColor  = WHITE;


            TYPE    MaxString     = STRING[80];
                    TitleString   = STRING[TitleLen];
                    AuthorString  = STRING[AuthorLen];
                    CondString    = STRING[CondLen];
                    DateString    = STRING[DateLen];
                    EditionString = STRING[EditionLen];
                    NoteString    = STRING[NoteLen];
                       {
                          The Edition may be 1st, 2nd, etc.
                          The Cover may be H or S for Hardcover or Softcover.
                          Notes can include miscellaneous notes on the book.
                       }
                    BookRecord    = RECORD
                                       Title:   TitleString;
                                       Author:  AuthorString;
                                       Cond:    CondString;
                                       PubDate: DateString;
                                       Edition: EditionString;
                                       Cover:   CHAR;
                                       Notes:   NoteString;
                                    END;
                    BookArray     = ARRAY[1..MaxNumBooks] OF BookRecord;

            VAR     gBookRec:   BookRecord;              { A user-defined type }
                    tBookRec:   BookRecord;
                    gBooks:     BookArray;
                    gBookFile:  FILE OF BookRecord; { Book datafile to use }
                    gBookFName: STRING[BookNameLen];

        PROCEDURE Color(FG,BG: BYTE);
           BEGIN
              TEXTCOLOR(FG);
              TEXTBACKGROUND(BG);
           END;  {Color}
```

```
PROCEDURE PaintScreen(FG,BG: BYTE);
   BEGIN
      TEXTCOLOR(FG);                       {Controls color of cursor}
      TEXTBACKGROUND(BG);
      CLRSCR;
   END;  {PaintScreen}

PROCEDURE PaintLine(y:  BYTE;
                   FG: BYTE;
                   BG: BYTE);
   BEGIN
      GOTOXY(1,y);
      TEXTCOLOR(FG);
      TEXTBACKGROUND(BG);
      CLREOL;
   END;  {PaintLine}

FUNCTION FillString(n:  BYTE;
                    Ch: CHAR): MaxString;
   VAR tStr: MaxString;
   BEGIN
      FILLCHAR(tStr[1],n,Ch);
      tStr[0] := CHR(n);
      FillString := tStr;
   END;  {FillString}

PROCEDURE ScrWrite(X,Y: INTEGER;
                   FG:  BYTE;
                   BG:  BYTE;
                   S:   MaxString);
   BEGIN
      GOTOXY(X,Y);
      TEXTCOLOR(FG);
      TEXTBACKGROUND(BG);
      WRITE(S);
   END;  {ScrWrite}

PROCEDURE ClearField(x,y: BYTE;
                     FG:  BYTE;
                     BG:  BYTE;
                     Len: BYTE);
   VAR tStr: MaxString;
```

```
        BEGIN
            tStr := FillString(Len,Spc);
            ScrWrite(x,y,FG,BG,tStr);
            GOTOXY(x,y);
        END;  {ClearField}


    FUNCTION Trim(s: MaxString): MaxString;
        BEGIN
            WHILE s[1] = Spc DO DELETE(s,1,1);
            WHILE s[LENGTH(s)] = Spc DO DELETE(s,LENGTH(s),1);
            Trim := s;
        END;  {Trim}


    FUNCTION Pad(s: MaxString): MaxString;
        BEGIN
            WHILE LENGTH(s) < 79 DO s := s + Spc;
            Pad := s;
        END;  {Pad}


    FUNCTION Caps(s: MaxString): MaxString;
        VAR i: INTEGER;
        BEGIN
            FOR i := 1 TO LENGTH(s) DO s[i] := UPCASE(s[i]);
            Caps := s;
        END;  {Caps}


    PROCEDURE FormFeed;
        BEGIN
            WRITELN(LST,#12);
        END;  {FormFeed}


            { Displays information at bottom of screen }

    PROCEDURE DispMessage(Msg: MaxString);
        BEGIN
            ScrWrite(1,YBot,BLACK,CYAN,Pad(Spc+Msg));
            GOTOXY(LENGTH(Msg)+2,YBot);
        END;  {DispMessage}


    PROCEDURE ErrorMsg1(Message: MaxString);
        VAR Ch: CHAR;
```

```
   BEGIN
      ScrWrite(1,YBot,WHITE,Red,Pad('*** '+Message+' ***'));
      ScrWrite(70,YBot,WHITE,RED,'Press Esc');
      REPEAT
        Ch := READKEY;
      UNTIL Ch = #27;
      ScrWrite(1,YBot,BLUE,BLUE,FillString(79,Spc));
   END;   {ErrorMsg1}


FUNCTION GetString( x,y:   BYTE;
                    FG,BG: BYTE;
                    Len:   BYTE;
                    s:     MaxString): MaxString;
   VAR tStr: MaxString;
       Ch:   CHAR;
   BEGIN
      GOTOXY(x,y);
      TEXTCOLOR(FG);
      TEXTBACKGROUND(BG);
      tStr := '';
      REPEAT
        Ch := READKEY;
        IF KEYPRESSED
           THEN Ch := READKEY
           ELSE IF Ch <> #13
                   THEN BEGIN
                          IF tStr = ''
                             THEN ClearField(x,y,WHITE,BG,Len);
                          WRITE(Ch);
                          IF Ch = #8
                             THEN BEGIN
                                    DELETE(tStr,LENGTH(tStr),1);
                                    GOTOXY(WHEREX,y);
                                    WRITE(Spc);
                                    GOTOXY(WHEREX-1,y);
                                  END
                             ELSE tStr := tStr + Ch;
                        END;
      UNTIL ((Ch = #13) OR (LENGTH(tStr) >= Len));
      IF tStr <> ''
         THEN s := tStr;
      GetString := s;
   END;   {GetString}
```

```
                    {
                      This routine ensures that the user types either
                      an H or S for Hardcover or Softcover, respectively.
                    }


        FUNCTION GetCover(Cover: CHAR): CHAR;
           VAR OK:  BOOLEAN;
               tCh: CHAR;
           BEGIN
             REPEAT
               OK := FALSE;
               GOTOXY( 58, 15 );
               tCh := READKEY;
               IF tCh = #13
                  THEN OK := TRUE
                  ELSE BEGIN
                          Cover := UPCASE(tCh);
                          ScrWrite(58,15,WHITE,BLUE,Cover);
                          IF Cover IN ['H','S']
                             THEN BEGIN
                                     OK := TRUE;
                                     ScrWrite(58,15,WHITE,BLUE,Cover);
                                  END
                             ELSE ErrorMsg1('You must type an H or S')
                       END;
             UNTIL OK;
             GetCover := Cover;
           END;  {GetCover}


                    {
                      If the title starts with "The..." this routine
                      will move ", The" to the end of the title.
                    }


        PROCEDURE FixTitle;
           BEGIN
             IF Caps(COPY(gBookRec.Title,1,4)) = 'THE '
                THEN BEGIN
                        {
                          Trim any trailing spaces, temporarily, off
                          the title. Then append ', The' to the end of
                          the book title and take off the prefix 'The'
                          before actually saving the "real" title.
                        }
```

```
                    DELETE(gBookRec.Title,1,4);
                    gBookRec.Title := Trim(gBookRec.Title) + ', The';
                    ScrWrite(12,6,WHITE,BLUE,gBookRec.Title);
                 END;
     END;  {FixTitle}


        {
            This routine lets the user press ENTER through data,
            changing whatever needs to be changed on the screen.
        }


PROCEDURE EditData(VAR tBookRec: BookRecord);
    BEGIN
       WITH gBookRec DO
          BEGIN
             Title   := GetString(12,6,WHITE,BLUE,TitleLen,
                              tBookRec.Title);
             FixTitle;
             Author  := GetString(13,8,WHITE,BLUE,AuthorLen,
                              tBookRec.Author);
             Cond    := GetString(16,11,WHITE,BLUE,CondLen,
                              tBookRec.Cond);
             PubDate := GetString(53,11,WHITE,BLUE,DateLen,
                              tBookRec.PubDate);
             Edition := GetString(14,15,WHITE,BLUE,EditionLen,
                              tBookRec.Edition);
             Cover   := GetCover(tBookRec.Cover);
             Notes   := Trim(GetString(12,18,WHITE,BLUE,NoteLen,
                                 tBookRec.Notes));
          END;  {with}
     END;  {EditData}



        { Prints new titles on the screen, by Author field. }


PROCEDURE DispScrnTitlesA;
    BEGIN
       ScrWrite( 1,1,WHITE,BLUE,'Author');
       ScrWrite(27,1,WHITE,BLUE,'Title');
       ScrWrite(58,1,WHITE,BLUE,'Edition');
       ScrWrite(69,1,WHITE,BLUE,'Cover');
       ScrWrite( 1,2,WHITE,BLUE,FillString(79,'-'));
    END;  {DispScrnTitlesA}
```

```
                  { Prints new titles on the screen, Title field first. }

      PROCEDURE DispScrnTitlesT;
         BEGIN
            ScrWrite( 1,1,WHITE,BLUE,'Title');
            ScrWrite(32,1,WHITE,BLUE,'Author');
            ScrWrite(58,1,WHITE,BLUE,'Edition');
            ScrWrite(69,1,WHITE,BLUE,'Cover');
            ScrWrite( 1,2,WHITE,BLUE,FillString(79,'-'));
         END;  {DispScrnTitlesT}


                  { Displays found book's data in highlighted fields. }

      PROCEDURE DispFieldData;
         BEGIN
            ScrWrite(12, 6,WHITE,BLUE,gBookRec.Title);
            ScrWrite(13, 8,WHITE,BLUE,gBookRec.Author);
            ScrWrite(16,11,WHITE,BLUE,gBookRec.Cond);
            ScrWrite(53,11,WHITE,BLUE,gBookRec.PubDate);
            ScrWrite(14,15,WHITE,BLUE,gBookRec.Edition);
            ScrWrite(58,15,WHITE,BLUE,gBookRec.Cover);
            ScrWrite(12,18,WHITE,BLUE,Trim(gBookRec.Notes));
         END;  {DispFieldData}

            {
               Simply prints the names of each field
               in their place on the screen, and a
               lot of spaces after them to clear
               whatever may still be on the line.
            }

      PROCEDURE DispFieldNames;
         BEGIN
            ScrWrite(5,6,FNameColor,BLUE,'Title:'+FillString(50,Spc));
            ScrWrite(5,8,FNameColor,BLUE,'Author:'+
                     FillString(50,Spc));
            ScrWrite(5,11,FNameColor,BLUE,'Condition:'+
                     FillString(20,Spc));
            ScrWrite(35,11,FNameColor,BLUE,'Publication Date:'+
                     FillString(20,Spc));
            ScrWrite(5,15,FNameColor,BLUE,'Edition:'+
                     FillString(20,Spc));
```

```
      ScrWrite(35,15,FNameColor,BLUE,'Hard/Soft Cover (H/S):' +
                FillString(20,Spc));

         {  Old notes on the screen may take more than 1 line. }

      ScrWrite(5,18,FNameColor,BLUE,'Notes:' +
                FillString(50,Spc));
      PaintLine(19,WHITE,BLUE);
      PaintLine(20,WHITE,BLUE);
   END;   {DispFieldNames}


         {
            This subroutine is called from the data-entry routine.
            It simply prints the data-entry screen title and
            prompts for each field.
         }


PROCEDURE DispPrompts;
   BEGIN
      ScrWrite(20,3,WHITE,BLUE,
             '*** Enter a Book''s Information ***' );
      ScrWrite(20,4,WHITE,BLUE,
             '    -------------------------' );

      DispFieldNames;
   END;   {DispPrompts}


PROCEDURE ChkForChange;
   VAR Ch:       CHAR;
       EditDone: BOOLEAN;
   BEGIN
      EditDone := FALSE;
      REPEAT
        DispMessage('Do you want to edit this record? (Y/N) ');
        Ch := UPCASE(READKEY);
        IF (Ch = 'Y')
           THEN BEGIN
                   ScrWrite(1,YBot,WHITE,BLUE,FillString(79,Spc));
                   EditData(tBookRec);
                   EditDone := TRUE;
                END;
      UNTIL ((Ch = 'N') OR EditDone);
      WRITE(gBookFile, gBookRec);
   END;   {ChkForChange}
```

```
                    {
                      This subroutine gets the user's input for a book.
                      That information is then written to the file.
                    }

        PROCEDURE EnterBook;
           VAR Ch: CHAR;
           BEGIN
              ASSIGN(gBookFile,gBookFName);
{$I-}
              RESET(gBookFile);
{$I+}
              IF IORESULT <> 0 THEN REWRITE(gBookFile);
              IF FILESIZE(gBookFile) >= MaxNumBooks
                 THEN BEGIN
                         ErrorMsg1 ('You have the maximum number of '+
                                      'books in this file');
                         CLOSE(gBookFile);
                         EXIT;
                       END;
              SEEK(gBookFile,FILESIZE(gBookFile));

           REPEAT
              PaintScreen(WHITE,BLUE);
              DispPrompts;
              WITH gBookRec DO
                 BEGIN
                    Title := GetString(12, 6,WHITE,BLUE,TitleLen, '');
                    IF (Title = '')          { If pressed ENTER }
                       THEN BEGIN
                                {
                                  Close data file without writing
                                  to it, and return to Main Menu.
                                }
                                CLOSE(gBookFile);
                                EXIT;
                             END;
                    FixTitle;                { Move 'The' to title end }
                    Author  := GetString(13, 8, WHITE, BLUE,
                                      AuthorLen,'');
                    Cond    := GetString(16, 11, WHITE, BLUE,
                                      CondLen, '');
```

```
               PubDate := GetString(53, 11, WHITE, BLUE,
                                      DateLen,'');
               Edition := Caps(GetString(14, 15, WHITE, BLUE,
                                           EditionLen,''));
               Cover   := GetCover(Cover); { get H or S only }
               Notes   := GetString(12, 18, WHITE, BLUE,
                                      NoteLen,'');
           END;  {with}
         tBookRec := gBookRec;

         ChkForChange;

         DispMessage('Do you want to enter another? (Y/N) ' );
         Ch := UPCASE(READKEY);
      UNTIL (Ch = 'N');
      CLOSE(gBookFile);
   END;  {EnterBook}


       {
         Asks the user for the name of the disk file to use.
         This allows for more than one data file. They might
         have a file of technical books, one for fiction, etc.
       }

 PROCEDURE GetFileName;
   CONST Prompt = ' New book file name? ';
   BEGIN
   Frame(1,22,1+LENGTH(Prompt)+BookNameLen+3,24,BLACK,CYAN,BLACK,'','');
      ScrWrite(2,2,BLACK,CYAN,Prompt);
      gBookFName := GetString(LENGTH(Prompt)+3,2,BLACK,BLACK,
                              BookNameLen,'');
      IF POS('.',gBookFName) = 0        { Append extension }
         THEN gBookFName := gBookFName + '.DAT';
      WINDOW(1,1,80,25);                    { restore full window }
   END;  {GetFileName}


       {
         Get a valid title to look for.
         User cannot begin a title with 'The' when searching.
       }
```

```
PROCEDURE GetLookTitle (VAR s: MaxString);
    VAR OK: BOOLEAN;
    BEGIN
       REPEAT
          OK := FALSE;
          DispMessage('* * Type a title, or first few letters '+
                      'of the title * *');
          PaintLine(6,WHITE,BLUE);
          ScrWrite(1, 6, WHITE, BLUE, 'Title = ');
             { Get the title to search for }
          s := GetString(9, 6, WHITE, BLUE, TitleLen,'');
          IF (s = '') THEN EXIT;         { If only ENTER, return. }
          IF (Caps(COPY(s,1,4)) = 'THE ')
             THEN ErrorMsg1('The title cannot begin with "The"')
             ELSE OK := TRUE;
       UNTIL OK;
       PaintLine(6,WHITE,BLUE);
    END;  {GetLookTitle}


          { Prompt for user to press ENTER. }


PROCEDURE PressEnter;
    VAR Ch: CHAR;
    BEGIN
       ScrWrite(1,YBot,BLUE,BLUE,FillString(79,Spc));
       DispMessage('Press ENTER to continue:' );
       Ch := READKEY;
    END; {PressEnter}



          {
             Searches for title (or partial title)
             that user typed.
          }

PROCEDURE FileSearch(     s:         MaxString;
                     VAR RecNum:    INTEGER;
                     VAR BookFound: BOOLEAN);
    VAR Ch:      CHAR;
        BookCnt: INTEGER;
```

```
    BEGIN
      RecNum    := 0;
      BookFound := FALSE;
      s         := Caps(s);
      ASSIGN(gBookFile,gBookFName);
{$I-}
      RESET(gBookFile);
{$I+}
      IF IORESULT <> 0
         THEN BEGIN
                 ErrorMsg1('No books in file');
                 EXIT;
              END;
      BookCnt := 0;
      WHILE (NOT EOF(gBookFile) AND (NOT BookFound)) DO
         BEGIN
            READ(gBookFile,gBookRec);
            IF POS(s,Caps(gBookRec.Title)) > 0
               THEN BEGIN
                       INC(BookCnt);
                       DispFieldNames;
                       DispFieldData;
                       PaintLine(YBot,BLUE,BLUE);
                       REPEAT
                        DispMessage('Is this the correct '+
                           'book you were looking for? (Y/N) ');
                           Ch := UPCASE(READKEY);
                           ScrWrite(55,YBot,WHITE,RED,Ch);
                       UNTIL Ch IN ['Y','N'];
                       BookFound := (Ch = 'Y');
                    END
               ELSE INC(RecNum);
         END;  {while}
      CLOSE(gBookFile);
      IF BookFound THEN EXIT;    { skip error messages if book found }
      IF BookCnt = 0
         THEN ErrorMsg1('Book not found in file, '+gBookFName)
         ELSE ErrorMsg1('Desired book not in file, '+gBookFName);
    END;  {FileSearch}
```

```
              {
                Requests a title, or partial title, and displays
                that book's information.
              }

PROCEDURE LookBook;
   VAR s:          MaxString;
       RecNum:     INTEGER;
       Ch:         CHAR;
       BookFound: BOOLEAN;
       EditDone:  BOOLEAN;
   BEGIN
      BookFound := FALSE;
      EditDone  := FALSE;
      ASSIGN(gBookFile,gBookFName);
{$I-}
      RESET(gBookFile);
{$I+}
      IF IORESULT <> 0
         THEN BEGIN
                 ErrorMsg1('No books in file');
                 EXIT;
              END;
      PaintScreen(WHITE,BLUE);
      ScrWrite(20,3,WHITE,BLUE,
              '*** Look at a Book''s Information ***');
      ScrWrite(20,4,WHITE,BLUE,
              '    --------------------------');
      GetLookTitle(s);                   { Get title to look for. }
      FileSearch(s,RecNum,BookFound);  { Search for the title. }
      IF NOT BookFound THEN EXIT;        { no book to update }
      REPEAT
         DispMessage('Do you want to edit this record? (Y/N) ' );
         Ch := UPCASE(READKEY);
         IF (Ch = 'Y')
            THEN BEGIN
                    PaintLine(YBot,WHITE,BLUE);
                    EditData(gBookRec);
                    EditDone := TRUE;
                 END;
      UNTIL ((Ch = 'N') OR EditDone);
```

```
            ASSIGN(gBookFile,gBookFName);
            RESET(gBookFile);
            SEEK(gBookFile,RecNum);
            WRITE(gBookFile, gBookRec);
            CLOSE(gBookFile);
        END;  {LookBook}


            { Prints new titles on the printer. }


PROCEDURE PrintTitles(VAR PrinterOK: BOOLEAN);
    BEGIN
        PrinterOK := TRUE;
{$I-}
        WRITELN(LST,'Title':TitleLen,'Author':AuthorLen,
                'Edition':8,'Cover':6 );
{$I+}
        IF IORESULT <> 0
            THEN BEGIN
                    ErrorMsg1('Printer not ready');
                    PrinterOK := FALSE;
                    EXIT;
                 END;
        WRITELN(LST, FillString(79, '-'));
    END;  {PrintTitles}


        {
            Prints a record on the printer. This subroutine keeps
            track of the printed lines and prints a title at each
            new page (after 66 lines) and form feeds at the end
            of each page. If the Init argument is equal to 1,
            this routine zeroes out the printing variables and
            assumes that this call is the start of a new listing.
            Otherwise, the typed constants keep their values.
        }


PROCEDURE PrinterPrintA(    Init:      INTEGER;
                        VAR PrinterOK: BOOLEAN);
    CONST LineCnt: INTEGER = 0;
    BEGIN
        IF (Init = 1)                    { If called first time: }
            THEN BEGIN
                    LineCnt := 3;
                    PrintTitles(PrinterOK);
```

```
                                EXIT
                        END;                        { Else, all later times. }


            IF (LineCnt = 2)
                THEN BEGIN
                        PrintTitles(PrinterOK);
                        IF NOT PrinterOK THEN EXIT;
                        LineCnt := 3;
                    END;


            WITH gBookRec DO
                WRITELN(LST, Title:TitleLen, Author:AuthorLen,
                        Edition:8, Cover:6);


            INC(LineCnt);
            IF LineCnt = 64
                THEN BEGIN
                        LineCnt := 2;
                        IF PrinterOK THEN FormFeed;
                    END;
        END;  {PrinterPrintA}


            {
                Prints a record on the printer. This subroutine keeps
                track of the printed lines and prints a title at each
                new page (after 66 lines) and form feeds at the end of
                each page. If the init% argument is equal to 1, this
                routine zeroes out the printing variables and assumes
                that this call is the start of a new listing.
                Otherwise, the typed constants keep their values.
            }


PROCEDURE PrinterPrintT (    Init:      INTEGER;
                         VAR PrinterOK: BOOLEAN);
    CONST LineCnt: INTEGER = 0;
    BEGIN
        IF (Init = 1)    { If this were called for 1st time.}
            THEN BEGIN
                    LineCnt := 3;
                    PrintTitles(PrinterOK);
                    EXIT;
                END;                        { Else, all later times. }
```

```
        IF (LineCnt = 2)
            THEN BEGIN
                    PrintTitles(PrinterOK);
                    LineCnt := 3;
                END;


        WITH gBookRec DO
            WRITELN(LST,Title:TitleLen, Author:AuthorLen,
                    Edition:8, Cover:6 );


        INC(LineCnt);
        IF LineCnt = 64
            THEN BEGIN
                    LineCnt := 2;
                    IF PrinterOK THEN FormFeed;
                END;
    END;   {PrinterPrintT}


        {
           Asks the user if he or she wants to print the list
           on the screen or printer.
         }


PROCEDURE ScrnOrPrint(VAR Dev: CHAR);
    BEGIN
        REPEAT
            DispMessage('Do you want to see listing on the Screen'+
                        ' or Printer? (S/P) ');
            Dev := UPCASE(READKEY);
        UNTIL (Dev IN ['S','P']);
        IF Dev = 'S' THEN PaintScreen(WHITE,BLUE);
    END;   {ScrnOrPrint}


        {
           Prints a record on the screen. This subroutine keeps
           track of the screen lines printed and prints a title
           at each new screen and pauses at the end of each.
           If the Init argument is equal to 1, this routine
           zeroes out the display variables and assumes that this
           call is the start of a new listing. Otherwise, the
           typed constants keep their values.
         }
```

```
PROCEDURE ScrnPrintA(Init: INTEGER);
    CONST LineCnt: INTEGER = 0;
    BEGIN
        IF (Init = 1)                      { If called for first time }
            THEN BEGIN
                    LineCnt := 3;
                    DispScrnTitlesA;
                    EXIT;
                END;                       { Else, all later times. }

        IF (LineCnt = 2)
            THEN BEGIN
                    DispScrnTitlesA;
                    LineCnt := 3;
                END;

        WITH gBookRec DO
            BEGIN
                ScrWrite( 1,LineCnt,WHITE,BLUE,Author);
                ScrWrite(27,LineCnt,WHITE,BLUE,Title);
                ScrWrite(58,LineCnt,WHITE,BLUE,Edition);
                ScrWrite(69,LineCnt,WHITE,BLUE,Cover);
            END; {with}

        INC(LineCnt);
        IF LineCnt = 22
            THEN BEGIN
                    PressEnter;
                    LineCnt := 2;
                    PaintScreen(WHITE,BLUE);
                END;
    END;   {ScrnPrintA}

        {
            Prints a record on the screen. This subroutine keeps
            track of the screen lines printed and prints a title
            at each new screen and pauses at the end of each.
            If the init% argument is equal to 1, this routine
            zeroes out the display variables and assumes that this
            call is the start of a new listing. Otherwise, the
            typed constants keep their values.
        }
```

```pascal
PROCEDURE ScrnPrintT (Init: INTEGER);
   CONST LineCnt: INTEGER = 0;
   BEGIN
      IF (Init = 1)                        { If called for first time }
         THEN BEGIN
                 PaintScreen(WHITE,BLUE);
                 LineCnt := 3;
                 DispScrnTitlesT;
                 EXIT;
              END;                         { Else, all later times. }

      IF (LineCnt = 2)
         THEN BEGIN
                 DispScrnTitlesT;
                 LineCnt := 3;
              END;

      WITH gBookRec DO
         BEGIN
            ScrWrite( 1,LineCnt,WHITE,BLUE,Title);
            ScrWrite(32,LineCnt,WHITE,BLUE,Author);
            ScrWrite(58,LineCnt,WHITE,BLUE,Edition);
            ScrWrite(69,LineCnt,WHITE,BLUE,Cover);
         END;  {with}

      INC(LineCnt);
      IF LineCnt = 22
         THEN BEGIN
                 PressEnter;
                 LineCnt := 2;
                 PaintScreen(WHITE,BLUE);
              END;
   END;  {ScrnPrintT}

PROCEDURE Swap(i,j: INTEGER);
   VAR tRec: BookRecord;
   BEGIN
      tRec      := gBooks[i];
      gBooks[i] := gBooks[j];
      gBooks[j] := tRec;
   END;  {Swap}
```

```
                    {
                      Prints a report alphabetically by the author's name.
                      (This implies that the user entered them in last
                      name order!) The file is read into parallel arrays
                      and sorted.
                    }

        PROCEDURE PrintBookAuth;
            VAR  i:        INTEGER;
                 j:        INTEGER;
                 RecNum:   INTEGER;
                 Dev:      CHAR;
                 PrinterOK: BOOLEAN;
            BEGIN
                ASSIGN(gBookFile,gBookFName);
        {$I-}
                RESET(gBookFile);
        {$I+}
                IF IORESULT <> 0
                    THEN BEGIN
                            ErrorMsg1('No books in file');
                            EXIT;
                        END;
                DispMessage('Please wait while sorting.');
                RecNum := 0;
                WHILE NOT EOF(gBookFile) DO
                    BEGIN
                        INC(RecNum);
                        READ(gBookFile,gBookRec);
                        gBooks[RecNum] := gBookRec;
                    END;  {while}
                CLOSE(gBookFile);

                FOR i := 1 TO RecNum DO
                    FOR j := i+1 TO RecNum DO
                        IF (Caps(gBooks[i].Author) > Caps(gBooks[j].Author))
                            THEN Swap(i,j);

                PrinterOK := TRUE;
                ScrnOrPrint(Dev);                    { Use screen or printer. }
                IF (Dev = 'S')
```

```
        THEN ScrnPrintA(1)
        ELSE PrinterPrintA(1,PrinterOK);


    i := 1;
    WHILE (PrinterOK AND (i <= RecNum)) DO
        BEGIN
            gBookRec := gBooks[i];
            IF (Dev = 'S')
                THEN ScrnPrintA(0)
                ELSE PrinterPrintA(0,PrinterOK);
            INC(i);
        END;  {for}
    CASE Dev OF
        'S': PressEnter;
        'P': IF PrinterOK THEN FormFeed;
    END;  {case}
  END;  {PrintBookAuth}


        {
            Prints a report alphabetically by the title. The
            file is read into parallel arrays and sorted.
        }


PROCEDURE PrintBookTitl;
    VAR RecNum:    INTEGER;
        i:         INTEGER;
        j:         INTEGER;
        Dev:       CHAR;
        PrinterOK: BOOLEAN;
    BEGIN
        PrinterOK := TRUE;
        DispMessage('Please wait while sorting.');
        ASSIGN(gBookFile,gBookFName);
{$I-}
        RESET(gBookFile);
{$I+}
        IF IORESULT <> 0
            THEN BEGIN
                    ErrorMsg1('No books in file');
                    EXIT;
                 END;
        RecNum := 0;
```

```
WHILE NOT EOF(gBookFile) DO
   BEGIN
      INC(RecNum);
      READ(gBookFile,gBookRec);
      gBooks[RecNum] := gBookRec;
   END;  {while}
CLOSE(gBookFile);

FOR i := 1 TO RecNum DO
   FOR j := i TO RecNum - 1 DO
      IF (Caps(gBooks[i].Title) > Caps(gBooks[j].Title))
         THEN Swap(i,j);

ScrnOrPrint(Dev);                  { Use screen or printer. }
IF (Dev = 'S')
   THEN ScrnPrintT(1)              { Initialize screen. }
   ELSE PrinterPrintT(1,PrinterOK);

i := 1;
WHILE (PrinterOK AND (i <= RecNum)) DO
   BEGIN
      gBookRec := gBooks[i];
      IF (Dev = 'S')
         THEN ScrnPrintT(0)
         ELSE PrinterPrintT(0,PrinterOK);
      INC(i);
   END;  {for}
CASE Dev OF
   'S': PressEnter;
   'P': IF PrinterOK THEN FormFeed;
END;  {case}
END;  {PrintBookTitl}

VAR MenuOption: INTEGER;

   {
      This subroutine simply displays the book database
      main menu. The user enters the option he or she
      desires. The menu keeps displaying until a valid
      option is entered.
   }
```

```
PROCEDURE DispMenu;
   VAR Ans:    CHAR;
       ErrCode: INTEGER;
   BEGIN
      PaintScreen(WHITE,BLUE);
      ScrWrite(20, 1,WHITE,BLUE,
               '*** Book Database Program ***' );
      ScrWrite(22, 3,YELLOW,BLUE,'Current File = '+
               Trim(gBookFName));
      ScrWrite(10, 6,WHITE,BLUE,'Here are your choices:' );
      ScrWrite(20, 8,WHITE,BLUE,'1. Type data for a new book' );
      ScrWrite(20,10,WHITE,BLUE,'2. Look at a book''s '+
               'information' );
      ScrWrite(20,12,WHITE,BLUE,'3. List all books by author' );
      ScrWrite(20,14,WHITE,BLUE,'4. List all books by title' );
      ScrWrite(20,16,WHITE,BLUE,'5. Get another file name' );
      ScrWrite(20,18,WHITE,BLUE,'6. Exit this program' );
      ScrWrite(10,21,WHITE,BLUE,'What is your choice? ' );
      REPEAT
        Ans := READKEY;
      UNTIL Ans IN ['1'..'6'];
      ScrWrite(31,21,WHITE,BLUE,Ans);  { Echo the user's input. }
      VAL(Ans,MenuOption,ErrCode);
   END;  {DispMenu}


BEGIN
   PaintScreen(WHITE,BLUE);
   gBookFName := 'Books.dat';
   REPEAT
      DispMenu;                       { Get menu option. }
      CASE MenuOption OF
         1: EnterBook;                { Get a book. }
         2: LookBook;                 { Look at an indiv book. }
         3: PrintBookAuth;            { Print books by author. }
         4: PrintBookTitl;            { Print books by title. }
         5: GetFileName;              { Get book file filename. }
      END;  {case}
   UNTIL (MenuOption = 6);
   PaintScreen(LIGHTGRAY,BLACK);
END.  {BookFileSystem}
```

Glossary

In the following definitions, italicized terms are cross-references to other terms in this glossary.

absolute value   The magnitude of a number (equal to the positive value of that number), regardless of its algebraic sign (positive or negative).

active directory   The directory the computer first looks to when it is given commands.

active drive   The *disk drive* the computer first looks to when it is given commands.

address   Each *memory* location (each byte) has a unique address. The first address in memory is 0, the second *RAM* location's address is 1, and so on until the last RAM location (which comes thousands of bytes later).

analog signals   How *data* is transferred over telephone lines. These signals are different from the binary digital signals used by your PC.

argument   The value sent to a *function* or *procedure*. The value (*constant*, type, or *variable*) is enclosed inside parentheses.

array   A list of *variables*, sometimes called a table of variables.

ASCII   An acronym for American Standard Code for Information Interchange.

ASCII file   A file containing ASCII characters that can be used by any *program* on most computers. Sometimes it is called a text file or an ASCII text file.

AUTOEXEC.BAT   An optional *batch file* that *executes* a series of commands whenever you start or reset your computer.

backup file   A duplicate copy of a file that preserves your work in case you damage the original file. Files on a *hard disk* commonly are backed up to *floppy disks.*

.BAK   A common *file extension* for a *backup file.*

.BAS   A common *file extension* for a BASIC *program.*

batch file   An *ASCII* text file containing *DOS* commands.

binary   A numbering system based on two digits. The only valid digits in a binary system are 0 and 1. See also *bit.*

bit   Short for *bi*nary digi*t*, the smallest unit of storage on a computer. Each bit can have a value of 0 or 1, indicating the absence or presence of an electrical signal. See also *binary.*

block   One or more statements treated as though they are a single statement.

bookmark   A placemarker in a file. When you have a large file in the editor, mark certain areas that you refer to frequently. In Turbo Pascal you create a bookmark with Ctrl–K–*n*, where *n* is a number from 0 to 9. To jump to a bookmark, you press Ctrl–Q–*n*.

BOOLEAN   A data type consisting of either True or False.

boot   To start a computer with the operating system *software* in place. You must boot your computer before using it.

bubble sort   A type of *sorting* routine in which values in an *array* are compared to each other, a pair at a time, and swapped if they are not in correct order.

buffer   A place in your computer's *memory* for temporary *data* storage.

bug An error in a *program* that prevents the program from running correctly. This term originated when a moth short-circuited a connection in one of the first computers and prevented the computer from working.

bullet-proof A way of writing your program so that the user cannot *crash* your program by typing invalid input.

byte A basic unit of *data* storage and manipulation. A byte is equivalent to eight *bits* and can contain a value ranging from 0 to 255.

carriage return-line feed Identifies the special ASCII characters #13 and #10. Typically separates lines of data in a text file.

cathode ray tube (CRT) The television-like screen of the computer, also called the *monitor.* It is one place to which the output of the computer can be sent.

central processing unit (CPU) The *microprocessor* responsible for operations within the computer. These operations generally include system timing, logical processing, and logical operations. The CPU controls every operation of the computer system.

CGA Color Graphics Adapter. Defines the *resolution* of the *display* (how many *pixels* show on the screen). CGA graphics have a maximum resolution of 640×200 pixels.

click To move the *mouse*-pointer over an object or icon and press and release the *mouse button* once.

Clipboard A section of *memory* reserved for *blocks* of *text*. The Clipboard holds only one block of text at a time.

clock tick A length of time based on the CPU's built-in timing clock. There are 18.2 ticks in one second.

code A set of instructions written in a *programming language.* See also *source code.*

code segment One of the main areas of memory used by your program. Your program code is stored here. Your main program and each unit can be up to 64K in size.

comment   Text you include in a program to clarify the code. Pascal comments are enclosed in either curly braces { } or parentheses with asterisks (**). Comments are ignored by the compiler.

compile   The process of translating a *program* written in a *programming language,* such as QuickBASIC or Pascal, into machine *code* your computer understands.

concatenation   The process of attaching one string to the end of another or combining two or more strings into a longer string. You can concatenate *string variables, string constants,* or a combination of both and assign the concatenated strings to a string variable.

conditional loop   A series of Turbo Pascal instructions that repeats while a condition is true (WHILE loop) or while a condition is false (REPEAT loop).

constant   *Data* that remains the same during a *program* run.

context-sensitive help   When you press F1 in Turbo Pascal, the editor displays a help window that is based on the current context.

CPU   *Central processing unit.*

crash   When the computer or your program stops working unexpectedly.

CRT   *Cathode ray tube.*

cursor   Usually a blinking underline, located on a *monitor.* Denotes the spot where the next character typed will appear on the screen.

cut   To remove *text* from your *program.* See also *paste.*

data   Information stored in the computer as numbers, letters, and special symbols (such as punctuation marks). *Data* refers also to the characters you input into your *program* so that the program can produce meaningful *information.*

data processing   When a computer takes data and manipulates it into meaningful output, called *information.*

data record   A package of information usually separated into parts called *fields.*

data segment   One of the main sections of memory used by your program. The data segment has a maximum size of 64K and stores all global variables and all typed constants.

data validation   The process of testing the values input into a *program*—for instance, ensuring that a number is within a certain range.

debug   The process of locating an error (*bug*) in a *program* and removing it.

debugger   A special *program* designed to help locate errors in a program.

default   A predefined action or command that the computer chooses unless you specify otherwise.

demodulate   The process of converting *analog signals* back to digital signals that the computer can understand. See also *modulate*.

dialog box   A box-like structure that appears on the screen after the user chooses a *menu* command with an ellipsis (...). You must type more information before Turbo Pascal can carry out the command.

digital computer   A term describing the fact that your computer operates on *binary* (on and off) digital impulses of electricity.

directory   A way of organizing files into categories on a *disk*. See also *subdirectory*.

disk   A round, flat magnetic storage medium. *Floppy disks* are made of flexible material and enclosed in $5^1/_4$-inch or $3^1/_2$-inch protective cases. *Hard disks* consist of a stack of rigid disks housed in a single unit. A disk sometimes is called *external memory*. Disk storage is non*volatile*. When you turn off your computer, the disk's contents do not go away.

disk drive   A device that reads and writes *data* to a *floppy disk* or a *hard disk*.

diskette   Another name for a removable *floppy disk*.

display   A screen or *monitor*.

display adapter Located in the *system unit*; determines the amount of *resolution* and the possible number of colors on the screen.

double-click To click the *mouse button* twice in rapid succession.

DOS Disk operating system.

dot-matrix printer One of the two most common PC printers. The laser printer is the other. A dot-matrix printer is inexpensive and fast; it uses a series of small dots to represent printed *text* and *graphics*. See also *laser printer*.

drag Pressing and holding the left *mouse button* without letting up while moving the mouse *cursor* across the screen.

EGA Enhanced Graphics Adapter. Defines the *resolution* of the *display* (how many *pixels* show on the screen). The EGA has a maximum resolution of 640×350 *pixels*.

element An individual *variable* in an *array*.

encrypt To transform text so as to hide its meaning.

enumerated type An ordinal data type consisting of identifiers defined by the programmer. Defined in a TYPE section. For example, Colors = (Red, White, Blue);.

execute To run a *program*.

expanded memory Extra memory in your system between 640K and 1 Meg (1,000 kilobytes) that can be accessed by only special programs. See *extended memory*.

extended memory The amount of *RAM* above 1 megabyte (1,000 kilobytes) in 286 or later PCs. You cannot access this extra RAM without special *programs*.

external modem A modem located in a box outside your computer. See also *internal modem*.

field An identifier denoting part of a record. See *record*.

file A collection of *data* stored as a single unit on a *floppy disk* or *hard disk*. A file always has a *filename* that identifies it.

file extension   A suffix to a *filename* consisting of a period followed by as many as three characters. The extension denotes the type of file it is.

filename   A unique name that identifies a file. Filenames can be as much as eight characters long and can have a period followed by an extension (normally three characters long).

file pointer   In a typed file, the pointer that Turbo Pascal uses to keep track of the current record.

fixed disk   See *hard disk.*

fixed-length records   A record in which each field takes the same amount of *disk* space, even if that field's *data* value does not fill the field. Fixed strings typically are used for fixed-length records.

fixed-length string variables   Variables that can hold only strings shorter than or equal to the length you define. These strings are not as flexible as *variable-length strings.*

floppy disk   See *disk.*

format   The process of creating a "map" on the *disk* that tells the operating system how the disk is structured. In this way, the operating system keeps track of where *files* are stored.

frequency   The number of cycles per second, in *hertz.*

function   A self-contained code module designed to do a specific task. A function is sometimes called a *subroutine.* Some functions are built-in routines that manipulate numbers, strings, and output.

function keys   Keys labeled F1 through F12 (some keyboards have only through F10) that provide special *functions.*

global variable   A variable that can be seen from (and used by) every statement in a *program.*

graphics   A video presentation consisting mostly of pictures and figures rather than letters and numbers. See also *text.*

graphics monitor   A monitor that can display pictures.

hard copy   The printout of a *program* (or its output). *Hard copy* refers also to a safe backup copy for a program in case the *disk* is erased.

hard disk   Sometimes called a *fixed disk.* A hard disk holds much more *data* and is many times faster than a *floppy disk.* See *disk.*

hardware   The physical parts of the machine. Hardware, which has been defined as "anything you can kick," consists of the things you can see.

heap   One of the main areas of memory that can be used by your program. The heap consists of all regular memory not used by your program's code segment, data segment, and stack segment. The heap is used for dynamic variables created with pointers.

hertz   A unit of measurement equal to one cycle per second.

hexadecimal   A numbering system based on 16 *elements.* Digits are numbered 0 through F, as follows: 0, 1, 2, 3, 4, 5, 6, 7, 8, 9, A, B, C, D, E, F. Hexadecimal numbers are often called "hex numbers."

HGA   Hercules Graphics Adapter. Defines the *resolution* of the *display* (how many *pixels* show on the screen).

hierarchy of operators   See *order of operators.*

identifier   A general term to describe the name of a constant, type, variable, record field, function, procedure, unit, or program.

indeterminate loop   A loop in which you do not know in advance how many cycles of the loop will be made (unlike with the FOR loop).

infinite loop   The never-ending repetition of a *block* of Turbo Pascal statements.

information   The meaningful product of a *program. Data* goes into a program to produce meaningful output.

input   The *data* entered into a computer through a device such as the keyboard.

input-process-output   This model is the foundation of everything that happens in your computer. *Data* is input and then processed by your *program* in the computer. Finally, *information* is output.

I/O   An acronym for input/output.

integer variable   A variable that can hold integers.

internal modem   A modem that resides inside the *system unit*. See also *external modem*.

key field   A field that usually contains unique *data* used to identify a *record*.

keyboard buffer   A special area in memory where all keystrokes are stored as bytes. The buffer is 32 bytes long. Each character in the buffer uses two bytes.

kilobyte (K)   A unit of measurement that refers to 1,024 *bytes*.

laser printer   A type of printer that in general is faster than a dot-matrix printer. Laser printer output is much sharper than that of a dot-matrix printer. Laser printers are more expensive than dot-matrix printers. See also *dot-matrix printer*.

least significant bit   The extreme-right bit of a *byte*. For example, a *binary* 00000111 has a 1 as the least significant bit.

length byte   The byte in a Turbo Pascal string that stores the current length of the string. It stores the number of bytes in character format and is in position 0 of the string.

line printer   Another name for your printer.

local variable   A variable that can be seen from (and used by) only the *code* in which it is defined (within a *function* or *procedure*).

loop   The repeated circular execution of one or more statements.

machine language   The series of *binary* digits that a *microprocessor executes* to perform individual tasks. People seldom (if ever) program in machine language. Instead, they program in assembly language, and an assembler translates their instructions into machine language.

main module   The first routine of a *modular program*. It is not really a *subroutine*, but is the main *program*. Also called the main program block.

maintainability   The computer industry's word for the capability to change and update *programs*.

math operator   A symbol used for addition, subtraction, multiplication, division, or other calculations.

MCGA   Multi-Color Graphics Array.

MDA   Monochrome Display Adapter.

megabyte (M)   In computer terminology, about a million bytes.

memory   Storage area inside a computer, used to store *data* temporarily. The computer's memory is erased when the power is turned off.

menu   A list of commands or instructions displayed on the screen. These lists organize commands and make a *program* easier to use.

menu-driven   Describes a *program* that provides menus for choosing commands.

microchip   A small wafer of silicon that holds computer components and occupies less space than a postage stamp.

microcomputer   A small version of a computer that can fit on a desktop. The *microchip* is the heart of the microcomputer. Microcomputers are much less expensive than their larger counterparts.

microprocessor   The chip that does the calculations for the computer. Sometimes it is called the *central processing unit* (CPU).

modem   A piece of *hardware* that *modulates* and *demodulates* signals so that your PC can communicate with other computers over telephone lines. See also *external modem, internal modem*.

modular programming   The process of writing your programs in several modules rather than as one long program. By breaking a program into several smaller routines, you can isolate problems better, write correct programs faster, and produce programs that are much easier to maintain.

modulate   Before your computer can transmit *data* over a telephone line, the *information* to be sent must be converted (modulated) into *analog signals*. See also *demodulate, modem*.

modulus   The integer remainder of division.

monitor   A television-like screen that lets a computer display *information*. It is known as an *output device*. See also *cathode ray tube*.

monochrome monitor   A monitor that can display only one foreground color, such as green or amber, on a black or white background.

mouse   A hand-held device you move across the desktop to move an indicator, called a mouse pointer, across the screen. The mouse is used rather than the keyboard to select and move items (such as *text* or *graphics*), *execute* commands, and perform other tasks.

mouse button   A button on top of a mouse that performs a specific action, such as executing a command, depending on the location of the mouse pointer on the screen.

MS-DOS   An operating system for IBM and compatible computers.

multidimensional arrays   As two-dimensional arrays, which have rows and columns, they sometimes are called tables or matrices.

nested loop   A loop within a loop.

null string   An empty string denoted by two single quotation marks.

numeric functions   Built-in routines that work with numbers.

object code   A "halfway step" between *source code* and executable *machine language.* Object code consists mostly of machine language but is not directly executable by the computer. It first must be linked to resolve external references and *address* references.

open   To load a *file* into an application.

order of operators   Sometimes called the *hierarchy of operators* or the *precedence of operators,* it determines exactly how Turbo Pascal computes formulas.

ordinal type   A type consisting of values that may be ordered. For example, all integer types also are ordinal types.

output device   Where the results of a *program* are output, such as the screen, the *printer*, or a *disk file.*

palette   A collection of possible colors, just like an artist's palette of colors.

parallel arrays   Two arrays working side by side. Each *element* in each array corresponds to one in the other array.

parallel port   A connector used to plug a device such as a *printer* into the computer. Transferring *data* through a parallel port is much faster than transferring data through a *serial port.*

parameter   A list of *variables* enclosed in parentheses that follow the name of a *function* or *procedure*. Parameters indicate the number and type of *arguments* that will be sent to the function or procedure.

.PAS   Common *file extension* for a Pascal *program.*

passing by address   Also called *passing by reference.* When an argument (a *local variable*) is passed by address, the variable's address in *memory* is sent to and assigned to the receiving routine's *parameter* list. (If more than one *variable* is passed by address, each of their addresses is sent to and assigned to the receiving *function*'s parameters.) A change made to the parameter within the routine changes also the value of the argument variable. In the receiving routine's parameter list, VAR prefaces each parameter passed by address.

passing by copy   Another name for *passing by value.*

passing by reference   Another name for *passing by address.*

passing by value   When the value contained in a *variable* is passed to the *parameter* list of a receiving routine. Changes made to the parameter within the routine do not change the value of the *argument* variable. Also called *passing by copy.*

paste   To insert text into your program.

path   The route the computer travels from the root *directory* to any subdirectories in locating a *file*. The path refers also to the subdirectories *MS-DOS* examines when you type a command that requires it to find and access a file.

peripheral   A device attached to the computer, such as a *modem, disk drive, mouse,* or *printer.*

personal computer   A *microcomputer*, sometimes called a PC.

pixel   A dot on the computer screen. The number of dots in a line and in a column determine the *resolution* of the *monitor*. See also *CGA, EGA,* and *VGA.*

precedence of operators   See *order of operators.*

printer   A device that prints *data* from the computer to paper.

procedure   A self-contained code module designed to perform a specific task, sometimes referred to as a *subroutine.*

program   A group of instructions that tells the computer what to do.

programming language   A set of rules for writing instructions for the computer. Popular programming languages include BASIC, QBasic, Visual Basic, C, C++, and Pascal.

quick sort   A type of *sorting* routine.

RAM   *Random-access memory.*

random-access file   A file in which *records* can be accessed in any order you choose.

random-access memory (RAM)   What your computer uses to temporarily store *data* and *programs.* RAM is measured in *kilobytes* and *megabytes.* Generally, the more RAM a computer has, the more powerful programs it can run.

read-only memory (ROM)   A permanent type of computer memory. ROM contains the BIOS (basic input/output system), a special chip used to provide instructions to the computer when you turn on the computer.

real number   A number that has a decimal point and a fractional part to the right of the decimal.

record   A unit of related *information* containing one or more *fields,* such as an employee number, employee name, employee address, employee pay rate, and so on. It is an individual occurrence in a typed *file.*

relational operators   Operators that compare *data*; they tell how two *variables* or *constants* relate to each other. They tell you whether two variables are equal or not equal, or which one is less than or more than the other.

resolution   The sharpness of an image in print or on the screen. Resolution usually is measured in dots per inch (dpi) for *printers*, and *pixels* for screens. The higher the resolution, the sharper the image.

ROM   *Read-only memory.*

runtime   The time when a program runs. For example, if you get an error while the program is running, this error is called a runtime error.

scientific notation   A shortcut method of representing numbers of extreme values.

sectors   A pattern of pie-shaped wedges on a *disk*. Formatting creates a pattern of *tracks* and sectors in which your *data* and *programs* will be stored.

sequential file   A file that must be accessed one *record* at a time beginning with the first record.

serial port   A connector used to plug in serial devices, such as a *modem* or a *mouse*.

set   A group of values of an ordinal type. A set may consist of a maximum of 256 elements and up to 32 bytes in length.

shell sort   A type of *sorting* routine in which each *array element* is compared to another array element and swapped if needed to put them in order.

simple type   Either an ordinal type or a real type. Ordinal types include integers, BOOLEAN types, CHAR types, enumerated types, and subrange types. Strings are not a simple type.

single-dimensional arrays   Arrays that have only one *subscript*. Single-dimensional arrays represent a list of values.

software   The *data* and *programs* that interact with your hardware. The Turbo Pascal language is an example of software. See also *hardware*.

sorting   A method of putting *arrays* in a specific order (such as alphabetical or numerical order), even if that order is not the same order in which the *elements* were entered.

source code   The Turbo Pascal language instructions, written by humans, that the Turbo Pascal compiler translates into *object code.*

spaghetti code   A term used when there are too many GOTOs in a *program*. If a program branches all over the place, it is difficult to follow. Trying to follow the logic resembles a "bowl of spaghetti."

stack segment   One of the main areas of memory used by your program. All local variables are stored on the stack. The maximum size of the stack segment is 64K.

string constant   One or more groups of characters inside single quotation marks.

string literal   Another name for a *string constant.*

string variable   A variable that can hold string *data.*

subdirectory   A directory within an existing directory.

subroutine   A self-contained code module designed to perform a specific task. In Turbo Pascal, a subroutine can be either a *procedure* or a *function*. Subroutines are sections of *programs* you can *execute* repeatedly.

subscript   A number inside brackets that differentiates one *element* of an *array* from another.

SVGA   Super Video Graphics Array, a nonstandardized type of *display adapter* based on extensions to the *VGA* standard. Defines the *resolution* of the *display* (how many *pixels* show on the screen).

syntax error   The most common error a programmer makes when trying to compile a program—usually a misspelled word or an omitted semicolon.

system unit   The large box component of the computer. The system unit houses the PC's *microchip* (the *CPU*).

text   A video presentation scheme consisting mostly of letters and numbers. See also *graphics.*

tracks   A pattern of *paths* on a *disk*. Formatting creates a pattern of *tracks* and *sectors* in which your *data* and *programs* will be stored.

truncation   When the fractional part of a number (the part of the number to the right of the decimal point) is taken off the number. No rounding is done.

two's complement   A method your computer uses to take the negative of a number. This method plus addition enables the computer to simulate subtraction. See Appendix D.

unary operator   The addition or subtraction operator used by itself.

unit   A self-contained module of code that can be compiled separately from the program.

user-defined functions   Functions that the programmer writes, as opposed to those supplied with Turbo Pascal. See also *functions*.

user-friendliness   A *program* is user-friendly if it makes the user comfortable and simulates what the user is already familiar with.

variable   *Data* that can change as the *program* runs.

variable-length records   A record that wastes no space on the *disk*. As soon as a field's *data* value is saved to the *file*, the next field's data value is stored immediately after it. A special separating character usually is placed between the fields so that your *programs* know where the fields begin and end.

variable-length string variables   The string *data* stored in the variable can be any length. If you put a short word in a variable-length string variable and then replace it with a longer word or phrase, the string variable grows to hold the new, longer data.

variable scope   Sometimes called the "visibility of variables"; describes how variables are "seen" by your *program*. See also *global variables* and *local variables*.

VGA   Video Graphics Array, a type of *display adapter*. Defines the *resolution* of the *display* (how many *pixels* show on the screen). This refers to 640 × 480 pixel resolution.

volatile   Temporary. For example, when you turn off the computer, all the *RAM* is erased.

white space   Empty space on a page. Spaces and tabs are two ways to generate white space.

word   In general usage, two consecutive *bytes* (16 *bits*) of *data*.

Index

F

encrypting, 688
moving, 70
    to Clipboard, 70-71
replacing, 88-89
searching for, 86-88
text files, 541
    creating, 543
    data
        appending, 543
        reading, 542
        writing, 543
    opening, 542-545
    viewing, 552
TEXTBACKGROUND
statement, 216-220
TEXTCOLOR statement,
    216-220
titles
    displaying in programs, 557
    multidimensional tables, 372
totals
    loops, 256-265
    variables, adding to, 259
TPU (Turbo Pascal Unit) file,
    510
tracks (disks), 18, 697
transistors, 16
trigonometric functions
    ARCTAN, 411
    COS, 411
    PI, 410
    SIN, 411-412
TRUNC function, 404
truncating, 404, 698
truth tables, 240-241
truths, internal, 243
Turbo Pascal
    editor, 516
    exiting, 51-52
    units, 507
Turbo Pascal Unit (TPU) file,
    510

two's complement, 698
TYPE command, 552
type mismatch error, 175
TYPE section, 270-272
TYPE statement, 514-522
typed constants, 341, 347-349
    declaring, 347
    records, 388-391
typed files, 541, 575
types
    arrays, elements, 339
    enumerated, 358-359, 401
    location, specifying, 481
    matching, 315
    ordinal, 314, 693
    SET, 280
    simple, 281, 696
typing programs, program
    editor, 63-65

U

unary operators, 145, 698
underscore (_) character, 82, 535
units, 110, 438, 507-523, 698
    compiling, 510
    creating, 509-512
    expanding, 512-514
    IMPLEMENTATION section,
        509
    INTERFACE section, 509
    naming, 508-509
    recompiling, 512, 513
    saving, 510
    ScrTool, updating, 521
    statements
        CONST, 514-522
        TYPE, 514-522
        VAR, 514-522
    storing in subdirectories, 511
    structure, 508
    Turbo Pascal, 507

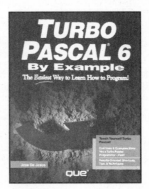
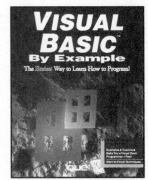

Personal computing is easy
when you're using Que!

Using 1-2-3 for DOS Release 2.3,
Special Edition
$29.95 USA
0-88022-727-8, 584 pp., $7^3/_8$ x $9^1/_4$

Using 1-2-3 for DOS Release 3.1+,
Special Edition
$29.95 USA
0-88022-843-1, 584 pp., $7^3/_8$ x $9^1/_4$

Using 1-2-3 for Windows
$29.95 USA
0-88022-724-9, 584 pp., $7^3/_8$ x $9^1/_4$

Using 1-2-3/G
$29.95 USA
0-88022-549-7, 584 pp., $7^3/_8$ x $9^1/_4$

Using AlphaFOUR
$24.95 USA
0-88022-890-3, 500 pp., $7^3/_8$ x $9^1/_4$

Using AmiPro
$24.95 USA
0-88022-738-9, 584 pp., $7^3/_8$ x $9^1/_4$

Using Assembly Language, 3rd Edition
$29.95 USA
0-88022-884-9, 900 pp., $7^3/_8$ x $9^1/_4$

Using BASIC
$24.95 USA
0-88022-537-8, 584 pp., $7^3/_8$ x $9^1/_4$

Using Borland C++, 2nd Edition
$29.95 USA
0-88022-901-2, 1,300 pp., $7^3/_8$ x $9^1/_4$

Using C
$29.95 USA
0-88022-571-8, 950 pp., $7^3/_8$ x $9^1/_4$

Using Clipper, 3rd Edition
$29.95 USA
0-88022-885-7, 750 pp., $7^3/_8$ x $9^1/_4$

Using DacEasy, 2nd Edition
$24.95 USA
0-88022-510-6, 584 pp., $7^3/_8$ x $9^1/_4$

Using DataEase
$24.95 USA
0-88022-465-7, 584 pp., $7^3/_8$ x $9^1/_4$

Using dBASE IV
$24.95 USA
0-88022-551-3, 584 pp., $7^3/_8$ x $9^1/_4$

Using Excel 3 for Windows,
Special Edition
$24.95 USA
0-88022-685-4, 584 pp., $7^3/_8$ x $9^1/_4$

Using FoxPro 2
$24.95 USA
0-88022-703-6, 584 pp., $7^3/_8$ x $9^1/_4$

Using Freelance Plus
$24.95 USA
0-88022-528-9, 584 pp., $7^3/_8$ x $9^1/_4$

Using GeoWorks Ensemble
$24.95 USA
0-88022-748-6, 584 pp., $7^3/_8$ x $9^1/_4$

Using Harvard Graphics 3
$24.95 USA
0-88022-735-4, 584 pp., $7^3/_8$ x $9^1/_4$

Using Harvard Graphics for Windows
$24.95 USA
0-88022-755-9, 700 pp., $7^3/_8$ x $9^1/_4$

Using LetterPoerfect
$24.95 USA
0-88022-667-6, 584 pp., $7^3/_8$ x $9^1/_4$

Using Microsoft C
$24.95 USA
0-88022-809-1, 584 pp., $7^3/_8$ x $9^1/_4$

Using Microsoft Money
$19.95 USA
0-88022-914-4, 400 pp., $7^3/_8$ x $9^1/_4$

Using Microsoft Publisher
$22.95 USA
0-88022-915-2, 450 pp., $7^3/_8$ x $9^1/_4$

Using Microsoft Windows 3,
2nd Edition
$24.95 USA
0-88022-509-2, 584 pp., $7^3/_8$ x $9^1/_4$

Using Microsoft Word 5.5: IBM
Version, 2nd Edition
$24.95 USA
0-88022-642-0, 584 pp., $7^3/_8$ x $9^1/_4$

Using Microsoft Works for Windows,
Special Edition
$24.95 USA
0-88022-757-5, 584 pp., $7^3/_8$ x $9^1/_4$

Using Microsoft Works: IBM Version
$24.95 USA
0-88022-467-3, 584 pp., $7^3/_8$ x $9^1/_4$

Using MoneyCounts
$24.95 USA
0-88022-696-X, 584 pp., $7^3/_8$ x $9^1/_4$

Using MS-DOS 5
$24.95 USA
0-88022-668-4, 584 pp., $7^3/_8$ x $9^1/_4$

Using Norton Utilities 6
$24.95 USA
0-88022-861-X, 584 pp., $7^3/_8$ x $9^1/_4$

Using Novell NetWare, 2nd Edition
$24.95 USA
0-88022-756-7, 584 pp., $7^3/_8$ x $9^1/_4$

Using ORACLE
$24.95 USA
0-88022-506-8, 584 pp., $7^3/_8$ x $9^1/_4$

Using OS/2 2.0
$24.95 USA
0-88022-863-6, 584 pp., $7^3/_8$ x $9^1/_4$

Using Pacioli 2000
$24.95 USA
0-88022-780-X, 584 pp., $7^3/_8$ x $9^1/_4$

Using PageMaker 4 for Windows
$24.95 USA
0-88022-607-2, 584 pp., $7^3/_8$ x $9^1/_4$

Using Paradox 4, Special Edition
$29.95 USA
0-88022-822-9, 900 pp., $7^3/_8$ x $9^1/_4$

Using Paradox for Windows,
Special Edition
$29.95 USA
0-88022-823-7, 750 pp., $7^3/_8$ x $9^1/_4$

Using PC DOS, 3rd Edition
$24.95 USA
0-88022-409-3, 584 pp., $7^3/_8$ x $9^1/_4$

Using PC Tools 7
$24.95 USA
0-88022-733-8, 584 pp., $7^3/_8$ x $9^1/_4$

Using PC-File
$24.95 USA
0-88022-695-1, 584 pp., $7^3/_8$ x $9^1/_4$

Using PC-Write
$24.95 USA
0-88022-654-4, 584 pp., $7^3/_8$ x $9^1/_4$

Using PFS: First Choice
$24.95 USA
0-88022-454-1, 584 pp., $7^3/_8$ x $9^1/_4$

Using PFS: First Publisher,
2nd Edition
$24.95 USA
0-88022-591-2, 584 pp., $7^3/_8$ x $9^1/_4$

Using PFS: WindowWorks
$24.95 USA
0-88022-751-6, 584 pp., $7^3/_8$ x $9^1/_4$

Using PowerPoint
$24.95 USA
0-88022-698-6, 584 pp., $7^3/_8$ x $9^1/_4$

Using Prodigy
$24.95 USA
0-88022-658-7, 584 pp., $7^3/_8$ x $9^1/_4$

Using Professional Write
$24.95 USA
0-88022-490-8, 584 pp., $7^3/_8$ x $9^1/_4$

Using Professional Write Plus for
Windows
$24.95 USA
0-88022-754-0, 584 pp., $7^3/_8$ x $9^1/_4$

Using Publish It!
$24.95 USA
0-88022-660-9, 584 pp., $7^3/_8$ x $9^1/_4$

Using Q&A 4
$24.95 USA
0-88022-643-9, 584 pp., $7^3/_8$ x $9^1/_4$

Using QBasic
$24.95 USA
0-88022-713-3, 584 pp., $7^3/_8$ x $9^1/_4$

Using Quattro Pro 3, Special Edition
$24.95 USA
0-88022-721-4, 584 pp., $7^3/_8$ x $9^1/_4$

Using Quattro Pro for Windows,
Special Edition
$27.95 USA
0-88022-889-X, 900 pp., $7^3/_8$ x $9^1/_4$

Using Quick BASIC 4
$24.95 USA
0-88022-378-2, 713 pp., $7^3/_8$ x $9^1/_4$

Using QuickC for Windows
$29.95 USA
0-88022-810-5, 584 pp., $7^3/_8$ x $9^1/_4$

Using Quicken 5
$19.95 USA
0-88022-888-1, 550 pp., $7^3/_8$ x $9^1/_4$

Using Quicken for Windows
$19.95 USA
0-88022-907-1, 550 pp., $7^3/_8$ x $9^1/_4$

Using R:BASE
$24.95 USA
0-88022-603-X, 584 pp., $7^3/_8$ x $9^1/_4$

Using Smart
$24.95 USA
0-88022-229-8, 584 pp., $7^3/_8$ x $9^1/_4$

Using SuperCalc5, 2nd Edition
$24.95 USA
0-88022-404-5, 584 pp., $7^3/_8$ x $9^1/_4$

Using TimeLine
$24.95 USA
0-88022-602-1, 584 pp., $7^3/_8$ x $9^1/_4$

Using Turbo Pascal 6,
2nd Edition
$29.95 USA
0-88022-700-1, 800 pp., $7^3/_8$ x $9^1/_4$

Using Turbo Pascal for Windows
$29.95 USA
0-88022-806-7, 584 pp., $7^3/_8$ x $9^1/_4$

Using Turbo Tax: 1992 Edition Tax
Advice & Planning
$24.95 USA
0-88022-839-3, 584 pp., $7^3/_8$ x $9^1/_4$

Using UNIX
$29.95 USA
0-88022-519-X, 584 pp., $7^3/_8$ x $9^1/_4$

Using Visual Basic
$29.95 USA
0-88022-763-X, 584 pp., $7^3/_8$ x $9^1/_4$

Using Windows 3.1
$27.95 USA
0-88022-731-1, 584 pp., $7^3/_8$ x $9^1/_4$

Using Word for Windows 2,
Special Edition
$27.95 USA
0-88022-832-6, 584 pp., $7^3/_8$ x $9^1/_4$

Using WordPerfect 5
$27.95 USA
0-88022-351-0, 584 pp., $7^3/_8$ x $9^1/_4$

Using WordPerfect 5.1, Special Edition
$27.95 USA
0-88022-554-8, 584 pp., $7^3/_8$ x $9^1/_4$

Using WordStar 7
$19.95 USA
0-88022-909-8, 550 pp., $7^3/_8$ x $9^1/_4$

Using Your Hard Disk
$29.95 USA
0-88022-583-1, 584 pp., $7^3/_8$ x $9^1/_4$

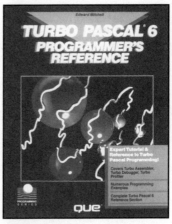

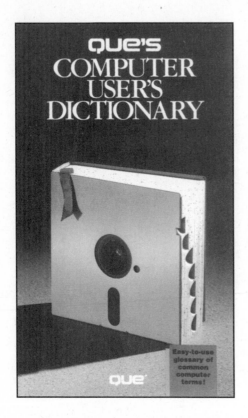

Order Your Program Disk Today!

You can save yourself hours of tedious, error-prone typing by ordering the companion disk to *Turbo Pascal By Example*. The disk contains the source code for all the complete programs, many of the shorter samples in the book, as well as answers to some of the review exercises. Appendix E's complete book-tracking database application is also included on the disk.

With this disk, you'll receive code that shows you how to use most of the features of Turbo Pascal. Samples include code for screen control, file I/O, control statements, and more, giving you many programs to help you learn Turbo Pascal.

Each 3 ½-inch disk is $10.

Just make a copy of this page, fill in the blanks, and mail with your check or money order to:

Turbo Pascal Disk
Greg Perry
P.O. Box 35752
Tulsa, OK   74153-0752

Please **print** the following information:

Number of 3^1/$_2$-inch disks: _____   @ $10 = _____

Name:_____

Street Address: _____

City: _____ State: _____ ZIP: _____

On foreign orders, please use a separate page to give your exact mailing address in the format required by your post office, and add $5 (U.S. currency only) to cover the additional postage.

Make checks and money orders payable to: **Greg Perry**

(This offer is made by the author,
not by Que Corporation.)